THE ANNALS

of The American Academy *of* Political
and Social Science

RICHARD D. LAMBERT, *Editor*
ALAN W. HESTON, *Associate Editor*
THOMAS FOGARTY *and* DAVID LUDDEN,
Acting Associate Editors

IMPLEMENTING GOVERNMENTAL CHANGE

Special Editor of this Volume

CHARLES E. GILBERT

Professor of Political Science
Swarthmore College
Swarthmore, Pennsylvania

THE ANNALS

© 1983 by The American Academy of Political and Social Science

MARY V. YATES, Assistant Editor

All rights reserved. No part of this volume may be reproduced or utilized in any form or by any means, electronic or mechanical, including photocopying, recording, or by any information storage and retrieval system, without permission in writing from the publisher.

Editorial Office: 3937 Chestnut Street, Philadelphia, Pennsylvania 19104.

For information about membership* (individuals only) and subscriptions (institutions), address:

SAGE PUBLICATIONS, INC.
275 South Beverly Drive
Beverly Hills, Calif. 90212 USA

From India and South Asia, write to:	From the UK, Europe, the Middle East, and Africa, write to:
SAGE PUBLICATIONS INDIA Pvt. Ltd. P.O. Box 3605 New Delhi 110 024 INDIA	SAGE PUBLICATIONS LTD 28 Banner Street London EC1Y 8QE ENGLAND

**Please note that members of The Academy receive THE ANNALS with their membership.*

Library of Congress Catalog Card Number 82-63181
International Standard Serial Number ISSN 0002-7162
International Standard Book Number ISBN 0-8039-1984-0 (Vol. 466, 1983, paper)
International Standard Book Number ISBN 0-8039-1983-2 (Vol. 466, 1983, cloth)

Manufactured in the United States of America. First printing, March 1983.

The articles appearing in THE ANNALS are indexed in *Book Review Index; Public Affairs Information Service Bulletin; Social Sciences Index; Monthly Periodical Index; Current Contents; Behavioral, Social, Management Sciences;* and *Combined Retrospective Index Sets.* They are also abstracted and indexed in *ABC Pol Sci, Historical Abstracts, Human Resources Abstracts, Social Sciences Citation Index, United States Political Science Documents, Social Work Research & Abstracts, Peace Research Reviews, Sage Urban Studies Abstracts, International Political Science Abstracts,* and/or *America: History and Life.*

Information about membership rates, institutional subscriptions, and back issue prices may be found on the facing page.

Advertising. Current rates and specifications may be obtained by writing to THE ANNALS Advertising and Promotion Manager at the Beverly Hills office (address above).

Claims. Claims for undelivered copies must be made no later than three months following month of publication. The publisher will supply missing copies when losses have been sustained in transit and when the reserve stock will permit.

Change of Address. Six weeks' advance notice must be given when notifying of change of address. Please send old address label along with the new address to insure proper identification. Please specify name of journal. Send change of address to: THE ANNALS, c/o Sage Publications, Inc., 275 South Beverly Drive, Beverly Hills, CA 90212.

The American Academy of Political and Social Science

3937 Chestnut Street   Philadelphia, Pennsylvania 19104

Board of Directors

ELMER B. STAATS	REBECCA JEAN BROWNLEE
MARVIN E. WOLFGANG	COVEY T. OLIVER
LEE BENSON	THOMAS L. HUGHES
A. LEON HIGGINBOTHAM, Jr.	MATINA S. HORNER
RICHARD D. LAMBERT	LLOYD N. CUTLER

RANDALL M. WHALEY

Officers

President
MARVIN E. WOLFGANG

Vice-Presidents
RICHARD D. LAMBERT, *First Vice-President*
STEPHEN B. SWEENEY, *First Vice-President Emeritus*

Secretary	Treasurer	Counsel
REBECCA JEAN BROWNLEE	ELMER B. STAATS	HENRY W. SAWYER, III

Editors, THE ANNALS

RICHARD D. LAMBERT, *Editor*   ALAN W. HESTON, *Associate Editor*

THORSTEN SELLIN, *Editor Emeritus*

Business Manager
INGEBORG HESSLER

Origin and Purpose. The Academy was organized December 14, 1889, to promote the progress of political and social science, especially through publications and meetings. The Academy does not take sides in controverted questions, but seeks to gather and present reliable information to assist the public in forming an intelligent and accurate judgment.

Meetings. The Academy holds an annual meeting in the spring extending over two days.

Publications. THE ANNALS is the bimonthly publication of The Academy. Each issue contains articles on some prominent social or political problem, written at the invitation of the editors. Also, monographs are published from time to time, numbers of which are distributed to pertinent professional organizations. These volumes constitute important reference works on the topics with which they deal, and they are extensively cited by authorities throughout the United States and abroad. The papers presented at the meetings of The Academy are included in THE ANNALS.

Membership. Each member of The Academy receives THE ANNALS and may attend the meetings of The Academy. Membership is open only to individuals. Annual dues: $26.00 for the regular paperbound edition (clothbound, $39.00). Add $6.00 per year for membership outside the U.S.A. Members may also purchase single issues of THE ANNALS for $6.95 each (clothbound, $10.00).

Subscriptions. THE ANNALS is published six times annually—in January, March, May, July, September, and November. Institutions may subscribe to THE ANNALS at the annual rate: $45.00 (clothbound, $60.00). Add $6.00 per year for subscriptions outside the U.S.A. Institutional rates for single issues: $10.00 each (clothbound, $15.00).

Second class postage paid at Beverly Hills, California.

Single issues of THE ANNALS may be obtained by individuals who are not members of The Academy for $7.95 each (clothbound, $15.00). Single issues of THE ANNALS have proven to be excellent supplementary texts for classroom use. Direct inquiries regarding adoptions to THE ANNALS c/o Sage Publications (address below).

All correspondence concerning membership in The Academy, dues renewals, inquiries about membership status, and/or purchase of single issues of THE ANNALS should be sent to THE ANNALS c/o Sage Publications, Inc., 275 South Beverly Drive, Beverly Hills, CA 90212. *Please note that orders under $20 must be prepaid.* Sage affiliates in London and India will assist institutional subscribers abroad with regard to orders, claims, and inquiries for both subscriptions and single issues.

THE EIGHTY-SIXTH ANNUAL MEETING OF THE AMERICAN ACADEMY OF POLITICAL AND SOCIAL SCIENCE

APRIL 22 AND 23, 1983
THE BELLEVUE STRATFORD HOTEL
PHILADELPHIA, PENNSYLVANIA

The annual meeting of The Academy is attended by hundreds of distinguished scholars, statesmen, authors, and professionals in diverse fields, including representatives of many embassies, academic institutions, and cultural, civic, and scientific organizations.

This 86th Annual Meeting will be addressed at each session by prominent scholars and officials and will be devoted to the topic of

NUCLEAR ARMAMENT AND DISARMAMENT

Members of the Academy are cordially invited to attend and will receive full information. Information on Academy membership can be found in each volume of THE ANNALS.

- Proceedings of the 86th Annual Meeting will be published in the September 1983 volume of THE ANNALS.

- FOR DETAILS WRITE TO: THE AMERICAN ACADEMY OF POLITICAL AND SOCIAL SCIENCE • BUSINESS OFFICE • 3937 CHESTNUT STREET PHILADELPHIA, PENNSYLVANIA 19104

CONTENTS

PREFACE .... *Charles E. Gilbert*	9
POLITICS, POLICY, AND BUREAUCRACY AT THE TOP .... *James W. Fesler*	23
POLICY INNOVATION AND THE STRUCTURE OF THE STATE: THE POLITICS-ADMINISTRATION NEXUS IN FRANCE AND BRITAIN .... *Peter A. Hall*	43
THE PUBLIC-SERVICE PROBLEM .... *Eugene B. McGregor, Jr.*	61
THE MANAGEMENT OF EXECUTIVE DEPARTMENTS .... *Alan L. Dean*	77
PUBLIC MANAGEMENT IN THE 1980s AND BEYOND .... *Fred A. Kramer*	91
PROGRAM EVALUATION AND APPROPRIATE GOVERNMENTAL CHANGE .... *Eleanor Chelimsky*	103
ORGANIZING FOR CHANGE .... *Louis C. Gawthrop*	119
NONHIERARCHICAL APPROACHES TO THE ORGANIZATION OF PUBLIC ACTIVITY .... *Vincent Ostrom*	135
CHANGING PUBLIC-PRIVATE SECTOR RELATIONS: A LOOK AT THE UNITED STATES .... *Bruce L.R. Smith*	149
INTERGOVERNMENTAL REDIRECTION .... *Donald H. Haider*	165
THE PRESIDENCY AND POLITICAL CHANGE .... *Lester G. Seligman*	179
INTEGRATION AND FRAGMENTATION: KEY THEMES OF CONGRESSIONAL CHANGE .... *Walter J. Oleszek*	193
BOOK DEPARTMENT	207
INDEX	251

BOOK DEPARTMENT CONTENTS

INTERNATIONAL RELATIONS AND POLITICS

BILDER, RICHARD B. *Managing the Risks of International Agreement.* James R. Silkenat 207

FLYNN, GREGORY et al. *The Internal Fabric of Western Security.* Richard E. Johe 208

MALLAKH, RAGAEI EL, ed. *OPEC: Twenty Years and Beyond.* Mary A. Holman 209

MEIBAR, BASHEER. *Political Culture, Foreign Policy, and Conflict: The Palestine Area Conflict System.* David H. Rosenbloom 210

WESTOBY, ADAM. *Communism Since World War II.* Ivar Spector 211

AFRICA, ASIA, AND LATIN AMERICA

KAUL, TRILOKI N. *Reminiscences: Discreet and Indiscreet.* Norman D. Palmer 211

LIANGYING, XU and FAN DAINIAN. *Science and Socialist Construction in China.* J. E. Spencer 212

McDONOUGH, PETER. *Power and Ideology in Brazil.* Donald L. Huddle 213

MILLER, BARBARA D. *The Endangered Sex: Neglect of Female Children in Rural North India.* Surinder K. Mehta 214

SILVERMAN, MILTON, PHILIP R. LEE, and MIA LYDECKER. *Prescriptions for Death: The Drugging of the Third World.* Harold L. Johnson 215

SMITH, BRIAN H. *The Church and Politics in Chile: Challenges to Modern Catholicism.* David M. Billikopf 217

TOTMAN, CONRAD. *Japan Before Perry: A Short History.* R. Kent Lancaster 217

WILES, PETER, ed. *The New Communist Third World.* Roy M. Melbourne 218

WILSON, A. JEYARATNAM. *The Gaullist System in Asia: The Constitution of Sri Lanka.* Minoo Adenwalla 219

EUROPE

BRAUDEL, FERNAND. *The Structures of Everyday Life: The Limits of the Possible.* Joseph A. Amato 220

CULLEN, L. M. *The Emergence of Modern Ireland, 1600-1900,* and BOYCE, D. GEORGE. *Nationalism in Ireland.* William M. Simons 221

LIEBERMAN, SIMA. *The Contemporary Spanish Economy: A Historical Perspective.* Carolyn P. Boyd 222

VITAL, DAVID. *Zionism: The Formative Years.* Harry N. Howard 223

YANOV, ALEXANDER. *The Origins of Autocracy: Ivan the Terrible in Russian History.* David Hecht . 223

UNITED STATES

DABNEY, VIRGINIUS. *The Jefferson Scandals: A Rebuttal.* Louis Filler 224

ECCLES, JAMES R. *The Hatch Act and the American Bureaucracy.* Robert P. Hay 225

GAVENTA, JOHN. *Power and Powerlessness: Quiescence and Rebellion in an Appalachian Valley.* Walter Licht 226

HOUSEMAN, GERALD L. *City of the Right: Urban Applications of American Conservative Thought.* Paul Kantor 227

JOHNSON, HERBERT A. *Essays on New York Colonial Legal History.* Jack P. Maddex, Jr. 228

LEVINE, ANDREW. *Liberal Democracy: A Critique of Its Theory.* Sidney Axinn 229

LINK, ARTHUR S. et al., eds. *The Papers of Woodrow Wilson,* vol. 38. Louis Filler 230

McGAUGHEY, WILLIAM, Jr. *A Shorter Workweek in the 1980's.* Martin E. Danzig 231

MUZZIO, DOUGLAS. *Watergate Games: Strategies, Choices, Outcomes.* Stephen W. White 232

SHUE, HENRY. *Basic Rights: Subsistence, Affluence, and U.S. Foreign Policy.* Donald T. Critchlow and Michael A. Payne 233

SOCIOLOGY

ABEL, ERNEST L. *Marihuana: The First Twelve Thousand Years.* Maureen Searle	233
ALEXANDER, JEFFREY C. *Theoretical Logic in Sociology, Vol. 1: Positivism, Presuppositions, and Current Controversies.* Adrian C. Hayes	234
BELLE, DEBORAH, ed. *Lives in Stress: Women and Depression.* Charlotte L. Beahan	235
BENDITT, THEODORE M. *Rights.* Hon. Gerald L. Sbarboro	236
HEISE, DAVID R., ed. *Microcomputers in Social Research,* and TAYLOR, JAMES B. *Using Microcomputers in Social Agencies.* George H. Conklin	237
LAPIDUS, GAIL WARSHOFSKY, ed. *Women, Work, and Family in the Soviet Union.* David Hecht	238
MORGAN, GORDON D. *America Without Ethnicity.* Abraham D. Lavender	239
PALMORE, ERDMAN. *Social Patterns in Normal Aging: Findings from the Duke Longitudinal Study.* George R. Sharwell	239
RICHARDS, DAVID A. J. *Sex, Drugs, Death, and the Law: An Essay on Human Rights and Overcriminalization.* Joseph E. Jacoby	240
WEAVER, W. TIMOTHY. *The Contest for Educational Resources.* William A. Harrington	241

ECONOMICS

BEATON, W. PATRICK, JON H. WEYLAND, and NANCY NEUMAN. *Energy Forecasting for Planners: Transportation Models.* Philip A. Viton	242
BURCHELL, ROBERT W. and DAVID LISTOKIN, eds. *Energy and Land Use.* Jack N. Barkenbus	243
DAM, KENNETH W. *The Rules of the Game: Reform and Evolution in the International Monetary System.* George T. McCandless, Jr.	244
SIMON, CARL P. and ANN D. WITTE. *Beating the System: The Underground Economy.* Anne Mayhew	244

PREFACE

Most issues of *The Annals* treat subjects already well endowed with definition—conventionally, pragmatically, or theoretically. The subject of this issue is not like that, and our assignment seems partly a challenge to define and justify it. There is no field, profession, or industry focused on (governmental) change per se; and the staff function of projecting or anticipating change that increasingly appears in the private sector has much more to do with strategic intelligence than with implementation. There is no general agreement that governmental change is problematic in the simple sense that there is not enough of it, though there may well be a widespread impression today of governmental inertia or intractability in general, and as to implementation of authorized change in particular.

Something like inertia or intractability is no doubt a problem—the other side of the coin variously denominated predictability, regularity, even responsibility or due process, and therefore a tolerable problem within broad limits. But perhaps the limits can be narrowed, either altogether or in certain subjects and sectors of government. "Implementing governmental change," in this view, has to do with enhancing rationality and effectiveness in governments—with institutional fine tuning. And our challenge in this volume, then, is to see what can be learned, and what is already known, about how purposeful change occurs in government, construed here primarily—not entirely—as American national government.

But the claims of stability make for constant complication.[1] They make change problematical as a value, not just operationally. Most of the topics in this volume—most aspects and attributes of public organization—have potentially to do both with resistance to change or redirection, and with facilitation of change or redirection. A little reflection turns up opposite potentialities, diversely conditioned, in most public institutions. And these need balanced analysis; we rarely consider a simple, generic change to be maximized without reference to a companion star, stability—which also is not a simple notion, standing as it does for various other concerns as well.

There are further complications. For example, some changes take more implementing than other changes—though few statutes or other (re)directions are simply self-executing. Insofar, then, as change, or capacity for change, is an issue, one might well focus on attributes of statutes and orders—for example, simplicity, specificity, automaticity—and also on ways of structuring public action that minimize reliance on bureaucracy, with its attendant problems of authority, communication, and interdependence; and one might in particular avoid intergovernmental management, in which the foregoing problems and other hangups seem especially to trammel implementation of allegedly national objectives.[2]

However, decentralization is often recommended as a way of rendering government more susceptible to change. By encouraging diversity, decentralization

---

1. The complication is considered in Herbert Kaufman, *The Limits of Organizational Change* (University: University of Alabama Press, 1971).
2. For some discussion of this, see Jeffrey L. Pressman and Aaron B. Wildavsky, *Implementation* (Berkeley: University of California Press, 1973).

may also encourage innovation through experiment and emulation; by multiplying centers of decision and of access for sources of suggestion, decentralization may enhance the chances of change; and by reducing the uses and the scale of bureaucracy, decentralization may diminish resistance to change. But this issue is complicated also, both empirically and in its criteria of comparison. Historically and politically it can be argued that decentralization tends to favor the preponderance of established interests in the relative absence of competition, and to render public policy and conduct less subject to political forces of change and to professional states of the art. In this view bureaucracy, with its intrinsic rigidities, may also be, as has often been argued, the necessary and appropriate instrument of homocentrically directed and connected change within the large or inclusive jurisdiction. Furthermore, whichever structural tendency—centralization or decentralization—more favors change, the functions subject to change and the interests served by change are unlikely to be the same under both tendencies. This is not to suggest that one tendency is preferable to the other: here the argument is merely that their susceptibility to rational redirection can rarely be measured by the same yardstick, given that change is not a simple category.

How, then, shall we understand change for purposes of this consideration? The editorial guidance given contributors to this volume was simply "appropriate change" or "rational redirection," leaving room for argument in the particular case, but tending to rule out the accidental and the inordinate. And pragmatically considered, even in complex balance with stability, the subject in such terms seems straightforward enough: what do we know about how to improve the capacity of government for rational and effective redirection? What experiences and expedients are particularly helpful? What are the principal resistances—those properly balancing circuits, and those blocking appropriate change? Are some sorts of change—on or off, more or less, left or right, large or marginal—characteristically easier than others?

"Implementing governmental change," then, implicates political capacities for the appropriate redirection of policy as well as administrative attributes of implementation—say, fidelity and facility, but also appropriate flexibility and administrative counsels on feasibility. This statement of the problem accepts some traditional distinctions between politics or policy and administration—let us say between politics, policy, and administration. If the title of this volume suggests greater emphasis on the implementation than on the generation, negotiation, and formulation of policy, these phases of governing are nevertheless in degree reciprocal; perhaps in reality inseparable. And if that is so, then the organization of each presumably conditions performance of the others; the balance and articulation of all presumably condition the performance of each. In particular, the provisions for administrative contributions to policy and for political control of administration may be critical.

Thus the institutionalization of the principal intersections of these governmental attributes seems crucial to capacity for appropriate governmental change. There surely are limits beyond which the political conditions of innovation or change—considered as initiative or responsiveness or both—and the administrative conditions of appropriate initiative and responsiveness within the political framework cease to exist well together and tend to frustrate one another. Political aggrandizement in wholesale patronage or in retail administrative interventions may damp administrative capacities for both the implementation of and contribution to policy in productive balance; and public bureaucracy can be so traditional, prestigious, or professionally intransigent as to blunt political direction. So the joinder of these elements—of political direction, administrative implementation, policy formulation—is a problem of some delicacy and difficulty; and the institutional fine tuning suggested by these terms may exceed our political and analytical capacities.

In any case, this volume begins with articles that consider issues in the politics-policy-administration joinder, both in their modern American manifestations and comparatively. It concludes with articles that deal primarily with the political branches of American government and their capacities for changing their own organization as well as for redirecting governmental policy and operations. Between these sets of articles, the bulk of the volume is concerned with aspects of the permanent government or public bureaucracy, and with issues of decentralization and devolution in governmental structure and conduct. Several of the articles in this group point to critical interdependencies between policy-formulating and policy-implementing capacities in large-scale government; some others consider departures from large-scale government and organization that would, at least incidentally, tend to minimize politics-policy-administration distinctions.

ALTERNATIVE CONCEPTIONS OF THE SUBJECT

Toward an inventory of the subject of governmental change, it may be useful to consider what the organization of this volume elides or combines, what strategies and categories might have been adopted alternatively. First, the entire volume might conceivably have been focused on the sociology of formal organization and the technology of management, as the heart of the matter. I shall argue later that these probably are not the heart of the matter; but in any case it seems unlikely that enough is known about the sociology of change in public bureaucracies to justify such emphasis here and now.[3] And a collection of articles on public-management methods seems likely, on the record, to tell us more about technique than about its consequences.

Second, in the planning of this volume, some topics of obvious relevance—budgeting methods, central planning agencies, administrative reorganizations—lost separate billing in the face of space constraints, mainly on the ground that their properties and prospects of contributing to appropriate change have been amply explored in print already.[4] As to all of them, it seems fair to say that the prevailing

---

3. *Change in Public Bureaucracies* is the title of a fine study of this problem in one type of agency by Marshall W. Meyer (Cambridge: Cambridge University Press, 1979). It stands pretty much alone in its focus and its conclusion that, depending on structure and circumstance, public agencies are surprisingly—my interpretation—open to change. See, on the other hand, James Q. Wilson, *The Investigators* (New York: Basic Books, 1978).

4. Just illustratively, in: Fred A. Kramer, ed., *Contemporary Approaches to Public Budgeting* (Cambridge, MA: Winthrop, 1979); Fremont J. Lyden and Ernest G. Miller, eds., *Public Budgeting:*

tendency of contemporary assessment is at best agnostic. While the logic of program budgeting and structural reorganization is in general cogent enough in its bearing on governmental change, the purposes of both approaches have been congenitally difficult to realize in practice. This is the more so as they approximate central planning in purpose, for the managerial logics of planning, budgeting, and integral organization apparently work best for conventionally cognate public functions, below global governmental levels.

Third, there are in theory, if less prominent in public practice, approaches to administrative reorganization beyond the customary recombining and realigning of agencies—approaches that break with traditional principles, for example, by mixing line and staff explicitly, by substituting invertible matrices and other permutable structures of purpose for invariable hierarchies, or by flattening hierarchy to enhance discretion and flexibility. But the most remarkable aspect of this topic probably is the lack of governmental attention to it, most notably in contrast with industrial practice. In prospective governmental application, such expedients for coping with multiple and mutable goals may seem too refractory to political, especially legislative, direction and control.

Fourth, the notion of appropriate change or rational redirection suggests attention to the intellectual structure and culture of public agencies—to development of more integrally evaluative, self-critically experimental, reflexively corrective modes of administration; of a more provisional approach to administrative missions and a more decisional emphasis in organization.[5] Certain agencies no doubt approach this heuristic, counterbureaucratic ideal less remotely than do others; but in general the program will be difficult to implement in its implicit competition with the claims of organizational authority, functional commitment, and political accountability. Some loosely kindred criticisms of the hierarchical-synoptic tradition ground their arguments rather more in claims to realism than in an ideal. This is especially so of radical incrementalism, recommended either as a program or as a selective strategy, in structure or in *modus operandi,* as "republic of science" or as "partisan mutual adjustment."[6] It is still so, if less so, of the neo-utilitarian, "public-choice" agenda for governmental decomposition and competition.[7] From the standpoint of this volume, what these several perspectives have in common are claims for modes of rationality and responsiveness considered superior to homocentric and hierarchical modes—and conceivably, then, if not just implicitly, superior capacities for appropriate change. The claims of radical incrementalism on this score, and counterclaims of its susceptibility to inertia and conservative clientelism, will be familiar to many readers of this volume. The claims for public-institutional morselization and functional specialization in the neo-

---

Program Planning and Evaluation, 3rd ed. (Chicago: Rand McNally College Publishing, 1978); Peter Szanton, ed., *Federal Reorganization* (Chatham, NJ: Chatham House Publishers, 1981).

5. Martin Landau, "On the Concept of a Self-Correcting Organization," *Public Administration Review,* 33:533 (Nov.-Dec. 1973).

6. Michael Polanyi, *The Logic of Liberty* (Chicago: University of Chicago Press, 1958); Charles E. Lindblom, *The Intelligence of Democracy* (New York: Free Press, 1965).

7. Vincent Ostrom, *The Intellectual Crisis in American Public Administration,* rev. ed. (University: University of Alabama Press, 1974), chs. 3-5.

utilitarian analysis may not be so familiar: they are represented here in Vincent Ostrom's contribution.

Finally, among change-facilitating possibilities not represented in this volume, one should mention two related and perennial tendencies toward distributing authority among the immediate parties to governmental endeavor: programs for enhancing either personal or community development within public administration, and programs for citizen participation through devolution or clientele involvement. These seem expectable tendencies in a liberal-democratic society; and, as they have waxed programmatically in the last 20 years, they have commonly been identified with change. They seem likelier in the long run, however, to be part of the problem of appropriate change, by vesting claims of personnel and clientele, than to contribute much to the solution, whatever their virtues in other respects. They might, then, have been considered in this volume from either perspective or from both: neither tendency gets extended analysis here, though they are noticed sympathetically in Louis Gawthrop's article.[8]

PERSPECTIVES ON RECENT GOVERNMENTAL CHANGE

So much by way of introduction to important explorations not centrally pursued in this volume, and to alternative conceptions of the subject. The topics that make up this volume can justify themselves article by article. In the large, however, the range and variety of the subject, with the intended diversity of authors' perspectives on it, pretty much rule out a unitary view of governmental change. So some explanation of the plan of this volume may be helpful in relating the articles to a common problem. I can approach that explanation through a few prefatory propositions about the common problem.

1. There has been no scarcity of change in the programs—substantive and procedural—of American government(s) in, say, the last 20 years. Every national administration elected since 1960 has had a package or even a program of changes to propose, if only as an obligatory aspect of the presidential campaign today. If there is a governmental-change industry, it must be the still discontinuous issues staffs, task forces, and consulting networks that function in presidential campaigns and transitions. They are not typically concerned with problems of implementation, nor has the remarkable growth of congressional staff helped much to link policy change with implementation. Still, most recent American administrations and Congresses have consummated or mediated plenty of change. Even those administrations that have failed to alter substantive policies nearly in accord with their ambitions have worked numerous, significant, organizational reforms. Thus this observation on the prevalence—incidence—of change has to do not only with adoption of policies but with procedural and structural departures: for example, administrative reorganizations; multifarious budgeting and managerial modifications; growth of staff functions for planning, analysis, and evaluation; civil-service

---

8. The program known as OD, for organization development, may be included in this category for its human relations and community-enhancement bases, though that is something of a forced fit. On OD in general, and as a change-inducing program, see, for example, "Symposium: Organization Development," *Public Administration Review,* 34:97 (Mar.-Apr. 1974).

reform; one new federalism after another; historic changes in the organization and operation of Congress; continuing changes in administrative procedures enjoined by courts, Congress, or functional exigency; and so on. In the sense simply of manifest redirection, our common topic is dubiously problematical: there has probably been more programmed or negotiated governmental change, 1963-83, than in any other 20-year period, in part but not solely because there is more government and a larger market for critical discussion of it than ever before.

2. Very little of this change was predictable in its pace and scale, let alone in its particulars. This was apparently so on the record; it was probably so in principle. Insofar as appropriate governmental change depends on prompt response to change, governmental or other, its planning and implementation are commonly disadvantaged.[9]

3. Moreover, policy change and operational change may not yield much change in product; or the change in product—there has been plenty of it—may not be the change projected and intended. Here matters become darkly problematical in any attempt to generalize. Of course there are difficulties of implementation, perhaps especially in the intergovernmental and public-private contractual undertakings that are now so prevalent. But there are also problems of intention. Procedural changes difficult to make and satisfactory to some for their own sake are for others insufficient, considered instrumentally. As to more substantive change, there is usually room for argument about what was projected: it was not stated and legislated perspicuously; it could not be, for lack of a cogent majority; however stated prospectively, it occasions surprise and discordant understandings in realization.[10] Thus the actual dimensions of accomplished change are hard to estimate for want of definitive intentions or targets, not to mention the contextual change in a dynamic society.

4. In any case, institutional patterns for implementing or inhibiting change have changed a lot since midcentury. Prominent among these changes have been a progressive layering of political appointees and program protagonists over and into the civil service; the further pluralizing of the federal establishment along functional-professional-industrial lines—programs, complexes, networks, syndicates, interests, constituencies, or whatever; and the public or private federal aspect of this tendency through the vast growth of government by grant and contract—the "new political economy" and the "new public administration."[11]

5. So in the generation since midcentury, once-conventional views of public management and organization have come under pragmatic pressure as well as

9. Advisory Commission on Intergovernmental Relations, *The Future of Federalism in the 1980s* (Washington, DC: Government Printing Office, 1981), ch. 1; William Ascher, *Forecasting: An Appraisal for Policymakers and Planners* (Baltimore: Johns Hopkins University Press, 1978); Robert U. Ayres, *Uncertain Futures* (New York: John Wiley, 1979).

10. Involved here are Chester A. Barnard's "two dilemmas of democratic administration": we adopt policies by more or less narrow majorities but apply them more or less uniformly to all; we contemplate policies in the abstract and experience them necessarily in hard particulars. *Organization and Management* (Cambridge, MA: Harvard University Press, 1948), ch. 2.

11. Bruce L.R. Smith, ed., *The New Political Economy* (New York: John Wiley, 1975); Frederick C. Mosher, "The Changing Responsibilities and Tactics of the Federal Government," *Public Administration Review*, 40:541 (Nov.-Dec. 1980).

under theoretical challenge. Both the practical and the abstract logics of hierarchy and integration have been questioned and qualified—for government altogether or in large segments, and also for many particular tasks. The consequential ordering of ends and means, or of policy and implementation, has tended to become less clear and more complex, not only from tendencies just mentioned but also through multiplication, mainly by legislative and judicial mandate, of the goals and constraints that appertain to governmental programs, through growth in governmental scale and scope, and through progressive acknowledgment of bureaucratic politics. Thus the question whether and when it is either productive or just quixotic to profess the norms of hierarchy and integration runs through the articles in this volume that deal with administrative organization and management.

6. The bureaucratic implementation of change must be problematical in any case, owing to both internal and external aspects of organization, especially at the operating level or the cutting edge of government. Bureaucratic resistance to change is probably common and presumably functional, reflecting rank-and-file commitments to established missions without which management would be much more difficult and less effective. Bureaucracy's logic—not its formal top-down program, but its morphology as an assemblage of established functions and professions—militates in general against change. The tendancy of organizations to compromise with apparent environmental imperatives, putting organizational longevity ahead of formal objectives, has become a commonplace of sociology. In government, this adjustment arguably reflects appropriate administrative and political economies of cultivating acceptance or consensus—save as environmental change or diversity may render such practice unduly protective and prejudicial to the public interest. The virtues of stability appear to lie not alone in predictability, prudence, and due process, but also, up to a point, in productivity.

7. As to the responsiveness of permanent government at the national level to legitimate political direction, the evidence is mostly mixed and unsystematic. Presidents who can sustain and concentrate priorities can also, apparently, alter governmental conduct and its results, though there is ample testimony to the special Sisyphean character of this task.[12] Twentieth-century experience pretty much requires us to expect the election of presidents to result in consequential change, however contingently and, as to particulars, unpredictably. But much of the contingency is constitutional in origin, grounded in the separation of powers—in the individuality and political instability of the presidential role; and in legislative-executive relations, or checks and balances. It may be a critical factor for American bureaucratic tractability—for its evaluation or measurement as well as for its intrinsic dimensions—that both the formulation of policy and control of its

---

12. A general survey may be found in, for example, Thomas Cronin, *The State of the Presidency*, 2nd ed. (Boston: Little, Brown, 1980). For an uncommon specific study, see Ronald Randall, "Presidential Power Versus Bureaucratic Intransigence," *American Political Science Review*, 73:795 (Sept. 1979). Some cogent essays on the problems appear in Hugh Heclo and Lester Salamon, eds., *The Illusion of Presidential Government* (Boulder, CO: Westview Press, 1981). And for a contemporary account, see Burt Schorr and Andy Pasztor, "Reaganites Make Sure that the Bureaucracy Toes the Line on Policy," *Wall Street Journal*, 10 Feb. 1982.

implementation, insofar as these are distinguishable, are subject to division and even to rivalry between the elective branches.

8. The presidency and Congress have changed a lot lately also, in their electoral linkages and in organization. Walter Oleszek's article in this volume considers the capacities of Congress for congressional change, the enduring interests of members in congressional decentralization, the continuities likely to flow from this interest for congressional direction and control of administration, and the unanticipated effects of reform of the congressional budgeting process. Lester Seligman's article on the presidency distinguishes ephemeral from institutional changes in that office, proposing a model of the institutional evolution of presidential functions and using the modern history of the president's role in macroeconomic policy to illustrate the model. One critical form of twentieth-century governmental change, or sea change, we learn, is the accumulation of and redefinition of presidential roles. Ultimately presidential effectiveness within this process depends on political support, on sustaining coalitions; and Seligman then remarks the growing coalitional fragility and instability of the modern presidency as presidents, their particular electoral coalitions, and party institutions have progressively separated, and as party institutions have progressively attenuated. It follows that contemporary presidents may lack political capacity to work sustained change in (economic) policy—to "stay the course," in the current president's recent campaign slogan. In general, Seligman suggests, presidents are less often original innovators than facilitators and ratifiers of political forces for change, often accomplished by cumulative institutionalization of presidential functions. One supposes that in this regard the political and the administrative conditions of effective presidential impetus will frequently conflict. And both Seligman and Oleszek remark that presidential institutionalization has lately, in various fields, been countered by institutional change in Congress.

9. In American society the agenda and terms of change in public policy and conduct are fixed not by electoral and bureaucratic politics alone but by litigation and courts as well. The judicial role in policy and conduct here includes constitutional and statutory interpretations that change the bearing of public policy on the conduct of private parties as well as rulings, similarly based, that regulate in degree the conduct of public agencies. Judicially induced change in both these sectors has bulked large in public policy during the last 20 years; and in certain fields of policy—most notably those subject to civil-rights standards—the federal courts have become implementers as well as mandators of change.

10. The problems of implementing governmental change, it thus appears, have constitutional roots in the partition of agencies for promulgating policy and for superintending its implementation. Surely this American constitutional arrangement influences pervasively the conventions and traditions by which, on the continuum of ends and means and in the blending of political, managerial, and operating jurisdictions, we conceive of policy and administration, thus distinguishing and articulating presumptively fundamental public functions in peculiarly American fashions. If the hypostasizing of hierarchy and integration is a persistent issue, so is its other face: the politics (or policy)/administration dichotomy. Arguably—perhaps even by definition—the successful implementation of change,

or of anything else, depends on the clarity and facility with which these levels and attributes of governing articulate institutionally.

THE COURSE OF OUR INQUIRY

Accordingly, this volume begins with some consideration of how politics, policy, and administration articulate at top levels of government—first in American government, then in the distinctively different constitutional structures of Britain and France. There is a long history of criticism to the effect that the American separation of powers greatly complicates the implementation of change—by diffusing power while confusing functions of decision and implementation, and by opening government to indefinite conflict, thus stunting an institutional balance of stability and adaptability.[13] British and French comparisons may lend perspective on this claim, but, whatever one's conclusion about the traditional attributes of contrasting systems, it seems likely that the American system has become increasingly muddled since, say, midcentury. As an incompletely operative ideal, the policy/administration distinction has lost intellectual support since the time of the New Deal; since the end of the Fair Deal the problem of how to adjust the claims of politics and administration amid partisan turnovers, an imperious presidency, and a large permanent government has become a modern constitutional problem of increasing urgency. During all this time particular public bureaucracies have, with their constituencies, matured and inured as public functions have multiplied. In this period, then, congenital rivalry between the elective agencies over direction and control of the bureaucracy has grown; both Congress and, especially, presidents have increasingly challenged regular administrative channels; and the progressive layering of temporary political appointees over and into the civil service has given us "a government of strangers."[14]

Why should of any of this matter for the central problem of this volume of *The Annals*? It should matter if the convention of "neutral competence" is attenuated, thus legitimating administrative resistance to change; it should matter if administrative competence of whatever genre is discouraged; it should matter if policy-making is diminishingly informed by experienced perspectives on administrative feasibility. Those who argue that the American constitutional structure puts any sure institutionalization of these relations out of reach may be right, notwithstanding modern dissatisfaction with and reorganization of these relations in Britain and France; or we may learn to do considerably better. The enhancing of capacity for appropriate change—short of more or less radical decentralization—seems critically dependent on the latter alternative. And our pursuit of this alternative—if we choose to pursue it—depends apparently, in turn, on how the public service develops in the future and in the unwritten structure of the Constitution.

---

13. Here, among the many critics, I have in mind particularly Samuel P. Huntington, *Political Order in Changing Societies* (New Haven, CT: Yale University Press, 1968), ch. 2, and especially pp. 109-21.

14. The problem of relating political and career levels of public service in Washington is the focus of Hugh Heclo, *A Government of Strangers: Executive Politics in Washington* (Washington, DC: Brookings Institution, 1977).

So this volume begins with two articles on the articulation of politics, policy, and administration, first in the American setting (Fesler), then in French and British comparison (Hall). In the juxtaposition of these articles, the problem of appropriately defining and balancing political and administrative interests turns out, as expected, to be delicate and difficult institutionally. Fesler suggests that political interests have overbalanced somewhat administrative interests in the United States lately—specifically that implementation and even policy might be improved by some upward extension and integration of the civil service; or may thus be improved through the new Senior Executive Service. Hall suggests that an opposite balance tends to stymie innovation in Britain, and that the special French institution of the minister's cabinet has facilitated innovation in France—where, however, ministerial cabinets, and, frequently, ministers as well, come from civil-service backgrounds within an elite administrative tradition. Any application of these comparisons in the American setting is prospectively complicated by legislative-executive competition over control of policy and implementation.

Eugene McGregor's article on the American public service reminds us of at least one further, related complication—that, perhaps more than France, and in different ways, we lack an integrated public service. The American federal establishment is a congeries of discrete services, mission oriented and mutually competitive—altogether, McGregor argues, a system that has served purposes of governmental change pragmatically and effectively, though it has done less well in helping to define common national interests or in facilitating political direction in such terms. In the latter connections, McGregor considers the prospects of the Senior Executive Service reform and proposes, as a route to better analytic and pragmatic understanding, a reformulation of the politics/administration dichotomy.

In constitutional and in classical administrative doctrine, the executive department is the key level for linking policy and administration, and for assembling public services; potentially the fulcrum for implementing politically determined change and for consolidating the tools of the managerial trade—all subject to appropriate organization of the public business into functionally coherent and perhaps symbolically significant departments. However, there is little informative literature on this topic; and there are at least apparent problems with the classical view of it in the traditions of bureau autonomy within most older departments, in the dense cross-departmental interdependence of much modern public policy, in the protean nature of interdepartmental priorities, and in political contingencies that figure in the selection of departmental leadership. Yet if the departments are not now, or perhaps never have been, able to carry the weight laid on them by classical theory and constitutional indication, how otherwise can the demands of politics, policymaking, and implementation be combined productively? In his article on the executive departments, reflecting his high-level experience in several of them, Alan Dean argues that we can identify the conditions of departmental management both strong enough and flexible enough to sustain this joinder; and he does so.

Modern managerial methods figure in Dean's prescription, subject, however, to appropriate functional definition, working structure, and high-level career staffing of the departments—subject, that is, to conditions of effective decision. Fred Kramer's article picks up here, evaluating public management as profession and methodology—even as ideology. And again, implications of the politics/administration joinder for the implementation of change appear: managerial methods will enhance efficiency in particulars of redirection; and effectiveness is in large degree a matter of intelligent decision—of getting the political and managerial elements together productively.

Here the new discipline of program evaluation enters the picture potentially. In classical logic, valid program evaluation depends on initial clarity of program objectives, and on prior provision for evaluation in program design. Eleanor Chelimsky, who directs program evaluation in a setting where the political elements of policymaking are endemic, writes an incisive review of evaluation as discipline and as institution, focusing on implications for implementing change, balancing problems and accomplishments. Evaluation, Chelimsky suggests, is not alone a retrospective activity: the "early-reconnaissance" and "planning" phases of evaluation can also figure in the original formulation of programs; and legislative anticipation of evaluation can contribute to the cogency of legislative action, enhancing the chances of appropriate change.

To this point in the exploration, all the articles can, in their several concerns and perspectives, be read as commentaries, at least partly and implicitly, on a generic paradigm and a common problem. In the paradigm, elective agencies of government, including their surrogates, and the civil service are the principal, respectively senior and junior partners in governing, with responsibilities variously and more or less continuously blending policy and implementation. The common problem has to do with how the two classes of activity and participant relate. On this score there appears to be some tendency in politically oriented governmental sectors to emphasize methods of implementation and the administrative conditions of efficiency, while persons concerned with the technologies and responsibilities of management and program evaluation stress their dependence on more cogent policymaking. There are, manifestly, different versions of the generic paradigm and different accommodations of the policy/implementation problem, but the similar conceptions figure in the first half dozen articles as focus or as presupposition. The following two articles, however, challenge these conceptions directly.

Louis Gawthrop considers governmental capacity for change in the light of theories of organization, certain traditions of which have long held that more or less distinct policy/administration or ends/means dichotomies distort reality. In a particularly original typology and analysis of theoretical positions, Gawthrop argues that public bureaucracies, left to themselves and to their political alliances, instinctively strive to occlude environmental pressures and suggestions for change. They can best be opened up to creative, anticipatory response to such influences by a combination of apparently opposite prescriptions, noticed earlier in this introduction: by sophisticating human relations and public participation in administration; and by grafting a formal analytic function into public administration. Thus bureaucracy can be sensitized and intellectualized; implementation is, presumably, much decentralized to agency and neighborhood; public functions, with their constituencies, may become still more autonomous. Gawthrop's analysis may imply, then, that we can only improve the practical prospects of governmental change by further distancing its direction and implementation from electoral institutions; and, if that is so, the implications are constitutionally fundamental.

Vincent Ostrom's analysis, directed not alone to tractability among governmental attributes, tilts still more explicitly and radically against contemporary governmental organization, and especially against centralization in all its forms. In Ostrom's argument, dispersion of public authority, organizational morselization of public functions, and federal provision for public-service diversity are critical desiderata, linked to something like consumer sovereignty through a combination of markets and contractual arrangements, elections, and contingent litigations. The argument can be read as an anachronistic program for recreating Jacksonian America—*sans* local mercantilism, perhaps—or, more accurately and also more radically, as an institutional analysis that reconceives values and possibilities, including conceptions of public and private, society and community, organization and authority. In its emphasis on voluntarism and diversity, institutional competition and decomposition, it reconceives the problem of governmental change: less large-scale interest-group bargaining and bureaucratic hierarchy; more reliance on marketlike competition and local electoral options. Critics will ask whether the thesis applies realistically to governmental change in even a pre-Johnsonian "great society."[15] One answer is that it challenges us to reconsider what public functions, or phases of public functions, require homocentric direction or administration, suggesting as it does that much centrally determined change is locally inappropriate and that much bureaucratically adjusted change is illegitimate.

Short of radical devolution and decentralization, there remain for consideration the changing arrangements of private federalism, or federal grants and contracts for nongovernmental institutions, and of conventional, intergovernmental federalism as factors and frustraters of public-sector change. Bruce Smith's comprehensive article reviews the changing dimensions and conventions of the public-private nexus over 50 years. His conclusions are appropriately mixed: government contracting and kindred expedients can, as end runs around bureaucracy, facilitate short-run change; but in the long run, cumulation of these arrangements brings complexity and vesting of positions that inhibit flexibility and redirection. But "the contract state is here to stay," and we shall have to improve its public management in support of both accountability and capacity for change.

Donald Haider's review of trends in public federalism since the beginnings of the Great Society reaches, in general, similar conclusions about the proliferation of intergovernmental programs, the viscidity of intergovernmental interests, and the progressive complexity of the federal system: change by accretion has been easier than either decremental change or comprehensive redirection, owing both to constituent tendencies of congressional politics abetted lately by political-party decline, and to the progressive effects of federal-system complexity; but changing economic conditions have at least induced decremental change and set the stage for more radical if still problematical change on presidential initiative. Electoral influence on state and local governments has been a source of retrenchment in

---

15. As in Graham Wallas, *The Great Society* (London: Macmillan, 1914).

public federalism; and the balance of states and nation in the system has shifted first one way, then the other, over the last 20 years. What happens next depends on the post-1982 balance of president and Congress—and we are back to the capacities and political bases of those institutions.

SOME INTRODUCTORY CONCLUSIONS

The contributors to this volume have been asked to orient topics of their scholarly concern or professional experience toward the problem of appropriate governmental change. With a little luck we shall have illuminated a common subject from diverse perspectives, sharpening its definition a little and shaping a beginning agenda for its further study. Needless to say, the articles that follow far transcend these introductory comments; altogether they frame the subject in several dimensions better left to readers' fresh perceptions than to summary delineation here.

But it will be consistent with this introduction and its surface interpretations of the articles to conclude that the problem of implementing governmental change is chiefly an aspect of other pervasive issues in modern American government. One such issue lies in the structural and logical bureaucratic complexity that goes with multiplicity of goals and proliferating foci of formal organization, governmental or intergovernmental. Another is the broadening theoretical and ideological emphasis on virtues of decentralization versus centralization, fragmentation versus consolidation—an issue or nest of issues over the claims of large-scale organization and professional management on the one hand and the current neo-utilitarian critique of classical bureaucratic values on the other. Still another related issue pits public institutional formality and ultimate electoral accountability against claims of devolution and direct participation for clienteles, and of liberal self-determination, individual or collective, for public servants. A fourth set of issues inheres in problems of the politics-policy-administration joinder, especially within the American checks-and-balances matrix. And in that context I shall mention finally the problem of political capacity for rational redirection of American government in the relative absence of electoral (party) institutions for supporting and sustaining direction.

CHARLES E. GILBERT

Publisher's Note: The following information is printed in accordance with U.S. postal regulations: Statement of Ownership, Management and Circulation (required by 39 U.S.C. 3685). 1. Title of Publication: THE ANNALS OF THE AMERICAN ACADEMY OF POLITICAL AND SOCIAL SCIENCE. 1A. Publication No.: 026060. 2. Date of Filing: September 30, 1982. 3. Frequency of Issue: Bimonthly. 3A. No. of Issues Published Annually: 6. 3B. Annual Subscription Price: institutions, $45.00 (paper); $60.00 (cloth); individuals, $26.00 (paper), $39.00 (cloth). 4. Location of Known Office of Publication: 3937 Chestnut Street, Philadelphia, PA 19104. 5. Location of the Headquarters or General Business Offices of Publisher, Editor, and Managing Editor: Publisher: The American Academy of Political and Social Science, 3937 Chestnut Street, Philadelphia, PA 19104; Editor: Richard D. Lambert, 3937 Chestnut Street, Philadelphia, PA 19104; Managing Editor: None. 7. Owner (If owned by a corporation, its name and address must be stated and also immediately thereunder the names and addresses of stockholders owning or holding 1% or more of total amount of stock. If now owned by a corporation, the names and addresses of the individual owners must be given. If owned by a partnership or other unincorporated firm, its name and address, as well as that of each individual must be given.): The American Academy of Political and Social Science, 3937 Chestnut Street, Philadelphia, PA 19104. 8. Known Bondholders, Mortgagees, and Other Security Holders Owning or Holding 1% or More of Total Amount of Bonds, Mortgages or Other Securities: None. 9. For Completion by Nonprofit Organizations Authorized to Mail at Special Rates (Section 132.122, PSM): Has not changed during preceding 12 months.

	Av. No. Copies Each Issue During Preceding 12 Months	Actual No. of Copies of Single Issue Published Nearest to Filing Date
10. Extent and Nature of Circulation		
A. Total no. copies printed (net press run)	12,000	12,000
B. Paid circulation:		
1. Sales through dealers and carriers, street vendors and counter sales	820	215
2. Mail subscriptions	7,677	7,289
C. Total paid circulation (sum of 10B1 and 10B2)	8,497	7,504
D. Free distribution by mail, carrier or other means: samples, complimentary, and other free copies	104	132
E. Total distribution (sum of C & D)	8,601	7,636
F. Copies not distributed:		
1. Office use, left-over, unaccounted, spoiled after printing	3,399	4,364
2. Returns from news agents	0	0
G. Total (sum of E, F1 and 2—should equal net press run shown in A)	12,000	12,000

11. I certify that the statements made by me above are correct and complete. (Signed) Ingeborg Hessler, Business Manager

Politics, Policy, and Bureaucracy at the Top

By JAMES W. FESLER

ABSTRACT: Innovation reflecting presidential priorities stems in part from the interplay among political appointees and senior civil servants. Members within each set share distinctive capabilities and disabilities. The brief tenure of political appointees, along with the two-year interval between elections, imposes short time perspectives on political executives, in contrast to those of career executives. The large number of political appointees and their initial distrust of the bureaucracy reduce the contribution that careerists might make to the development and implementation of policies. This is a serious loss, given many political appointees' lack of governmental experience and weak preparation for managing or operating within large organizations. Most career executives are disposed to adapt to a new administration's policy initiatives; resistance is as likely among political executives when the president changes course. Centrifugal forces disperse policymaking into overly discrete, semiautonomous compartments. Centripetal forces draw policymaking to the White House staff, whose members are only occasionally qualified for such responsibility. Reducing the number of political appointees would permit more discriminating selection and lead to greater involvement of careerists. However, careerist's preparation for a larger role needs improvement.

James W. Fesler is the Alfred Cowles Professor Emeritus of Government at Yale University. As a member of the staffs of the National Resources Planning Board, the President's (Brownlow) Committee on Administrative Management, and the War Production Board, he acquired civil-service status. He has been vice-president of the American Political Science Association, editor-in-chief of the Public Administration Review, *and associate editor of the* American Political Science Review. *He is a member of the National Academy of Public Administration and of the editorial board of* Presidential Studies Quarterly. *His most recent books are* Public Administration: Theory and Practice; *and* American Public Administration: Patterns of the Past, *which he edited and coauthored.*

THE exceptional nature of the American governmental system has attracted many interpreters, some grandly addressing the whole complexity, others focusing on particular sectors of the system. Our concern here is the sector in which the president, political executives, and career executives interact in the formulation of policy initiatives and in responding to policy decisions. The character of this sector is unique to the United States. In a major study of bureaucrats and politicians in seven Western democracies, the authors frequently interrupt their main course of cross-national generalization to acknowledge "American exceptionalism" and "the American aberration."[1]

Though our focus is on only one part of the whole system, that part is remarkably interactive with other elements of the system, most prominently Congress, interest groups, communications media, public opinion, and the courts. Even within this sector the dynamics of interactions among officials with different capabilities and time frames, and the dynamics energized by competing values—the free market and government intervention, politics and neutral competence, innovation and continuity, for instance—are so complex as to have uncertain outcomes. It is not clear whether and when these dynamics work synergistically to effect forward movement, are so constructively conflictual as to assure prudence, or immobilize government when action is needed.

AT THE TOP

The upper reaches of the executive branch are a curious mélange. They include roughly 9000 officials: about 100 in the White House and other parts of the Executive Office of the President; about 700 cabinet and subcabinet posts, commissionerships, and bureau chiefships filled by presidential appointment, usually with the advice and consent of the Senate; some 7000 members of the Senior Executive Service, of whom 700 are political appointees and 6300 are senior civil servants; and about 1200 scientists and other specialists without managerial responsibilities.[2] Altogether these top officials amount to four-tenths of one percent of total federal civilian employment.

Except immediately under the cabinet, no line can be drawn across the executive branch, or across a single department, above which all senior officials are political executives and below which all are civil-service careerists. By law, some bureau chiefs are presidential appointees confirmed by the Senate, some are noncareer appointees of a cabinet member, and some are career appointees. A further complexity is that some civil-service careerists accept appointment as political executives, though until recently they thereby lost civil-service status, including tenure.

The United States outdoes all other modern democracies in its provision for change when party control of the executive branch shifts. About 1600 higher positions are filled by political appointment. This contrasts with the approximately 100 top officials in Britain and

1. Joel D. Aberbach, Robert D. Putnam, and Bert A. Rockman, *Bureaucrats and Politicians in Western Democracies* (Cambridge, MA: Harvard University Press, 1981).

2. U.S. House Committee on Post Office and Civil Service, *United States Government Policy and Supporting Positions,* 96th Cong., 2nd sess., 18 November 1980 (Washington, DC: Government Printing Office, 1980); "The Pick of the Plums," *National Journal,* 12:1 (29 Nov. 1980), Special Insert. The Senior Executive Service, with an authorized strength of 8500, is not fully staffed.

360 in France—though 85 percent of France's are drawn from the civil service—that a new administration is entitled to choose afresh. In a typical American department, the secretary, deputy and under secretaries, assistant and deputy assistant secretaries, administrators of large aggregates, chiefs of several bureaus, and regional directors are replaced by a new set of officials. In the Department of Commerce, 93 high political incumbents can be displaced; in the Department of Agriculture, 65.

For three decades the number of politically filled posts has increased. This occurred partly by interposition of new layers of political appointees and partly by multiplication of executives' staff assistants. But existing positions were also shifted from the career service to political appointment; examples are department's assistant secretaries for administration and regional directors. If political executives are the principal means by which a president and a department head can grasp control of the bureaucracy and institute changes in policy and program, the United States has abundantly provided for it.

THE PRESIDENT'S ENTOURAGE

Nearest the president are the White House staff and the agencies housed in the Executive Office of the President, especially the mostly career-staffed Office of Management and Budget (OMB). Between them one might expect a happy melding of short-term political and long-term careerist points of view in service of the president's policy and management responsibilities.

The White House staff

Every president needs near him a few intimate advisers who are politically astute and personally loyal. He turns to those with whom he has been closely associated in the campaigns for nomination and election and to friends in his home state. The problem that arises is twofold. One is that his closest advisers are often poorly qualified for the responsible governmental roles in which they are suddenly cast, roles that have become magnified by the centripetal pull of policy and short-term decision making to the White House and by the president's delegation of the tangle of domestic affairs to his aides as he increasingly becomes absorbed in foreign affairs.

The other form of the problem is extension downward in White House staffing of the same recruitment criteria, except for prior intimacy with the president: personal loyalty, campaign service, and congruence of substantive policy views, if any, with those voiced in the election campaign. In 1981, runs one report, "with few exceptions, the professionals on the policy development staff were active in Reagan's 1980 campaign for the presidency." Two of them, in their mid-twenties, had been campaign speech writers.[3] In the Carter administration, the then associate OMB director recalls, "OMB felt that the Domestic Policy Staff was too pervasive, too concerned with short-term political considerations and that some of its junior people were not too capable."[4]

3. Dick Kirschten, "Reagan Sings of Cabinet Government, and Anderson Leads the Chorus," *National Journal,* 13:824-27, 827, 824 (9 May 1981). In 1982, Martin Anderson's resignation as director of the staff was accepted.

4. W. Bowman Cutter, quoted in Dick Kirschten, "Decision Making in the White House: How Well Does It Serve the President?" *National Journal,* 14:584-89, 588 (3 Apr. 1982).

Characterizations of the presidential assistants constituting the White House staff vary more in tone than in essentials. One, kinder than most, reads, "They tend to be young, highly intelligent, and unashamedly on the make. They take chances, they cut corners, and unlike most politicians they sometimes have a little spontaneity and irreverence left in them. This accounts for much of their charm and most of their problems."[5] The words are from Patrick Anderson's study of assistants serving presidents from Roosevelt to Johnson. Characterizations of assistants to Nixon, Ford, Carter, and Reagan have a darker cast.

Efforts to strengthen the president by furnishing him with a staff of several hundred creates more problems than it solves. The White House itself becomes a complex, layered bureaucracy that is difficult to manage. The number of aides with the ready access to the president that propinquity promotes reduces his opportunities for conferring with cabinet members and seeking counsel from knowledgeable persons outside the government. The number, energy, and policy-area assignments of lower-level aides draw business to the White House that might well be left to cabinet departments. Such aides' intrusiveness into departmental affairs often bypasses department heads, thus weakening the prestige of those on whom the president depends for departmental management. The policy-formation process is slowed and complicated by in-house clearance procedures and by substantive and personal controversies among aides.[6] The White House contribution, then, becomes not the comprehensive, long-range view of policy and honest brokering of conflicting departmental advocacy positions, but often a poorly coordinated battle for the president's mind among his own assistants.

The Office of Management and Budget

Established in 1921 and brought into the new Executive Office in 1939, the Bureau of the Budget was a major resource for management of much of the presidential-level policy-formation process. It was staffed with unusually able careerists and generally headed by a well-qualified presidential appointee. Its skeptical review of departments' budget requests gave it control, under the president's direction, over one of the two major presidential policy instruments: the budget and the State of the Union Message. Additionally, its legislative clearance role enabled it to review all departments' legislative proposals and positions in support of or opposition to pending legislation, all with a view to advising whether they were in accord with the president's program. And its review of bills passed by Congress, including gathering of concerned departments' reactions, gave it a key role in advising the president whether to approve or veto the bills. Its administrative management staff had broad

---

5. Patrick Anderson, *The President's Men: White House Assistants of Franklin D. Roosevelt . . . Lyndon Johnson* (Garden City, NY: Doubleday, Anchor Books, 1969), p. 469. In the 1976 campaign, Anderson was a speech writer for Jimmy Carter; he declined appointment to the White House staff.

6. "The Carter decision loop covered well over a dozen separate offices within the White House; the process could take several weeks to complete, and it often generated considerable conflict." Paul C. Light, *The President's Agenda: Domestic Policy Choice from Kennedy to Carter* (Baltimore: Johns Hopkins University Press, 1982), p. 55.

responsibility for improving the organization and efficiency of executive agencies.

After 1960, while its budgetary power did not decline, presidential aides largely superseded the bureau's policy-level role in legislative clearance and review of enrolled congressional bills. And its work on administrative management declined as the budgetary staff gained dominance, so much so that it could not monitor compliance with its own administrative directives.

Despite Nixon's change of its name, in 1970, to the Office of Management and Budget, and despite its sizable staff, now about 600, these tendencies have persisted and new tendencies have appeared. Appointees to director and deputy director positions are more often political men, closely associated with the president, lobbying with Congress, and soliciting public support of his policies. A layer of noncareer appointees has been inserted between the director and the civil servants on the staff. New presidents and their aides initially distrust the bureaucrats in OMB, so that its rich fund of knowledge about the executive branch, the fate of earlier presidential initiatives, and the policy-affecting potential of the budget process are rarely tapped in the crucial first year. Though OMB mounts specific administrative management undertakings for particular presidents—as in executive branch reorganization, regulatory review, and paperwork management—the management staff for longer-range responsibilities has been successively cut, most recently in mid-1982. Informed observers believe that OMB needs reinvigoration, greater high-level participation by senior careerists, and either strengthening of its nonbudgetary activities or transfer of them to a new staff agency.

CABINET MEMBERS

The initial selection of members of the cabinet receives more personal attention by the president-elect than that of any other set of political executives, save his few top aides. Recent presidents have had such confidence in those they select as to assert an intention to institute cabinet government, meaning reliance on cabinet members for counsel and for the staffing and running of their departments.

Cabinet members are an abler lot than the conspicuous exceptions lead us to believe. Many have achieved distinction in their careers and, for good or ill, are members of the establishment. Eisenhower appointed nine millionaires and Reagan at least eight. Carter's 1977 cabinet included five members with Ph.D.s and five who were lawyers.[7] Most have had federal government experience. From 1953 to 1976, this was true of 55 percent of the initial appointees and of 85 percent of replacement appointees.[8] They often are generalists who have served in other cabinet posts, at the subcabinet level in the same or other departments, or as top presidential aides. Early exemplars of the pattern are George Marshall, Dean Acheson,

7. Nelson Polsby, "Presidential Cabinet Making: Lessons for the Political System," *Political Science Quarterly*, 93:15-25 (Spring 1978); "Financial Reports Show that 10 Members of Cabinet Are Worth $1 Million or More," AP dispatch in *New York Times*, 26 Jan. 1981, p. A24. Our text's count excludes cabinet members without departmental portfolios.

8. James J. Best, "Presidential Cabinet Appointments: 1953-1976," *Presidential Studies Quarterly*, 11:62-66, 65 (Winter 1981).

Robert Lovett, Averell Harriman, and Douglas Dillon. Later ones are Elliot Richardson, James Schlesinger, Rufus Vance, Harold Brown, Joseph Califano, Alexander Haig, Caspar Weinberger, and George Shultz. Many are highly qualified, whether by public or private experience, for the processes of advocacy, negotiation, and compromise that are at the heart of governmental policymaking—lawyers more so, corporate executives and academics somewhat less so, the few ideologues not at all.

However able and experienced they are, the president's early promise of cabinet government soon evaporates. Why should this be so? A too easy explanation, favored by White House aides, is that cabinet members "marry the natives"; each, headquartered in his department, is captured by the bureaucracy and by the clientele groups in the department's immediate environment. Responsiveness to the president, and to his aides, lapses.

An explanation that receives too little attention is that each cabinet member, as department head, is obligated to see to the faithful execution of the laws that fall within his department's jurisdiction. In most of its statutes, Congress vests authority directly in departments and their heads, not in the president. A department head is bound to resist White House aides' urging that he neglect or distort any of his principal statutory responsibilities. Should he not resist, he will alienate his career executives and will have to answer to clientele groups, congressional committees, and the courts.

A political element helps to poison the well. Though the president may initially promise cabinet members free hands in filling their subcabinet and other executive posts, this commitment eventually yields to the White House staff's insistence on clearance of nominees and, often, appointment of candidates centrally identified and preferred.

A variety of factors set cabinet members and White House aides on a collision course. In addition to those mentioned, petty and not-so-petty behaviors play their part. Cabinet members' access to the president is denied, White House aides fail to return cabinet members' telephone calls, and deliberate slights of protocol signal that individual members are out of favor. President Carter's purge of his cabinet in 1979 focused on those who had incurred White House aides' displeasure.

Joseph Califano quotes from his exit interview with Carter: "'Your performance as Secretary has been outstanding,' the President said. 'You have put the Department in better shape than it has ever been before. You've been the best Secretary of HEW.... The problem is the friction with the White House staff. The same qualities and drive and managerial ability that make you such a superb Secretary create problems with the White House staff.'"[9] The secretary must have sensed an odd reversal of role, for in the Johnson White House, "serving as the chief expediter for an impatient and demanding President, Califano made many enemies," some among cabinet members. "Time and again . . . Califano fought to impose Johnson's interests over the narrower interests of the departments of government."[10]

9. Joseph A. Califano, Jr., *Governing America: An Insider's Report from the White House and the Cabinet* (New York: Simon & Schuster, 1981), pp. 434-35.
10. Anderson, *The President's Men*, pp. 443, 446.

Whether by their own or the president's choice, cabinet members' median term since World War II has been barely more than two years. Over one-fifth of the secretaries were in place for less than 11 months.[11] From 1953 through 1976, there were 5 presidents, but 12 secretaries of commerce, 11 secretaries of HEW, 10 attorneys general, 9 secretaries of labor and of the treasury, and 8 secretaries of defense.[12]

Brevity of tenure, perhaps because it is not anticipated, does not deflect cabinet members from according highest priority to the making and influencing of policy. This is no doubt appropriate, but there is a price to pay. Many give very low priority to departmental management, which is the key to assuring responsiveness and effectiveness of the bureaucracy. This is as true of able corporate executives as of their colleagues from other walks of life. Secretary of the Treasury Michael Blumenthal, formerly head of the Bendix Corporation, made the point: "You learn very quickly that you do not go down in history as a good or bad Secretary in terms of how well you ran the place, whether you're a good administrator or not. You're perceived to be a good Secretary in terms of whether the policies for which you are responsible are adjudged successful or not. . . . But that's not true in a company. In a company it's how well you run the place."[13]

POLITICAL EXECUTIVES

Below cabinet members and other major agencies' heads are most of the 1600 political executives. A president intent on effecting change within the executive branch normally transmits his intentions through these appointees and, at least in theory, should be able to rely on them for vigorous translation of intentions into action. Yet the multiplicity, qualifications, and tenure of political executives probably hamper the effecting of change more than does any obduracy of the permanent bureaucracy.

Numbers

The large number of political appointments available guarantees that errors of choice will be made, and the earlier the more. In the 10-week post-election rush, self-nomination, others' recommendations, the old-boy network, the BOGSAT technique ("a bunch of guys sitting around a table"), and a variety of other means provide the large pool of candidates and the disorderly modes of selection.

The numbers also account for how deeply political appointments extend into the bowels of departmental administration. The proliferation of subcabinet posts, strictly defined, affords one clue. These positions—of under secretary, deputy under secretary, and assistant secretary—increased from 55 in 1950 to 84 in 1960, 113 in 1970, and 145 in 1978.[14] The secretary may have as many as 15 politically appointed assis-

---

11. G. Calvin Mackenzie, *The Politics of Presidential Appointments* (New York: Free Press, 1981), p. 7. The period covered was 1945-77; in 1979, President Carter replaced five cabinet members.

12. Best, "Presidential Cabinet Appointments," p. 63.

13. W. Michael Blumenthal, "Candid Reflections of a Businessman in Washington," *Fortune*, 99(2):36ff., 39 (Jan. 1979).

14. Thomas P. Murphy, Donald E. Nuechterlein, and Ronald J. Stupak, *Inside the Bureaucracy: The View from the Assistant Secretary's Desk* (Boulder, CO: Westview Press, 1978), pp. 5-6.

tants attached to his own office, and the subcabinet officials may average two such assistants apiece.[15] Below the subcabinet level are a number of political appointees with such titles as deputy assistant secretary, bureau chief, deputy bureau chief, and regional director.[16]

The large number of political executives and their penetration of departments, bureaus, and the field service distance able careerists from the centers of decision making. Their rich potential remains untapped, especially in the early period when the administration's and departments' major policy proposals are formulated.

Qualifications

By most standard criteria, especially educational level and subject-matter knowledge relevant to their particular program-area responsibilities, political executives are a well-qualified elite. Three other criteria concern us here. These are partisan and policy compatibility with the president, governmental experience, and capacity to manage large organizations.

Political executives are less partisan than their designation suggests. From 1961 to 1978, members of the president's party averaged only 58 percent among the four administrations' sets of political appointees, with a range of 47 percent under Johnson to 65 percent under Nixon. Within cabinet departments, two-thirds of the political appointees, on average, belonged to the president's party, with State and Defense on the low side (44 and 47 percent) and Housing and Urban Development and Agriculture (89 and 86 percent) on the high side.[17]

Old images of party patronage have largely ceased to reflect reality. White House personnel staffs try to deflect partisan pressures by rewarding large financial contributors and taking care of defeated candidates for electoral office by minor, though sometimes major, ambassadorships; membership in multimember bodies—regulatory boards and commissions, presidential advisory commissions, and departmental advisory committees—and invitations to White House galas for foreign dignitaries.

The politics of policy, if not of party, plays a large role in recruitment. This politics takes two forms: loyalty to the president and his policies throughout his term, including the possibility of his changing course, and inflexible loyalty to particular policies, most of them compatible with the president's campaign rhetoric but selectively erosive during his term. The second kind of loyalty can turn antipresidential. Initial selection of subcabinet and subordinate executives depends heavily on nominations and recommendations from the economic and professional communities interested in particular programs. A

---

15. Based on the Interior Department's management pattern, as charted in Hugh Heclo, *A Government of Strangers: Executive Politics in Washington* (Washington, DC: Brookings Institution, 1977), p. 58.

16. In 1977, political appointees in the Department of Health, Education and Welfare included 13 deputy assistant secretaries, 12 bureau chiefs, 10 deputy bureau chiefs, and 10 regional directors. James W. Fesler, *Public Administration: Theory and Practice* (Englewood Cliffs, NJ: Prentice-Hall, 1980), pp. 135-36.

17. Calculated from tables in Roger G. Brown, "Party and Bureaucracy: From Kennedy to Reagan," *Political Science Quarterly*, 97:279-94, 283, 285 (Summer 1982). These and related data in the text partly reflect the promotion of civil servants to political-executive posts, especially in the last half of a president's term.

number of those chosen are likely to be drawn from interest groups, single-cause movements, conservative or liberal think tanks, and congressional staff members who share the president's initial orientation. Many such are advocates, with agendas of their own. There is little assurance that such political appointees will flexibly respond to the president's initiatives for change rather than firmly adhere to their convictions, constituencies, political patrons. Yet they are arrayed in many layers between the good to be done, as the president perceives it, and those who can do it, the career executives in closest touch with implementation.

Advocates, it is true, have a strong impulse to innovate, whether to turn the clock forward or backward. But innovations can be good or bad, well timed or ill timed, contributors or embarrassments to a larger strategy of change. Advocacy-oriented political executives are not the president's men and women. They march to a different drummer.

Prior experience in the federal government is a criterion closely linked to political executives' performance. Looking back, former appointees confess that they were poorly prepared for the Washington setting of interest groups, congressional committees, the White House staff, the goldfish-bowl exposure to the media, the budget process, and the permanent bureaucracy. In 1970 over two-thirds of presidential and two-fifths of departmental political appointees had less than two years of federal governmental experience.[18]

Another two-fifths of the departmentally appointed political officials had over 10 years of federal experience and, like the top civil servants, were better prepared. Hugh Heclo notes the anomaly, that "unlike the situation in most private organizations, in the U.S. executive branch those in the top positions of formal authority [that is, presidential appointees] are likely to be substantially less familiar with their working environment than both their civil service and political subordinates."[19]

Capability for the management of large organizations or for operating in them is a third criterion of executives' effectiveness. Few of the political executives who are lawyers or who are recruited from universities and research institutes, interest-group organizations, congressional staffs, and small business firms have had experience that prepares them for running a bureau of 5000 employees, let alone for operating in one of the cabinet departments, which range from 15,000 to one million employees. Sometimes, as Dean Acheson and George W. Ball have noted, even the head of a major corporation may have served only an ornamental function there and can do no more in government.[20]

Tenure

Independently of other attributes, the brief tenure of political executives suffi-

18. Heclo, *A Government of Strangers*, p. 101 (drawing on a study by Joel D. Aberbach). The year 1970 may seem unrepresentative, as the Nixon administration had followed almost a decade of Democratic administrations. However, experienced Eisenhower executives had aged no more than 10 years in the decade.

19. Ibid.
20. Both write acidly about Edward R. Stettinius, who had been vice-president of General Motors and chairman of the board of United States Steel. Between 1939 and 1945, he served as a defense production official, land-lease administrator, under secretary of state, and secretary of state. Dean Acheson, *Present at the Creation: My Years in the State Department* (New York: W. W. Norton, 1969), pp. 88-91; and George W. Ball, *The Past Has Another Pattern: Memoirs* (New York: W. W. Norton, 1982), pp. 29-30.

ces to explain the marginality of their impact. In the period of 1960 to 1972, over half of the under secretaries and assistant secretaries moved out within less than two years, including a fifth who left in less than one year.[21] How much time does a new political executive need to achieve effectiveness? Maurice Stans, former secretary of commerce, said, "A business executive needs at least two years to become effective in government, to understand the intricacies of his programs, and to make beneficial changes."[22]

Rapid turnover not only reduces individual effectiveness, it impairs three relationships that are at the heart of the administration's effectiveness. First, it complicates a department head's effort to establish teamwork among his principal subordinates, for they are ever changing. Second, rapid turnover near the top recurrently breaks up interdepartmental networks of political executives sharing concern with, and perhaps having divergent views on, particular policy and program areas extending across several departments. For these, especially, there need to be what Heclo terms "relationships of confidence and trust."[23] The chemistry involved in these interpersonal relations takes time to develop and is upset if new elements are constantly being introduced. Third, top civil servants' relations with political superiors that are here today and gone tomorrow cannot faithfully follow copybook maxims. Some careerists, if called on, will patiently tutor one after another political executive to speed his learning process. Others, particularly those in charge of bureaus and programs, will take protective measures to minimize the damage an ill-prepared and very temporary political executive can do.

Political executives share a number of attributes that limit their effectiveness as the president's agents of change. Their number is too large. Partisanship is too weak to make them a cohesive group. In its place is the politics of policy. For some this means a commitment to support the president and, so, to adapt flexibly to his changing policy agenda and priorities. But for many it means tenacious devotion to particular program areas and particular policies, whether or not they comport with the president's strategic emphases. Too few political executives have prior governmental experience; fewer know how to run a large organization well. Finally, political appointees' stay is short and their comings and goings erratic.

CAREER EXECUTIVES

Recent presidents campaigned against the bureaucracy and complained during their terms of the unresponsiveness of the bureaucracy. Most political appointees enter office with a stereotypical view of bureaucrats. This inhibits their seeking a collaborative relation with those best informed on departmental programs and best prepared to warn inexperienced superiors of minefields in the surrounding terrain. The three elements of the president's and political executives' stance are an assumption that the bureaucracy is swollen, a doubt of careerists' competence, and an expectation of their unresponsiveness to the administration in

---

21. Arch Patton, "Government's Revolving Door," *Business Week*, Sept. 1973, pp. 12-13.

22. Quoted, ibid., p. 12. The same estimate is made in Frederick V. Malek, *Washington's Hidden Tragedy* (New York: Macmillan, 1978), p. 49.

23. Heclo, *A Government of Strangers*, p. 158 and passim.

power. The first is quickly disposed of. For three decades the number of federal civilian employees has been substantially stable, in contrast to increases in the nation's population, its employed labor force, and the range of governmental responsibilities.

Doubt of careerists' competence is ill founded. Elmer Staats, after a distinguished career in politically appointive posts, said on ending his term as the comptroller general of the United States that ever since World War II days, "I have worked with business people who have been in the government.... And I have yet to find a single one of those business executives after their experience here who doesn't go out and have nothing but praise for the calibre and the hard work of the people in the government."[24] And Alan K. Campbell, an executive vice-president of ARA Services, Inc.—and earlier a Carter appointee—reports that "the quality of top managers I knew in the federal government... is every bit as high as we have at ARA; and on the whole, the people at ARA are paid from 1½ to 3 times more than their public sector counterparts."[25]

An expectation that the bureaucracy will be unresponsive to the administration in power is too simplistic to fit comfortably with the complexity of factors determining senior civil servants' behavior. Top careerists are remarkably diverse in ideological orientation and in party identification. On a scale of attitudes ranging from state intervention to free enterprise, Joel D. Aberbach and his colleagues found that their sample of such American careerists was "more heterogeneous than any of the European bureaucratic samples." The basic picture is a distribution of attitudes that is not only wide but substantially congruent with the distribution pattern in Congress.[26]

Party affiliations of careerists are weaker predictors of behavior. In social-service agencies in 1970, "even Republican administrators... were not wholly sympathetic to the social service retrenchments sought by the Nixon administration."[27] Sample surveys in 1970 and 1976 found that top careerists were 47 percent Democratic (38 percent in 1976), 36 percent Independent (48 percent in 1976), and 17 percent Republican (16 percent in 1976). Using different tests of Independents' leanings, the surveyors drew different conclusions. For 1970, Joel Aberbach and Bert Rockman held that "the belief that a Republican administration does not have natural political allies within the federal bureaucracy seems well-justified."[28] For 1976, Richard Cole and David Caputo believed that "Independents and party identifiers combined assure either a Republican or a Democratic president substantial support at

---

24. Transcript, *The MacNeil/Lehrer Report: Elmer Staats Interview*, 6 Mar. 1981, pp. 6-7.

25. Alan K. Campbell, in a symposium, "The Public Service as Institution," *Public Administration Review*, 42:304-20, 315 (July-Aug. 1982).

26. Aberbach, Putnam, and Rockman, *Bureaucrats and Politicians*, pp. 122, 124-25. On congruence with Congress, see Joel D. Aberbach and Bert A. Rockman, "The Overlapping Worlds of American Federal Executives and Congressmen," *British Journal of Political Science*, 7:38 (Jan. 1967), Table 6.

27. Joel D. Aberbach and Bert A. Rockman, "Clashing Beliefs Within the Executive Branch: The Nixon Administration Bureaucracy," *American Political Science Review*, 70:456-68, 467 (June 1976).

28. Ibid., p. 458.

the senior career levels of the federal bureaucracy."[29]

Beyond ideologies and party affiliations, and often overriding them, is another attitudinal orientation. Most careerists perceive their role as one entailing the obligation to serve loyally the people's choice as president. Because senior careerists have served through several changes in administration, this is a well-internalized commitment. It is qualified, to be sure, by resistance to illegality, a resistance that served the nation well in the Watergate era.

This basic commitment, however, can be attenuated by another attitude toward role performance. Typically, senior civil servants identify with their agency and its responsibilities. Their finding fulfillment in achieving the purposes of statutes entrusted to them, instead of being passively neutral, generally strengthens the faithful execution of the laws. But it lures some into bureaucratic politics—protection of the agency's turf, development of a degree of autonomy, and mobilization of allies in Congress and clientele groups.

How responsive careerists are to presidential policy shifts is a complex product of ideologies, party affiliations, the civil-service doctrine of loyalty to the incumbent president, and devotion to particular programs and agencies. The relative weights of these factors vary with circumstances. The most negative reactions can be expected when the president orders termination of an agency or of well-established programs, reduction of funds, or slashing of staff.

Yet when, by President Reagan's order, the Community Services Administration, an antipoverty agency, was dismantled in three months, the agency director reports, "The career service had demonstrated in a dramatic way the best of professional integrity in executing a difficult assignment most of them opposed." It shows, he adds, that "the mythology of an untrustworthy bureaucracy poised to undermine a policy with which it disagreed was simply not true."[30]

THE SHARED WORLD OF
POLITICAL AND
CAREER EXECUTIVES

Though political and career executives differ in important regards, the considerable degree of congruence of orientations permits expectation that they might harmoniously collaborate in their shared world. The recent institution of the Senior Executive Service is designed to facilitate such collaboration. Yet careerists' morale has fallen to perhaps its lowest point, and their career paths often poorly prepare them for engagement in the fashioning of broad policy.

Some congruent orientations

Political executives and top careerists have a good deal in common. Both groups are highly educated; more than half the members of each hold graduate or professional degrees. However, more of the senior civil servants, 40 percent, majored in technology and natural science; only 10 percent of political executives did so. Members of the two

29. Richard L. Cole and David A. Caputo, "Presidential Control of the Senior Civil Service: Assessing the Strategies of the Nixon Years," *American Political Science Review,* 73:399-413, 412 (June 1979).

30. Dwight Ink, "CSA Closedown—A Myth Challenged," *Bureaucrat,* 11:39-43, 39, 43 (Summer 1982).

groups do not differ substantially in the proportions that see their role, or roles, as that of advocate, legalist, broker, trustee, facilitator, policymaker, or ombudsman. The civil servants, though, are twice as likely as political executives to have a technician-role focus, and half as likely to have a partisan-role focus. Their external activities disclose a common pattern: nearly two-thirds of each group have regular contacts with members of Congress; over 90 percent of each have regular contacts with representatives of clientele groups. Internally, not surprisingly, political executives have about twice as much contact with their department heads as do senior civil servants.[31] But, if not surprising, it indicates exclusion or filtering of counsel from members of the permanent government.

Top careerists share political executives' frustrations with bureaucratic obstacles to effective performance, particularly the pervasiveness of red tape and the constricting personnel system. At least two-thirds of those sampled in 1981 answered no when asked whether "the administrative support systems" provide a pool of qualified professional and managerial talent to hire from, make it easy to hire employees, or make it easy to fire or to apply lesser sanctions against poorly performing employees.[32]

Finally, the infiltration of political-executive ranks by career civil servants fosters congruence of outlook with those continuing in civil-service status. Former careerists filled 25 percent of assistant secretaryships in the 1933-61 period—an average for the three presidencies. In the mid-1970s they held nearly half of such posts, and in 1978, under Carter, 61 percent.[33] Below the assistant secretaries, Heclo reports, "one-third to one-half of the noncareer ... posts ... are usually filled by career civil servants."[34] In the period Heclo deals with, such cooptation by the incumbent administration required sacrifice of civil-service status and possible dismissal from government service by the next administration. This has changed.

The Senior Executive Service

The 1978 Civil Service Reform Act pooled most political executives and top career executives in a Senior Executive Service (SES). The service currently includes about 7000 executives, 90 percent of them careerists and 10 percent political appointees. This is a specified governmentwide ratio; within it an individual agency's political appointees may rise as high as 25 percent. Except for presidential appointees requiring senatorial confirmation, or requiring White House clearance, a department head freely chooses political appointees who meet his previously established qualification standards. In making career appointments to the SES, he must adhere to competitive merit principles.

The key feature is the new flexibility with which the department head can assign and reassign SES members,

---

31. Aberbach, Putnam, and Rockman, *Bureaucrats and Politicians,* pp. 52, 94, 230-31, 234; Aberbach and Rockman, "The Overlapping Worlds," p. 28. On meagerness of bureau chiefs' contacts with department heads, see Herbert Kaufman, *The Administrative Behavior of Federal Bureau Chiefs* (Washington, DC: Brookings Institution, 1981), pp. 59-62, 184-90.

32. Thomas D. Lynch and Gerald T. Gabris, "Obstacles to Effective Management," *Bureaucrat,* 10:8-14, 9-10 (Spring 1981).

33. Murphy, Nuechterlein, and Stupak, *Inside the Bureaucracy,* pp. 7, 195.

34. Heclo, *A Government of Strangers,* p. 131.

whether political or career, to particular positions. Only two restrictions apply. A careerist is protected against involuntary reassignment for the first 120 days after appointment of a new department head, or of a political executive with reassignment authority. And in about 45 percent of the positions, the department head can assign and reassign only careerists, not political appointees. These are posts reserved for civil servants "to ensure impartiality, or the public's confidence in the impartiality of the Government," as the statute phrases it.[35]

These necessary protections accounted for, the system is one in which the department head can assemble his large management team, mixing political and career executives as suits his purpose. Additionally, advised by performance-review boards, he can at any time remove from SES a career member rated "less than fully successful."

Morale

The Senior Executive Service had a troubled start.[36] Pay was a major problem. Though the Reform Act directs the president to establish SES pay levels, Congress later set a pay ceiling that in 1982 put 84 percent of SES members at the same pay, $6000 below the president's top pay level. The performance awards and substantial bonuses for abler SES careerists, provided in the act, were also later curtailed. The most basic problem was eased when, at the end of 1982, Congress authorized pay increases of up to 15 percent for some 32,000 senior government employees.

For nonpay reasons, too, the morale of SES career members fell to a lamentably low point. They tired of being flayed as bureaucrats by a succession of recent administrations. They believed that "the quality of political leadership in the agencies has been declining" in the last several years, so that "career staffs are being directed by persons who are simply not capable of providing the kind of leadership and guidance that the programs of agencies and the public deserve."[37] They were disturbed by political executives' short time frames. In 1981 over three-fifths of top careerists sampled said that rapid turnover of political appointees made long-term planning difficult, and that such appointees focus on short-term projects "nearly all the time" or "rather often."[38] And, rightly or wrongly, they reacted negatively to the reversal of programs by foxes in the chicken coop.

Whatever the causes, an alarming exodus of top careerists occurred. About 1600 career executives left the federal service between July 1979 and June 1981. In 1981 about 95 percent of the most experienced senior careerists, those eligible for voluntary retirement at ages 55 to 59, with 30 years' service, were deciding to leave, compared to about 18 percent in 1978.[39]

Career paths

Two features of the careers of senior civil servants weaken their potential

35. *U.S. Code,* Title V, secs. 3395, 3132 (b).
36. Panel on the Public Service, National Academy of Public Administration, *The Senior Executive Service: An Interim Report, October 1981* (Washington, DC: National Academy of Public Administration, 1981).

37. Ibid., pp. 34-35.
38. Lynch and Gabris, "Obstacles to Effective Management," pp. 9-10.
39. Annette Gaul, "Why Do Executives Leave the Federal Service?" *Management* (published by the U.S. Office of Personnel Management), 2:13-15 (Fall 1981); William J. Lanouette, "SES—From Civil Service Showpiece to Incipient Failure in Two Years," *National Journal,* 13:1296 (18 July 1981).

contribution to high-level policymaking and management. Most were initially recruited in their twenties and thirties as specialists—scientists, engineers, economists, and the like. What they know about public affairs and the management of large organizations must, therefore, be haphazardly acquired as they move forward in their careers. The second career feature is confinement of most of their experience to one agency. The two specializations, by discipline and by agency, reinforce each other. Top careerists, therefore, have depth of expertness but not the breadth of training and experience that in other countries produces generalist administrators. For the same reasons, many American senior civil servants develop a myopic loyalty to particular agencies and programs.

These disabilities are not necessarily compensated for by political executives. Many of them qualify for particular political positions because their professional specialties and private-sector activities closely relate to the programs they are to administer. Though this may make for some congruence of outlook with that of top careerists, it also imposes blinders that remove much of the world from their field of vision.

POLICYMAKING PROBLEMS

Formation and effectuation of an administration's policies are plagued by two major problems. One is the counterpull of centrifugal and centripetal forces. The other is the prevalence of short time perspectives.

Centrifugal and centripetal forces

The multiplication of governmental responsibilities has generated a geometrical growth of interrelations among programs and among departments. Whether the focus is on reduction of poverty, environmental protection, or foreign policy, the range of relevant factors and of concerned departments casts a shadow of quaintness on classic organizational doctrines of compartmentalization of authority and responsibility. Everything seems to be connected with everything else. Yet centrifugal forces create narrowly oriented, substantially autonomous policy communities in the governmental system.

George P. Shultz and Kenneth W. Dam, before becoming the secretary and deputy secretary of state, wrote of the costs of such partitioning: "In a balkanized executive branch, policymaking is necessarily a piecemeal affair; policymakers are under the constraint that they are not permitted to view problems whole."[40] Many share their concern that "the trend of events is toward greater fragmentation" and inveigh against iron triangles—enduring alliances of bureau, relevant congressional committees, and special-interest groups concerned with the bureau's programs. Joseph Califano believes that "the severest threat to governing for all the people" comes from the pernicious fact that "we have institutionalized, in law and bureaucracy, single-interest organizations that can accede only in the narrow interest and are incapable of adjudicating in the national interest." "We must," he says, "have people and institutions ... that will render national policy more than the sum of the atomistic interests. We must design bureaucratic structures that permit and encourage top govern-

---

40. George P. Shultz and Kenneth W. Dam, *Economic Policy Beyond the Headlines* (New York: W. W. Norton, 1977), p. 173.

ment officials to assess special interests, rather than pander to them."[41]

How to counter these tendencies is a problem far from solution. The principal, though problematic, counterstrategy is the centripetal pull to the White House of matters that earlier might have been left for resolution within individual departments. Elliot Richardson, holder of four cabinet posts, writes that "the delegation of responsibilities and their interposition between the President and department or agency heads are symptoms, not causes. The fundamental problems are the growth of Presidential tasks and the inescapable burdens of interrelatedness which lead inexorably to the enlargement of staff functions."[42] White House assistants, we have seen, are weakly prepared for the formulation of broad, long-range policies.

A hazard that attends the centripetal tendency is the swamping of deliberative policymaking at the top by strong pressures on the White House for quick decisions on myriad problems, which arise seriatim in no discernible pattern and are mistakenly thought to be discrete. Responses to sudden surprises can rarely be tested for compatibility with recent and pending actions or checked for consistency with long-range policy. Shultz and Dam attest to the phenomenon: "Most decisions in government . . . are made . . . in the day-to-day process of responding to crises of the moment. The danger is that this daily firefighting leaves the policymaker further and further from his goal. . . . Many of the failures of government in dealing with the economy can be traced to an attempt to solve minor problems piecemeal."[43]

Efforts are made, of course, to involve cabinet members in top-level policymaking. The Reagan administration, with six Cabinet Councils, was not the first to assemble cabinet members concerned with the same policy area in hopes of a coordinated approach to policy formation. But, as Richardson says, "Interdepartmental committees cannot do the job alone because their disagreements can all too easily end in deadlock. To prevent deadlocks some external authority is needed—and here is a role that invites reliance on the anonymous Presidential staff."[44] Furthermore, cabinet-level committees, including the Reagan Cabinet Councils, though they were staffed by White House aides, do not monopolize policymaking channels. In 1981 and 1982, major presidential policy decisions and proposals emerged without cabinet input.

Time perspectives

George W. Ball, the under secretary of state under Kennedy, recalls, "When one tried to point out the long-range implications of a current problem or how it meshed or collided with other major national interests, Kennedy would often say, politely but impatiently, 'Let's not worry about five years from now, what do we do tomorrow?'"[45]

---

41. Califano, *Governing America*, pp. 451, 452. "Government by advocacy" (Shultz and Dam's term) has invaded the White House itself. Charged with "public liaison" are assistants and deputy assistants to the president for the elderly, youth, women, consumers, Hispanics, Blacks, the Jewish community, and other groups.

42. Elliot Richardson, *The Creative Balance: Government, Politics, and the Individual in America's Third Century* (New York: Holt, Rinehart & Winston, 1976), p. 80.

43. Shultz and Dam, *Economic Policy*, p. 18.
44. Richardson, *The Creative Balance*, p. 73.
45. Ball, *The Past Has Another Pattern*, p. 167.

This attitude pervades the White House staff, is less operative among cabinet members and their deputy and under secretaries, gets strongly reinforced among assistant secretaries and other political executives, and is the despair of career civil servants. Systemic factors, not personal quirkiness, account for its prevalence.

The president's major opportunity for formulating his major policies with an expectation of favorable congressional action falls in the period between the popular election and the end of his first six months in office. He can, or does, claim a mandate for change, his public-approval ratings quickly register 70 percent or so, Congress grants a honeymoon period, the president can usually focus on domestic rather than principally foreign policies, and his cabinet members are not yet alienated by the White House staff.

Most presidents seize the opportunity offered. They initiate more requests for legislation in the first than in any later year. If wise, they act early in that year, for, Paul C. Light reports, 72 percent of requests introduced in January to March of the first year are eventually enacted, but only 25 percent of third- and fourth-quarter requests are so successful.[46]

The period of greatest opportunity is also the period when the administration may be least capable of carefully fashioning a policy program. Legislative proposals advanced in the first three months are largely products of the campaign staff and pro tem transition advisers. Though the cabinet is completed in December, appointment of subcabinet and other political executives stretches through several months. The permanent bureaucracy is not fully available in the preinaugural period. After the inauguration the bureaucracy is not trusted. So the new administration deprives itself of data, expertness, sophisticated understanding of the Washington environment, and longer time perspectives, all of which could strengthen the policy-formation process.

Coming elections, congressional and presidential, soon cast their shadows. That, together with the president's increasing absorption in foreign affairs, explains why, as John Helmer writes, "for only one year, the first for a one-term president, can it be said that he has time and some political incentive to consider longer-term problems and to make decisions and commitments whose results may not be immediately apparent."[47] In the second year, seeking to minimize loss of his party's congressional seats, he and his aides prefer initiatives with quick impact. The presidential reelection campaign begins in the third year and becomes all-important in the fourth year. Furthermore, neither Congress nor foreign governments welcome major policy proposals for which negotiation must bridge the current and a possibly different successor administration.

The irony is that by the second half of the presidential term, the administration has become better equipped to formulate long-range policies. The White House usually has achieved a clearer structure and more orderly processes,

---

46. Light, *The President's Agenda,* pp. 44-45. See p. 42 for comparison of the number of the first and later years' requests.

47. John Helmer, "The Presidential Office: Velvet Fist in an Iron Glove," in *The Illusion of Presidential Government,* eds. Hugh Heclo and Lester M. Salamon (Boulder, CO: Westview Press, for the National Academy of Public Administration, 1981), pp. 78-79.

though it may have increased friction with cabinet members. Half the initial political appointees have left their posts and replacements have been more prudently chosen, often by promotion or transfer of able and responsive political executives and by promotion of careerists.[48] Continuing political executives have acquired Washington experience, discovered that civil servants are colleagues, not enemies, and learned that the designing of policies needs to take account of their implementability.[49] Regrettably, these resources cannot be exploited in a period dominated by short time perspectives.

A MODEST PROPOSAL

Deficiencies in the making and implementing of policy at the top levels of the executive branch derive from many sources. Some of the most basic lie outside the scope of this article. Within our framework one thing is clear: exhorting officials to behave differently than they do is profitless unless incentives are created that will alter their behavior. That daunting task might be circumvented by changing the mix of top executives.

Reducing the number of political executives would permit greater care in their selection and would open opportunities for experienced careerists, with their longer time perspectives, to contribute to the design and implementation of programs that embody the administration's innovative policies. Surprisingly, this is strongly advocated by President Nixon's top political recruiter. Frederick Malek writes,

The solution to problems of rigidity and resistance to change in government is *not* to increase the number of appointive positions at the top, as so many politicians are wont to do. . . . An optimum balance between the number of career and noncareer appointments . . . should be struck in favor of fewer political appointees, not more. In many cases, the effectiveness of an agency would be improved and political appointments would be reduced by roughly 25 percent if line positions beneath the assistant secretary level were reserved for career officials.[50]

If his prescription were followed, top careerists would play a more significant role, one that is common in Europe and one that would bolster their morale and reduce the rate of prime-age resignations and retirements.

James L. Sundquist compared the policymaking capacity of the United States with that of five Western European countries that successfully developed and applied policies to influence the regional distribution of their populations—largely a matter of incentives for private investment in declining areas and disincentives for investment in regions growing too rapidly. By 1970 the United States had a clear national policy, in principle. It was embraced in both major parties' platforms, was frequently set forth by President Nixon, and was partially reflected in two congressional statutes. But, in contrast to European countries, "the institutional structure in the United States did not respond to the political directives."[51] Why not?

---

48. This staffing strategy partly reflects reluctance of persons in the private sector to accept appointments in the terminal years or months of an administration.

49. However, negative factors are the fall in the president's public-approval ratings, the shift of his personal energies to foreign affairs, and, consequently, substantial delegation of domestic affairs to his aides.

50. Malek, *Washington's Hidden Tragedy*, pp. 102-3.

51. James L. Sundquist, "A Comparison of Policy-Making Capacity in the United States and

Among several reasons, Sundquist emphasizes the "gulf between the career bureaucracy, which was familiar with the data and had some degree of competence to analyze it, and the [White House] staff advisers who had responsibility for developing policy recommendations." In Europe a typical participant "was at the same time the long-time career civil servant and the respected policy adviser." In the United States, "many of the most competent and ambitious of the career officials—the kind that rise to the top in European civil services—find themselves excluded from the inner policy-making circles, or subordinated to younger, less experienced political appointees, and so depart. The capability of the career service is reduced, which leads to pressures for further politicization, in a vicious circle."[52]

If the quality of senior civil servants has been declining and if the policy-making process needs greater participation by careerists, we urgently need to repair the damage and strengthen careerists' capabilities for high-level responsibilities. Raising the level of positions to which able careerists can aspire will help. Beyond that, the top civil service needs strengthening of executive development programs. These are a mix of identifying the comers, moving them among a variety of broadening assignments, and providing sabbatical-leave years in university graduate programs and shorter training periods at federal academies such as the Federal Executive Institute. Such leaves and training opportunities should come at the career point when a careerist's special professional discipline and narrow, single-agency experience are inadequate preparation for the work that lies ahead. This includes management of large organizations, negotiations with other agencies, the White House, Congress, and interest groups, shaping of legislative and presidential-directive drafts to assure successful implementation, and relating of policy ideas to one another and to the social fabric of America.

From 1953 on, says Sundquist, "no administration devoted any appreciable attention to training and developing a new generation of career managers, or even seemed to care."[53] The reason is a familiar one. This requires a long time perspective and yields no credit for an administration in its short life.

Five European Countries: The Case of Population Distribution," in *Population Policy Analysis*, eds. Michael E. Kraft and Mark Schneider (Lexington, MA: D. C. Heath, 1978), pp. 67-80, 71.

52. Ibid., p. 73. The theme is more fully developed in James L. Sundquist, "Jimmy Carter as Public Administrator: An Appraisal at Mid-Term," *Public Administration Review*, 39:3-11, 6-8 (Jan-Feb. 1979).

53. Sundquist, "Jimmy Carter as Public Administrator," p. 8.

Policy Innovation and the Structure of the State: The Politics-Administration Nexus in France and Britain

By PETER A. HALL

ABSTRACT: Democratic governments often promise political change, but have difficulty delivering it. The capacity of each state to formulate and implement innovative forms of policy varies across nations. In particular, it is affected by the structural features of the state itself, of state-society relations, and of social institutions in each nation. This article focuses on one facet of the structure of the state, the organization of the politics-administration nexus, in Britain and France. Its purpose is to compare the impacts of different forms of politician-civil-servant relations on the capacity of governments to innovate. After a consideration of the general problems associated with governmental innovation, four conditions conducive to innovation are identified. The dimensions of the politics-administration nexus associated with the position of the chief executive, interministerial coordination, departmental innovation, and the character of the higher civil service in both nations are examined, with a view to ascertaining the extent to which these conditions are present in Britain and France. Finally, the implications of this analysis for the United States are reviewed.

Peter A. Hall is an assistant professor of government at Harvard University and a research associate of the Center for European Studies there. After receiving a B.A. in political economy from the University of Toronto, he completed an M.Phil. at Oxford and a Ph.D. at Harvard in political science. In 1974-75 he served as a legislative aide at the Canadian Parliament. He is the author of several articles on national planning and comparative economic policy, and currently teaches courses at Harvard in European government, comparative public policy, and the historical analysis of the state.

DEMOCRATIC governments are more than the guardians of social stability. From time to time they must also be the agents of social change and renewal. Special circumstances, such as the appearance of a depression or the conclusion of a war, may provide a critical juncture at which the state finds it expedient to redesign institutions and redirect its policies. Alternatively, the electorate may call for a change. The administrations of Ronald Reagan in the United States, Margaret Thatcher in Britain, and François Mitterand in France were all elected by voters who looked forward to the change of direction that their platforms promised.

It is easier to promise political change, however, than it is to deliver it. As they solicit the cooperation of those who must help formulate the policies, the agreement of those who must administer them, and the acquiescence of those who will be affected by them, the advocates of innovation will encounter resistance from those who have a vested interest in the status quo, both inside and outside the state apparatus itself. Therefore, a series of factors that determine the balance of power between innovators and traditionalists will affect the innovative capacity of a government.

Some of these are conjunctural: the auspices for change will be more favorable at some times than at others. But the most important factors are structural. Upon taking office, each government, however radical, inherits an institutional apparatus that was constructed by its predecessors and confronts a network of societal relations the configuration of which is determined by history. The structures of power and rationality implicit in these institutionalized sets of relations can have a profound impact on the ability of a government to formulate and implement innovative policies.

Three kinds of structural factors affect the ability of a government to innovate. The first are those associated with the structure of the state itself. These include the elements of internal organization that determine the balance of power and genre of relations between the executive and legislature, between the political leadership and civil service, among departments, between the judiciary and administration, and between various echelons within the departments themselves.

A second set of organizational features characterize state-society relations. To a large extent, these determine the leverage state managers wield when seeking the acquiescence of societal groups in new policies. The French state, for instance, controls most of the banking sector and 30 percent or more of the equity in over 800 French corporations.[1] Thus its managers are in a better position to press new investment policies on most sectors of industry than are their British or American counterparts. Similar variation can be found in other segments of state-society relations.

Finally, the institutional relations implicit within society itself exercise an important influence over the capacity of the state to innovate in certain areas. Income policies, for instance, can be implemented much more readily in nations where the trade-union movement is centrally organized along industrial lines than in nations where it is fragmented and craft based.[2] Similarly,

1. Vincent Wright, *The Government and Politics of France* (London: Hutchinson, 1978), p. 85.

2. See Philippe Schmitter and Gerhard Lehmbruch, eds., *Trends Toward Corporatist*

the conventional relationships between a nation's financial institutions and its industrial sector can affect the facility with which new forms of industrial policy may be implemented through the financial system.[3]

It should be apparent that these sorts of structural factors vary across nations. Accordingly, the innovative capacity of different states will vary as well, both in aggregate and in specific policy areas. Through cross-national analysis, we can trace the impacts of differing structural features on policy outcomes. However, this is an immense field of enquiry. The purpose of this article is to examine only one small dimension of the problem: namely, the impact that differing forms of politician-civil-servant relations have on the capacity of a state to formulate and implement innovative forms of policy.

Two nations, Britain and France, provide the focus for this comparison. Both are advanced industrial democracies in which governmental operations enjoy a reputation for efficiency. Each has a large and diverse civil service, some branches of which operate more effectively than others.[4] As a result, many of the problems that confront political innovators can be observed in both countries. However, the structure of relations between politicians and civil servants, or the politics-administration nexus, is very different in the two states; and we can trace the impact of these differences on the capacity of these governments to innovate.

THE PROBLEM OF GOVERNMENTAL INNOVATION

Governmental innovation would not be especially problematic if states were unitary or rational actors. In that case, we might expect the government to think strategically and to act with dispatch when conditions warrant a change in policy. However, all states are fragmented entities, in which policies are produced only after many individuals have been persuaded of their desirability, and actions taken only by way of massive interpersonal coordination. In effect, administrations are miniature polities in themselves.[5]

Power and rationality in the policy process

As a consequence, the conceptions of power and rationality that we apply to governmental decision making must be refined. First, no matter how hierarchical the organization of a state, power over its actions is always diffused among a multitude of persons. Even the power of a head of state to choose any course he or she likes is only nominal. Real power consists of the ability to find means that will accomplish one's ends; and for that, a head of state is dependent on the expert advice of bureaucrats he or she may not even know. As John F. Kennedy found, heads of state are also dependent on the willingness of others

---

Intermediation (Beverly Hills, CA: Sage, 1979); and Suzanne Berger, ed., *Organizing Interests in Western Europe* (London: Cambridge University Press, 1980).

3. See Peter A. Hall, "Patterns of Economic Policy: An Organizational Approach," in *The State in Capitalist Europe*, eds. Stephen Bornstein, David Held, and Joel Krieger (London: Allen & Unwin, 1983).

4. For overviews of each system, see R.G.S. Brown and D. R. Steel, *The Administrative Process in Britain* (London: Methuen, 1979); and Francis de Baecque, *Le gouvernement et l'administration de la France* (Paris: Colin, 1973).

5. See Graham T. Allison, *The Essence of Decision* (Boston: Little, Brown, 1971).

to implement the policies chosen.[6] Therefore, to amass enough power to get a decision made and to enforce its implementation is a perpetual problem for modern states, especially when a change in the direction of policy is involved.

Similarly, the intelligence of a state is always a collective intelligence, and the rationality of such an organization, as Herbert Simon has shown, is always a "bounded rationality."[7] That is to say, major policy decisions are the result of a process that aggregates the perceptions and judgments of many individuals. In most cases, there is an inherent incrementalism to this process. Each individual contributes only a component, based on his or her own preoccupations and experience, to the final decision. In a separate series of steps, that component must then be adjusted to fit with those contributed by others, if a policy recommendation is to move though the bureaucracy and acquire enough of a consensus to result in action.[8]

In the process, many individual rationalities are brought to bear on the question, but there is no guarantee that the amalgam that emerges from these steps will be rational from a strategic point of view for the state. Therefore, every government that hopes to produce innovative policies appropriate to evolving social conditions must find a way of integrating the individual rationalities of its officials that produces strategically appropriate outcomes for the state as a whole. Where a policy innovation is concerned, this is especially problematic because it will be rational for officials whose vested interests are disturbed to oppose it, however desirable the policy might be from an overall point of view.

The conditions for innovation

From these considerations we can derive a more specific conception of the organizational conditions likely to be most conducive to effective governmental innovation. In this case, the capacity for governmental innovation refers to the ability of a state's managers to anticipate the evolving social problems that will confront the state, to design new policies appropriate to those problems, and to implement those policies successfully. The foregoing analysis suggests that the presence of four organizational conditions will improve a government's capacity for innovation.

First, to the degree that it is possible, power over a particular area of policy must be concentrated in the hands of relatively few individuals. The greater the number of persons who must pass on a policy innovation, the more likely it is that such an innovation will be delayed by one of them. And the more people with power over the decision, the more likely it is that the policy outcome will reflect the vagaries of partisan mutual adjustment rather than rational consideration of the state's needs.

Second, the government's capacity to innovate in a particular field will be enhanced if a preponderant share of power over policymaking lies in the hands of actors who are relatively free of vested interests in the existing pattern of policy within that field. This is a simple truth. Those with such vested interests

---

6. Thomas E. Cronin, *The State of the Presidency* (Boston: Little, Brown, 1975), p. 17. See also Richard Neustadt, *Presidential Power* (New York: John Wiley, 1960).

7. Herbert Simon, "Theories of Bounded Rationality," in *Decisions and Organization,* eds. C. B. McGuire and R. Radner (Amsterdam: North Holland, 1972), pp. 161-76.

8. See Charles Lindblom, *The Intelligence of Democracy* (New York: Free Press, 1965).

are most likely to resist any elements of a new policy that adversely affect the position they have attained under the old one. For this reason, it is also desirable that power should be concentrated in the political executive and advisers appointed by them. As Joel Aberbach and others have found, political leaders are more likely to be the "energizers" behind policy innovation than are civil servants, who are usually "equilibrators" in a policy area.[9]

Third, a government's capacity to innovate effectively will be enhanced if its organizational structures maximize the access to information and relevant expertise of those who hold principal responsibility for making the policy decisions in a particular area. On the one hand, since information is power within the policy environment, this facilitates the concentration of power deemed conducive to policy innovation. On the other hand, it also reduces the likelihood that those officials will select policies that prove inappropriate for achieving the ends they have in mind. Senior officials with some expertise will be in a better position to cut through any technical objections raised concerning a new policy and better equipped to tailor the final proposal to actual policy needs.

Finally, effective innovation is more likely to occur under a system of organizational arrangements that encourages the formation of informal alliances between members of the political executive and civil servants. The old model of policymaking, as a process in which politicians formulate a policy and then require civil servants to enforce it, is seriously outdated.[10] The formulation and implementation of policy requires the active cooperation of civil servants and politicians at virtually all stages. If one side balks, only rarely can the other force through a new policy alone. Thus the formation of an alliance between innovators within the civil service and political executives is a virtual prerequisite for the introduction of a new policy.

These are the four conditions that improve a government's capacity for policy innovation. Let us examine the organization of the politics-administration nexus in Britain and France with a view to assessing the extent to which these conditions are present there.

THE FRENCH SYSTEM

The structure of administrative relations in France is far from perfect, as a number of distinguished commentators have pointed out.[11] But several features of the French system of political-administrative relations significantly enhance its government's capacity for innovation. Like much that is French, the origins of these features go back to the *colbertisme* of the Old Regime that ruled prerevolutionary France. However, their outlines were etched most deeply into the French polity during the Fifth Republic, which followed Charles de Gaulle's accession to power in 1958.

The president and interministerial coordination

The most striking characteristic of the French system, of course, is the

---

9. Joel Aberbach, Robert Putnam, and Bert A. Rockman, *Bureaucrats and Politicians in Western Democracies* (Cambridge, MA: Harvard University Press, 1981), p. 242 and passim.

10. See C. H. Sisson, *The Spirit of British Administration* (London: Faber, 1952).

11. Michel Crozier, *Strategies for Change* (Cambridge: MIT Press, 1982); and Alain Peyrefitte, *The Trouble with France* (New York: Knopf, 1981).

power accorded its president. Like his American counterpart, the French president is the active director of the government. However, unlike the American chief executive, France's president exercises considerable power over the legislature. Not only does he appoint the prime minister and all other ministers, but he also enjoys the right to dissolve the National Assembly, to call for new elections, and to govern for substantial periods of time without legislative assent, under Article 16 of the Constitution. Moreover, his government has access to several tactics for pressing bills through the Assembly without amendment or substantial debate.[12]

In the administrative sphere, the president is even more powerful. In addition to ministers, he also appoints, directly or indirectly, most senior members of the judiciary, all ambassadors, councillors of state, division heads within the ministries, and the prefects who superintend the regions of France. Although some of these appointments are supposed to be made in consultation with the Council of Ministers and in accordance with conventions of seniority, recent presidents have arrogated much of this power to themselves. As one scholar put it, "By this liberal interpretation of the Constitution, the President has increasingly turned the Government into an instrument of his own ascendancy. He has become the principal dispenser of political rewards and revenge, able to make or break the career of the aspiring and the ambitious."[13]

In a nation that habitually handles conflict by looking upward for guidance, the president stands at the top of the pyramid. Nothing conveys a sense of his preeminent position more dramatically than accounts of meetings of the Council of Ministers, the French equivalent of the British or American cabinets. These reveal that even when decisions on the most controversial social problems are being made, there is virtually no debate. The president, who has set the agenda and appointed the participants, may solicit opinions from a few of those in attendance, but for the most part they listen in silence as he announces what they have decided.[14] On matters of foreign policy, national defense, and an increasing range of economic topics, the Council of Ministers may not even be consulted. Under the French system, power is heavily concentrated at the top.

Of course, the president cannot govern alone. He depends in the first instance on a handpicked staff in the Elysée palace, equivalent to the White House staff in America. Although many of those who work in the Elysée come from the French civil service, they are chosen by the president and his counselors. There are usually 20 to 30 senior members of the General Secretariat and about 100 subordinate officials at the Elysée.[15]

The primary work of governmental coordination in France is carried on by this staff and a series of interministerial

12. Wright, *The Government and Politics of France*, chs. 1-5.
13. Ibid., p. 29.
14. William G. Andrews, "The Collective Political Executive Under the Gaullists," in *The Impact of the Fifth Republic on France*, eds. W. G. Andrews and Stanley Hoffmann (Albany: State University of New York Press, 1981), pp. 26ff.
15. Samy Cohen, "Le Secrétariat général de la présidence de la République," in *Administration et politique sous la Cinquième République*, eds. F. de Baecque and J.-L. Quermonne (Paris: Fondation National des Sciences Politiques, 1981), pp. 104-28.

bodies, composed of both ministers and civil servants whose appointments are subject to presidential approval. The president himself presides over interministerial councils, and the prime minister convenes interministerial committees. Some of these bodies, which can range in size from 5 to 30 members, are quasi-permanent institutions established to deal with recurring issues, such as the allocation of funds to industrial sectors, defense issues, and regional policy. Others are convened on an ad hoc basis to handle periodic problems that transcend the boundaries of one ministry.[16] In addition, when he wishes to take an initiative that may be opposed by the relevant ministry, the president frequently appoints a special commission, usually headed by one or two senior civil servants with political ambitions, to select a course of action on the matter. With the power of the president behind them, these commissions are able to sidestep traditional departmental rivalries when a new policy is required.

One of the factors undermining the flexibility of the French system has been the tendency of its officials to deal with problems by promulgating and adhering to formal rules and regulations in each area of policy. This is tied to the preeminent status accorded administrative law in France.[17] In recent years, however, the growth of interministerial committees has given rise to a culture of bargaining within the French administration that has significantly reduced the extent to which officials proceed solely according to the rule book. This has increased the room available for innovation.[18]

Departmental administration

The structure of political-administrative relations at the departmental level in France is a reflection of those at the Elysée. The most significant facet of departmental organization is the institution of *cabinets ministériels*. These consist of a small body of advisers, generally chosen by the minister himself, who form his private office and take responsibility for the overall coordination of policy within the department. On average, there are about 15 officials in a cabinet, although some ministers have employed up to 50 or 60. In general, a minister will select about 90 percent of his staff from those who look most promising in the civil service, although not necessarily from his current department.[19] A few members are usually longstanding advisers to the minister, and many may be chosen because they share his policy orientations.[20]

The significance of these cabinets stems from the fact that most French departments do not have an equivalent of the British permanent secretary, who coordinates the work of the department and acts as its spokesman to the minis-

16. Jean-Luc Bodiguel, "Conseils restreints, comités interministériels et réunions interministérielles," in *Administration et politique*, eds. de Baecque and Quermonne, pp. 139-62.

17. Brian Chapman, *The Profession of Government* (London: Allen & Unwin, 1966), pp. 229ff.

18. Albert Mabileau and Pierre Sadran, "Administration et politique au niveau local," in *Administration et politique,* eds. de Baecque and Quermonne, pp. 268-69.

19. Ezra Suleiman, *Politics, Power and Bureaucracy in France* (Princeton, NJ: Princeton University Press, 1974) p. 234 and passim.

20. The Mitterand government has been more inclined than most to use trade unionists and other outsiders in ministerial cabinets; see Stanley Hoffmann, "Year One," *New York Review of Books,* 12 Aug. 1982, pp. 37-43.

ter. Only two French ministries had such *secrétaires généraux* in 1974. Instead, the minister and his cabinet deal directly with the directors (*directeurs*) who superintend the branches of the department, such as under secretaries do in Britain and the United States. The cabinet functions as a kind of collective permanent secretary. Because they are chosen directly by the minister, however, and serve at his pleasure, its members are likely to be much more responsive to political initiatives than the permanent secretaries, whom British ministers can only rarely unseat. The ministerial cabinet is the center of power in a French department. Catherine Grémion, who studied three cases of policy reform in France, asked all the civil servants involved to identify the actors with the most influence over the result: 80 percent named the members of ministerial cabinets.[21]

Directly below the cabinet in a French department are the directors of its branches. They too can be replaced by a minister, unlike British under secretaries, but with greater difficulty than the members of the cabinet. In general, equivalent jobs must be found for them elsewhere in the administration. As technical experts, thoroughly familiar with the complex work of the branches they supervise, the directors are also powerful civil servants.

The higher civil service

The approximately 600 civil servants at directorial level or above form the *hauts fonctionnaires* of the French administration. In France, as elsewhere, a distinction can be drawn between the upper and lower levels of the civil service. A state's capacity for innovative policymaking seems to depend most heavily on the configuration of its senior civil service. At lower levels, bureaucracies appear to be similar across many nations. However, several characteristics of the senior civil service are special to France.

In particular, the French state has set about creating an elite corps of fonctionnaires who are trained and destined to move in and out of higher administrative office throughout their lifetimes. The twin pillars of this system are the *Ecole Nationale d'Administration* (ENA) and the *grand corps*. ENA was established after the war to train about 150 university graduates per year in law, economics, and the skills of administration. It complements a sister institution, the *Ecole Polytechnique*, which performs a similar function for those involved in scientific pursuits or engineering. Roughly half of ENA's two-year program is spent at internships in government departments, and the course concludes with a competitive examination that determines which graduates will go on to the grands corps.[22] The latter are highly structured professional associations, each associated with a functional specialization such as civil engineering, administrative law, or finance, whose members traditionally exercise a monopoly over many of the most senior positions in the state. Upon entry, a member may spend two or three years working in one of the traditional occupations associated with his corps, and then move on to relatively responsible positions in several ministries, often secured for him by the senior

21. Catherine Grémion, *Profession: décideurs* (Paris: Gauthier-villars, 1979), p. 317.

22. Jean-Luc Bodiguel, *L'Ecole National d'Administration* (Paris: FNSP, 1978).

officials of his corps.[23] The career patterns of this elite are characterized by the assumption of considerable policymaking responsibility at a relatively young age and by a high degree of mobility among jobs.

In recent years, two new dimensions have been added to the career pattern of France's senior servants. First, an increasing portion of the political executive has been drawn from the ranks of the civil service. By the end of 1977, the president, prime minister, and 30 out of 36 ministers were former civil servants.[24] Moreover, as members of the grands corps, many of these politicians can return to the civil service after resigning from office, if they so desire. The roots of this development are not difficult to discern. French law has traditionally allowed members of the grand corps to hold public office, and French presidents are not required to select their ministers exclusively from parliamentarians, as are the British. President Valerie Giscard d'Estaing, perhaps because of his own background in the administration, was especially partial to ministers drawn from the civil service. Thus the most successful or politically adept civil servants can look forward to a ministerial appointment, and many ministers arrive with a firsthand knowledge of the administration.

At the same time, an increasing number of civil servants have been moving back and forth between government employment and the private sector. This is termed *pantouflage*. In general, a civil servant will acquire 5 to 10 years experience with the state before moving into a senior post in the private sector. The majority of those who move go to large firms in the most dynamic sectors of the economy or to the financial sector. A recent survey found that 43 percent of the heads of the largest 100 companies in France were former civil servants.[25] This vastly increases the flow of ideas and influence between the private and public sectors of France.

The French system assessed

Each of these organizational features has implications for the innovative capacity of the French state. In some measure, each contributes to the fulfillment of the four conditions conducive to governmental innovation that were cited previously.

First, it should be apparent that this system tends to concentrate power over policy in the hands of a few individuals. The president, who wields great influence himself, can and frequently does place that influence behind a few officials appointed to spearhead policy initiatives in difficult areas. As *chargés de mission* or members of a special interministerial commission, a small group of innovators can circumvent the bureaucratic procedures of the large departments and bring a recommended course of action directly to fruition in a short space of time. Such was the case with the housing policy of 1976 and the regional assemblies established in 1966.[26]

In an extension of this technique, French governments have frequently

---

23. Ezra Suleiman, *Elites in French Society* (Princeton, NJ: Princeton University Press, 1978).
24. Wright, *The Government and Politics of France,* p. 91.
25. Pierre Birnbaum, *The Heights of Power* (Chicago: University of Chicago Press, 1982), p. 103.
26. Catherine Grémion, "Le Milieu décisionnel central," in *Administration et politique,* eds. de Baecque and Quermonne, pp. 205-24.

established independent agencies to take the supervision of new projects out of the hands of the slower-moving ministries. Again, this was a way of ensuring that a new policy would be fully implemented. The model for many of these agencies was the Planning Commission, established in 1948 under Jean Monnet to act as an *agent provocateur,* both within the state and outside it, for policies favorable to modernization and economic growth. Indeed, many commentators believe that the greatest contribution of this commission, in the ensuing 25 years, was to tilt the balance of power inside the state itself toward such policies.[27] In other spheres, the French state has used independent agencies of this sort to push through such ventures as the Charles de Gaulle Airport at Roissy and the French nuclear energy program, despite substantial political and administrative opposition.[28] The danger, of course, is that these juggernauts, once launched, acquire powerful resources to defend vested interests of their own.

On the whole, however, the organizational framework of the French state is well suited for placing power over new projects in the hands of individuals without strong vested interests of their own in the area. For the most part, the hauts fonctionnaires of France are generalists. Despite its image abroad, ENA gives only a generalist training in techniques of administration; and many members of the grands corps function primarily as troubleshooters, moving rapidly from one job to the next in widely divergent areas.[29] They pick up technical expertise on the way, but relatively few entrenched interests. Therefore, when they are parachuted into a ministerial cabinet, they are often favorably diposed to new policy initiatives that would unsettle longer-serving members of the department. Grémion's intensive study of innovation within the French administration revealed that the officials most likely to support new policy initiatives were those who had spent time *hors machine,* in other departments, overseas, and in the private sector.[30] The elements of the French system that encourage this kind of mobility, including increasing forays into the private sector, therefore, also increase the capacity of the state for policy innovation.

Third, the politics-administration nexus of the French state is organized so as to maximize the access to technical information and expertise of the political decision makers at its apex. The ministerial cabinets place a repository of expertise at each minister's disposal, as does the staff at the Elysée and Matignon. It is customary for a *conseiller technique* within the cabinet to supervise each *direction* of a department; and, as Suleiman shows, the loyalties of these officials tend to be to their minister rather than to the vested interests of the department.[31] Thus political decision makers can depend on minimally biased

27. Peter A. Hall, "Economic Planning and the State: The Evolution of Economic Challenge and Political Response in France," in *Political Power and Social Theory,* eds. Gosta Esping-Andersen and Roger Friedland (Greenwich, CT: JAI Press, 1982), pp. 175-213.

28. See Elliot Feldman and Jerome Milch, *Technocracy vs. Democracy* (Boston: Auburn House, 1982); and Robert J. Lieber, "Energy Policies of the Fifth Republic," in *The Fifth Republic at Twenty,* eds. W. Andrews and S. Hoffmann (Albany: SUNY Press, 1980).

29. Suleiman, *Elites in French Society,* p. 164.
30. Grémion, *Profession: décideurs,* ch. 16.
31. Suleiman, *Politics, Power and Bureaucracy in France,* p. 234.

advice from individuals conversant with the day-to-day complexities of the ministry's branches. Similarly, one of the consequences of promoting civil servants to ministerial positions has been to supply the French government with ministers who have some administrative and technical expertise themselves, useful for piloting innovative programs through the bureaucracy.[32]

Finally, several features of this system facilitate the formation of alliances between civil servants and politicians behind innovative policies, and enhance the responsiveness of administrators to political leadership. The ministerial cabinet, for instance, vests responsibility for the ultimate appraisal of policy and coordination of departmental initiatives in a small group of young civil servants who owe their current position to the minister. There is no doubt that this, and the practice of elevating civil servants to ministerial rank, has rendered many of them more sensitive to political initiatives.[33] At the same time, ministers with experience in the administration are better equipped to find allies there. The French system is ideally suited to the formation of such alliances. If the Americans have a "government of strangers," the French have *un gouvernement de familiers*.[34] The common formation of the higher civil service through ENA, the *Ecole Polytechnique,* the grands corps, and ministerial cabinets provides a ready-made set of lines along which alliances can be formed.

It is not surprising, then, that the French state became the agent of modernization for postwar French society. The institutions of the Fifth Republic, in particular, enabled socioeconomic innovators within the political executive and bureaucracy to overwhelm the legislators who were often the defenders of traditional interests in society.[35] On many fronts, including those of housing, industrial expansion, technological development, energy, and transport, new policies were introduced to supplant a status quo often a century old. In Stanley Hoffmann's words, the state became "the incubator and promoter of the new economic and social order."[36]

In conclusion, however, several qualifications should be added to this picture. First, it should be noted that the institutional characteristics that facilitate innovation from the top of the state do not always render the lower levels of the bureaucracy responsive to local needs. On the contrary, the centralization of power that has given momentum to the initiatives emanating from Paris has frequently made it difficult for local officials to secure the regulatory flexibility required to answer local needs or to introduce changes at the municipal level. To build a secondary school in France, a municipality needs to secure approval from 14 different agencies via a procedure that involves 24 separate

---

32. See Pierre Birnbaum, *La classe dirigeante française* (Paris: Presses Universitaires de France, 1978).

33. Anne Stevens, "Politicisation and Cohesion in the French Administration," in *Conflict and Consensus in France,* ed. Vincent Wright (London: Cass, 1979), pp. 68-80.

34. See Hugh Heclo, *A Government of Strangers: Executive Politics in Washington* (Washington, DC: Brookings Institution, 1977).

35. See Suzanne Berger and Michael Piore, *Dualism and Discontinuity in Industrial Societies* (Cambridge: Cambridge University Press, 1980).

36. Stanley Hoffmann, "The Fifth Republic at Twenty," in *The Impact of the Fifth Republic on France,* eds. Andrews and Hoffmann, p. 285.

administrative steps.[37] Viewed from the bottom, the French state still appears to be a relatively inflexible entity.

Similarly, although the president and key ministers are capable of pressing a few innovative projects through to completion, the number of fronts on which they can operate at any one time is limited. Therefore other problem areas may be neglected for long periods of time. French presidents, for instance, have tended to concentrate on initiatives in the foreign and economic arenas, dealing with social problems only when they reached intolerable levels of intensity.[38] This is not a system that encourages grass-roots renewal organized around multiple centers of power. The decentralization program of the Mitterand government seems to be designed to reorient the nation to this model of social change, but, as we have seen, that will require a massive alteration in the structure of the state.[39]

Finally, to say that the state is relatively well equipped to formulate and impose innovative policies on the nation is not to say that these policies are always the ideal ones for the circumstances. Some of the French state's most ambitious projects, while carried through to completion, have displayed serious defects in operation. Among these must be listed the Concorde airliner, the food-processing facility at La Villette, the Charles de Gaulle Airport, the Plan Calcul for the computer industry, and the Rhine-Rhone canal.[40] As these examples indicate, the real problem of the French government in many instances lies not in getting something accomplished, but in figuring out what to do. The very capacity to ram through a project sometimes seems to induce French governments to do so rather hastily. In other areas, where the power of peripheral actors is still deeply entrenched, some initiatives from the center have also been unsuccessful, notably in the sphere of local government. Local politicians have often proved better defenders of traditional interests than government departments in France.[41] Thus, like all systems, the French network of political-administrative relations has both advantages and drawbacks from a policy point of view.

THE BRITISH SYSTEM

The French system stands in some contrast to the structure of the politics-administration nexus in Britain. Since the British system is more familiar to American readers, it will be reviewed more briefly.

---

37. Peyrefitte, *The Trouble with France*, p. 199.

38. Anne Stevens, "The Higher Civil Service and Economic Policy-Making," in *French Politics and Public Policy*, eds. Philip G. Cerny and Martin A. Schain (London: Methuen, 1980), pp. 93ff.

39. See Hoffmann, "Year One," and the articles on the changes in administration under the new regime in *Le Monde* (Paris) 29, 30, and 31 July 1982.

40. See Stephen Cohen, "Informed Bewilderment: French Economic Strategy and the Crisis," in *France in the Troubled World Economy*, eds. Peter Gourevitch and Stephen Cohen (London: Butterworths, 1982); and Suzanne Berger, "Lame Ducks and National Champions: Industrial Policy in the Fifth Republic," in *The Impact of the Fifth Republic on France*, eds. Andrews and Hoffmann, pp. 160-78.

41. Douglas Ashford, "Are Britain and France Unitary?" *Comparative Politics*, 9(4):483-99 (July 1977); see also Pierre Grémion, *Le pouvoir périphérique* (Paris: Le Seuil, 1976) and Howard Machin, "Local Government Change in France—The Case of the 1964 Reforms," *Policy and Politics* (London), 3 (1974).

The prime minister and cabinet

At the apex of the British polity stands the prime minister, who is the leader of his or her party in the House of Commons. In recent years, the balance of power within the British government, as elsewhere, has definitely shifted toward the prime minister.[42] However, he or she enjoys nothing like the authority of the French president. Whereas French ministers behave as subordinates, indeed often as functionaries, of the president, there is still a tone of *primus inter pares* to the British prime minister's role. By corollary, most of the government's major decisions are made by the cabinet after considerable debate among its members. The cabinet, rather than the prime minister, is the center of executive power in Britain. The prime minister controls its agenda and conclusions, and can afford some resignations by disgruntled ministers; but when something approaching a majority of the cabinet remains opposed to a major policy initiative, he or she cannot usually afford to proceed with it alone. This confers slightly more power on individual ministers and their departments in Britain than in France.

Although some cabinet committees bring civil servants into their discussions, the cabinet system also means that the ultimate stage of decision making in Britain, at which substantial revisions of a policy may be made, takes place in a forum where politicians are the only participants.[43] By contrast, in France, where the final stage of executive decision making usually entails securing the president's approval, civil servants are frequently involved in last-minute consultations and revisions. This brings greater technical expertise to bear on the final decision.

Departmental administration

If individual departments are more powerful in Britain, ministers there have far fewer personal resources at their disposal than do their French counterparts. There are no ministerial cabinets in Britain. Instead, each cabinet minister is assisted by several junior ministers also drawn from Parliament, by one or two personal advisers, and by a private office composed of 4-10 civil servants, usually chosen by the permanent secretary of the department. Although the most promising young principals are often selected for private office work, their loyalties tend to remain much more solidly with the civil service than with the minister, who has only a marginal influence on their positions and careers. Even more significantly, their duties are primarily clerical rather than policy oriented. A minister's private office simply organizes his itinerary, appointments, correspondence, and flow of memoranda.[44] Departmental civil servants at under-secretary level and above tend to remain the minister's main source of policy advice. In particular, each department has a permanent secretary, usually with at least 25 years of experience in the service, who is the conduit for all the department's advice to the minister and the supervisor of its subordinate branches.[45]

42. See Richard Crossman, *Inside View* (London: Jonathan Cape, 1972).

43. See John Mackintosh, *The British Cabinet* (London: Stevens, 1962).

44. See Gerald Kaufman, *How to Be a Minister* (London: Sidgwick & Jackson, 1980).

45. See Kenneth Waltz's suggestion that the combination of low civil-service turnover and a high ministerial turnover in office is the formula

With one eye on the French system, critics of the innovative capacity of the British state have often complained of the generalist, homogeneous, and insulated character of the British civil service.[46] Paradoxically, however, the overall character of the senior civil service in Britain is very similar to that of France. As we have seen, ENA tends to produce administrative generalists rather than specialists. Like their French counterparts, most senior civil servants in Britain acquire specialized knowledge through the pursuit of their jobs. As in France, the majority of senior British officials have been in government service for most of their lives, but enjoyed considerable job mobility for most of that period, spending only two or three years in each post until they reached the senior positions at which they would build up expertise over 5 to 10 years.[47]

The British system assessed

What distinguishes the British civil service from that of France is not primarily the character of the higher civil service, but the structure of the politics-administration nexus there. On all four of the dimensions associated with governmental innovation, the British structure compares unfavorably with the French.

In the first place, power is much more widely diffused among various actors in the British system, not only because the prime minister's office is less powerful, but because there is a cavernous gap between the politicians who have the political motivation to innovate and the civil servants who have the technical expertise to render innovation effective.[48] In France that gap is filled by ministerial cabinets and the *chargés de mission* who serve the Elysée. British ministers lack an equivalent set of policy experts whose energies and loyalties are attached to their personal projects. They must depend almost entirely on being able to elicit the enthusiasm of their permanent secretary for each project, always a chancy endeavor. Since they are isolated to such an extent from technical advice, British ministers, for all their nominal authority, are not nearly as powerful vis-à-vis civil servants as those in France.[49]

Of equal importance, there is very little provision within the senior levels of the British state for project-oriented missions of the sort that figure prominently in the French administration. Almost all projects must be implemented through traditional departmental hierarchies, in short, by those bureaucrats who have the greatest vested interest in existing policies. Even the small Central Policy Review Staff created in 1970 lacks the capacity to follow through on its ideas.[50] It is not

---

for a low rate of governmental innovation, in *Foreign Policy and Democratic Politics* (Boston: Little, Brown, 1967).

46. F. F. Ridley, ed., *Specialists and Generalists* (London: Allen & Unwin, 1968); D. W. Buck, *Amateurs and Professionals in British Politics* (Chicago: University of Chicago Press, 1963).

47. Brown and Steel, *The Administrative Process in Britain*, pp. 86ff.

48. See Bruce W. Headey, "A Typology of Ministers: Implications for Minister-Civil Servant Relationships in Britain," in *The Mandarins of Western Europe,* ed. Mattei Dogan (Beverly Hills, CA: Sage 1975), pp. 63-86.

49. Many years ago, Harold Laski suggested that the British should be given ministerial cabinets to remedy this situation in "The British Civil Service," *Yale Review*, 26:342 (1936-37).

50. See Christopher Pollitt, "The Central Policy Review Staff, 1970-74," *Public Administration,* 52:375-92 (1974).

surprising that this should stifle innovation. Management theorists have long maintained that project-oriented forms of organization are more likely to be innovative than the administration-oriented forms that predominate in Britain.[51]

This problem is exacerbated by the hierarchical nature of British administration. Unlike their French equivalents, British ministers have very little access to the under secretaries and assistant secretaries who run the branches of their departments. Almost all communication is funneled through the permanent secretary. The opportunities for politicians to form alliances with innovators among their middle-level civil servants are very limited. The problem is intensified by the fact that permanent secretaries are invariably older officials who have become accustomed over long periods of time to traditional ways of proceeding. Far younger officials are much more likely to have direct access to ministers in France. The British situation is mitigated only slightly by the fact that permanent secretaries are often drawn from the upper ranks of other departments.

Finally, whatever its disadvantages, the French system of blurring the lines between politicians and administrators, through the use of ministerial cabinets, joint committees, and civil servants as ministers, ensures that a broad group of politico-administrators will be created to share responsibility for the design and initiation of new policies.[52] In Britain, by contrast, civil servants have a tendency to believe that politicians are responsible for the initiation of new policies, while the latter lack the expertise needed in many specific policy areas to undertake this task.[53] As a result, the group with the wherewithal to do the job tends to feel that the responsibility lies elsewhere, and those with the responsibility lack the technical skills to do the job. Policy innovation gets lost between two stools.

This is not to say that British government cannot innovate. From time to time, the happy coincidence of a savvy minister with a sympathetic permanent secretary produces effective new policy initiatives. The 1971-73 reform of the taxation system, the postwar institution of the National Health Service, and the military cutbacks east of Suez in the 1960s provide evidence that this can be done. For the most part, however, British governments have been dependent on party manifestos to suggest new policy initiatives, often in very crude form, while French administrations managed to innovate under one-party rule for over 20 years.

The leaders of Britain's governments have been unhappy about this situation for almost two decades, but have not yet been able to alter it significantly. The reforms that followed the report of the Fulton Committee on the civil service in 1970 were supposed to tackle some of these issues, but most of them have come to naught.[54] The Civil Service Col-

51. C. Argyris, "Today's Problems with Tomorrow's Organizations," *Journal of Management Studies,* 4:32 (1974).

52. Aberbach, Putnam, and Rockman describe this joint sharing of responsibilities as the image of politician-administrator relations that most countries are moving toward, in *Bureaucrats and Politicians in Western Democracies,* pp. 228-39.

53. See Richard Rose, "The Making of Cabinet Ministers," *British Journal of Political Science,* 1:406 (1971); and Michael Gordon, "Civil Servants, Politicians and Parties: Shortcomings in the British Policy Process," *Comparative Politics,* 4:29-58 (Oct. 1971).

54. Great Britain, *The Civil Service, I Report of the Committee,* CMND 3638 (London: Her Majesty's Stationery Office, 1968).

lege created at this time plays nothing like the role of ENA that its advocates expected. The creation of a unified class of administrators to replace many of the old civil-service divisions has done little to bring more specialized personnel to top administrative positions; and the social background of the senior civil service is almost as homogeneous as it was before new entry provisions were introduced in the early 1970s.[55] Yet these were the principal results to follow from Fulton. If this analysis is correct, the thrust of the Fulton report was misplaced from the outset. When appointing the Fulton Committee, the prime minister ruled any consideration of the basic structure of the politics-administration nexus beyond its purview on the grounds that this would interfere with the doctrine of ministerial responsibility.[56] However, the configuration of this nexus seems to be the structural feature of the state that most hampers governmental innovation in Britain.

CONCLUSION

In this article it has only been possible to sketch the broad outlines of the politics-administration nexus in Britain and France and to explore some of its effects on policy innovation. However, in-depth studies of several policy areas in these nations tend to support the analysis presented here.[57] In conclusion, we might ask what implications this analysis has for the United States.

Overall, on the four dimensions associated with governmental innovation, the American state seems to stand between those of Britain and France. On the one hand, the capacity of American governments to fill the top administrative positions in each new administration with several hundred outside experts significantly increases the exposure of its civil servants to new ideas and the responsiveness of the bureaucratic apparatus to political direction.[58] The relative ease of access that officials, politicians, and the public alike have to departmental information in America also appears to encourage the flow of new ideas into government and stimulates the sort of critical scrutiny of policies that should improve their quality. Americans unhappy with the apparent secrecy of some of their agencies should recall that even ministers in Britain and France are often denied access to the most elementary economic forecasts of other departments. Similarly, these facets of the American system encourage the formation of alliances between political leaders and their administrators around innovative policies; and they limit the extent to which vested departmental interests are allowed to dominate the upper echelons of the American administration, even if senior officials always fight their department's corner to some extent.

On the other hand, power is relatively dispersed among the different branches and agencies of the U.S. government. The presence of a Congress whose

---

55. For a review, see Peter Kellner and Lord Crowther-Hunt, *The Civil Servants* (London: Macdonald, 1980).

56. Harold Wilson observed that the establishment of the Fulton Committee "does not imply any intention on [the part of the Government] to alter the basic relationships between Ministers and civil servants." *Hansard,* 8 Feb. 1966, col. 210.

57. For a review of many specific policy studies, see Douglas Ashford, *Policy and Politics in Britain* (Philadelphia: Temple University Press, 1981); idem, *Policy and Politics in France* (Philadelphia: Temple University Press, forthcoming).

58. See Heclo, *A Government of Strangers.*

power rivals that of the executive branch must be the major factor differentiating the American case from that of Britain and France. There is no doubt that long-standing civil servants, seeking to block an innovation that affects the interests of their agency, can often do an end run around the White House, by appealing to the congressional committees with which they are accustomed to working. In league with affected societal lobbyists, these groups can form an "iron triangle" that has greater resilience than analogous alliances in the two countries studied here.[59] And even within the executive itself, power seems to leak out of the White House to the cabinet secretaries and their departments, as a succession of presidents have discovered.[60] In issue areas where power is dispersed in this way, the government's capacity for policy innovation should be attentuated correspondingly.

In all of these nations, the government's capacity for innovative action will vary from one policy field to another, as the specific organizational structures associated with the administration of that field vary. Only individual case studies of each policy area can establish the degree of variation. At the moment, new governments seeking a change in direction have come to power in all of these nations. In most instances the outcome of their efforts is still in doubt, but before long, we will have a test case against which to reassess the innovative capacity of each state. This article has attempted to provide an analytic framework capable of outlining the factors associated with the politics-administration nexus that can affect the success that each of these new governments will have in redirecting governmental action.

59. See Theodore Lowi, *The End of Liberalism* (New York: W. W. Norton, 1976).
60. See Cronin, *The State of the Presidency.*

The Public-Service Problem

By EUGENE B. McGREGOR, Jr.

ABSTRACT: Current government size and complexity require career officials to manage an experimental and service-based system of public administration. A problem-solving executive service is an effective means of managing a diverse public-service system without stifling its productive potential.

Eugene B. McGregor, Jr., is a professor of public and environmental affairs at Indiana University. He is currently working on two book-length manuscripts dealing with the design and management of complex systems of public administration and the problem of workforce management. He teaches courses in the fields of public policy and management. He holds an A.B. degree from Dartmouth College and a Ph.D. in political science from the Maxwell School, Syracuse University.

The question for us is, how shall our series of governments within governments be so administered that it shall always be to the interest of the public officer to serve, not his superior alone but the community also, with the best efforts of his talents and the soberest service of his conscience? How shall such service be made to his commonest interest by contributing abundantly to his sustenance, to his dearest interest by furthering his ambition, and to his highest interest by advancing his honor and establishing his character? And how shall this be done alike for the local part and for the national whole?[1]

Woodrow Wilson was, even as a junior professor at Bryn Mawr, exceedingly shrewd about matters of government and public affairs. The problem is to render his classic query sensible to current public-service realities.

One looming reality is that the current size and complexity of government conspire to make public enterprise unresponsive to the manipulations of public-service amateurs. Clearly, citizen-politicians and gifted inners and outers can, through an efficient use of spare time, have a profound effect on public affairs, especially during periods of national mobilization; and law firms, universities, corporations, and consultancies can be useful bases of public-affairs operations.[2] However, the real point remains. Professional expertise developed over a lifetime of public service is indispensable to the effective conduct of public business.[3]

The emerging professionalization of U.S. public service is not surprising. Economic historians have charted the ascendancy of professional managers in modern business enterprise.[4] The rise of professions in U.S. civil service systems has long been noted.[5] Even Woodrow Wilson clearly understood the effect of government size and structure on public service:

There was (in early times) little or no trouble about administration. . . . The functions of government were simple, because life itself was simple. . . . There was no complex system of public revenues and public debts to puzzle financiers; there were, consequently, no financiers to be puzzled.[6]

Wilson also understood the converse argument: large and complex public policy requires a commensurate system of public service.[7] How to design and staff such a system constitutes the core of what will be referred to here as the public-service problem.

PUBLIC-SERVICE SIZE AND STRUCTURE

That public-service size and structure should be determined by the operating requirements of public missions is axio-

---

1. Woodrow Wilson, "The Study of Administration," *Political Science Quarterly*, 2(2):221 (June 1887). Born on 28 December 1856, Wilson was 30 when the essay was published; his first book, *Congressional Government*, was published in January 1885. See also Norton E. Long's discussion of the SES, "The S.E.S. and the Public Interest," *Public Administration Review*, 41(3):305, 312 (May-June 1981).

2. Leonard P. White, ed., *Civil Service in Wartime* (Chicago: University of Chicago Press, 1945), pp. 36-44.

3. Eugene B. McGregor, Jr., ed., "Symposium: The Public Service as Institution," *Public Administration Review*, 42(4):304, 320 (July-Aug. 1982).

4. Frederick C. Mosher, *Democracy and Public Service* (New York: Oxford University Press, 1968).

5. Alfred D. Chandler, Jr., *The Visible Hand: The Managerial Revolution in American Business* (Cambridge, MA: Belknap Press, 1977).

6. Wilson, "Study of Administration," p. 199.

7. Ibid., pp. 200-1.

matic. When governments fight wars, conduct research and development programs, stimulate economic development, or care for the indigent, personnel requirements result. Thus when government decides that a competitive push must advance the state of the art in aerospace, an array of sophisticated scientific and technical skills are required. When stimulating economic growth in depressed areas is the policy goal, entrepreneurial, financial, and industrial development skills are prized. If policy moves public capital into the construction of homes, offices, and urban rehabilitation, then banking, insurance, and real estate skills are needed for successful program execution. If public policy expands cash entitlement programs, then skills associated with computerized disbursement systems are required. If, to take a final example, the aim is to expand the regulation of enterprise, then legal training and technically trained inspectors are required to work on such regulatory problems as pollution control, environment impact analysis, plant safety, and consumer product safety.

Trend data on public finance and employment provide clues about the history of public service in the United States. One simple way to display the data is a two-point comparison by which gross shifts in aggregate totals can be summarized. Two-point snapshots allow the simultaneous comparison of several government employment and finance indicators.

Figure 1 displays the U.S. public finance and employment comparisons for 1950 and 1980. Since federal research and development (R&D) funding was not recorded before 1951, the R&D spending totals span only a 29-year period. The solid and slashed lines refer to the financial side of government. The dotted lines record numbers of people. In neither case are the raw data adjusted to discount the effects of inflation and shifts in work-force size. To simplify the data, a logarithmic scale shows the magnitude of change over three decades, where 1950 represents the base year of one, and the amount of the calculated 30-year increase, presented in parentheses, is represented by the slope of each line.

Several findings obtain. First, growth of public finance outstripped personnel growth by substantial margins. For example, growth in federal government outlays and state and local own-source revenues vastly outstripped the growth in government employment. We return shortly to the implications of financial outlays growing by factors of 13 to 40 while work forces grew by factors of only one and one-half to three. Clearly budgets and bureaucrats have not been growing at the same rate, and the disparity reveals much about public-service structure.

A second finding is that the most dramatic federal spending changes have occurred not in federally delivered services but in the 30-year growth in federal grants-in-aid and transfer payments. In effect, the federal government has increasingly become a major purchaser of public-policy services from nonfederal levels of government. Furthermore, to the extent that it relies on entitlement cash transfers and service reimbursements as a means of implementing welfare, health, education, housing, unemployment, and disability policies, the federal government may even be subsidizing the avoidance of governmental service-delivery mechanisms altogether.

FIGURE 1
UNADJUSTED TWO-POINT TRENDS IN U.S. PUBLIC FINANCE AND PUBLIC EMPLOYMENT: 1950 to 1980

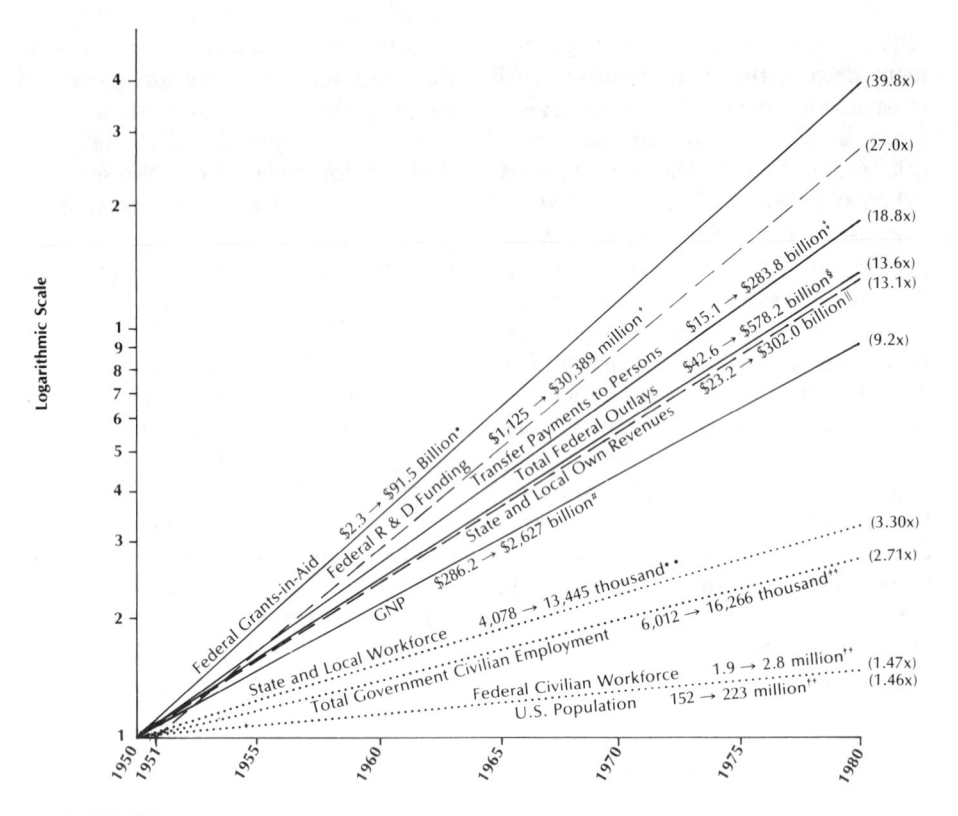

SOURCES:

*Intergovernmental Perspective, 4:8 (Winter 1978); Budget of the U.S. FY 1982, Special Analyses (Washington, DC: Government Printing Office, 1981), p. 242.

†Budget of the U.S., FY 1952/53 through Budget of the U.S., FY 1982.

‡Business Statistics, 1951; Survey of Current Business, June 1981, p. 8.

§Census Bureau, Department of Commerce, 1977 U.S. Statistical Abstract (Washington, DC: Government Printing Office), p. 247; Budget of the U.S., FY 1982, Special Analyses, p. 44.

‖1977 U.S. Statistical Abstract, p. 278; 1981 U.S. Statistical Abstract, p. 288.

#1977 U.S. Statistical Abstract, p. 429; Budget of the U.S., FY 1982, Special Analyses, p. 8.

**Budget of the U.S., FY 1982, Special Analyses, p. 288; Budget of the U.S., FY 1979, Special Analyses, p. 210.

††Budget of the U.S., FY 1982, Special Analyses, p. 288; Budget of the U.S., FY 1979, Special Analyses, p. 210.

A third finding pertains to the growth in government work forces. It is true that total government employment has grown nearly twice as fast as the U.S. population. But it is also true that the growth is due to the growth of government at state and local levels. The federal work force has grown at almost exactly the same rate as the population, and since the early sixties—with the exception of a peak employment level during the Vietnam war in 1970—it has remained virtually stable at 2.8 million employees. Clearly spectacular growth in policy responsibilities and spending do not have to result in commensurate increases in the size of government work forces. That programmatic and budgetary responsibilities can grow while government work-force size remains constant is one of the lessons revealed in Figure 1.

But work forces somewhere are affected by the programmatic and spending growth implied in Figure 1. In the case of governmental work forces, an explosion in the use of the federal grant-in-aid mechanism has had an enormous impact on the growth of state and local work forces. State and local government hired the caseworkers, police officers and fire fighters, planners, inspectors, health professionals, teachers, and administrators to implement the programs funded by categorical and block grants and revenue sharing. In effect, the federal government has become a major purchaser of services produced by other levels of government. That the federal government also became the regulator of state and local governments accepting federal largesse is a confounding issue[8] that affects the skill mix and organization of a federal work force operating under a fixed personnel constraint.

Figure 2 adds two major insights. One is the immensity of the public-service enterprise. With expenditures

8. George E. Hale and Marian Lief Palley, *The Politics of Federal Grants* (Washington, DC: Congressional Quarterly, 1981); Jean J. Couturier and Stephen E. Dunn, "Federal Colonization of State and Local Governments," *State Government*, 50(2):65, 71 (Spring 1977).

again indicated by solid lines and personnel indicated by dotted lines, the magnitudes can be summarized for a period spanning the last two years of the Truman administration to the end of the Carter administration. Total government outlays exceeded one-third of the gross national product (GNP) in 1980, and federal outlays alone consumed over 22 percent of GNP. Federal grants-in-aid totaled one-fourth of state and local expenditures. Governmental transfer payments consumed over 10 percent of GNP. Federal research and development (R&D) budgets (Figure 1) have grown from 1.1 billion dollars in fiscal year 1951, the first year in which R&D totals could be estimated, to over five percent of the federal budget—over $30 billion—in 1980. Total government civilian employment employs nearly 15 percent of the U.S. labor force.

By any estimate, government is big business, big enough to consume the efforts of thousands of Wilson's financiers. A more immediately relevant point is that the business is so large and complex that it cannot conceivably be run by amateurs, no matter how talented they might be. Business of the size and complexity of U.S. government can really be run only by trained professionals who pursue full-time public-affairs careers.

A second conclusion is that federal service appears unusually dynamic, considering the juxtaposition of an enormous growth of policy responsibility—as indicated by spending changes—coupled with a decline in its work force relative to other levels of government. How can both trends—that is, growth in service and financial demands and a decline in relative work-force size—occur simultaneously? The answer can only be that federal service has developed productive instruments that rely

FIGURE 2
TWO-POINT PERCENTAGE TRENDS IN U.S. PUBLIC FINANCE AND PUBLIC EMPLOYMENT: 1950 to 1980

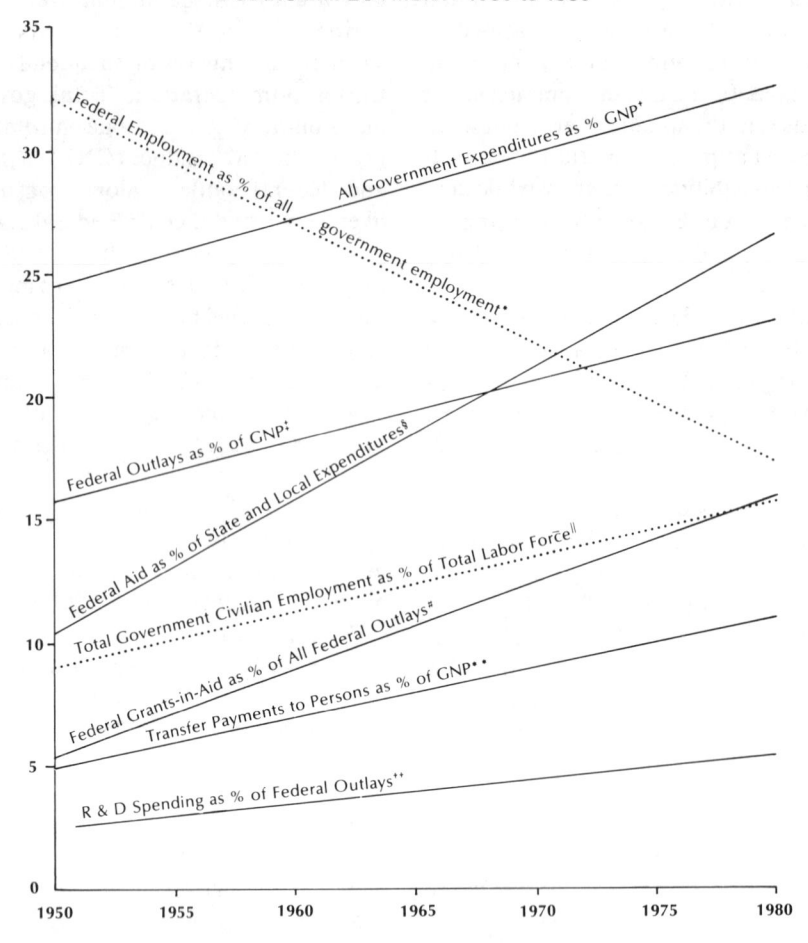

SOURCES:

*Budget of the U.S., FY 1982, Special Analyses, p. 288.

†1977 U.S. Statistical Abstract, pp. 276, 429; Budget of the U.S., FY 1982, Special Analyses, p. 253.

‡Budget of the U.S., FY 1982, Special Analyses, p. 48.

§Budget of the U.S., FY 1982, Special Analyses, p. 252; Budget of the U.S., FY 1979, Special Analyses, p. 184.

‖Budget of the U.S., FY 1979, Special Analyses, p. 210; 1977 U.S. Statistical Abstract, p. 387; Budget of the U.S., FY 1982, Special Analyses, p. 288.

#Budget of the U.S., FY 1979, Special Analyses, p. 184; Budget of the U.S., FY 1982, Special Analyses, p. 242.

**Business Statistics, 1951, p. 8; Survey of Current Business, June 1981, p. 8.

††Budget of the U.S., FY 1952/53, p. 1170; Budget of the U.S., FY 1981, Special Analyses, p. 306.

less on federally produced services and more on financial assistance that takes the form of direct payments to individuals, grants, cooperative agreements, subsidies, loans, loan guarantees, insurance, technical services, and information and property donations to persons, government, or other institutions that do produce final public products and services. Well over one-half of the federal budget is now funneled through such public-assistance mechanisms.[9]

CURRENT PUBLIC-SERVICE DESIGN ASSUMPTIONS

Constant change also appears to have been one of the unappreciated realities of U.S. public administration. Quite contrary to the metaphors of bureaucratic intransigence and inertia, the operating ethic of administration in the United States appears highly dynamic and fully consistent with a pragmatic and problem-solving American public policy. Clearly Figures 1 and 2 demonstrate that public policy has not been standing still. The magnitude of spending and employment changes belies the argument that public bureaucracy is static.

Federal service has been constantly shifting its skill mix within the constraint of a fixed work-force ceiling in order to accommodate a constantly changing portfolio of missions. The enormous expansion in spending relative to personnel suggests a highly professional work force, capital-intensive

---

9. *Managing Federal Assistance in the 1980's: A Report to the Congress of the United States Pursuant to the Federal Grant and Cooperative Agreement Act of 1977, Public Law 95-224* (Washington, DC: Executive Office of the President, Office of Management and Budget, Mar. 1980).

methods of service production—such as computers, satellites, and modern airport safety equipment—and a changing task structure in which the delivery of many of the final products of federal policy is accomplished by nonfederal workers under a variety of contractual mechanisms. Only through such a highly professionalized work force implementing large and sophisticated programs can one conceive of something less than one-fourth of the nation's annual productive capacity being dispersed by a mere 2.8 million workers.

This gross generalization is not meant to imply that agencies of the federal government do not deliver final services and products to citizens. The Bureau of Labor Statistics, the Federal Bureau of Investigation, the Public Health Service, the Social Security Administration, the Internal Revenue Service, the Federal Aviation Administration, the National Park Service, and the U.S. Forest Service are all federal services operating at the delivery end of public policy, which is to say that they produce government's final products as well as supervise public-assistance mechanisms through which public services are also produced at other levels of government.

This summary suggests the logic of American administrative structure. Public service, in reality, is a bundle of discrete services that have accrued in response to citizen demand for solving public problems. The system is highly competitive and mission-oriented. It also resists the rationalizing efforts of centrally located managers.

A repetitive, problem-solving cycle appears to typify American practice. First, a problem is discovered. Several programmatic remedies are suggested, debated, separately authorized, and funded. Cutbacks are competitively administered only when the problem abates, funds are depleted, or some initial investments are found to produce no results. The administrative structure and public service resulting from such problem solving is predictably messy, but precisely of the sort one might expect when multiple public firms, sometimes called bureaus or agencies, compete for the honor of fixing public problems. That such problem solving occurs within a constitutional environment of checks and balances only ensures an outcome of adventure, for in the Madisonian constitutional scheme, governmental and policy actors are accorded several points of access to each of the problem-solving stages. Thus if the game is lost in one arena, another committee or executive-branch agency can be approached.

Furthermore, courts are available to require certain services and enjoin others. Protected civil liberties, sunshine laws, and the Freedom of Information Act help citizens and interest groups probe relevant files and gather visibility and support through the public media. In short, the environment in which American public administration operates is highly active, sustained both by constitutional design and an active public opinion, which, in Wilson's view, is "a pupil apt to think itself quite sufficiently instructed."[10]

The administrative result was inevitable. Public service has developed in a manner compatible with other U.S. political, economic, and technological institutions. In short, through experimentation with the myriad ways to do public business, American administrative technology has responded to the programmatic problem-solving requirements of American public policy. In this important regard, American public service diverges significantly from the rationalized theories of administration put into practice in such countries as France, Great Britain, and Germany. Historian Daniel J. Boorstin supplies the leitmotif of the American administrative and political technology:

This experimental spirit, which had made the new nation politically possible, would explain much that would be distinctive of the nation's life. . . . The American limbo—a borderland between experience and idea, where old absolutes were dissolved and new opportunities discovered—would puzzle thinkers from abroad. With their time-honored distinction between fact and idea, between materialism and idealism, they labeled a people who had so little respect for absolutes as vulgar "materialists." In the gloriously filigreed cultures of the Old World it was not easy to think of life as experiment. But American life was experiment, and experiment was a technique for testing and revising ideas. In this American limbo all sorts of novelties might emerge. What to men of the Old World seemed a no-man's-land was the Americans' native land.[11]

The result is a potentially chaotic public service. Public service defies neat rationalization because its administrative structure derives from problem-based services.[12] In a service-based

---

10. Wilson, "Study of Administration," p. 215.

11. Daniel J. Boorstin, *The Republic of Technology: Reflection on Our Future Community* (New York: Harper & Row, 1980). That Woodrow Wilson exulted in the same pragmatic and experimental approach to problem solving seems clearly implied in "Study of Administration"; see his comments on the transferability of European practice to the United States, p. 216, and the role of theory in practical administration, pp. 220-21.

12. Observers from outside the United States find U.S. public-service structure anomalous. As the Fulton Committee report noted, "'Agencies' proliferate on a considerable scale, and they may

system, overarching agency and bureau objectives are nominal. Goals exist, but they are stated only loosely. When an agency's mission portfolio becomes outdated, unnecessary, or badly performed, new services spring up to compete in the new markets. The mission portfolios of all affected agencies are then adjusted to suit a new policy environment.[13] Experimental problem solving has been the traditional basis of American public-service design.

ASSESSING AN EXPERIMENTAL PUBLIC SERVICE

The design is both promise and problem. One advantage of an experimental public service is that a polycentric, service-based system of public administration possesses an inherent capacity for change. An absence of neatly rationalized administrative structure means, for example, that there is neither an administrative theory nor a centralized bureaucratic elite hostile to experiments threatening bureaucratic stability. The result is that competing service-delivery prototypes can be continuously invented, nurtured, and entered in the public-service sweepstakes. In such a competitive environment, the public wins because unproductive experiments lose the competition to more productive administrative technology.

The second advantage is that a competitive environment fosters a performance-based, managerial excel-

lence. Public managers and executives emerge not because of personal connections, pedigree, or some bureaucratically designed screening device that may or may not be relevant to public needs. Managerial excellence is proven by an ability to get things done. James Webb's account of the National Aeronautics and Space Administration (NASA) experience is germane to the technology metaphor:

There appears to be little use in attempting to select an executive scientifically through a long period of complex matching and testing. In my earlier experience I often spent months seeking just the right key executive for a job. But I have found that such approaches can be counterproductive. When you put an undue effort into a selection and persuasion process and a man fails, you find yourself committed to him. Furthermore, the failure rate is not greatly lessened by such an arduous process. Today, in NASA, we search until we find a man who seems to be qualified, and then we put him to the test. If he works out, well and good. If not, we try another.[14]

A third advantage is that it encourages the maintenance of redundancy in policy areas where failure results in enormous public pain and suffering. The case for administrative redundancy is well stated elsewhere,[15] but it bears

---

or may not eventually be brought together under one ministerial head." *Report of the Committee on the Civil Service to Parliament* (London: Her Majesty's Stationery Office, 1968), p. 144.

13. Louis Bragaw's analysis of the "hidden stimulus" describes nicely how agency missions change over time: *Managing a Federal Agency* (Baltimore: Johns Hopkins University Press, 1980).

14. James E. Webb, *Space Age Management: The Large Scale Approach* (New York: McGraw-Hill, 1969), p. 162.

15. Martin Landau, "Redundancy, Rationality, and the Problem of Duplication and Overlap," *Public Administration Review,* 29:346-58 (July-Aug. 1969). For an even earlier account of the structure and operation of governmental redundancy, see, for instance, Charles A. Beard, *American Government and Politics* (New York: Macmillan, 1936), pp. 382-83, on the role of American government in the advancement of foreign trade.

repeating that the use of triads for strategic weapons delivery, or a troika for the purposes of economic forecasting, or duplicate sets of equipotential agencies provides options for public decision makers. The point must also be made that the mere availability of options ensures neither intelligent maintenance nor pointed employment of redundant systems, a subject to be taken up in the last section of this article.

Finally, an administrative structure based on experimental problem solving creates natural checks and balances through which bureaucratic power is controlled. Experimental design involves generous amounts of administrative decentralization buttressed by bureau-based budgets and career structures and iron-triangle subgovernments.[16] In an open, experimental system, a thicket of independently chartered public-service systems stimulates the competitive search for productivity.

There are problems. One is that a diffuse system of administration is clumsy and expensive. The danger of profligacy is inherent in any system that maintains redundant and competing systems of public businesses. The problem is particularly revealed when administrative complexity must be managed in times of fiscal constraint accompanied by continued demand for government problem solving. Scarcity mandates a reassessment of the need to maintain multiple sets of potentially competitive services.

A second problem is found in the potential for goal displacement where bureaucrats, interest groups, and legislative subcommittees supplant public goals with private aims by combining to protect and enlarge the advantages of specific programs and agencies. The problem is only compounded when administrative designs are based on the merger of public and private interests. Charles Beard supplies incisive historic illustration of the problem of administrative accountability and responsibility:

Although the armed officers of the United States do not form a caste founded on a feudal aristocracy, they are an estate in themselves. . . . Enlisted on their side are powerful private interests—industrialists who annually sell millions of dollars' worth of war materials to the Government. Capitalists subscribe to private societies engaged in propaganda for increased armaments, and sometimes employ agents to promote policies likely to multiply their profits. For example, an investigation initiated by the Senate on motion of President Hoover in 1929 showed that three important corporations, which did a lucrative business building warships for the Government, had hired a professional agitator to represent them at the Geneva conference on the reduction of armaments, two years before, and had made large expenditures with a view to securing congressional aid for the mercantile marine—an auxiliary arm of naval defense. Inevitably such incidents make it difficult for Congress to differentiate between military proposals founded on the merits of the situation and those which arise from interested machinations. It is on this ground that many advocates of civilian supremacy demand that the Government manufacture its own munitions without profit to anyone, or at least "take all the profits out of war."[17]

A third problem is that administrative systems based on decentralized and redundant experimentation do not re-

---

16. Eugene B. McGregor, Jr., "Politics and Career Mobility," *American Political Science Review*, 68(1):18, 26 (Mar. 1974).

17. Beard, *American Government and Politics*, pp. 300-1.

spond easily to nonprofessionals who would manage the instruments of government. The sheer number of operating units prevents easy mastery. Use of privatized instruments of policy implementation only compounds the complexity by removing government operations from the direct control of government managers. Whether modern administrative complexity is a contributor to the current decline of citizen confidence in government is only a speculative question. The question is not entirely idle. It seems likely that citizens in democracies will not long finance large, complex, obtuse, and expensive mysteries. And yet if the current operating reality is that costly professional training and years of continuous participation are required to master the details of government management, how can citizens trust that their affairs are well managed and that they have not surrendered their freedoms to an expensive and impenetrable monster or to experimental chaos?

PUBLIC-SERVICE REDESIGN

The Wilsonian problem is perpetual. How can a public service be constituted to serve both "the local part and the national whole"? A simple schematic, shown in Figure 3, restates the problem in functional terms. All public-service systems must solve three classic problems of governance, policy, and administrative operations. Solution of only one or two of the problem areas risks systemic failure. In the absence of governance, public service will be incapable of forming coalitions of interests strong enough to set purposes and stick with them. In the absence of policy, public service will become contentless and irrelevant to the solution of substantive problems. In the absence of administrative operations, policy cannot be implemented.

The point of Figure 3 is that what has been commonly referred to as the Wilsonian politics-administration dichotomy derives in fact from the interaction of three political-administrative arenas. Indeed, the dichotomy cannot be understood until the three arenas are clarified. Administration derives from the organizational need for standard operating procedures through which the productive efforts of large numbers of people are combined. Thus administrative structure, rules, and regulations exist precisely because they are capable of achieving enormous economies through division of labor and repetitive performance of tasks. That numerous bureaucratic pathologies derive from red tape and organizational architecture is not the issue here.

What is arrayed against administration, however, is only nominally labeled "politics." In reality, the label "politics" covers two distinct activities. One is steerage. "Governance" is the term assigned to the process by which a government or a society mobilizes itself and allocates resources to meet its public-policy commitments.[18] Steerage necessarily involves a partisan exercise of power, for only through advocacy can winning coalitions be formed behind the rules of authority necessary to governance.

The second activity is substantive problem solving. Whereas governance depends on the partisan advancement of cause, the issues for policy are the definition of public problems, assessment of options, and selection of action strate-

---

18. Richard Rose, ed., *Challenge to Governance: Studies in Overloaded Polities* (Beverly Hills, CA: Sage, 1980), pp. 6-7.

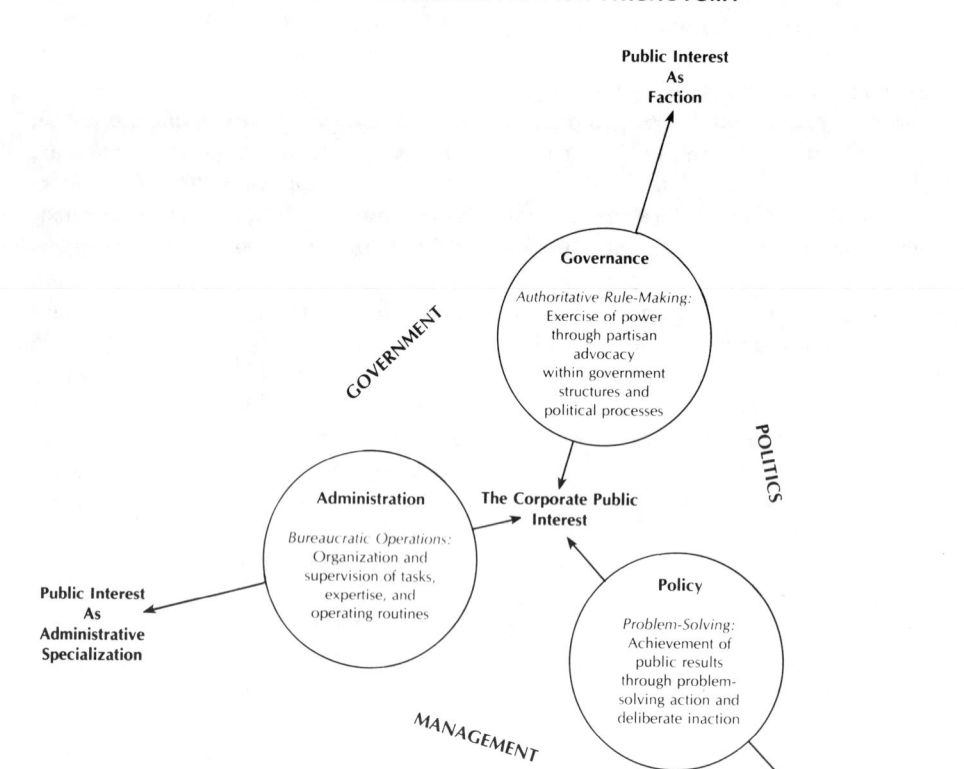

FIGURE 3
THE POLITICS-ADMINISTRATION TRICHOTOMY

Governance
Authoritative Rule-Making: Exercise of power through partisan advocacy within government structures and political processes

Administration
Bureaucratic Operations: Organization and supervision of tasks, expertise, and operating routines

Policy
Problem-Solving: Achievement of public results through problem-solving action and deliberate inaction

- Public Interest As Faction
- Public Interest As Administrative Specialization
- Public Interest As Interest Group Liberalism
- The Corporate Public Interest
- GOVERNMENT
- POLITICS
- MANAGEMENT

gies. In the governance arena, partisanship is *sui generis* since winning coalitions can only be established by prevailing in the establishment of authority.[19] In the case of the policy arena, however, partisanship is either ignored or viewed as instrumental—for example, "politics as the art of the possible"; what counts is solving problems.

---

19. An excellent illustration of the governance process is found in Robert Caro, *The Power Broker* (New York: Vintage Books, 1974); see ch. 33, "Leading Out the Regiment."

The three arenas are also useful descriptors of public-service reform. For example, the Pendleton Act of Wilson's day (1883) was a governmental reform. The installation of merit principles had as its chief aim the separation of partisan politics from personnel operations. Thus civil-service commissions, classified—that is, merit—positions, certificates of eligibility, and rules-of-three became the instruments of governmental change.

Separation of administrative operations from partisan politics does not *ipso facto* solve public problems, and, in some instances, an overzealous use of merit machinery and technology becomes a positive impediment to problem solving. On this point is based the premise of the Civil Service Reform Act (CSRA) of 1978, implementation of which is currently under way. The CSRA is largely a managerial reform aimed at enhancing the productivity of governmental employees. The basis for this claim is seen in the key provisions of the act (Public Law 95-454), to wit:

1. The act abolishes the U.S. Civil Service Commission, whose existence depended upon a procedural control of personnel operations, and authorizes the establishment of three agencies with new governmental missions. The Office of Personnel Management now holds the managerial portfolio with respect to personnel administration; the Merit Systems Protection Board plays the regulatory role of protecting merit principles and hearing appeals of employee grievances; the Federal Labor Relations Authority administers the federal collective bargaining process.

2. The position of managers closest to the production of final products is strengthened through several devices:

   —the requirement of agency-based performance appraisals (Title II);

   —the requirement that merit pay, including incentive awards, be allocated on the basis of performance effectiveness (Title V);

   —the authorization of administrative experiments which demonstrate new methods of managing personnel at agency levels of government (Title VI);

   —the authorization of a study of federal government decentralization (Title IX);

   —the authorization of a delegation of personnel management authorities including competitive examination to agency managers (Title II, Section 1104);

   —the authorization of flexibility in the staffing of agencies both in terms of loosening rules of selection (Title III, Section 3309) and using student volunteer services (Title III, Section 3111).

3. The establishment of a capstone management structure in the form of a Senior Executive Service (Title IV)—the SES—to enhance the recruitment and retention of qualified executives and to facilitate the effective assignment of executives to the management of agency functions.[20]

The most important change of the CSRA reforms is the establishment of the Senior Executive Service (SES), which replaces the old general schedule supergrades and executives grades V and IV. The strategic nature of the shift lies in the establishment of a class of public servant whose portfolio is not limited to a single service or agency. The use of a rank-in-the-person strategy, rather than the rank-in-the-job concept, potentially frees members of the SES from agency operations and interest-group captivity. Under the rank-in-person theory, SES members are

20. Alan K. Campbell, "Testimony on Civil Service Reform and Reorganization," Testimony before the Committee on Post Office and Civil Service, U.S. House of Representatives (14 Mar. 1978). The establishment of a statutory basis for federal labor relations appears not to have been the strategic issue addressed by CSRA. The subject was omitted in the original arguments for reform (see Campbell, "Testimony"). The subsequent appearance of what became the labor-management relations provisions of Public Law 95-454 confirms that Title VII of CSRA was designed to secure the support of federal labor unions whose help was needed to pass the rest of the legislation. In effect, the key part of CSRA lies with those subjects for which the support of labor was solicited.

assignable to problems. In a rank-in-job system, SES positions would have been the property of bureaucratic operations and agency-interest-group-subcommittee subgovernments.

In essence, the SES symbolizes public recognition that a professional policy establishment is now required. The use of executives who are sworn officers of government is strategic. The oath of office (Standard Form 61), for example, binds government officials to the Constitution of the United States.[21] Government executives are pledged, therefore, not simply to the maintenance of agency and program but to the constitutional principles that make community service possible. Thus they possess a legitimacy to discharge the executive function of government not enjoyed by civil-service operatives and contractual government employees who, in reality, are professors, lawyers, corporate executives, and consultants.

The appearance of the SES is deceiving, however. On the surface, the SES inauguration appears to be modeled after a European senior civil service on the assumption that a corporate structure of governance will inject coherence and continuity into a fragmented governmental system that does not appear either to work very well or to inspire public confidence in its efficacy. The idea now circulating implies that the development of a new class of governmental mandarins will restore competence and governance[22] to a highly fragmented public service. The argument is certainly based on a correct factual premise: the authorization of the SES establishes the higher civil service as a new institution of government. But the basis of the reform and the defense of this new institution lies elsewhere.

The SES exists because no other institution has been able to integrate policy, governance, and administrative operations and do so in a way that balances the centrifugal interests of agency and faction with the corporate needs of whole communities. Executives are traditionally called upon to define clearly the public business, assign operational goals and objectives to administrative instruments, manage the public-service resource base, close down unproductive governmental exercises, and reallocate available resources to more hopeful ventures. Simply to throw money at redundant systems produces no final products and may undermine democratic governance and policymaking in the bargain. The specter of public servants prowling aimlessly about dispersing loose change does not inspire confidence in the problem-solving potential of government. Neither is public service encouraged to rise above the parochialism of agency and bureau to solve problems that invariably cut across agency boundaries.

The creation of a governmentwide executive personnel system has risks. Members of the SES will undoubtedly be used to create order and problem-solving coherence, should other institutions fail to discharge their governance and policy functions. It might therefore

---

21. John A. Rohr, "Ethics for the Senior Executive Service: Suggestions for Management Training," *Administration and Society*, 12(2):203, 215 (Aug. 1980).

22. A useful account of the friction between career bureaucrats and political executives is Hugh Heclo, *A Government of Strangers: Executive Politics in Washington* (Washington, DC: Brookings Institution, 1977). See also James L. Sundquist, "The Crisis of Competence in Our National Government," *Political Science Quarterly*, 95(2):207, 208 (Summer 1980).

appear that increased executive command of public bureaucracy in the form of a single executive service poses a threat to democratic values, for administrative efficiency seems forever at odds with the messy and time-consuming interactions characteristic of democratic community.[23]

The bureaucratic threat to democratic governance is not without plausibility. But such a risk should not be assigned to the SES. The very definition of the executive function as integrative problem solving militates against the proposition that democracy is threatened by an official executive establishment. The risk is not that the SES can tyrannize. The danger is that it can be misconceived and become useless and ignored. Given the extensive constitutional and governmental checks on bureaucracy already in place, it is difficult to conceive of the SES as dangerous. It seems more likely that an executive service will enhance the productivity of a currently overloaded public-service system. In short, there is potentially much to gain and little to lose by experimenting with a new form of public service.

This is a different position from defending the idea of a monotonic, hierarchic, and corporate administrative class as European mandarins are alleged to be. What is corporate is the holistic view of the public service that constantly envisions programmatic change engineered across the boundaries of traditionally autonomous agencies and interests. The nature of problems, not theoretical ideas about governance and administration, dictates the structure and operation of an executive service. Problems of national security, for example, are not solved simply by maintaining an independent and increasingly expensive army, navy, and air force. Solutions to defense problems derive from explicit conceptions of threats for which the maintenance of force levels are adequate to cover risks.[24] The executive point of view also recognizes that national security problems are a partial function of national economic strength and industrial capacity, and that economic power in a postindustrial world is tied to technological competitiveness for which an educated population is an economic necessity. Thus it is that defense problems fold into economic development problems, which fold into the delivery of educational services.

The point is not that an overarching public-service elite is needed to unravel all the issues associated with a large and complex problem such as national security. Problems do not get solved by government overlords. The point is that a large public problem decomposes into problem subsets, and the executive function is to solve the specific problems that stand in the way of community achievement. In the example already cited, the problem subsets range across military strategy, industrial and economic development, educational policy, research and development, public finance, and so forth. Each problem, in turn, defines executive skill requirements and, therefore, who should be an executive and who should not. That executives must be generalists able to move pieces with an eye to the whole

---

23. Douglas Yates, *Bureaucratic Democracy: The Search for Democracy and Efficiency in American Government* (Cambridge, MA: Harvard University Press, 1982).

24. I am indebted to Long's analysis of the problem of administrative fragmentation and problem solving in the Pentagon, "S.E.S.," pp. 307-8.

chessboard seems implicit in this conception of executive problem solving.[25] It also follows that when problems are solved, become intractable, or cease to be interesting, problem-solving executives move on to new lines of work.

I do not suggest—nor did Woodrow Wilson—that public service be reduced to a uniform and rationalized entity. What is concluded is that several versions of the SES experiment should be tried in states and localities as well as at the federal level.[26] That executives should be independent of parochial interests, well paid, and endowed with prestige, and should enjoy reasonably secure appointments is implied by the role they will be required to play in balancing the centrifugal pressures of factional interests with the interests of corporate society. Should the experiment fail, auxiliary measures are always available to deal with what remains the public-service problem.

25. It is important to emphasize that what Harlan Cleveland has referred to as a "situation-as-a-whole" generalist does not imply the absence of specialized training and experience: *The Future Executive* (New York: Harper & Row, 1972), ch. 9, "Shapers of Values."

26. Arthur L. Finkle, Herbert Hall, and Sophia S. Min, "Senior Executive Service: The State of the Art," *Public Personnel Management Journal,* 10(3):299, 312 (Fall 1981).

The Management of Executive Departments

By ALAN L. DEAN

ABSTRACT: One of the most important aspects of the management of the executive branch of the federal government relates to the organization and administration of the 13 executive departments. Yet there has been little attention given to this aspect of public administration in the literature. If the functions of the government of the United States are to be efficiently executed, it is vital that the executive departments be well conceived, structured, and managed. This means that they should be set up to carry out definable major purposes of the government, the enacting statutes should provide for adequate authority in the secretaries, there should be substantial freedom to adapt the departments to changes in priorities, greater attention should be given to the design and implementation of modern management systems, and reliance should be placed on the career civil servants who alone have the knowledge and continuity to assure efficient and consistent administration. It is likely, however, that there is so little agreement as to how the shortcomings of our departments can be remedied that something like a new Hoover Commission may be required to identify solutions and raise public awareness of the urgency of the situation.

Alan L. Dean is a trustee and recent chairman (1977-81) of the National Academy of Public Administration. Before serving as vice-president for administration of the United States Railway Association (1974-79), he was the management adviser to the under secretary of the Department of Health, Education and Welfare, deputy assistant director of the Office of Management and Budget, and coordinator of the President's Departmental Reorganization Program. He was the first assistant secretary for administration of the Department of Transportation (DOT), and served on the interagency task forces that drafted the DOT legislation and planned its implementation. He had previously held the post of associate administrator for administration of the Federal Aviation Agency. He received a B.A. in political science from Reed College and an M.A. in public administration from American University, and has published many articles on the administration of public agencies.

THE Constitution of the United States contemplated that executive departments would be created to carry out the functions of the new government, but it wisely left to the Congress and the president the tasks of determining what departments would be created, what responsibilities would be assigned to them, and how they would be organized and managed.[1]

The first Congress turned promptly to the establishment of the departments needed to discharge urgent functions entrusted to the new federal government, and by the end of 1789 the Departments of State, Treasury, and War were in operation. Since then, presidents and the Congress have relied on the executive department as the primary mechanism for the administration of federal programs. The number of departments has grown to reflect increases in the magnitude and diversity of the activities of the federal government, and by 1980 the original 3 had expanded to 13.[2]

The crucial role played by the departments in today's government is illustrated by the fact that over 80 percent of all federal civilian employees and virtually all military personnel are on the rolls of the executive departments. It is also estimated that nearly 90 percent of federal fund outlays for the 1982 fiscal year will be accounted for by the departments.

In citing the dominant place of the departments in federal program administration, note should be taken of the existence of a large number of independent agencies.[3] Although a few of these entities, such as the U.S. Postal Service, the Veterans Administration, the National Aeronautics and Space Administration, and the Environmental Protection Agency, have come to play important roles within the executive branch, most are small agencies with limited missions and resources. Few even approach the cabinet departments in influence, prestige, or scope of functions.

From the administration of President Washington, the heads of the departments have been included in the cabinet[4] by virtue of their positions. Although the cabinet has not evolved into the powerful instrument that similarly designated councils have become in some parliamentary systems, membership in the president's cabinet carries a great deal of prestige and a reasonable assurance of access to the president and his principal advisers.

Unfortunately, from the standpoint of effective administration, the executive departments as they now exist vary widely in size, importance, and traditions of management. Having been created at different times and having developed different approaches to internal administration, today's departments present numerous urgent issues with

---

1. The Constitution's Article II authorizes the president to "require the Opinion, in writing, of the principal Officer in each of the executive Departments." The Congress is also authorized to vest by law the appointment of "inferior Officers" in the heads of departments.

2. President Reagan has recommended the elimination or the conversion to nondepartmental status of the Departments of Energy and Education.

3. The term "independent agency" is used here to mean any entity of the executive branch created outside of the departments and, in theory, accorded a direct reporting relationship to the president.

4. The cabinet in the United States has no constitutional or legal basis. Its functions are based on custom and the style of management of individual presidents.

respect to their roles, relationships, and effectiveness. Consequently, improving the management of the executive departments has become one of the most important challenges now facing the United States.

In spite of the importance of the subject, matters relating to the organization and management of executive departments have received only the most cursory attention in public administration literature. There has been no authoritative treatment of departmental management, and those who would seek guidance in administering these entities must draw upon past studies, which tend to be out of date or to treat only portions of the subject matter.

In its report on *Departmental Management* in 1948, the first Hoover Commission[5] helped to identify some of the deficiencies of the departments as they then existed and made a number of important recommendations. Most of these were directed toward strengthening the position of the secretaries with the objective of converting them into real, rather than nominal, managers of their departments.

In 1966, a task force led by the Bureau of the Budget made a special effort to develop and implement advanced management concepts in drafting the legislation creating a Department of Transportation (DOT). Because there was no nucleus agency on which to base the department, as had been the case when the Departments of Health, Education and Welfare (HEW) and Housing and Urban Development (HUD) were established,[6] there was both a need and an opportunity to design the best possible way of organizing transportation functions and units assembled from many locations in the government. Consequently, the Department of Transportation proposal, as transmitted to the Congress, reflected the best available thinking as to how a department should be organized and managed. The legislation proved relatively noncontroversial, and the Congress incorporated the bulk of the task force's recommendation in the Department of Transportation Act as approved on 15 October 1966. The DOT concepts, which will be treated later in this article, had substantial influence on the content of later proposals relating to the reform of the departments.

The most comprehensive and useful of recent efforts to address the need for improved departmental organization and management grew out of President Nixon's decision in 1971 to replace seven of the existing domestic departments with four larger and better designed entities. Based in part on the 1970 recommendations of the Ash Council,[7] the president's Departmental Management Program became a major Nixon administration effort. A central staff in the Office of Management and Budget and several task forces were established to draft legislation to create the proposed Departments of Community Development, Natural Resources,

5. Commission on Organization of the Executive Branch of the Government, which conducted its studies from 1947 to 1949 and issued a number of important reports.

6. The Department of Health, Education and Welfare was established by Reorganization Plan 1 in 1953 through the conversion of the Federal Security Agency into a department. HUD was basically a departmental version of the predecessor Housing and Home Finance Agency accomplished through legislation in 1965.

7. Advisory Council on Executive Organization (1969-71), chaired by Roy Ash.

Human Resources, and Economic Affairs. A special task force was charged with developing and articulating concepts of structure and management to be reflected in all four bills. Although an imminent election and a subsequent change in the president's approach to the supervision of the executive agencies prevented the enactment of any of the departmental bills, much documentation resulted that is of value to anyone concerned with matters of departmental management. In addition to drafts of legislation and the usual section-by-section analyses, the task forces turned out analytic reports, which described in detail how each of the departments would be organized and administered. These documents were published in a volume entitled *Papers Relating to the President's Departmental Reorganization Program*, which was compiled by the Office of Management and Budget and issued in a revised edition in February 1972.[8]

Little of value or significance on the subject of departmental management has appeared in print since 1972. The messages, hearings, and other records relating to the establishment of the Department of Energy in 1977 and the Department of Education in 1979 reveal little in the way of conceptual thinking and say more about how not to approach the management of departments than anything else. Recent proposals aimed at abolishing these departments seem to have been developed with little or no understanding of the role of an executive department or of executive branch organization generally.

---

8. This volume was available by purchase from the superintendent of documents, U.S. Government Printing Office.

MAJOR ASPECTS OF DEPARTMENTAL MANAGEMENT

If a department is to be susceptible to effective management and the successful pursuit of its goals or purposes, a number of prerequisites must be satisfied. A viable department must be justified by the importance and character of its programs, it must have a sufficient breadth of responsibility to enable it to advance successfully some major purpose of government, the secretary must be given adequate administrative authority to manage the department, and the legislation creating it should avoid the excessive prescription of structural and procedural detail.

Criteria for establishing executive departments

Generally an executive department should be provided for when the programs relating to some definable purpose of the government become so numerous, so large, and so complex that an official of secretarial rank with membership in the cabinet and immediate access to the president is needed to bring about effective oversight and coordination. At the outset of our government under the Constitution, it was evident that departments were needed for foreign affairs (State), revenue collection and financial management (Treasury), and defense (War). Except for the splitting off of the Navy Department in 1798, no new executive department was established until 1849, when the Department of Interior was set up to reduce the clutter in the Treasury Department and to assume the responsibility for emerging programs involving the public domain, Indians, and minerals. On the whole, the Congress has been conservative in its approach to establishing new departments, and most have been fully justified, or even overdue, at the time of establishment.

Occasionally, however, political forces emerge that lead to the establishment of a department the existence of which cannot be persuasively justified and that may complicate, rather than facilitate, the administration of federal programs. A notable example of this is the creation of the Department of Labor in 1913 through the break-up of the 10-year-old Department of Commerce and Labor. This unfortunate development was the result of insistence on the part of organized labor for a voice in the cabinet. This first example of a clientele department raised troublesome questions as to whether or not the secretary of labor was to administer his department in the public interest or as an advocate for and representative of an organized segment of the society. The emergence of the Labor Department has caused many subsequent problems of relationships with other departments, especially Commerce and Health and Human Services. Such anomalies as the placement of the Census Bureau in Commerce and the Bureau of Labor Statistics in the Labor Department stand in the way of a strong central statistical office with the capability of serving the economic data needs of the government and the public.

An equally unfortunate example of a department failing to meet the criteria of scope and importance of functions is provided by the recently established Department of Education. Because education in the United States is chiefly a responsibility of the state and local governments, the country has had no need for the equivalent of a European ministry of education. The Carter administration was unable, however, to resist the pressure of the National Education Association for its own department, and the president conducted a strong and narrowly successful campaign to break education away from the Department of Health, Education and Welfare. The consequences have been a retreat from the goal of building a genuine department of human resources around HEW and the emergence of a small, narrowly oriented department, which the Reagan administration is now seeking to abolish.[9]

The evidence remains strong that what President Nixon tried to do in 1971-72 made sense and that his proposals should be given careful consideration by those who would improve departmental management. There is a need to reduce the number of departments, to use major purpose as the criterion for grouping functions, and to equip each secretary with a scope of responsibilities broad enough to enable him to bring about meaningful coordination of related programs on behalf of the president.

The case for pulling together all the programs that relate to a single major purpose within one department can be further made by citing the sad predicament of the Department of Interior. For years after its creation in 1849, the department was noted chiefly for the scandals involving its programs and secretaries. With the accession of Harold Ickes as secretary in 1933 and the increased interest in natural resources conservation that emerged in the 1930s, the integrity of the department's management was improved and an

---

9. This tiny department now contains only 6000 employees. The next in size is the Department of Housing and Community Development, with a staff of 16,000.

effort was made to convert it, or have it evolve, into a Department of Natural Resources. Virtually every president from Roosevelt to Carter endorsed this objective, and many efforts were made to establish the Natural Resources Department. Unfortunately, the largest programs involving water resources on a national scale are administered by the anachronistic Corps of Engineers of the Department of the Army. Other important programs relating to flood prevention and forest management are lodged in the Department of Agriculture. The National Oceanic and Atmospheric Administration is a unit of the Department of Commerce. Opposition from groups fearing the disruption of existing relationships has over the years been sufficient to block the Department of Natural Resources. Consequently, the secretary of the interior remains powerless to provide effective leadership in land or water resource matters, and many problems of coordination rise to the president's level that under better arrangements would be susceptible to disposition at the departmental level.

On the positive side, the Department of Transportation has provided many examples of the benefits produced by a successful effort to place virtually all transportation programs in a single major-purpose department. Since the activation of the department in April 1967, important progress has been made in bringing more balance in federal assistance to the various transportation modes, in enhancing safety, and in encouraging each element of the department to take a broader view of the public interest.

A final word on the importance of having departments based primarily on groupings of related programs associated with major purposes of government: efforts to bring about fundamental realignment of the departments are occasionally denigrated as mere box shuffling, or as too costly in terms of the effort required to produce results. It is sometimes argued that by appointing able officials and by fostering interdepartmental coordination, the need for more fundamental reform can be avoided. My own view, after many years of direct involvement in reorganization efforts and in the management of departments, is that we can never attain the quality of management that our citizens have a right to expect until the departments of the executive branch are converted into more viable entities capable of coping with the problems of government instead of adding to them. Less drastic measures tend to be mere palliatives that seldom produce much in the way of beneficial results.

Structural organization of major-purpose departments

Assuring that a department has a valid basis for existing is only the first step in facilitating good departmental management. It is also essential that the department be so organized as to be able to achieve its potential. Both headquarters and field structures need to be designed to reflect the department's mission and its special problems in serving the public efficiently.

It is important that legislation establishing a department should avoid excessive detail in prescribing internal structure and the placement of authority. The Department of Transportation represents a reasonable balance between the desire of Congress to determine the major features of departmental organization and the need of the secretary for authority to manage his department. In the case of DOT, only a small number of major operating administrations are set up by law. These statutory constituents include the Federal Aviation Administration, the Coast Guard, the Federal Highway Administration, the Urban Mass Transportation Administration, and so on. The Department of Transportation Act generally avoids prescribing the subordinate structures of these first-tier program entities. Furthermore, the program authority is for the most part placed in the secretary with the power to delegate. The result is that the basic organization established in 1967 has held up very well. The principal changes have involved adjusting to the receipt of additional functions such as those relating to mass transportation and maritime programs.[10] There has been a dubious splitting of the original Federal Highway Administration into construction- and safety-oriented administrations,[11] but this is the only major change in a program entity included in the original departmental plan.

The use of assistant secretaries in DOT provides a model for other departments. Most DOT assistant secretaries have no functions assigned to them by law. The secretary alone decides what each assistant secretary shall do and adjusts his or her title accordingly. Thus one assistant secretary may be assigned a general policy role, another can be given governmental-affairs functions, and another budget and program review. If the secretary wishes to make changes in how he uses his assistant secretaries, he can do so administratively without seeking legislation. There have, in fact, been many adjustments in the roles and titles of DOT assistant secretaries since 1967.

A significant and potentially dangerous departure from the rule that secretaries should be permitted to use their assistant secretaries in the manner that will be most helpful in managing the department is the recent creation of statutory inspectors general. These officials are of assistant-secretary rank and are appointed by the president and confirmed by the Senate. Each secretary is required to fill the position even if there are better ways of arranging the audit and investigations functions now assigned to the inspectors general. The proliferation of the inspectors general is a result of the distrust that so bedevils government today. It is also an example of prescribing structure by law with little or no evidence that it will serve any constructive purpose. The inspectors general have served to fragment the distribution of staff management functions among the secretarial officers of the departments. Moreover, there is also a temptation for such politically chosen officials to seek to make their reputations at the expense of the secretary and to become negative rather than positive factors in the search for improved management. It would be preferable for the president and Congress to require department secretaries to organize their offices so that the functions now lodged in inspectors general would be efficiently performed by officers designated by the secretary. The adequacy of such arrangements could easily be verified by the General Accounting Office through its audit program.

---

10. In 1978, urban mass-transportation functions were transferred from HUD to DOT by Reorganization Plan. It was not until 1981 that the maritime functions of the Commerce Department were moved to DOT.

11. These are, respectively, the Federal Highway Administration and the National Highway and Traffic Safety Administration.

Another attractive feature of the Department of Transportation is the exclusively staff role given the assistant secretaries.[12] All program administrators report to the secretary and are able to work directly with him without having to go through intervening assistant secretaries. The assistant secretaries are used only to handle cross-cutting functions and do not become the advocates of particular programs or their administrators.

The DOT approach to internal organization closely resembles that used by the Department of Defense. In the Department of Defense, the principal operations are conducted by the three services, and the assistant secretaries are charged with such matters as logistics, personnel, budgets, and research and technology.

The DOT-Defense concept of management is in contrast to the bureau-oriented organization of older departments such as the Department of Interior. These departments have been characterized by a large number of statutory bureaus, each of which tends to be managerially self-sufficient and to be concerned with only a narrow slice of the department's total mission. The large span of control caused by these numerous bureau-type entities is bridged by so-called program assistant secretaries. Thus over the years Interior Department assistant secretaries have been used to oversee and to provide theoretical coordination of the bureaus concerned with water resources, lands, mineral resources, and wildlife and recreation.

The bureau approach, with its reliance on line assistant secretaries, has generally been found wanting from the standpoint of a capacity to foster effective management. The bureaus tend to be insulated from the secretary by the intervening assistant secretaries, yet the program-oriented assistant secretaries rarely have the experience or resources needed to exercise meaningful supervision over the bureaus assigned to them. In addition the cross-cutting functions that should be handled out of the secretary's office tend to be neglected or poorly led because the assistant secretaries are being used as line program officials.

Field organization and management

Of great importance to the efficacy of departmental administration is the design of the field organization and the degree to which operational authority is decentralized to the field officials close to the public served. Even a casual review of how existing departments approach their field organizations reveals much diversity, but this situation does not lend itself to easy or standardized solutions.

In contrast to such aspects of departmental management as the organization of the office of the secretary or the structuring of headquarters program elements, where certain preferred approaches have been suggested, there is no such thing as a single universally applicable field organization. Since the field structure is directly concerned primarily with the delivery of services, it must be tailored so as to assure that those services are competently, consistently, and effectively provided. Thus the nature of a department's mission and

---

12. All four departments proposed by President Nixon in 1971 utilized the DOT approach to the role of assistant secretaries.

the complexity of the interfaces between its various programs will normally dictate what is feasible in the way of field organization.

Suggesting that each department should design its system of field administration to meet its special needs does not imply that what the departments are currently doing cannot be improved, or that it is impossible to develop helpful doctrine in this area. Far from it. Some departments have clearly failed to move in directions that analysis suggests they should pursue in the interest of improved services delivery. We will not, however, find a single mold into which we can fit the field organization needs of all departments.

At the present time, the executive departments differ most markedly in the way in which they use departmental regional directors. In HUD, the regional director is, in theory at least, a comprehensive official, and virtually all program responsibilities of the department carried out within the geographical confines of a region are under the line supervision of the regional director. This concept in effect removes from the headquarters the direct control over field activities. Program directors—in HUD these are usually assistant secretaries—may be empowered by the secretary to issue directives to the regional directors, but since only the secretary can hire or fire the regional directors, the headquarters program officials are heavily dependent on the secretary's support. At the other end of the spectrum are several departments that have no departmental regional officials. This is true of Justice, Commerce, and Treasury, and, except for certain overseas commands, is true of the Department of Defense.

In the three cited domestic departments, there are no departmental regional directors for a very good reason. Their programs require little or no coordination in the field. If coordination is not a problem at the services delivery level, it is obvious that there is little need for an official to do the coordinating. In the Treasury Department, there are few relationships between the Mint and the Internal Revenue Service, or between the Bureau of Accounting Operations and the Secret Service. In the Department of Commerce, the Patent Office, the Census Bureau, and the National Oceanic and Atmospheric Administration deal with few matters of common concern in the field. While it may well be that the field organizations of the individual bureaus of these departments may need strengthening, there is little indication that improvement would result from the insertion of departmental regional directors into the field structure.

Between the extremes of the HUD departmental regional directors and the Commerce-Justice-Treasury reliance on bureau field structures are found a number of intermediate arrangements. An example of regional directors without comprehensive program oversight authority was provided by the Department of Health, Education and Welfare in the 1970s. Especially during the secretaryships of Elliot Richardson and Caspar Weinberger, the regional directors were given much of the authority and resources they needed to make themselves felt as general managers, program coordinators, service providers, evaluators, and general secretarial vicars in their regions. Yet HEW avoided making the regional director directly responsible for those technical programs in which field operations lent themselves to direct oversight by program officials in Washington. Consequently, food and drug enforcement, processing of social security payments, and most other program activities in the department took place in the field under the direct command of Washington. On the other hand, because the interrelationships between the various human resources programs were so complex, the regional directors of the department were compelled to play a strong role in bringing about needed coordination and in representing the department in dealings with units of general government within the regions.

HEW regional directors were also given line authority over a number of programs that did not readily lend themselves to direct administration through the separate field organizations of the program agencies. This was especially true of activities involving the needs and problems of special groups in our society, for example, the programs relating generally to children, youth, native Americans, the aging, the mentally retarded, and the users of skilled nursing facilities.

For reasons never clearly explained, the Carter administration through Secretary Califano abruptly abolished the HEW regional directors in 1977 and replaced them with greatly weakened principal regional officials. This reversed the promising evolutionary process that had appeared to be producing a field management structure well adapted to HEW's needs.

Other departments, such as Interior, Agriculture, and Transportation, do not have regional directors but have instead from time to time provided for a departmental field presence through secretarial representatives. These representatives usually report, actually or nominally, to the secretary, but they are given little or no programmatic authority. They are supplied with only limited managerial or analytic staffs. Secretarial representatives do, however, serve their departments in matters of interagency and intergovernmental relations, and they can frequently act as conveners of the field directors of the program elements. Such representatives may also function as the eyes and ears of the secretary in the field and may serve as members of such interagency bodies as the Federal Regional Councils.

Much skepticism has been expressed concerning the efficacy of secretarial representatives, and it must be conceded that the evidence to date is inconclusive. Observance of the DOT use of secretarial representatives suggests that the efficacy of the concept depends chiefly on the experience and skill of the individual secretarial representatives and the degree to which they have direct access to the secretary and other senior headquarters officials.

It is sometimes incorrectly assumed that departmental regional directors are prerequisite to decentralized management. This is simply not the case. The term "decentralization" applies to the placement of the authority to take definitive action on matters within the responsibility of a department in its field officials. It is entirely possible to operate a decentralized system through the bureaus or program administrations of a department such as DOT or Treasury. Within DOT, the Federal Aviation Administration, the Federal Highway Administration, and the Coast Guard are among the most decentralized organizations in the executive branch. The same is true of the Internal Revenue Service of the Treasury Department. In these instances the departmental program entities create their own regional systems and pass authority received from the secretary on to their own field officials. Most of these units do have regional organizations under regional directors or the equivalent, but such field officials report to the head of the service, bureau, or administration—not to the office of the secretary.

The weight of experience favors departmental management on a decentralized basis, but a truly decentralized system is not easy to install or maintain. Many headquarters officials are reluctant to rely on field staffs to take action on important matters of departmental business. Successful decentralization also depends on the central development of policies and standards to guide field officials in their actions, and the introduction of reporting, audit, and evaluation systems to verify that delegated authority has been wisely and correctly used.

Congress has always been ambivalent about decentralization—supporting it for the most part in DOT and strongly resisting it in HEW. Secretary of Transportation John Volpe had little trouble in the 1969-72 period in advancing a philosophy of decentralized management, in spite of the fact that he had to rely on his program administrators for implementation. In contrast, Secretary Weinberger and Under Secretary Frank Carlucci encountered strong resistance, including legislative interventions, when they sought to advance decentralization in HEW. A department that seeks to foster decentralization as a more efficient and responsive way of doing business will need to give careful attention to the concerns of the involved committees in Congress.

Management systems

It is possible to establish a department with an appropriate major purpose and to provide for a sound internal organization and still have disappointing management. One explanation is neglect of the systems needed to convert opportunity into sound decision making, skilled use of resources, a competent and motivated staff, and genuine responsiveness to the needs of the public.

A well-functioning department must spend much effort in designing, implementing, and fine tuning systems for policy development, for the preparation and issuance of regulations, for the determination of budget priorities, for keeping accounts of costs and outlays, for recruiting, compensating, retaining, and developing competent people, for evaluating the effectiveness of existing programs and identifying opportunities for their improvement, for assembling program information needed by agency management and the public, for exploiting new technologies, and for procuring and utilizing facilities, equipment, and supplies.

In most departments there is considerable variation in the degree to which the management systems meet their current needs. Some departments have excellent programs for developing their employees, supervisors, and managers, while others do little or nothing on a departmentwide basis. Some develop first-rate financial information, including usable data on program costs, while other departments have accounting systems that do little more than reduce the number of violations of the Antideficiency Act. Some have advanced management-by-objectives systems that facilitate careful monitoring of program accomplishments at the highest levels of the department, while others approach the setting of targets and the holding of officials accountable for results in haphazard ways.

In general, the departments have a long way to go in designing and bringing into effective operation the management systems that complex agencies need to serve the public well. The generally poor progress in these areas may be attributed in part to the lack of recognition or interest on the part of top officials, in part to inadequate or poorly led staffs concerned with management systems, and in part to resistance among program elements affected by the systems.

Another obstacle to the implementation of well-conceived and effective management systems is the long period usually associated with their design and installation. The time needed to do something tangible may be due to the complexity of the organization and the difficulty in getting concepts understood and accepted. In other instances, the designers themselves undertake ambitious and global assaults on systems needs that falter under their own weight and wear out the patience of even the most supportive managements. It is often necessary to approach systems needs on a modular basis so that the management can see the utility of each piece as it becomes operational. Such an approach is particularly desirable in areas such as management information, productivity improvement and measurement, and cost accounting.

It is also essential that a department understand the importance of building the in-house capability needed for successful design, implementation, and operation of management systems. While external experts and contractors may be able to help in carefully selected areas, the long-haul nature of systems improvement normally requires highly qualified staffs whose members stay with the problems from the earliest stages of design through debugging and evaluation.

The role of career staff

In recent years, the quality and continuity of departmental management has been jeopardized by assaults on the career civil servants on whom the political leadership of any agency must ultimately depend for the skilled execution of programs.

From the beginning of the second term of Franklin Roosevelt (1937) through the tragically shortened term of John F. Kennedy, steady progress was made in developing the institutions needed to foster improved management. At the same time, career staffs were accorded an opportunity to contribute directly to decisions bearing on the quality of administration. The emergence in 1939 of a highly respected Bureau of the Budget in the Executive Office of the President was a particularly significant development. This influential office was staffed almost exclusively by career civil servants and it was able to provide any president with objective advice carefully analyzed by the staff on matters of government funding and management. During this period, the Division of Administrative Management and its successor organizations were headed and staffed by career analysts who had developed an encyclopedic knowledge of how the federal government functioned and had evolved helpful doctrines to guide decisions bearing on government organization and management.

The first Hoover Commission articulated the need of each department to have a career official of assistant-secretary rank who could advise the transient political officers on matters relating to the internal management of their agencies. The result was the emergence of the post of assistant secretary for administration as a point of departmental continuity and institutional memory. This official also served as the overseer of a variety of administrative functions. These assistant secretaries stayed in close communication with each other and utilized a council called the Executive Officer's Group for the purpose of exchanging ideas and maintaining an interface with the Bureau of the Budget. It was understood that assistant secretaries for administration would bridge changes in secretaries, including those involving shifts in party control.

In other areas of the government, career people played challenging and useful roles and helped the political appointees design effective strategies in pursuing their policy and administrative goals. During this period, many bureau directors were drawn from the career service, all regional officials had competitive status, and the entire staff of the U.S. Civil Service Commission, including the executive director, had career tenure.

Beginning with the Nixon administration, a concept gained ground that has done grave damage to the management of agencies and threatens to prevent significant improvement in the future. This was the view that career staff could not be counted on to carry out loyally and efficiently the policies of the political appointees. The feeling spread that the head of a department or agency needed his own people around him if he were to control his agency. Among the results of this fallacious and mischievous view were the politicization of many senior positions in the Office of Management and Budget—successor agency to the Bureau of the Budget—in the Office of Personnel Management—which succeeded the Civil Service Commission—and in the field service—especially departmental regional directors and secretarial representatives. The post of career assistant secretary for administration was replaced in most departments by political assistant secretaryships with similar titles, and many political appointees began surrounding themselves with noncareer special assistants who brought chiefly confusion and mistrust to the agency management.

This tendency toward placing often uninformed political appointees in erstwhile career posts and the denigration of persons who had chosen public service as a career has not been limited to a single political party or president. The situation has become progressively more serious since President Nixon and his aides first launched a concerted effort to place persons with political credentials in senior posts once filled on a career basis.

No matter how well-conceived or important a department may be, it can never achieve or maintain a high level of management effectiveness without a cadre of higher civil servants who are respected and skillfully utilized. It is to be hoped that this fact, which once was so widely accepted, will again be recognized as a part of a future comprehensive and serious attack on the shortcomings of today's departmental management.

LOOKING TO THE FUTURE

From time to time, issues of government management require addressing by external commissions or similar groups in order to focus public, congressional, and executive-branch attention on both the nature of the problems and potential solutions. The Brownlow Committee of the 1930s, the first Hoover Commission, and the President's Commission on Postal Organization (Kappel Commission) played key roles in creating climates favorable to important reforms and in developing specific courses of constructive action.

It is unlikely that serious attention will again be devoted to the improvement of departmental organization and management on a governmentwide basis without the stimulus of some new group such as the Commission on More Effective Government proposed in legislation introduced in the Ninety-seventh Congress by Senator William Roth and Congressman Richard Bolling. The National Academy of Public Administration's Panel on Management of Governance has selected the area of departmental management for priority attention, but the resources needed for a full exploration of the problems and needs of the executive departments can best be mobilized by a mechanism such as that which the Roth-Bolling bills envisaged.

Public Management in the 1980s and Beyond

By FRED A. KRAMER

ABSTRACT: Critics of public management lament government's failure to use more businesslike methods. This criticism implies that the private sector is better managed than the public sector. Although this is not always the case, there are many techniques that have proved successful in the private sector that can be applied to public management problems. Public management traditions are changing. More sophisticated measures of program effectiveness are being developed. Some aspects of competition can be harnessed for better public management. Public managers are increasingly aware of such techniques and have used them when there has been political support. Under conditions of fiscal stress, for example, political forces have sometimes encouraged managers to use the spirit of budget reforms rather than just the rationalistic facade of such reforms. New public management techniques will be used only if political support for the consequences of these techniques can be mobilized.

Fred A. Kramer is an associate professor of political science at the University of Massachusetts (Amherst). He is author of Dynamics of Public Bureaucracy, *2nd ed. (Little, Brown, 1981) and has edited* Perspectives on Public Bureaucracy *and* Contemporary Approaches to Public Budgeting. *He has contributed to the* Public Administration Review, Public Personnel Management, American Political Science Review, *and other scholarly and professional journals. Professor Kramer has also been involved in management training programs for state, local, and foreign governments. He holds a Ph.D. in political science from the Maxwell School of Syracuse University.*

CRITICS of public administration often lament government's failure to use more businesslike management methods. If only government managers, the claim goes, adopted the correct style, used the right technique, developed the right information, processed it correctly, and so on, government would be more efficient and effective. The implication of the term "businesslike" is that the private sector is well managed and the public sector is not. "Businesslike" to many observers, is a synonym for "good management."

The notion of employing businesslike methods in public management raises several questions. What are the differences between private- and public-sector management? Does good management in the public sector mean the same thing as good management in the private? Is the private sector really well managed? Have governmental managers ignored private management techniques? In short, can government be well managed?

Several years ago, Robert Anthony posed a similar question. Dealing with nonprofit organizations, Anthony concluded that better management in such organizations, including government, was inhibited by several features that characterized them. Among the features of nonprofit organizations that concerned Anthony were (1) tradition, (2) the absence of the profit measure, (3) the absence of competition, (4) politics, (5) weak governing boards, and (6) low management salaries.[1] In this article, I want to look at some changes that have taken place in the past decade in the American public administration environment that have affected the first four of these features, and to assess the effects of these changes on public administration in the 1980s and beyond.

Before moving into these areas, let us briefly deal with the notion that private management using businesslike methods is necessarily good management. Impressionistically, the private sector enjoys a favorable reputation for managerial skill. But if the private sector is so well managed, why the record number of bankruptcies during the 1981-82 recession? One can appreciate the difficulties of operating in an economic environment defined by high interest rates and lack of economic activity caused, in large part, by misguided macroeconomic policies. But should not good management have been able to cope with such policies and their effects? If one believes that good management in organizations solves organizational problems, then one might conclude that private businesses are not so well managed as the myth of private-sector management competence might have it.

Bankruptcy, capitalism's most potent sanction, generally affects smaller businesses. Perhaps these smaller businesses cannot afford to practice the businesslike methods of modern management, and therefore they drown in the red ink that indicates management failure. But poor management, even with the extensive use of modern management techniques, affects some large private organizations that do survive. Detroit automobile manufacturers chose to cling to the big-car philosophy for too long. American steel makers chose to distribute divi-

---

1. Robert N. Anthony, "Can Nonprofit Organizations Be Well Managed?" in *Managing Nonprofit Organizations,* eds. Diane Borst and Patrick J. Montana (New York: Amacom, 1977), pp. 7-8. Anthony presents these features in different order. I have moved "tradition" from fifth place to first.

dends rather than reinvest in plant modernization. United States Steel even used its cash to acquire Marathon Oil rather than invest to produce steel more efficiently. Choices of inappropriate organizational goals can quickly bring disaster when these choices are coupled with inefficient means to attain them. Clearly, there is not a managerial skills membrane with all the good managers on the private-sector side and all the poor ones on government's side.

To a degree, management is a generic activity. Although there is wisdom in the late Wallace Sayre's often-quoted remark that "business and government administration are alike in all unimportant respects,"[2] public management can learn and is learning from some successful private management practices.

PUBLIC MANAGEMENT TRADITIONS

There are two major traditions of public management that have inhibited governmental change and effectiveness in the past: (1) managers have been undervalued, and (2) managers have been slow to adopt modern management techniques. Despite the long-standing view that experts should be "on tap, not on top,"[3] substantive experts have held secure positions at or near the top in career services of public bureaucracies. Frederick Mosher and Richard Stillman have shown the strong role that professionals continue to play in many public organizations.[4] These are not management professionals but professionals with training in substantive fields. One only has to think of lawyers in the Justice Department, political officers within the Foreign Service at the State Department, psychiatrists in state mental health departments, or civil engineers in public works. Unlike the situation in private corporations, management skills in the public career service have traditionally been subordinated to substantive and political skills.

In the past decade, this tradition has been changing. At the federal level, the creation of a Senior Executive Service (SES) by the Civil Service Reform Act of 1978 reflects an enhanced recognition of managerial professionals. At the state and local levels, there have been numerous efforts to recognize and develop a managerial identity. These efforts can be seen in managerial pay plans, such as New York City's plan, and different performance appraisal criteria for managers, such as those of the Commonwealth of Massachusetts. These efforts are barely out of the gestation stage, but they promise to bear fruit in the coming years.

Furthermore, in recent years there has been the interest and the capacity for training and developing public-sector managers. Graduate schools dedicated to this purpose have greatly expanded since the National Association of Schools of Public Affairs and Administration (NASPAA) was founded in the

---

2. Quoted in Joseph L. Bower, "Effective Public Management," *Harvard Business Review*, 55(2):132 (Mar.-Apr. 1977).

3. A. E. Buck, quoted by Luther H. Gulick, "Notes on the Theory of Organization," in *Papers on the Science of Administration*, eds. Luther H. Gulick and Lyndall Urwick (New York: Institute of Public Administration, 1937); reprinted in *Perspectives on Public Bureaucracy*, 3rd ed., ed. Fred A. Kramer (Cambridge, MA: Winthrop, 1981), p. 71.

4. Frederick C. Mosher, *Democracy and the Public Service*, 2nd ed. (New York: Oxford University Press, 1982), pp. 110-42. See also two symposium issues of the *Public Administration Review*, 37(6) (Nov.-Dec. 1977), and 38(2) (Mar.-Apr. 1978).

early 1970s. Graduates of these programs have brought managerial professionalism to many public programs. Greater recognition of managerial skills was spurred by the now debilitated Intergovernmental Personnel Act (IPA), which encouraged managerial training and development at all levels through grants and mobility assignments. Hardly a public-sector manager working at the GS-15 level for the federal government or equivalent levels in the states has not been exposed to the management theories of Douglas McGregor or Frederick Herzberg, for example. In many cases, state and at least the larger local governments have seen the value of managerial training and have continued to fund such programs even under conditions of fiscal stress.

THE SINS OF PUBLIC ADMINISTRATION

The second element of the public management tradition is that government has not applied modern management techniques to the extent that they might be effective. Peter F. Drucker, an influential consultant to private industries and the father of management by objectives (MBO), has chastised public managers for this failing. Only in the past 10 years or so has he devoted much energy to public management problems.

Drucker has suggested six deadly sins in public administration:

1. The first thing to do to make sure that a program will not have results is to have a lofty objective—"health care," for instance, or "to aid the disadvantaged." ...
2. The second strategy guaranteed to produce nonperformance is to try to do several things at once. . . .
3. The third deadly sin . . . is to believe that "fat is beautiful," despite the obvious fact that mass does not do work; brains and muscle do. . . .
4. "Don't experiment, be dogmatic" is the next. . . . "Whatever you do, do it on a grand scale at the first try. Otherwise, God forbid, you might learn how to do it differently." . . .
5. "Make sure that you cannot learn from experience" is the next prescription for nonperformance in public administration. . . .
6. The last of the administrator's deadly sins is the most damning and the most common; the inability to abandon.[5]

Drucker feels that public managers will guarantee failure of their programs if they commit any two of these sins. He suggests that to avoid these pitfalls, public managers should follow the private-sector practice of specifically spelling out objectives, focusing on priority items rather than trying to achieve all goals, avoiding overstaffing, trying pilot programs, learning from experience, and getting out of programs that can be better accomplished by other means.

Traditions die hard, but in many jurisdictions, public-sector managers have made progress in avoiding Drucker's sins. Public budgeting practice has absorbed many of the management lessons taught by successful private-sector consultants like Drucker. Although the big name public budgeting innovations of the last two decades have rarely been used in their pure forms with any success, program budgeting, planning-programming-budgeting (PPB) systems, management by objectives (MBO), and zero-base budgeting (ZBB) have contributed to a climate of management change that will continue to

5. Peter F. Drucker, "The Deadly Sins in Public Administration," *Public Administration Review*, 40(2):103-6 (Mar.-Apr. 1980).

affect governments at all levels in the coming years.

Each of these budgetary techniques calls upon agency managers to state objectives and set priorities. In the 1960s and early 1970s, most of these techniques provided a rationalist facade for budget politics as usual, but as the noose of fiscal stress tightened around some jurisdictions, they adopted the spirit of these reforms rather than the forms. New York City's Program to Eliminate the Gap (PEG) in the late 1970s forced agency managers to determine objectives, set priorities, and cut staff without the strict formal controls of a scientifically sound program structure, or a formal MBO system, or the rampant ranking games often associated with ZBB. As cutback conditions affected other jurisdictions, they too had to use the spirit rather than the form of these budgeting reforms. We will return to this later when we deal more with the political influences on public management.

Drucker's warning that public managers should try pilot programs and learn from experience has not been ignored. Traditionally this has been a problem. During the 1960s the Model Cities Program was to have been a pilot program, but political pressures soon expanded it to more cities than could be properly served, given the level of resources. In the 1960s, the federal government initiated a rigid governmentwide PPB effort without a pilot program in domestic agencies. But there is evidence that the federal government learned from such experiences. The social experiment dealing with a federally funded guaranteed annual income during the early 1970s was a pilot program. The full program, however, was never implemented. Efforts to incorporate the ZBB reforms during the Carter years suggest that the Office of Management and Budget (OMB) had learned from its earlier experience with PPB.

Pilot programs are reported at all levels of government. Many grants to state and local governments under categorical grant programs encouraged innovative responses to societal problems. In some cases, such as the Department of Housing and Urban Development's Capacity Building Program, successful innovations were shared with other jurisdictions. In the past decade, pilot programs have been used in a variety of jurisdictions on a variety of problems ranging from crime prevention to quality circles.[6] Fiscal constraints have provided political support for managers seeking to try some ideas on a small scale, evaluate them, then proceed either to implement or to discard them.

Although government is generally reluctant to abandon programs since each one develops a political constituency, there are examples of such abandonment. The Model Cities Program was folded into community development block grants. In a rare case, the Community Services Administration of the federal government actually closed its doors.

In short, public management traditions are changing. Governments are developing stronger managerial capacities and are adopting some private-sector management strategies. These trends will continue when there is political sup-

---

6. Stephen Bryant and Joseph Kearns, "'Workers Brains as Well as Their Bodies': Quality Circles in a Federal Facility," *Public Administration Review*, 42(2):144-50 (Mar.-Apr. 1982). See Joseph S. Wholey, *Zero-Base Budgeting and Program Evaluation* (Lexington, MA: D. C. Heath, 1979). The press often reports instances of pilot programs.

port to apply private-sector techniques to public-policy problems.

ALTERNATIVES TO PROFIT MEASURES

Traditionally government managers have claimed that people cannot measure what government programs do. Certainly the simple profit measure, which is available to private businesses, is lacking in most government work. Success in the private sector is often measured by the amount of profit that is generated by investment in the company. By comparing rates of return on capital, observers have a criterion that enables them to determine which companies are more effective. Although some have challenged this criterion as an indicator of long-term corporate health,[7] the bottom line remains a key indicator of corporate effectiveness.

Government agencies, however, do not have such a simple criterion for success. This does not mean they have no criteria by which they should be judged; the criteria are just more complex. Most government agencies render services, and the criteria for success—or effectiveness—are how well these services are rendered.

Evaluating the effectiveness of governmental agencies—an essential part of modern management—depends on two factors: (1) program goals must be clearly stated, and (2) appropriate measures must be devised that will really show whether those goals are being achieved. While it may be true that the goals of governmental programs may be harder to define than those of some private-sector organizations, there is a certain sting to George Odiorne's admonition, "If you cannot count it, measure it or describe it, you probably don't know what you want and you can often forget it as a goal."[8]

Developing reliable and valid measures to assess how close an agency is coming to its goals, however, is not always easy. In areas where the process itself, rather than any specific service, is valued, it is virtually impossible to establish measurable goals. How can we measure the extent to which the Department of Justice protects freedom of speech? By the number of arrests of speakers? By the number of arrests of those trying to stop the exercise of free speech? Although there are some areas of government where measures of objectives are not useful at all, in most agencies some goal-related measures can be developed.[9]

Some measures, however, may not really show how close an agency is getting to its goal. A program's goal might be to improve health in inner-city areas. The number of nurses that the particular program might train would be a measure of output of the program, but it does not necessarily measure how close the program comes to achieving its goal. The number of nurses trained would give a manager some notion of the cost of training each nurse, but relatively little knowledge of whether the program

---

7. Robert H. Hayes and William J. Abernathy, "Managing Our Way to Economic Decline," *Harvard Business Review*, 58(4):67-77 (July-Aug. 1980).

8. George S. Odiorne, *Personnel Management by Objectives* (Homewood, IL: Dorsey Press, 1971), p. 119.

9. A Government Accounting Office study of productivity measures in 1971 reported that half the work done in government was susceptible to output or impact measurement. Thomas D. Morris, William H. Corbett, and Brian L. Usilaner, "Productivity Measures in the Federal Government," *Public Administration Review*, 32(6):755 (Nov.-Dec. 1972).

was contributing to its real goal—better health care in the affected area. Impact or effectiveness measures attempt to assess program performance in relation to goals. Such measures are more difficult to develop than output measures.

Public management can benefit by using the valid and reliable measures that have been developed in the past decade for a wide variety of programs. The Urban Institute has tested many such indicators for many of the functions of local governments.[10] Among the kinds of measures developed was a scale for assessing street cleanliness. The scale values were related to photographic and written descriptions; trained observers assigned a scale rating based on the degree of cleanliness of the assigned area. For example, condition 1 would be used to describe a clean area; condition 2 would be moderately clean; condition 3 would be littered; and condition 4 would be heavily littered. The trained observer would have a set of photographs that corresponded to each of these conditions, so he or she could keep a standard idea of what a moderately clean area would be, for example. This technique has been used in New York City under the name Project Scorecard. Similar photographic rating scales have been used in Washington, Savannah, Nashville, and St. Petersburg.

AVOIDING PERVERSE MEASURES

There is a danger that the choice of a measure, especially some kinds of output measures, might contribute to an agency's failure to achieve its goal. Harry Hatry has raised the problem of perverse measures. According to Hatry, some measures encourage some employees to take actions that appear good on the measures but might not be in the interest of the agency's overall goal.[11] Measures with a high potential for encouraging perverse action occur regularly in public agencies. At least one community action program took the number of meetings held as an indicator. If an individual is being evaluated on the basis of the number of meetings held, how does that person act? If professors at a public university are evaluated by the number of students currently writing dissertations under their direction, does it make sense for a professor to push those students to complete their work? Any measurement system can be perverted to serve individual rather than agency goals.

Perverse measurement is likely to occur if public agencies haphazardly adopt a limited number of measures as criteria for effectiveness. Hatry suggests developing several complementary measures as standards. Assessments of agency effectiveness can be developed, to a degree, from a series of well-chosen output measures. Modern public management practice supports the development of multiple measures through greatly improved management information and reporting systems that can tap a variety of fiscal, personnel, and programmatic information. Many of the larger jurisdictions are building the foundation for computerized data processing that will have a great effect on public management within the next decade.[12] Many smaller jurisdictions,

10. Harry P. Hatry et al., *How Effective Are Your Community Services?* (Washington, DC: Urban Institute, 1977).

11. Harry P. Hatry, "Issues in Productivity Measurement for Local Government," *Public Administration Review*, 32(6):777-78 (Nov.-Dec. 1972).

12. For an interesting survey of some management problems involving computerized informa-

however, have not been able to devote resources to information handling.

One area in which management information in the public sector is making great strides is that of governmental accounting. Only since 1979, with the publication of the National Council on Governmental Accounting's statement on *Governmental Accounting and Financial Reporting* (GAAFR) have there been recognized standards for governmental accounting.[13] By adhering to these standards, most state and local governments will greatly improve their financial information. The changeover to more modern accounting practices will encourage elements of modern cost accounting and the development of cost and responsibility centers, which will support modern budgeting. The development of better accounting information will provide the basis for improved auditing.

Traditionally, auditing in the public sector has been limited to financial compliance audits. At the federal level, the General Accounting Office (GAO) has pioneered performance audits through the *GAO Reports* series. Performance auditing, which is sometimes called operational auditing, management auditing, or program results auditing, is a kind of program evaluation. The only way to learn from experience is to evaluate that experience. By improving accounting information, governmental jurisdictions will improve their analytical capability. Once better information is available to public managers, there is a better chance that they will use program evaluation routinely.

COMPETITION

In the private sector, competition is the source of many management changes designed to improve services or reduce costs. The role of competition as a means of improving management is not so sharply defined in the public sector, although in recent years there have been some efforts to use elements of competition to make government more efficient and effective. The most obvious way in which management has been able to use competition to deliver services within its jurisdiction is to contract out for services, or to threaten to do so. Virtually everything a government does can be contracted out to private vendors or to other governments. Aside from the obvious examples of garbage collection or computer services, some jurisdictions have experimented in contracting for elementary educational services and even police services. E. S. Savas calls such efforts "privatizing the public sector."[14]

Aside from contracting out, public managers can sometimes encourage competition within their own jurisdictions. A results-oriented public manager may be able to encourage competition among street-cleaning crews by using a Project Scorecard-type scale, for example. Furthermore, in some jurisdictions the manager may be able to reward financially the crew that wins the competition. Such direct competition within jurisdictions, however, is rare because of

---

tion systems, see Alena Northrop, William H. Dutton, and Kenneth L. Kraemer, "Management of Computer Applications in Local Government," *Public Administration Review*, 42(3):234-43 (May-June 1982).

13. National Council on Governmental Accounting, *Statement 1: Governmental Accounting and Financial Reporting Principles* (Chicago: Municipal Finance Officers Association, 1979).

14. E. S. Savas, *Privatizing the Public Sector: How to Shrink Government* (Chatham, NJ: Chatham House, 1982).

legal restraints on linking pay to performance in many jurisdictions.[15]

Another aspect in which competition comes into play in public-sector management is the use of comparative cost data, which may be mobilized at union contract time. State and local governmental managers have access to comparative cost information on a variety of services. One can compare the costs of garbage collection, for example, in major cities as well as costs for private carters in the city negotiating the contract. Cost data are not limited to wages and benefits. Modern information systems in many jurisdictions provide information on work rules, equipment, and various socioeconomic data that may be relevant at the bargaining table. What can be done with sanitation workers can also be done with teachers, police, fire, transportation, and general clerical workers, and others.

The possibility of using competition as a tool for improving management is contingent upon a strong information base. It is contingent upon developing valid performance measures and accurate cost data. As developments in these areas improve, it may be possible to harness competition to improve service delivery. In the long term, by using competition to hold career civil servants accountable, other internal demands for accountability could be relaxed. This would free many bureaucratic work hours. Perhaps far into the future it may be routine to see several work groups within a governmental agency competing with each other to provide services for the people. Such competition might inspire individual creativity among the bureaucrats themselves. Perhaps competition among work groups might encourage increased cooperation within each work group. Perhaps competition would lead to greater job satisfaction. Perhaps this might lead to a healthier organizational atmosphere in which the bureaucrats were more open to environmental changes and legitimate political demands.[16]

Although the potential exists for using competition to alter public management drastically, that potential will not be realized for many years, if at all. Instead, we can expect to see competition in the form of contracting out for services and impacts on union contracts continue to affect public sector management in a marginal way.

POLITICS

Improvements in public management depend on certain secular changes in knowledge and technology. Among these are the development of valid impact indicators, information-processing techniques, and the new techniques that may be developed in any of the substantive fields in which government operates. Whether public managers will use the new knowledge depends on their awareness of its existence and political factors.

In the past decade, great strides have taken place in developing managerial identity, managerial skills, measures of effectiveness, and information to support program evaluation. In many cases, these advances have been used by public managers to improve the efficiency and effectiveness of public service

---

15. John M. Greiner et al., *Productivity and Motivation* (Washington, DC: Urban Institute, 1981), pp. 95-105.

16. For examples of some negative consequences of intraorganizational competition, see Heywood Klein, "Pitting Workers Against Each Other Often Backfires, Firms Are Finding," *Wall Street Journal*, 15 July 1982, p. 33.

when there has been political support to do so. Political support for adopting modern management techniques has been most clearly seen in budgeting practices of those jurisdictions facing fiscal stress. Fiscal stress is the condition in which pressure for expenditures exceeds the revenue-generating capacity for a particular jurisdiction. This condition is more acute than the conditions of revenue scarcity that have faced governments at all levels in the United States since World War II. Ever since the Great Depression of the 1930s, there has never been enough money to allow government to do all the things it would like to do. As Aaron Wildavsky put it, "The budgetary situation is always tight, terribly tight, or impossibly tight."[17] For many jurisdictions today, however, there appears to have been an attitudinal change that has affected the incremental budget making of the past.

Wildavsky's incremental model should not be thrown out completely, but we must recognize that we are in a period of uncertainty, instability, and change with regard to public budgeting. As Naomi Caiden has observed, the overall budgeting environment has changed.

Public needs were conceived as finite and public resources infinite. The ability of governments to raise revenues and manage large expenditures was accepted as a matter of course. . . . We now have to work on a different assumption, namely, that public resources are finite and public needs infinite. . . . Lately, concern about the amount and equity of taxation, fears that the public sector is reaching its limits in a mixed economy, and mistrust of proliferating public bureaucracy indicate that the era of expanding public revenues may be coming to a close.[18]

For those jurisdictions or programs operating under cutback conditions, such an era has already arrived.

The politics of budgeting has been quite straightforward since World War II. In times of increasing revenues, special interests can be accommodated as the pie increases. The political system roughly dishes out fair shares of the expanded pie with relatively little conflict. Powerful political participants are interested more in the parts than in the whole. Conflict can be resolved at a low level. If political leadership is able to focus budgetary attention on the whole rather than the parts and mobilize the political support to make that focus remain a high priority to keep the pie from growing, the game changes. Rather than having special interests fighting one another in an incremental game, these special interests also have to fight the generalized interests concerned with the whole. Under such conditions, conflict becomes more visible and the level of conflict rises, making the stakes greater for all the participants.

Under these new conditions, arguments based on rational analysis may find great political support among those concerned more with the whole pie than with the pieces. If political support for controlling the whole is strong, program cuts will be made. Ideally, a public manager may want to weed out, in David Stockman's phrase, "weak programs

17. Aaron B. Wildavsky, "Budgeting as a Political Process," in *International Encyclopedia of the Social Sciences,* ed. David L. Sills (New York: Crowell Collier and Macmillan, 1968), 2: 195.

18. Naomi Caiden, "Public Budgeting Amidst Uncertainty and Instability," *Public Budgeting and Finance,* 1(1) (Spring 1981); reprinted in *Current Issues in Public Administration,* 2nd ed., ed. Frederick S. Lane (New York: St. Martin's Press, 1982), pp. 349-50.

rather than weak clients,"[19] but often political power means staying power. Even in managerial-oriented budgeting, politics counts for much. Certainly this was the case in federal cutbacks in fiscal 1982 and 1983. The poor seem to have taken more than a fair share of the cuts, whereas the military have prospered. Within agencies serving basically the same clientele, however, managers seem to have made some program decisions based on effectiveness criteria.

Cutback management has encouraged concern for evaluation at all levels of budgeting, but, as Charles Levine has implied, decisions to cut certain programs might not be made strictly by rational analysis. Levine points to the management science paradox. According to Levine, the evaluation and management information capacity is rarely used in good times because agencies prefer to put their efforts into maintaining political constituencies. In bad times, however, the analytic capacity is not used, because

first, the most capable analysts are lured away by better opportunities; then freezes cripple the agency's ability to hire replacements; and finally, the remaining staff is cut in order to avoid making cuts in personnel with direct service responsibility. All the while, organization decision on where to take cuts will be made on political grounds with important constituencies fully mobilized to protect their favorite programs.[20]

There is much truth in this, but public managers operating under extreme resource constraints cannot ignore the necessity to make some program decisions. The old games, such as the Washington Monument syndrome—threatening to cut a popular program—simply do not work anymore. Neither does the notion that Levine calls "the tooth fairy syndrome"—the hope that if one chooses to ignore the call for cuts, other programs will voluntarily sacrifice themselves or more money will mysteriously be found, thus allowing the manager to win by not taking any action.[21]

Modern management techniques applied to budget making have been used under cutback conditions. Such techniques, as knowledge of them becomes more widespread, will be used increasingly in the future. But political criteria, rather than managerial rationality, will continue to define basic budgetary decisions.

CONCLUSION

One cannot expect public management to operate exactly like private management. Government management operates within a complex social environment that sometimes inhibits the acceptance of businesslike management methods. During the 1930s and early 1940s, John Gaus noted that knowledge of "people, place, physical technology, social technology, wishes and ideas, catastrophe, and personality" can help one understand "why particular activities are undertaken through government and the problems of policy, organization and management" resulting from such factors.[22] Politics is a key factor

---

19. Quoted in William Greiner, "The Education of David Stockman," *Atlantic Monthly*, 248(6):38 (Dec. 1981).

20. Charles H. Levine, "More on Cutback Management: Hard Questions for Hard Times," *Public Administration Review*, 39(2):180 (Mar.-Apr. 1979).

21. Ibid., p. 181.

22. John M. Gaus, *Reflections on Public Administration* (University: University of Alabama Press, 1947), p. 10.

influencing this management environment.

Management in the private sector is seen as running things. Private-sector managers decide on the goals of the organization. They decide on the products or services that will be provided. They determine which criteria will determine effectiveness for their organizations, and they determine the ways in which the organization will mobilize resources to achieve these goals. In short, private-sector managers deal with both effectiveness and efficiency matters.

Public managers, however, have substantially less power to determine the basic goals of their agencies. Politics continually sets and resets program goals. Of course, as political actors, career managers in the public sector can greatly influence the goals of their organizations. Few citizens, however, expect public managers—the often pejorative "bureaucrats"—to run things. Rather than running things, citizens expect public managers to operate their agencies efficiently. Somehow, they seem to believe, if things operate efficiently, the agencies will also be effective.

Public managers in the 1980s and beyond will often have the tools to improve efficiency of operations. Increasingly they will use these tools. It does not necessarily follow, however, that increased use of management tools in government will automatically lead to greater effectiveness. Political decisions as to what direction government will take and at what level government will operate will continue to be key factors determining program effectiveness.

Program Evaluation and Appropriate Governmental Change

By ELEANOR CHELIMSKY

ABSTRACT: Examining the potential and the limitations of evaluation, this article envisions an essential role for evaluation in achieving appropriate governmental change. That role is a deliberate one that seeks to improve the basis for policymaking, rather than to influence the direction of policy. Evaluation can do this by bringing objective information to bear on whether a proposed change—in any policy direction—is likely to reach its goals. Current limitations of evaluation are identified as resulting from the newness of the evaluation field, from differing perspectives among evaluation producers and users, and from various systemic situations which block or vitiate the evaluative effort. New uses of evaluation methodologies are proposed, along with creative management of evaluation performance. Finally, a clearinghouse to ensure the cumulative use of evaluation findings is recommended.

Eleanor Chelimsky is the first director of the General Accounting Office's Institute for Program Evaluation, created by Elmer Staats in April 1980. For 10 years before that, she was associated with the MITRE Corporation, whose work she directed in the areas of program evaluation, policy analysis, and research management. Between 1966 and 1970 she was an economic analyst at the United States Mission to NATO, first in Paris and then in Brussels. She is a past president of the Evaluation Research Society.

NOTE: The views and opinions expressed by the author are her own and should not be construed to be the policy or position of the General Accounting Office.

IT is difficult to obtain agreement on what constitutes appropriate governmental change: initiatives that seem appropriate to some may be inappropriate to others. This, of course, is the case because judgments about governmental change are necessarily shaped and constrained, a priori, by an assortment of factors, many of which are matters of opinion. The individual perspective of the judger, based on his or her age, sex, race, politics, or self-interest, for example, is important in the way a change is viewed. But the climate of the period in which the observer makes his or her judgment is also important. Is the period one of reform or counterreform? Is big government viewed as good or bad? Is it a time of economic prosperity and generosity to the poor, or one of penury and retrenchment in social programs? Both of these quite subjective factors, then—the judger's perspective and the general climate of opinion—affect beliefs about what is or is not an appropriate change in government policy, whether or why it is needed, and what it will do.

Subjective factors such as these do not merely influence whether governmental change is perceived as appropriate, however. They also determine, in large part, what kind of change will be proposed. In effect, in our society and others, beliefs and opinions have been extremely powerful as drivers of change, and sometimes those beliefs and opinions have not even been very widely held; one need think only of the Spanish-American war, for example, or of the Soviet revolution. Recommendations for governmental change have often been put forward with little if any objective evidence that the change is likely to achieve what its advocates claim for it. A noteworthy example is the Law Enforcement Assistance Administration (LEAA) legislation of 1972, which had little empirical basis for predicting crime reduction as a result of federal expenditures, but did. The Model Cities Program, agricultural and merchant marine subsidies, supply-side economics, among a host of others, are further examples of programs or policies the likely effects of which were largely speculative when they were promulgated.

Objective evidence is important, not because it automatically reconciles conflicting perspectives about what is a good change and what is a bad one—of course, it cannot do that—but because such evidence can, at very least, bring nonpartisan understanding of the likelihood that a given change, whatever its goals, will be able to reach those goals. Thus, although the debate about what, according to belief and opinion, is or is not appropriate necessarily and properly continues, objective evidence can supply empirical weight to that debate and can reduce hyperbole and exaggerated claims for policies and programs, can lessen the possibility of costly mistakes, and can avoid, over the longer term, the weakening of public confidence in government that must inevitably proceed from a record of failed shots in the dark.

Objective evidence thus allows a stronger basis for predicting the success or failure of proposed changes and hence serves to protect the public from the vicissitudes of change that cannot possibly do what it sets out to do, from change with many costs and few benefits, from change for the sake of change. This, again, is important because while change often fails to bring the benefits hoped for, it always carries at least one cost: the major cost of disruption and discontinuity. Although this cost may not be immediately obvious in the euphoria that tends to accompany change, it is nonetheless real and sometimes even measurable both in its collective aspect—that is, the unachieved goals of programs or research interrupted by the change—and in its individual aspect—that is, the careers, habits, security, and health of people adversely affected by or inadequately protected from the change.

The appropriate governmental change defined here, then, is not a matter of a particular political, economic, or social direction; that direction is imposed by the aggregate of individual perspectives expressed through the electoral process. Instead, a special kind of change is envisaged, one that may move in any political—or economic or social—direction but is characterized by these traits:

- It is undertaken rationally, not only on the basis of belief that the change is needed and is likely to work, but also on the basis of objective evidence to support that belief.

- It is promulgated after responsible consideration not only of the likely benefits but also of the likely costs.

- It is accompanied by self-corrective mechanisms built into the change itself, which ensure that the results of the change will be documented so that there is accountability for the change and so that constructive modification or even reversibility of the change will be possible, depending upon the results.

"Appropriate," in this article, thus refers not to the direction of a change but to its deliberate, prudent character; not to its substance but to the objective manner in which it is proposed, executed, and assessed.

This is not, of course, to assert that evidence exists to support or weaken all claims for proposed changes; on the contrary, the realization that there is no evidence is also useful in that it should inspire reasonable caution in setting objectives. Nor is it argued here that all governmental change can be deliberate and prudent: rapid action and reaction are daily critical requirements of politics and of policymaking. However, it is certainly not the case that all policymaking must be performed in a hurry, and the ability to estimate whether a given change is likely to reach its goals is a function neither of belief nor of rapid action, but rather of two other things: first, the quality of the evidence amassed in support of the change, and second, the general existing knowledge about the experience and result of similar efforts tried elsewhere or in the past. It is here that evaluation finds its opportunity: the assessment techniques used in program evaluation represent some of the most powerful tools available for developing these kinds of information.

THE CONTRIBUTION AND POTENTIAL OF EVALUATION

The Congress recognized the importance of program evaluation some time ago, delegating statutory authority for its performance to the General Accounting Office, under Title VII of the Congressional Budget Act of 1974,[1] and—over the past 10 years or so—levying many requirements on executive

---

1. Title VII, Program Review and Evaluation, Conference Report, H.R. 7130, Congressional Budget and Impoundment Control Act, passed Senate 21 June 1974, P.L. 93-344.

branch agencies, either by statute or by committee report language, to evaluate their programs and report their findings to the Congress.

Senator Roth, in 1972, attributed his own interest in program evaluation to a desire to find "a practical path to true fiscal responsibility," pointing out that evaluation contributes to this end "by allowing us to better determine whether programs are accomplishing their intended goals; how these programs could be improved; and what new programs should be undertaken in the future."[2] For Senator Brock, in 1975, evaluation was rather a path to understanding the success or failure of a program in human terms. As he put it:

We in Congress tend to talk in terms of financial audits dealing with whether there is fraud or corruption or something like that. You just don't get people in Congress talking in terms of human effectiveness. We are very good at establishing economic accounts but we don't have a social account. Yet if these programs that we write, enact and administer are not subject to ongoing oversight using evaluative techniques . . . they're just not going to do the job.[3]

For others in the Congress, "evaluation has been useful in the development of legislation by: (a) showing new directions for policy; (b) clarifying issues; (c) assessing compliance with legislative intent; (d) showing program impact; (e) providing information for program advocacy, and (f) clarifying the status of legislation."[4]

The sense that evaluation can contribute to appropriate governmental change in quite diverse ways is thus widely shared in the Congress. This may well be a function not only of the evaluation process itself, but also of the uncertain objectivity characterizing other processes that coexist with it. That is, despite problems in the state of the evaluative art, evaluation is clearly superior to anecdotal evidence, and it happily supplements, in Weidenbaum's phrase, "existing rules-of-thumb and other subjective approaches."[5]

Without evaluation, an administration is in a poor position either to advocate and defend its proposed changes or even to say precisely what has been learned from them. Moynihan noted, in 1968, "the wreckage of crash programs that were going to change everything, in fact changed nothing,"[6] and about which understanding is still very dim. Again today, important claims have been made about the coming impacts of, say, tax reductions on productivity, of cuts in social programs on the work ethic, of large defense expenditures on deterrence. Yet if the evaluative base is lacking that can help establish the range and frequency of program effects, an

---

2. Statement of the Honorable William V. Roth on the floor of the Senate, "Public Program Analysis and Evaluation for the Purposes of the Executive and the Congress," *Congressional Record,* 8 June 1972, S9026.

3. Statement of the Honorable Bill Brock, "A Congressional View of Program Evaluation," at the WORC/TIMS Congressional Series, 27 Feb. 1975.

4. David H. Florio, Michael M. Behrmann, and Diane L. Goltz, "What Do Policymakers Think of Educational Research and Evaluation? Or Do They?" *Educational Evaluation and Policy Analysis,* 1(6):68 (Nov.-Dec. 1979).

5. Murray L. Weidenbaum, Dan Larkins, and Philip N. Marcus, *Matching Needs and Resources: Reforming the Federal Budget* (Washington, DC: American Enterprise Institute, 1973), p. 11.

6. Daniel P. Moynihan, cited in Peter Marris and Martin Rein, *Dilemmas of Social Reform* (Hawthorne, NY: Aldine, 1973), p. 241.

administration is without the empirical data it will eventually need to establish and support its record. It will be continually at the mercy of this or that individual case, typically generalized to the universe by the press: the welfare mother discovered driving a Cadillac, the totally disabled worker inexplicably cut from a disability program, block grant money used to finance the personal expenditures of a state official, and so forth. How different is the position of an administration with programs like Head Start or the Alcohol Safety Action Program, which have been evaluated over 10 years, and have produced clear evidence of the postprogram gains to their participants.

Not only can evaluation establish the effects of a change, however, but also, because it is a neutral tool, it can assure the continuity and cumulativeness of information across different administrations, with different social, economic, or political goals. This is, of course, as important to the Congress as it is to the executive branch or the public, both in the performance of congressional functions and in the assurance of congressional accountability. The Congress has to be able to tell whether its purposes in appropriating funds have been carried out. It also needs objective information based on prior program performance to move meaningfully in its budgetary, oversight, and legislative processes. When there has been, in the past, a dearth of evaluation data on that performance, on program problems, on their extent or degree, and on their causes, the Congress has often acted to increase reporting requirements placed on programs. It is for this reason that categorical grants have carried sometimes quite extensive mandates for evaluation, audit, and other means of ensuring accountability for federal funds, and for this reason also that, when those requirements were missing in some of the early block grants promulgated by the Nixon administration, the Congress gradually put them back, through a process known as "creeping categorization."[7]

This is not a very satisfactory method of implementing evaluation requirements, however, because when an evaluation is mandated post hoc, the information to be derived will typically suffer from the lack of baseline data. If the need for evaluation is not recognized early enough, so that evaluation plans can be established in time to capture meaningful information about how things were before the initiation of change, the range of evaluation designs—and hence the ability of evaluation to speak conclusively to the questions posed—will be severely constrained.

In sum, evaluation has an important contribution to make to the achievement of appropriate governmental change, whatever the direction of that change, and it can do a better or worse job in developing information, depending on how it is built into the warp and woof of programs. Even so, its potential has as yet barely been glimpsed because of various problems that have impeded its progress. While nearly all of these problems seem likely to be tractable over the short or long term, many are only now beginning to be confronted.

SOME MAJOR CURRENT LIMITATIONS OF EVALUATION

A taxonomy of evaluation's difficulties is obviously beyond the scope of this

---

7. Eleanor Chelimsky, "Making Block Grants Accountable," in *Evaluation in Change,* ed. Lois-ellin Datta (Beverly Hills, CA: Sage, 1981), p. 100.

short article. However, it is important to mention here at least the chief kinds of impediments to the fulfillment of evaluation's potential. Some of these impediments result from the newness of the evaluation field. Others result from inattention by evaluators to user needs. Still others result from the inadequate integration of evaluation with other systems already in place.

Newness of the evaluation field

Because evaluation is a fairly recent phenomenon, not yet 20 years old, it has been plagued by the same problems that have afflicted other new fields: ambiguity of definition, uncertainty about the interpretation of results, and lack of standards for performance and reporting.

Although there still is no single, universal, established definition of program evaluation, most evaluators would agree[8] that the essence of evaluation is comparison, and that the kind of comparison drawn dictates the strength of the conclusions that can be made. Thus an evaluation compares what happened in a program with what happened before the program, without the program, with a different program, and so on, to arrive at conclusions about the program that are based on those comparisons. If the comparison is weak—before and after data on the same program, for example—conclusions must be correspondingly weak. If the comparison is strong—before and after data on both experimental and control populations, randomly selected, for example—then changes observed can be attributed with confidence to the experimental intervention. If there is no comparison at all, but only, say, a survey taken at one point in time, then nothing whatever can be said about program effects; this is not, in fact, an evaluation of program effectiveness but is rather a description of program process, of what is happening within a program at a particular moment.

From this, the importance of the design phase of an evaluation can easily be grasped. It is the evaluation design that operationally defines the study question, determines what comparison base will be used, establishes criteria for success, pinpoints likely measures—already available or needing to be developed—to represent those criteria in quantitative form, indicates the data to be systematically collected on those measures, and shows how comparing the results to the criteria that were set will bring answers to the study question posed.

The fact that there has existed no specific definition of evaluation, however, has meant that many studies that have been called evaluations have been weak or entirely lacking in design, weak in data collection and analysis, weak in reporting their methodologies, and weak in specifying confidence levels for results. This is simply to say that in evaluation, as in other fields, good and less good studies are to be found. However, with the development of more general-

---

8. The discussion of evaluation given here is a synthesis of views derived from the following works: Joseph S. Wholey et al., *Federal Evaluation Policy* (Washington, DC: Urban Institute, 1970); Carol H. Weiss, *Evaluation Research* (Englewood Cliffs, NJ: Prentice-Hall, 1972); Eleanor Chelimsky, *Analysis of a Symposium on the Use of Evaluation by Federal Agencies,* M77-39 (McLean, VA: MITRE Corporation, July 1977), vol. 2; and Harry P. Hatry, Richard E. Winnie, and Donald M. Fisk, *Practical Program Evaluation for State and Local Governments* (Washington, DC: Urban Institute, 1981).

ized agreement among evaluators and nonevaluators alike with regard to the elements an evaluation should contain, and the way in which the presence or absence of those elements dictates the reporting and interpretation of results, this situation is notably improving. It has now become commonplace to see evaluations generally applauded for their methodological competence or pilloried on the basis of their technical inadequacies, an implicit reinforcement of the developing consensus on definition.

A lack of standards for performance has been a problem similar to that of definition in that there are no accepted procedures for planning, conducting, and reporting an evaluation, and, consequently, little agreement about the training required for the evaluation discipline: knowledge of research design, quantitative and qualitative methods, instrument design, sampling, data analysis, and so on. Happily, this problem is being resolved rapidly by the appearance of evaluation standards for education[9] and for evaluation in general,[10] as well as by increasing university attention to the evaluation discipline. More and more academic institutions now have evaluation departments—for example, Harvard, Stanford, Massachusetts Institute of Technology, Northwestern, University of California, George Washington University, and University of Maryland—that are developing competent practitioners.

A second problem related to the newness of the field is the way in which evaluation units in government have been organized to produce evaluations. Because the evaluation field emerged from a number of different disciplines, agency evaluation units have tended to mirror one or another of these disciplines. Mental health evaluation, for example, has been dominated by methods taught in the field of psychology, energy and defense, evaluations have been dominated by those of economics, criminal justice evaluation has been dominated by those of sociology, and so forth. This insular approach has meant, first, that little communication of methods has occurred across the various discipline-oriented approaches to evaluation; evaluation requests-for-procurement have differed enormously across agencies, ranging from requests-for-procurement specifying highly detailed evaluations to those that seem uncertain of what an evaluation is. Second, the insular approach means that evaluations have tended to be producer focused rather than user focused. For example, a study of federal evaluation units in fiscal year 1980, performed by the General Accounting Office's Institute for Program Evaluation, showed that in nearly three-fourths of the cases, evaluators had little if any knowledge of how or whether their evaluations had been used by the Congress.[11]

No centralized place has yet been established where evaluators beginning an evaluation can go to find out about and consult prior efforts in their area of interest, or to determine what other evaluations are currently taking place that

---

9. The Joint Committee on Standards for Educational Evaluation, *Standards for Evaluations of Educational Programs, Projects, and Materials* (New York: McGraw-Hill, 1981).

10. Standards Committee, *Standards for Program Evaluation* (Columbus, OH: Evaluation Research Society, May 1980).

11. U.S. General Accounting Office, *A Profile of Federal Program Evaluation Activities*, IPE-82-8 (forthcoming).

might impinge upon their own. Yet these functions are very important: to facilitate the literature review that normally precedes every evaluation, to avoid unintended duplication of work, and to alert the evaluator to possible competing sources of effects, as when a population to be studied is the focus of several different programs and evaluations. Instead, most of the debate with regard to the organization of evaluation units has centered on whether an evaluation unit should be a decentralized part of agency programs, with each program responsible for its own evaluation, or whether the unit should be centralized so as to be objective or independent of the programs to be evaluated.

This debate continues, with little convincing evidence for superiority as yet amassed by either side. In effect, a central, independent unit is protected from pressures by program managers but often is held at arm's length and not listened to by the managers it seeks to influence. On the other hand, an evaluation unit that is colocated with a program may capture the confidence of managers and learn a great deal more about the program and its problems than a centralized unit will be allowed to learn, but may then be prevented from even developing or documenting indicated negative findings on the programs.[12] An argument can thus be made for either type of organization, depending on whether one sees independence or good information as the primary value to be emphasized. In any case, institutional corrections are always possible; for example, an evaluation unit can be housed with a program but report to a higher echelon of authority.

12. Chelimsky, *Analysis of a Symposium.*

Agency evaluation units have thus suffered from the evaluation field's newness essentially through isolation and insulation—that is, organizational separation from each other and from users, as well as what appears to be little communication with either. This condition has been encouraged by the differences of approach that have characterized discipline-oriented evaluation, by uncertainties of definition and standards, and by the time that has been needed to develop university programs in evaluation.

A third problem resulting from the newness of evaluation is one familiar to most students of innovation transfer. That is, although the field now includes a large number of highly competent practitioners and the many university programs are continuing to develop new ones, evaluators are still only at about the second level of innovation use, to employ Gene Hall's paradigm.[13] That is, although practitioners are becoming more and more comfortable with the planning and performance of evaluation, they do not yet appear to be at the stage where, having learned the rules, they can now use their knowledge creatively. Thus, evaluations largely continue to be performed along traditional lines, with the major practitioner efforts applied mostly toward ensuring methodological quality while holding constant evaluation's familiar profile: that of a retrospective study, designed to answer a researchable question, oriented toward the production of new knowledge, taking whatever time and resources are needed to bring it to completion,

13. Gene E. Hall et al., "Levels of Use of the Innovation: A Framework for Analyzing Innovation Adoption," *Journal of Teacher Education,* 26(1):52 (Spring 1978).

envisaging the research community as its essential user, and searching for a policy user only when the evaluation is completed. This profile, however, fails to confront the criticisms made of evaluation by its users.

Evaluator inattention to user needs

Another kind of impediment to evaluation's potential, then, is the differing perspective among evaluation producers and sponsors about what an evaluation should be and do. Agency decision makers and program managers, along with congressional policymakers and other users, have been concerned essentially about the usefulness of evaluations to themselves, about the relevance of evaluations to policy questions, about their timeliness in regard to particular decision points of the budgetary or policy cycles, about their presentation and interpretation of findings, and about their cost.[14] Users who sponsor evaluations to obtain policy-focused information are not comfortable when that work is diverted to basic research with a knowledge focus; that is, they feel that evaluations funded for a policy use should either produce information relevant to that use or should not be performed with public monies. Their sense is that evaluators will often go off and study what interests them, veering subtly, or sometimes totally, away fom the question of policy interest.[15]

Timeliness also has been a major problem to users, since an evaluation is not helpful when it arrives after the decision for which the information was needed has been made. Although it is true that such an evaluation may indeed build new and important knowledge in a particular subject area over time, it has failed, at least from the user's viewpoint, to serve the purposes for which its sponsor intended it.

The presentation problem is more complex than may be commonly perceived by evaluators. It is not just that users would like to see evaluators dispense with jargon and reduce technical language to a minimum; it is also that users typically have little time at their disposal, so that reports, even very well-presented reports, may simply not be read. This points up a deeper problem of the relation between the evaluator and the user: a close and continuing interaction throughout the evaluation—from the establishment of the study question to the submission of the final report—is what users tend to feel would not only ensure relevance and timeliness but would mean that reading the report was almost unnecessary, given numerous briefings on the findings prior to the delivery of the final report.

Finally, many users are troubled about the costs of evaluation at a time of shrinking resources. However, costs need to be assessed not in absolute terms but in terms of both technical quality and usefulness, that is, appropriateness with regard to the user's information requirements.[16] For example, a full-bore evaluation taking two years is in fact overcostly to a user needing infor-

---

14. Elmer B. Staats, "Remarks to the Evaluation Research Society's Annual Convention," Austin, TX, 3 Oct. 1981.

15. Thomas L. Lalley, cited in Eleanor Chelimsky, *Interviews for a Symposium on the Institutionalization of Federal Programs at the Local Level*, M78-80 (McLean, VA: MITRE Corporation, May 1979), appendix, pp. 792-93.

16. Eleanor Chelimsky, "Improving the Cost Effectiveness of Evaluation," in *The Costs of Evaluation*, ed. Marvin C. Alkin (Beverly Hills, CA: Sage, forthcoming).

mation at the end of six months. Similarly, the costs of a rigorous evaluation using an experimental design, for example, could well be acceptable if highly conclusive information were needed, say, for a program reauthorization two years hence.

Users, then, have been troubled by their sense that evaluators have not focused adequately on the relevance, timeliness, presentation, and costs of their products in relation to the users'—rather than the evaluators'—needs. In this sense, the problem, like that of agency evaluation unit organization, is one of isolation and insulation, again facilitated by differing perspectives and different understandings of evaluation on the part of producers and users, but especially by clearly inadequate interactions between those producers and users.

Integration of evaluation with other systems

A third kind of impediment to the fulfillment of evaluation's potential has been that evaluations have often been hostage to other systems or system incentives already in place. It has often been the case, for example, that social program and other evaluations have been performed too soon,[17] long before it is reasonable to expect that effects will be measurable. This may occur not only because agencies feel pressured to defend their annual budget requests via evaluation, but also, and more importantly, because "there is a mismatch between the administrative, bureaucratic, and budgetary needs of agencies in marshalling support for programs, and the time-span of the normal diffusion process."[18] Evaluation is thus caught in agency pressures not only to show good results but to show them fast.

On the other hand, with complex technology to improve productivity, or weapons systems, for example, evaluations may in fact be performed too late either (1) to help the technology or system developer improve the product at the least possible cost, or (2) to ensure eventual user acceptance of the product—here the user may be a foot soldier or pilot, in the case of a weapons system, or a clerical worker, in the case of a productivity-improving technology—by incorporating that user's needs in early designs for product manufacture. By conducting evaluation too late in these types of programs, it becomes both difficult and prohibitively expensive to pinpoint specific component or subsystem failures; this encourages premature procurement on the basis of costly but inadequate testing. Further, the ways in which user needs and capabilities have or have not been built into product design and operating procedures must be tested early enough to ensure a reasonable match between developer and user goals; later evaluation thus increases the possibility of expensively developed, tested, and procured products that fail to meet their performance objectives.

Again, evaluation may be caught in promotional activities on behalf of agencies' programs. For example, expected achievement of a program may be heavily inflated, perhaps to obtain bigger appropriations from the Congress, or to get state and local agencies to buy into the program. On too many occasions, federal agencies have overstated the benefits that would accrue

---

17. Irwin Feller, cited in Chelimsky, *Interviews for a Symposium*, p. 140.

18. Ibid.

through implementation of a new program. Not only does this overoptimism build in disappointment in the program's eventual takers and in the public, it also ensures a negative if not a disastrous evaluation if that evaluation has structured its criteria for success based on agency rhetoric.

Another aspect of this problem is that, because of a presumed agency bias in favor of its own programs, many evaluations sponsored by agencies have become suspect. This, however, may be a problem that is more apparent than real, since careful methodological review of any evaluation will reveal its assumptions and their objectivity, as well as the way in which threats to validity were handled. Thus the credibility of an evaluation can be clearly established through methodological review: it lies less in the eye of the beholder than in the technical capabilities of the reviewer.

Finally, evaluations have not been cumulative. Questions raised by one evaluation have failed to be addressed in the next one performed. While this may occur in an operating agency because of the fear of negative findings, especially in a costly program, it is also the case that lack of continuity and cumulativeness is fostered both by the isolation of agency evaluation units and by the factors discussed before: evaluations have been disciplinary rather than multidisciplinary, users and evaluators have not worked together, and no clearinghouse has enabled evaluators to keep cogently in mind the current state of the art in terms of evaluation findings and studies performed. This is a real problem in that, if evaluation is to live up to its potential for helping government achieve appropriate change, then (1) the various studies already performed should be available to evaluators and users alike on an ongoing basis, and (2) evaluators with few resources available should be able to direct those resources to a study question that may be able to accommodate an inexpensive design and also produce needed information. Evaluators need some mechanism to ensure the availability of knowledge about current findings and questions, so as to achieve the cumulativeness that has marked other scientific and technological enterprises and that has permitted so much progress in those areas.

SOME OPTIONS FOR RESOLVING THESE PROBLEMS

In looking at the potential and at the limitations of evaluation, this article has posited an essential role for evaluation in achieving appropriate governmental change. That role is a deliberate one that seeks to improve the basis for governmental policymaking by bringing objective information to bear on whether a proposed change is likely to reach its goals. Evaluation can accomplish this through reviewing the quality of the evidence amassed by proponents in support of the change, and by synthesizing the available evaluation and other research findings that result from the experience of similar efforts elsewhere or in the past.

In examining the limitations of evaluation, this article has identified three types of problems having to do with the newness of the evaluation discipline, criticisms by evaluation users, and systemic difficulties that impede evaluation's usefulness. Some of these problems, such as those resulting from external systemic causes, may possibly be overcome by finding new ways to think about and use evaluation methodologies. Others may be resolvable through the development of ways to treat technical adequacy, costs, timeliness, presentation, relevance to user needs, appropriate costs, and quality control together as routine components of evaluation management. The General Accounting Office's Institute for Program Evaluation (IPE) is working to improve methods and applications in both of these areas. The problem of evaluation cumulativeness, however, appears to transcend the efforts of either evaluation managers or single agencies, and probably needs to be addressed with regard to the whole multidisciplinary evaluation community, including universities, research firms, and agency evaluation units at different governmental levels.

New uses of evaluation methodologies

Probably because evaluation is such a new tool and because so much effort has had to go into defining it, into developing procedures and standards for its conduct, and into training people in how to perform and use it, it has until now been used only in fairly limited ways and purely as a retrospective tool. Although many have recognized the ability of evaluation to address a range of questions about the costs, management, operations, and effects of a program, evaluations have usually been structured on an after-the-fact basis. However, evaluation also has the potential for informing prospectively on new programs and policies, as Senator Roth grasped early on,[19] that is, for providing evidence in support of or against a proposed change in a particular program or policy area. This is because the evaluation process typically consists of four stages, which take place in the course of routinely performing an evaluation, and because two of those stages can be used independently of the evaluation process to bring information to bear prospectively on changes proposed by government.

To illustrate, evaluators always begin an evaluation with a review and synthesis of past evaluation findings and other analytical information, so as to understand whatever evidence has already been amassed about a particular problem and about the programs or policies, if any, that have already addressed it. In the usual evaluation process, this synthesis typically serves as a preparation for the evaluation design. It is a way of determining the scope of issues to be confronted in the evaluation, of becoming aware of the designs and measures used in the past or that need to be developed, and of collecting evidence already available on those issues.

But when a change in policy or programs is being considered, an evaluation synthesis, performed alone, can inform, both quickly and reasonably well, on what is known about the problem and program being addressed, what is not known, and what is scientifically or analytically controversial. The synthesis can speak to the results, including benefits, costs, and unanticipated effects, of similar policies or programs undertaken in the past—or currently operational in individual states or in foreign countries—where evaluations have been or are being conducted and findings developed. The synthesis can specify the information gaps that exist with regard to a new program or policy so that extravagant claims of knowledge and feasibility cannot be made without proper dispute, and so that appropriate methods for developing the lacking

---

19. Roth, "Public Program Analysis," S9026.

information can be built into initial operations and activities, should the proposed change be enacted. The synthesis can guide a new program with respect to lessons already learned, so that its focus can be concentrated on areas likely to be productive in the sense of the desired goals and so that errors committed in the past can be avoided.

The second stage in preparing and performing an evaluation is evaluation planning, or setting up the activities that must be accomplished before an evaluation can be conducted. Some of these planning activities are, for example, the delineation of operationally defined questions, the selection of outcome and activity objectives and measures, the choice of the evaluation design—that is, the basis for comparison that will be used to identify and quantify the program's effects—the determination of the method of analysis, the preparation of data collection instruments, and so forth. Although the choice of issues to examine in this phase of the evaluation effort is based on the evaluation synthesis, it is important to recognize that the direction and thrust of evaluation planning—like all planning and unlike the rest of the evaluation process—is prospective or forward looking: it seeks to establish the design and operational strategy of an evaluation to be performed. In so doing the plan defines the criteria or outcomes by which success or failure will be determined and examines how the program's activities can be linked to those outcomes. While this is, of course, standard practice for evaluation planning, the process can be applied independently to a proposed new program as a validity check in three areas:

—the quality of the evidence used to support the need for the program;
—the feasibility of the activities proposed; and
—the reasonableness of the results expected, given that evidence and those activities.

Evaluation planning can thus expose assumptions about cause-and-effect relationships that are, in reality, uncertain. It can show the need for activities different from the ones proposed, if the program objectives stated are to be achieved; or it can show the need for different program objectives if the activities proposed cannot be changed. By demonstrating logically, in advance, that program objectives are not likely to be achieved given the proposed activities, or that the proposed activities are based on uncertain assumptions about what will cause a desired effect, or that the proposed activities are not feasible in light of conditions in the field or some other impediment, evaluation planning used independently offers the capability to assess rigorously, before the fact, the probability of success of a new program or policy.

Evaluation performance and reporting—which are, respectively, the third and fourth stages of evaluation—involve the actual execution and documentation of the assessment work, including the collection of data, its coding and analysis, the tabulation of results, and the timely presentation of those results to the evaluation's user, in a format and language congenial to the user's need. These two stages are the final steps in developing evidence on a program's achievements and costs.

In summary, then, these four stages of the program evaluation process can serve appropriate governmental change in several important ways. First, if prior evaluations and other analytical information exist, the evaluation synthesis can be used to develop evidence on the degree of need for a program and on the successes already achieved by that type of policy or program, either in the past or elsewhere. If there is little or no evaluative information, the lack of that information might itself indicate the need of a developmental form and character for the program. Second, evaluation planning can validate the reasonableness of a new program's objectives and activities and alert decision makers to gaps discovered in the available information at the same time that actual planning for the program's evaluation, per se, takes place. This has several advantages. It ensures that programs can be evaluated, that the questions asked and answered about their achievement will be relevant to decision makers' needs as well as to future programs, and that—most important of all—the policies and programs undertaken on the basis of such planning will have a reasonable chance of success. At the third stage, the evaluation conducted informs on the results of the new program, and the findings are then compared and consolidated with the information already developed in the evaluation synthesis. This reinforces at least one aspect of cumulativeness, in the sense that new information explicitly reports and confronts what was originally available. Finally, the evaluation report serves, in the conventional way, as a focus for debating the issues raised with regard to resource allocation and accountability for public funds.

The evaluation process evoked here is certainly deliberate, but it is both normal and feasible. Only the separate use of the components distinguishes it in any way. At the General Accounting Office, a methodology for performing the evaluation synthesis is currently being completed. Thus far, the synthesis has been used five times by IPE to inform the Congress with regard to access by the handicapped to special education, lessons learned from the block grants of the past, home health care for the elderly, Comprehensive Employment and Training Act (CETA) program effectiveness, and issues in the strategy and conduct of chemical warfare.[20] Efforts to develop the evaluation planning review, on the other hand, are just getting under way.

Evaluation management

Some of the problems of definition and nearly all of the user criticisms discussed earlier can be addressed by means of fairly rigorous evaluation management. IPE is developing a management system that seeks to ensure the technical quality of evaluations performed, to address those user criticisms and definitional problems, and to provide a way of documenting changes—improvements or declines—in the cost-effectiveness of evaluations performed.[21]

20. Two of these papers are now published. They are: U.S. General Accounting Office, *Disparities Still Exist in Who Gets Special Education*, Report to Chairman, Subcommittee on Select Education, House Committee on Education and Labor, IPE-81-1, 30 Sept. 1981; and U.S. General Accounting Office, *CETA Programs for Disadvantaged Adults—What Do We Know about Their Enrollees, Services, and Effectiveness?* Report to Chairman, Subcommittee on Employment Opportunities, House Committee on Education and Labor, GAO/IPE-82-2, 14 June 1982. The other three are pending.

21. Eleanor Chelimsky, "Some Thoughts on the Nature, Definition, and Measurement of Quality as a Component of Evaluation Management," in *The Management of Program Evaluation, New Directions for Program Evaluation*, ed.

Both usefulness and methodological adequacy are considered in this system as integral parts of every evaluation, and management control is established through two interventions. The first of these occurs at the end of the design phase, when the manager assesses the appropriateness of the design chosen for answering the evaluation question within the user's time and cost constraints. The second intervention involves a review at the end of the evaluation focusing on methodological soundness, actual costs incurred, and time elapsed, emphasizing a comparison between what was achieved and what had been expected at the end of the design phase. Two kinds of feedback are needed at this point: first, information on design feasibility, especially the experience of field staff in implementing the design; and second, information on user satisfaction with regard to relevance, timeliness, and presentation. Finally, follow-up on actual use of the report is made and compared with planned use; lessons learned are documented.

This management system will be tested and used in conjunction with all IPE evaluations so that progress can be assessed over time against a host of measures such as diversity of methods employed, average cost of evaluations, average time for delivering products, numbers of product rejections, timeliness, and numbers of reports achieving use or failing to be used.

The assumption here, of course, is that careful managerial attention over time can resolve many of the criticisms directed against evaluation, and should result in better evaluation quality, lower costs, greater timeliness, more user satisfaction, and wider impact.

Cumulative use of evaluations

As discussed earlier, some sort of central clearinghouse for evaluation findings should be established. It is needed for several reasons: first, it would save time and money during the literature review to have easy access to syntheses already performed and to completed evaluations. Second, knowledge of current work would help evaluators to direct their questions and resources to needed information that is not currently available, thus again saving money by avoiding duplication. Third, it would create a body of evaluative knowledge allowing continuous update. Finally, it could inform evaluators about the status of current programs and evaluations likely to affect their work in the field. While establishment of such a clearinghouse seems a very important thing to do, it must nonetheless await initiative either by government or by the private sector, because it will require some funds and because it goes beyond the responsibility of any one group or agency.

In conclusion, this article has taken a favorable view of evaluation's current progress and of its potential for helping government achieve appropriate change. By performing, managing, and using evaluations creatively, it should be possible over the long run (1) to develop a continuous, cumulative evaluation data bank that can serve government decision makers in the formulation and implementation of public policy, (2) to improve the rationality of program initiation, execution, and assessment, (3) to find a practical path to fiscal responsibility that makes sense within the policy-

---

Robert St.Pierre (San Francisco: Jossey-Bass, forthcoming).

making context of the executive and legislative branches of government, and (4) eventually to reach the point where it can be assumed, as a matter of course, that a proposed governmental change is one with a very good chance of achieving its goals.

Organizing for Change

By LOUIS C. GAWTHROP

ABSTRACT: The implementation of government policy decisions is the responsibility of designated public organizations. Thus the implementation of public policy has always been viewed as a function of internal organizational design and procedures. Until recently, organizational theory generally described this as a simple mechanistic process determined only by the canons of internal operating efficiency. Now, however, political stability, social equity, and policy effectiveness no longer appear to be automatic by-products of organizational efficiency. Depending on which of these concepts prevails in any public agency at any time, different organizational configurations may be identified and reorganization efforts in the public sector may be an exercise in shifting the emphasis of organizational systems from any one of these conceptual approaches to any other. Moreover, no one of these organizational value sets, or the organizational systems each engenders, appears more effective than any other in adapting to the relevant forces of change in every organization's external environment. As external complexity increases, the ability of public-sector agencies to absorb the forces of change decreases. To reverse this relationship, either external variety can be attenuated or the organization's internal capacity to absorb complexity can be amplified: strategies can thus involve either "changing organizations" or "organizing for change."

Louis C. Gawthrop is professor of public and environmental affairs at Indiana University—Bloomington. He formerly taught at the State University of New York at Binghamton and the University of Pennsylvania. He graduated from Franklin and Marshall College, Lancaster, Pennsylvania, and received his M.A. and Ph.D. degrees from the Johns Hopkins University. He is the author of three books—Bureaucratic Behavior in the Executive Branch, The Administration Process and Democratic Theory, *and* Administrative Politics and Social Change—*and a contributor to several edited volumes on public administration. He is currently the editor-in-chief of* Public Administration Review.

TO address the topic of administrative organization and reorganization in the public sector within an overall context that focuses on change, certain assumptions must be stated at the outset. For example, it must be viewed as axiomatic that organization is an inherent element of every purposeful system. A system may be defined as any set of components that are integrated in some fashion to achieve a purposeful end, and the manner of such integration represents the system's organization. Thus every organization—and specifically every public-sector organization—may be described and discussed in terms of its systemic structure. A corollary to this axiom is that purposefulness assumes rationality. Therefore, one focus of this article will be how government organizations in the United States organize their resources to achieve their purposes in a rational manner.

A second basic proposition is that every organization is characterized by an internal and an external environment. The systemic relationships that characterize every organization are formed by the linkages among component parts. These components directly supply the needs of the organization and, in turn, they are directly controlled by the demands of the system. Thus any element or phenomenon whose behavior is subject to the direct and consistent control of the organization must be included as a component of the organization's internal environment. Conversely, an element or phenomenon whose behavior is not directly and consistently controlled by the organization is part of the organization's external environment.[1] As a corollary of this proposition, it must also be assumed that every rational organization limits the scope of its perceived external environment to include only those elements or phenomena that are relevant to the organization's sense of purposefulness. Thus for each system or organization a clear distinction must be made between its internal operating environment and its relevant external environment. Although occasional references will be made to the former, this article will focus primarily on the relationship between public-sector organizations and their relevant external environments.

The third assumption that must be accepted as axiomatic is that change is an inherent and ever-present element of every organization. As a conceptual abstraction, the theoretical notion of change can be developed in extensive detail. As a practical concept, however, it may be viewed as a relational term that applies to every situation resulting from the interactions of two or more forces over time. Such resulting situations may be described as change and may be scaled on a continuum ranging from the benign to the turbulent. In similar fashion, every organization is affected by the rate, magnitude, and amplitude of change forces. A baby-boom year gives educational planners at the primary, secondary, and postsecondary levels a 6-, 14-, and 18-year lead time to prepare for the influx. The discovery of cures for all cancers would have an immediate, high-intensity impact—organizationally speaking—on the National Institute of Health. Thus to the element of organization as an inherent feature of every purposeful system must be added the element of change. For this reason, a second focus of this article will be the manner in which public-sector systems in the United States have organized their resour-

---

1. C. West Churchman, *A Systems Approach* (New York: Dell, 1979), pp. 64-67.

ces in a rational and purposeful manner to respond to change.

A FEW BASIC FACTS

Given these three basic assumptions, are there any generalizations that may be advanced relating to organizational change? Or, to restate the question, after 200 years of practical operating experience in the public sector and at least 100 years of serious, extensive, intensive, rigorous, thoughtful, and reflective scholarly study, what is the extent of our knowledge base—not our information or data bases, but the extent of our knowledge, or what we know for certain—as it relates to organization responses to the external forces of change?

We know that the survival of any system, biological or social, is directly related to its ability to adapt successfully to change. Organizational adaptation is simply another way of describing an organization's ability to respond to change. Thus, viewed in an organizational context, an integral relationship exists between the external forces of change and organizational responses to change.

On the basis of this initial proposition, several other generalizations can be offered. For example, in a public-sector organization the relationship between external forces of change and the organization's response to those forces cannot be explained in terms of a simple stimulus-response relationship. Between the demand and response mechanisms, every public-sector organization must insert an intervening variable that serves an assessment function. This variable must be built into the system; it guides the organization in determining how and when it will respond to the forces of change. At this point, however, our knowledge base begins to break down.

Within the universe of responses to change, we do know that there is a subset that can be labeled "objective solutions." That is to say, certain types of demands for change, which lend themselves nicely to a purely objective assessment of their validity, are received regularly by every public organization. In the policy areas of environmental, consumer, and occupational regulation and protection, the public-sector organizations charged with these responsibilities are extensively involved in dealing with this subset of demands, many of which—but by no means all—can be assessed on the basis of objective criteria. However, it is also a well-recognized fact that the effectiveness of objective assessment diminishes as the complexity of the external demand force increases. It is at this point that the extent of our firm knowledge of organizational responses to change begins to crumble. Clearly, sensor devices for assessing demands are still at work, but in dealing with highly complex sets of demands for change, it is not at all clear how the organization should proceed. We do know, however, that the ambiguity associated with these situations explains why external demand groups attempt to expand the scope and intensity of their demand, while the organization follows the opposite strategy of attempting to restrict the scope and minimize the intensity of change.

Still another fact that can be applied to the demand-response relationship concerns the manner in which the organization responds to nonobjective situations. A public organization can respond to change in only one of two ways: it can react to change after it manifests itself in fully developed form, or it can attempt to anticipate such change before it becomes fully manifest. These are by no means mutually exclusive responses. Indeed, every organization utilizes reactive and anticipatory strategies in varying degrees.[2] Again, at this stage our knowledge base continues to diminish; however, there is one proposition that emerges as conclusive. The total set of organizational costs associated with maintaining a fully committed anticipatory response mechanism is much greater than the costs required to maintain a fully developed reactive response mechanism. This gives rise to an interesting paradox increasingly evident in our society today. While an increasing number of observers conclude that government's failure to develop an anticipatory scanning, planning, and change capacity will seriously threaten the effectiveness of the entire system,[3] public-sector organizations throughout the United States, at all levels of government, continue to operate primarily under the assumption that a reactive response to change is the least costly and, over the long term, the most efficient, the most beneficial, and the most desirable.

---

2. For a more detailed elaboration of this point, see Louis C. Gawthrop, "The Political System and Public Service Education," *American Behavioral Scientist*, 21(6):917-36 (July-Aug. 1978); idem, *Bureaucratic Behavior in the Executive Branch* (New York: Free Press, 1969), pp. 172-88.

3. Stafford Beer, *Designing Freedom* (New York: John Wiley, 1974), pp. 87-100; Carl W. Stenberg, "Beyond the Days of Wine and Roses: Intergovernmental Management in a Cutback Environment," *Public Administration Review*, 41(1):10-20 (Jan.-Feb. 1981); Frederick C. Mosher, "The Changing Responsibilities and Tactics of the Federal Government," *Public Administration Review*, 40(6):541-52 (Nov.-Dec. 1980).

The synthesis of knowledge

Turning from the relationships between organizations and the forces of change, there is another segment of our knowledge base that needs to be discussed, concerning the relationship between public-sector organizations and the public policy process in general. As applied here, the term "public policy process" may be taken to mean the levels of recursion that flow from normative policy pronouncements to specific organizational strategies (programs), to rational organizational designs (structures), and, finally, to explicitly articulated organizational operations (procedures). In other words, policies must be transformed into specific programs; programs must be implemented within a structured context; and structures are meaningless without sets of operating procedures designed to control the flow of information, people, or things.

Assuming rational and purposeful behavior, the nature of the organizational process should be determined by the purposeful goals of policy; that is, policy precedes process—the end determines the means. However, it is also a generally recognized fact that the manner in which purposeful policies are implemented in an environment of persistent, pervasive, and uncertain change is determined by the organizational process network of programs, structures, and procedures. Viewed in this context, logic would clearly suggest that, in fact, process precedes policy, or the means shape the ends.

The distinction being made here between policy and process is simply a more elaborate and, I think, a more precise way to express the relationship that for years we have referred to simply as the policy-administration dichotomy. Regardless of how we may choose to describe this relationship, some kind of interaction does exist between policy and administration, or between policy and process. It is the nature of this relationship, when confronted with the forces of change, that determines the basis of governmental organization and reorganization in the United States. Moreover, it is the nature of this relationship that contributes significantly in determining how the limited resources of public-sector agencies can be organized most rationally to achieve purposeful goals in an environment of perpetual change.

Indeed, it might be argued that the basis of an organization's choice of responses to the forces of change— reactive or anticipatory—is a function not of policy but of process, that is, organizational structure and procedure, in which case—as with Warren Bennis—one could speak of "changing organizations."[4] Another way of viewing this relationship, however, is that an organization's structural design and procedural mechanism are functions of the nature of its response to the forces of change, in which case—as with this article—one could speak of "organizing for change." The fact that both of these propositions can be argued persuasively is an unfortunate commentary on the state of our knowledge of public organizations. The extent of our data and information base concerning public organizations has expanded substantially over the past 100 years. The extent of our knowledge base, however, has expanded modestly at best.

4. Warren Bennis, *Changing Organizations* (New York: McGraw-Hill, 1966).

One reason for this is that while it is relatively easy to generate and aggregate data into blocks of information, the conversion of information into knowledge is a function of deliberate and effective synthesis. As has already been noted, one essential feature of every viable system is its ability to adapt to change. A second essential feature for every organization is its ability to integrate or synthesize new information into its existing knowledge base. It is important to emphasize, however, that although these two change-related organizational functions are not mutually exclusive, it does not automatically follow that they are mutually inclusive. Organizational effectiveness, if viewed in terms of intellectual development, may be studied as a function of the extent to which these two subfunctions— adaptation and integration—are integrally related. Any cycle of organizational development must presume a growth and expansion in the organization's knowledge base. However, in the development of U.S. public-sector organizations, if viewed simply over the course of the twentieth century, no such presumption is valid. A summary assessment of the various contemporary approaches to organizing public agencies in the United States should be sufficient to confirm this assertion.

FOUR APPROACHES TO ORGANIZING

During this century, the theory and practice of public administration have been confronted with four major and different organizational perspectives or approaches as to how the limited resources of government bodies may be organized most rationally in order for these public agencies to achieve their purposeful goals in an environment of variable change. These four approaches may be characterized as different methods of organizing for change, and they may be described as

—organizing for control,
—organizing for bargaining,
—organizing for responsiveness, and
—organizing for analysis.

Organizing for control

The most obvious and basic approach for any organization to ensure the attainment of its ultimate purpose is to ensure maximum control over all relevant resources, including, most importantly, maximum control over the organizational behavior of its personnel. Virtually the entire span of history confirms Max Weber's generalized tenet that the most effective and efficient way to assure maximum control over a large group of individuals employed to achieve some stated objective is to organize them within the context of a vertically structured, hierarchical organization.[5] The notions of centralized authority, unity of command, precisely defined superior-subordinate relationships, and strictly delineated ranks of graded authority are all means designed to impose effective constraints on the unpredictable behavior of individuals. Driven by the motivation of reward and constrained by the fear of punishment, individuals operating within this format are expected to demonstrate loyalty, obedience, and willing subordination.

Within public-sector organizations, the notion of professionalism is introduced to alleviate the punitive, repressive, and coercive elements of the control model. Moreover, the notion of a professionalized public administration dovetails nicely with the theoretical rationale of the policy-administration and fact-value dichotomies.[6] The net result is a professionalized cadre of public administrators operating in a value-free framework of total detachment and objective impersonality, totally committed to the sole organizational purpose of operating efficiency. In this context, efficiency is a function of internal operational control, with organizational structures and procedures viewed solely as instrumental and mechanistic means for ensuring behavioral conformity.[7] Viewed from this perspective, the external organizational environment is, at best, an inert form and, at worst, a serious threat to the internal order of the organization. Therefore, control must also be maintained over who and what gain access to the internal recesses of the organization. The boundary must be guarded and, inevitably, one very important function of any public agency organized along these lines falls to the boundary-guarding agents who defend the organization's outer perimeter. Thus

---

5. Max Weber, "Bureaucracy," in *From Max Weber,* eds. Hans Gerth and C. Wright Mills (New York: Oxford University Press, 1946), pp. 196-244; idem, *Theory of Social and Economic Organization,* trans. A. M. Henderson and T. Parsons (New York: Oxford University Press, 1947), pp. 324-40.

6. Woodrow Wilson, "The Study of Administration," *Political Science Quarterly,* 2:197-222 (June 1887); Luther Gulick, "The Theory of Organization," in *Papers on the Science of Administration,* eds. Luther Gulick and L. Urwick (New York: Institute of Public Administration, 1937), p. 45; Luther Gulick, "Science, Values and Public Administration," ibid., p. 192.

7. Frederick W. Taylor, *The Principles of Scientific Management* (New York: Harper & Row, 1911), pp. 114-44.

the notion of control not only becomes a method of organizing the internal resources of an organization, but it also represents a perceptual attitude, which the organization applies in defining its relevant external environment.

A second function characteristic of public-sector agencies organized under the rubric of control is a transfer function. That is, a primary responsibility of the organization is to effect the most efficient transfer of authorized resources from the organization to its external clientele. Legislative authorizations represent the basic inputs, and the organization has the responsibility to deliver these mandated resources in the most efficient, cost-effective manner. The notion of service delivery—a term currently in vogue—is but a synonym for the age-old transfer function of public-sector organizations.

Of course, the transfer function is effected in a thoroughly impersonal, detached, and objective manner. The what and why of resource allocation from government to the body politic are solely policy questions to be decided among elected and top-level politically appointed officials. The how of resource allocation is an operational and administrative question. The criteria for gauging the effectiveness of the what and why questions are based solely on political values. The criterion for assessing the effectiveness of the transfer function is based solely on the measure of efficiency; and efficiency can be maximized only in a tightly controlled, hierarchically structured organizational setting.

Organizing for bargaining

The notion of a Weberian control structure, built around the prime value of operating efficiency, makes sense where a strict dichotomy between policy and administration prevails, and where pure economic rationalism affects the decision-making process. Given this approach to organizing public-sector agencies, it logically follows that operating efficiency is only incidentally, and often quite insignificantly, related to the political efficacy of public-sector implementation.

Political efficacy becomes a valid consideration for public-sector organizations to the extent that professional career employees are perceived—and perceive themselves—as being directly involved in the policy process. If viewed in this context, operating efficiency becomes synonymous with political efficacy, which, in turn, may be equated with the Madisonian notion of political stability in a pluralist society. Thus if career civil servants are perceived as principal professional participants in the maintenance of political stability in their relevant external environments, the essential focus of organizational design for public-sector agencies must undergo a substantial modification.

An organization designed around a basic value framework of political efficacy reflects the wide range of reciprocal exchange interactions between professional career administrators and all other legitimate professional political participants involved in the policy process—that is, elected and appointed executive branch officials, legislators, and interest-group representatives.[8] As a result of this modification, public-sector administrators are transformed from passive instruments, used simply to receive and transmit informa-

8. Louis C. Gawthrop, *Administrative Politics and Social Change* (New York: St. Martin's Press, 1971), pp. 18-40.

tion signals on a single channel frequency, to active and dynamic quasi-independent brokers of data and information, working on a multichannel frequency. The effects of this transformation on organizational structures and procedures are significant. First, the narrowly defined, vertically structured chains of communication of the hierarchical control model are substantially weakened; second, to the extent that information is perceived as a valuable resource in the public policy process, the significance of any public agency vis-à-vis other collaterally related organizations is determined by the extent and quality of its information holdings.[9]

In practical operating terms, this approach to organizing places public-sector career personnel on an informational parity with the elected and appointed top-level executive officials, legislators, and interest-group representatives. Moreover, this approach mandates that public policy decisions reflect a consensus of agreement among these four groups, no one of which enjoys direct, unilateral control over any other. Under any situation in which decisions are hinged to consensus in the absence of direct control, such consensus gathering can be effected only through bargaining. Hence organizing for bargaining becomes an exercise in political efficacy.[10]

This still leaves the nagging question of efficiency unanswered. How is one to decide rationally when confronted with multivariant change situations? How are the organization's limited resources to be allocated rationally among competing programs and diverse clientele groups? The answers to these questions may be obtained from two well-established sources. Decision-making rationality in the face of multivariant change complexity is built into the bargaining model by Herbert Simon's concept of satisficing, whereby the decision maker "satisfices—looks for a course of action that is satisfactory or 'good enough'"; and the rational allocation of limited budgetary resources is attained in the bargaining model through the application of Aaron Wildavsky's politics of incrementalism.[11] Thus, in answer to the first question, a rational decision is attained through the selection of that alternative which is satisfactory—that is, good enough—and, in answer to the second question, rationality is most closely approximated when it is recognized that the future is determined by the present, which, in turn, is based on the past. If one draws together the notions of pluralism, bargaining, and incrementalism, and incorporates them into an integrative framework, what emerges is a working formula in which the incremental allocation of limited resources within a pluralist society is accomplished by a closed group of professional political participants on the basis of bargained political agreements.

It is important to note that although the bargaining model does introduce some significant departures from the control model, in actual practice the ramifications of the former are superim-

---

9. Stafford Beer, "Managing Modern Complexity," in *The Management of Information and Knowledge* (Washington, DC: U.S. House of Representatives, Committee on Science and Astronautics, 1970), pp. 41-62.

10. Gawthrop, *Administrative Politics and Social Change*, pp. 41-56.

11. Herbert A. Simon, *Administrative Behavior*, 3rd ed. (New York: Free Press, 1976), p. xxix; James G. March and Herbert A. Simon, *Organizations* (New York: John Wiley, 1958); Aaron Wildavsky, *The Politics of the Budgetary Process*, 3rd ed. (Boston: Little, Brown, 1979).

posed on the latter to form a deceptively simple composite design. The bargaining model does modify the internal operating environment of the control model, but it does not alter either the transfer or the boundary-guarding functions of that approach. To ensure the effective working of the pluralist-bargaining-incremental formula already noted, external forces for change may legitimately be introduced into the public policy discussion process only by individuals who are recognized as bona fide professional political participants. Within this closed subset of individuals, the interactions may be intense, complex, and highly volatile, but once consensus is reached, the primary function of the public organization involved is to effect the implementation of the decision in the manner of an automatic transfer function. Moreover, insofar as the boundary-guarding function is concerned, it must be recognized that the effectiveness of the consensus-building process is critically dependent upon the maintenance of a relatively high degree of comity among the closed set of professional political participants. Thus it is essential that the boundary be guarded against the unwarranted intrusion of amateurs into the politically sensitive bargaining complex. If anything, the boundary-guarding function assumes an even greater significance in the bargaining model.

Organizing for responsiveness

Viewed in terms of administrative responsibilities, proponents of both the control and bargaining models stoutly defend their respective organizational designs as thoroughly consistent with the democratic values of justice and equity. Moreover, if viewed in terms of administrative accountability, both models reveal linkages to other system components that enjoy direct political oversight of administrative activities. Public organizations, designed either in the control or bargaining context, are directly accountable and responsible to legitimately elected political representatives of the body politic—that is, chief executives and/or legislators. In both approaches to organizing, however, the relationships between public-sector agencies and their relevant external constituencies have been criticized as formal, objective, civil, officious, punctilious, and inflexible—responsible yes; responsive, no.[12]

The notion of organizing public agencies to be directly responsive to the forces of change is specifically intended to shift the nexus of administrative purposefulness from the internal to the external environment, from structural and procedural processes to delivery systems, from performance to consequences. To attain this type of modification, however, some significant alterations must be made in the organizational designs of the control and bargaining models.

In the first place, the passively detached, formalistic transfer function must be replaced by the active engagement of tailoring organizational resources to meet specific external demands

12. For example, see H. George Frederickson, *New Public Administration* (University: University of Alabama Press, 1980); idem, ed., "Symposium on Social Equity and Public Administration," *Public Administration Review,* 34(1):1-51 (Jan.-Feb. 1974); Frank Marini, ed., *Toward a New Public Administration* (San Francisco: Chandler, 1971); Dwight Waldo, ed., *Public Administration in a Time of Turbulence* (Scranton, PA: Chandler, 1971); Orion White, "The Dialectical Organization: An Alternative to Bureaucracy," *Public Administration Review,* 29(1):32-42 (Jan.-Feb. 1969).

for change. Second, change must be viewed as value enhancing rather than value threatening, and this means that third, the forces of change are to be actively sought rather than assiduously avoided. Fourth, the boundary-guarding function must be redefined to become a boundary-spanning function. And, finally, the primary responsibility of public organizations must be gauged by their responsiveness to their external clienteles and not to their politically elected or appointed overseers.

The organizational implications of these modifications should be apparent. Organizational agents who have direct, face-to-face contact with their clientele are to be expected to operate with wide discretion, minimal constraints, and imaginative, creative innovation. Moreover, they are to have broad access to the organization's resources, direct contact with the agency's highest-level officials, if necessary, and the unswerving support of these top-level individuals. Project team clusters, situationally defined leadership roles, ad hoc problem-solving mechanisms, personalized change strategies, free and open communication exchange, and horizontal pathway search processes are all standard operating procedures in such a design framework.[13]

Viewed in this context, change not only becomes a positive force for the qualitative enhancement of the external target group, but it also becomes the catalyst, so to speak, for converting the organization's passive transfer agents into dynamic change agents. The creative challenges facing change agents are (1) to establish an integrated sense of problem-solving self-confidence within the clientele groups through the fully developed participatory involvement of all members of the group, and (2) to establish the clientele groups as fully recognized and authorized participants in the organization's programmatic and resource allocation decision-making system. Hence the notion of responsiveness is drawn quite clearly to indicate that the sole *raison d'être* of public-sector agencies is to serve the problem-solving needs of clientele groups as determined by the groups themselves on the basis of the self-actualized and self-enlightened forces of participatory democracy.[14]

Organizing for analysis

The fourth approach to organizing may simply be characterized as organizing for analysis. This approach incorporates the basic designs of systems theory; as a consequence, it is the only approach that is explicitly committed to rational decision making on the basis of a comprehensive information source of all known and available data. By contrast, the bargaining or pluralist-bargaining-incremental approach is explicitly committed to nonrational, political decision making on the basis of a pragmatically selective information source,[15] while the responsiveness approach is committed

---

13. For Example, see Robert Golembiewski, ed., *Organizational Development in Public Administration* (New York: Marcel Dekker, 1978), vol. 2; idem, *Organizing Man and Power* (Chicago: Rand McNally, 1967); Martin Landau and Russell Stout, Jr., "To Manage is Not to Control: Or the Folly of Type II Errors," *Public Administration Review*, 39(2):148-56 (Mar.-Apr. 1979); Chris Argyris, "Some Limits of Rational Man Theory," *Public Administration Review*, 33(3):253-67 (May-June 1973).

14. David Korten, "The Management of Social Transformation," *Public Administration Review*, 41(6):609-18 (Nov.-Dec. 1981).

15. Paul Diesing, *Reason in Society* (Urbana: University of Illinois Press, 1962), pp. 198, 203-4.

to a purely normative decision-making agenda. Only the control model makes any pretense of adopting a rational decision-making posture, but the pure economic rationalism incorporated in this design, with its myopic commitment to the notion of classical efficiency, can be viewed as a simplistic caricature of objective reality. Moreover, the satisficing approach to decision making as advanced by Herbert Simon and endorsed by the bargaining model is categorically rejected as analytically indefensible, programmatically inefficient, and operationally noncontrollable.

The attractiveness—and indeed the effectiveness—of the control and bargaining approaches is directly dependent upon the existence of two indispensable conditions: a relatively stable external environment and an expanding national economy. If either of these conditions does not prevail, the programmatic and operational effectiveness of the two approaches is seriously strained. If neither condition prevails, both of these approaches can become severely dysfunctional and counterproductive. The primary criticism by the analytical rationalists of the bargaining approach is aimed at the latter's fundamental insufficiency to respond effectively to the rapid acceleration of dynamic change in an external environment of increasing complexity, particularly when this insufficiency is further exacerbated by either a static or a contracting national economy. One central feature of the analytical approach, therefore, is the rank ordering of change demands on the basis of rational, comprehensive, and comparative analysis.

The relationship between the analytical and control models is somewhat less strained and distorted. Although the decision-making assumptions of the control model are dismissed out of hand by analytical rationalists, this concept has always been the weakest link in the control framework. The strengths and persistence of the control approach come from the clarity of its hierarchical design, its attendance to the internal orderliness of its operational procedures, and its heavy emphasis on individual discipline, loyalty, and obedience. In connection with each of these elements, the rational-comprehensive-analytical approach introduces significant and clearly distinctive modifications while retaining the essence of each. A second central feature of the analytical model, therefore, is its adaptation of hierarchy, order, discipline, and loyalty.

In considering the relationships between organizational designs and the forces of change, the common feature in both the control and bargaining models is a purely reactive response to change. Moreover, the forces of change are viewed solely in terms of the organization's past experiences. Given a relatively high level of stability, continuity, and predictability in the organization's external environment, a purely reactive response to change is undoubtedly the most rational and efficient approach. However, it also follows that such effectiveness diminishes as the causal texture of the external environment becomes complexly joined by more numerous components likely to emit more frequent and more forceful perturbations.[16] The effectiveness of a reactive response is a function of the relaxation

16. F. E. Emery and E. L. Trist, "The Causal Texture of Organizational Environments," *Human Relations,* 19(2):21-32 (Feb. 1965).

time any system enjoys between perturbations. As the relaxation time diminishes, the forces of complex change can seriously damage the decision-making process of any system. Thus a third central feature of the analytical model is the conscious and explicit development of a future-focused, anticipatory scanning capacity to detect the latent, embryonic forces of change before they coalesce and manifest themselves in the present.

The combined central features of an analytical approach to change, therefore, consist of an efficiently ordered and disciplined hierarchical structure designed to anticipate the relevant forces of change in order to achieve a rank ordering of change priorities on the basis of rational, comprehensive, and comparative analysis.

SOME COMPARATIVE ASSESSMENTS

Each of these four approaches to organizing may be viewed from various perspectives, but the manner in which each system is designed to accommodate change is of central concern here. Although each can be characterized by significant differences, there are some important similarities that, if appropriately linked together, could provide the basis for a synthesis of our knowledge of organizing for change. Certainly the role of the public agency as the primary receptor of the forces of change and the manner in which this role is affected and effected by the agency's organizational design need to be studied in much more detail than they have been in the past. More important, however, the aggregation and synthesis of our knowledge of the relationship between organizational design and organizing for change must be advanced. Only through the tentative exploration of similarities and commonalities can such progress be realized. It is with this in mind that the four approaches could be integrated into two organizational redesigns for change.

Commonalities of the control and bargaining approaches

Both the control and bargaining systems are constituted to maintain a purely reactive response to the external forces of change. Obviously, a certain latent, opportunistic, anticipatory capacity exists in every astute administrator or manager, and, although this capacity can be activated under the appropriate circumstances, the predominant operating pattern in response to change is essentially reactive and guarded. What this means is that neither system need be too concerned about the state of the future. If any system only reacts to change demands when they are evidenced in manifest form, that system, by definition, is active solely in the present.

Problem situations, clientele needs, change demands, and malfunctions in existing programs that do emerge in legitimately expressed form are assessed and evaluated in an effort to devise the most appropriate solutions. But where does a control or bargaining organization turn to find such solutions? To ask the question is to answer it—to the agency's repertoire of experience, to its past. How has it dealt with similar situations in the past? The key word here is "similar." Obviously there is a certain uniqueness about every change situation, but in public agencies organized for control and bargaining there is a clear assumption that all change demands can be specified according to the existing functional line operations of the agency. In other words, all demands for change can be accommodated within the agency's existing programmed, routinized responses. Programmed routines reflect the accumulated experience of the past. Thus, for control and bargaining organizations, the future is determined by the past.

The effectiveness of such an organizational tactic depends on the agency's ability to maintain a relatively high degree of control over the change forces generated from the external environment. Forces of change generate conflict, and virtually all available evidence suggests that the scale of conflict is directly related to its scope and intensity. For any agency to maximize control over conflict, it must limit the scope of conflict and minimize its intensity. This task is not too difficult for public agencies that serve a homogeneous or homologous clientele or purpose, but it may prove to be a major problem for organizations with highly heterogeneous clienteles. The Federal Bureau of Prisons, like the Bureau of Indian Affairs, may perceive that it is confronted with clienteles highly diversified in many respects, but certainly the variety in the clientele groups is minimal when compared to the variety in the external clienteles of the Bureau of Land Management and the Bureau of Consumer Protection. External variety, therefore, becomes a variable of important concern for all public agencies.

In this regard, if an agency is concerned about limiting the scope and intensity of conflict as a means of controlling the forces of change, then it becomes essential that the variety in its external environment be attenuated to the fullest extent necessary. And in fact this is precisely the primary stabilizing tactic employed by control and bargaining organizations in the public sector. The U.S. Department of Agriculture is an excellent example of a public agency that has, over the years, skillfully employed the tactic of variety attenuation. The Department of Health, Education and Welfare was created as a variety-attenuating department, as were the Departments of Housing and Urban Development and Transportation. The Department of Education, with its genesis, seemed to focus on a single-entity clientele, while, in fact, its subdivision into primary, secondary, and higher education served a clearly designed variety-attenuating purpose. Indeed, a very strong argument could be made that the primary value of executive reorganization is the variety-attenuating function it serves. At least in the context of control and bargaining organizations, all else seems secondary.

Commonalities of the responsive and analytical approaches

As opposed to the purely reactive response to change that is characteristic of the control and bargaining designs, both the responsive and analytical approaches are geared to maintain an anticipatory response to change. To attempt to anticipate anything is, by definition, to be involved in the future, and although the analytical approach is more committed to a longer-term, future-focused continuum than the responsive design, both see the future as a prime source of open opportunities for change, and both reject any suggestion of being bound by the past.

Although the specific organizational procedures of these two approaches are fundamentally different, both draw energy primarily from the common assumption that change—and the conflict it may engender—is a positive, value-enhancing, basic, and inevitable component of any complex system. Thus in both approaches the open and explicit acceptance of conflict is viewed as vital to maintaining organizational effectiveness.

The manner in which any public agency organized for analysis views change is, of course, quite distinct from that revealed by responsive organizations. In both, change is a given. However, in the former change is perceived as an exercise in systems analytical problem solving, while in the latter it is perceived more as a heuristic challenge in problem dis-solving. Elaborate, rationally devised feedback loops in the one instance, and intuitive sensors attuned to experimental learning in the other, result in active and adaptive approaches to change. In this regard, one of the basic characteristics of these two approaches—and probably the one that most sets them apart from the control and bargaining designs—is the emphasis placed on amplifying the internal capacity of the organization to deal effectively with increasing variety in the external environment rather than concentrating organizational resources solely on the attenuation of such variety. Variety amplification does assume different forms in these two organizational settings, but in both instances the emphasis is on organizational redesign in a manner primarily intended to expand the range of creative, imaginative, innovative, and rational thought and action that may be applied to any given policy situation or program demand. If Ashby's Law of Requisite Variety is to be taken seriously, and only variety can absorb variety,[17] then the principal concern of responsive and analytical agencies is to ensure an internal organizational capacity for stabilizing the external forces of change effectively. Both approaches to organizing are preeminently committed to this end.

In this regard, the most rationally developed amplifying system is that of analysis. Although grossly distorted and seriously discredited when unilaterally mandated for the entire federal executive branch from 1965 to 1969, the systems analytical principles incorporated in planning-programming-budgeting (PPB) were then, and are now, viewed by many as the only viable organizational approach to an external environment marked by increasing diversity or variety, dynamic change, turbulent instability, exponentially greater interconnective linkages, and a diminishing national resource base. The notions of explicitly demanding (1) that policy purposefulness be openly articulated and directly linked to policy planning, (2) that operational programs be designed to relate to both plans and purposes, and (3) that budgetary decisions be integrally related to purposefulness, plans, and programs provided the core principles of organizing for analysis. Moreover, the concepts of program priority ranking, ongoing program monitoring and program adjustments, early detection of first-, second-, and third-order consequences and effects of existing programs, and the future-focused, anticipatory scanning of the beginning trajectories of change are all designed to amplify the internal sophistication of the organization to deal with external variety.

The commitment of responsive organizations to amplify their own internal variety capacity is as basic as

17. W. R. Ashby, *Introduction to Cybernetics* (New York: John Wiley, 1956), pp. 202-18.

with the analytical design, but the manner in which this commitment is developed differs significantly. This approach focuses mainly on interpersonal relations. The basic operating assumption is that as a result of procedural and normative constraints, a substantial source of positive intellectual and creative potential lies dormant in most professional public-sector administrators. In order to amplify the capacity of public agencies to absorb the level of variety in their external environments, the full creative capabilities of all agency personnel must be realized. However, to realize the full potential of each individual and to focus this combined source of energy on the collaborative and consensual enterprise of the organization, an internal operating environment that is conducive to, and supportive of, an open system of interpersonal relations must be established. Such an environment must, of necessity, encourage the explicit expression of individual self-confidence, mutual respect and trust, reciprocal support, willing collaboration, information and knowledge exchange, rational criticism, a personalized sense of transcendent purposefulness, and—most important of all—a self-conscious sense of individual responsibility for one's own intentions as well as actions. Such a patterned environment is the keystone of the organizational development (OD) field, and the hallmark of the extensive body of OD literature is the amplification of individual potential in an organizational context.[18]

18. For example, see Robert Golembiewski, *Managing Organizations* (Washington, DC: American Society for Public Administration, 1981); Larry Kirkhart and Neely Gardner, eds., "Symposium on Organizational Development," *Public Administration Review,* 34(2):97-140 (Mar.-Apr. 1974).

AN ORGANIZATIONAL SYNTHESIS FOR CHANGE

On the basis of the preceding discussion, it seems reasonable to conclude that (1) there exists no single approach to organizing or reorganizing in the public sector—rather, a multiplicity of approaches prevails; (2) the approaches that do currently prevail are complementary in many respects, although it is just as important to understand their differences as it is to understand their similarities; (3) different organizations can employ different approaches, and even a single agency can incorporate more than one approach simultaneously; and, finally, (4) the net results of such diffuse, conflicting, confusing, and often contradictory composite approaches to organizing and reorganizing are the additional fragmentation of the forces of change in the external environment and the continued frustration and debilitation of administrative and managerial purposefulness in the internal operating environments of all public-sector organizations.

However, if organizing for change can be viewed as a more significant and instructive conceptual focus than simply changing organizations, and if a valid distinction can be drawn between organizational mechanisms for variety-attentuation and variety-amplification purposes, then some initial steps are suggested that could yield a synthesized approach to organizing public agencies in a manner designed to capture and direct the forces of change in a positive, value-enhancing direction.

In this regard, the strategy of choice would appear to lie in the direction of combining the rational, future-focused, policy-planning capacity of analysis with the ethical, present-oriented, program-implementation capacity of responsiveness. Two different sets of organizing values are clearly evidenced in these seemingly diverse approaches, but the value sets are by no means mutually exclusive. They share a commitment to a sense of transcendent purposefulness, a holistic perspective, an anticipatory response to change, and an internal amplifying capacity as the most appropriate means to manage the dynamic forces of change. The techniques employed by each for variety amplification are complementary, not contradictory. If integrated correctly, the resulting synthesis would yield an organizational design featuring the close collaboration of policy planners and program managers.[19]

Given the common value base shared by each, such a collaborative endeavor would force program managers to interact with their clienteles more rationally, and it would force the analytical planners to devise their macro projects in a fashion more directly responsive to the needs of their agencies' clienteles. To maximize the internal variety-amplification capacity of any organization, planners must learn to scan their futures and managers must learn to span their boundaries with a shared sense of responsibility stemming from a mutual appreciation of each other's primary concerns. Each group must be utilized to supplement the needs of the other to the point where analysis and responsiveness become fused in an indistinguishable and inseparable organizational design. At that stage, the contorted process that our public-sector agencies frequently follow in attempting to organize for change may be concluded with the institutionalization of a system designed for critical consciousness. Organizational adaptation to change in the face of rapidly increasing complexity calls for a creative approach to the internal processes of management. However, such an approach is but a facade if not infused with a sense of critical consciousness. Thus organizing for change is a challenge that still confronts and eludes our public-sector agencies. To end its elusiveness means to confront its challenge. This would be the required first step toward a more rational and responsive public bureaucracy.

19. Gawthrop, *Administrative Politics and Social Change*, pp. 92-108.

ANNALS, *AAPSS*, **466**, March 1983

Nonhierarchical Approaches to the Organization of Public Activity

By VINCENT OSTROM

ABSTRACT: Recent emphasis on the management of intergovernmental relations raises questions about patterns of governance in a federal system that rely more upon the nonhierarchical modes of organization implied by management principles. Tocqueville, in *Democracy in America,* explicitly recognized that the American system of administration relied on nonhierarchical methods of control that manifest an invisible-hand effect in the exercise of administrative power. Modern developments in public choice theory provide another explanation for nonhierarchical patterns of organization in a public economy. Such modes of organization are consistent with the patterns of multiorganizational arrangement that one would expect to occur in a federal system of administration, in contrast to a bureaucratic system of administration.

Vincent Ostrom is a professor of political science at Indiana University, Bloomington. He served as a research fellow at the Center for Interdisciplinary Research, Bielefeld University, during 1981-82, when this article was prepared. His principal publications include The Intellectual Crisis in American Public Administration *(University of Alabama Press, 1974)* and The Political Theory of a Compound Republic *(Center for Study of Public Choice, 1971).*

MUCH of the implementation literature is based on theoretical assumptions that Congress is the authoritative decision-making body responsible for the formulation of public policy.[1] In its formulation of policy, Congress performs the basic political function of specifying the policy goal to be attained. From this perspective, the task of implementation is to create the appropriate technical and institutional means for realizing the goals specified by Congress.

The task of implementation is one of managing command structures so that policies are appropriately implemented. Hierarchical principles of bureaucratic organization are assumed to apply so that those who have administrative responsibility can maintain a sufficiently narrow span of control to assure proper performance of administrative responsibility at each level of organization. Earlier applications of the span-of-control principle were assumed to be operable only within the internal structure of administration. Since the development of the War on Poverty, increasing attention has been given to the management of intergovernmental relations.

Conceptualizing the management of intergovernmental relations has involved an extension of command principles to the structure of relationships among different units of government. Span of control, in this context, requires simplification in the structure of subordinate units of government so that rules can be uniformly applied to a manageable number of units of government. This implies both a simplification in structure to assure managerial responsibility in a hierarchy of command and a reduction in the number of units to conform to the requirements of span of control.

In *Making Federalism Work,* James L. Sundquist provides both a critique of the traditional theory of federalism and a conception of changes in government structure necessary for the management of a federal system as a single integrated system. He considers the traditional federal system to be so complex as to be unworkable. The coordination of intergovernmental and interagency relationships calls for a new management structure directed from the Executive Offices of the President, where the whole system of federal-state-local relationships can be viewed as a single structure. Ultimate responsibility for managing federal-state-local relationships will, in Sundquist's formulation, reside with the president.[2]

In Reorganization Plan 2 of 1970, creating the Office of Management and Budget, President Nixon made provision for a system of Washington-based coordinators who would serve as presidential surrogates to coordinate interagency and intergovernmental relationships throughout the country.[3] Implicit in these arrangements is the creation of a system of prefectoral

---

1. Paul A. Sabatier and Daniel A. Mazmanian, "Implementation of Public Policy: A Framework of Analysis," in *Effective Policy Implementation,* eds. D. A. Mazmanian and P. A. Sabatier (Lexington, MA: Lexington Books, 1971), pp. 3-35, provide an excellent review of implementation research with reference to both its methodological and its normative implications.

2. James L. Sundquist, *Making Federalism Work: A Study of Program Coordination at the Community Level* (Washington, DC: Brookings Institution, 1969). See especially the introductory and concluding chapters.

3. *United States Codes Congressional and Administrative Laws,* 91st Cong., 2d sess., 1970 (St. Paul, MN: West Publishing, 1971), 3:6318.

administration analogous to the French system. The French prefect is a surrogate for central authorities responsible for managing interagency relationships and local units of government within each department or province of France.

The new emphasis on managing intergovernmental relations such that the whole system of federal-state-local relations is made the subject of a command relationship entails a radical transformation of the American system of government. Sundquist quite explicitly recognizes that his proposals entail "the final burial, perhaps, of the traditional doctrines of American federalism."[4] Before such steps are irrevocably taken, it may be important to make an assessment of what is being sacrificed in the creation of command structures in the Executive Offices of the President that make the whole system of federal-state-local relationships look like a single, unified command structure subject to presidential direction and control.

In an exploration of nonhierarchical approaches to the organization of public activities, I propose first to explore Alexis de Tocqueville's comparison of the American system of administration with the French system of bureaucratic administration, with reference both to *Democracy in America* and to *The Old Regime and the French Revolution*. I shall then refer to modern developments in public choice theory that suggest the relevance of nonhierarchical modes of coordination in the operation of a modern public economy. Following these assessments, I shall conclude by drawing attention to the implications these analyses have for rethinking the theory that applies to a federal system of administration.

4. Sundquist, *Making Federalism Work*, p. 6.

TOCQUEVILLE'S CHARACTERIZATION OF NONHIERARCHICAL ORGANIZATION OF PUBLIC ACTIVITIES IN AMERICA

The potential for nonhierarchical organization of public activities is indicated by two key observations in Tocqueville's *Democracy in America:*

Nothing is more striking to a European traveler in the United States than the absence of what we call the government, or the administration. Written laws exist in America, and one sees the daily execution of them; but although everything moves regularly, the mover can nowhere be discovered. The hand that directs the social machinery is invisible.[5]

In no country in the world does the law hold so absolute a language as in America; and in no country is the right of applying it vested in so many hands. The administrative power in the United States presents nothing either centralized or hierarchical in its constitution; this accounts for its passing unperceived. The power exists, but its representative is nowhere to be seen.[6]

The conception of an invisible hand operating in a competitive market economy has been generally recognized since Adam Smith's formulation of that thesis. Its application to the public realm is a different matter. Tocqueville's formulation of an invisible-hand thesis implies that special attention needs to be given to patterns of nonhierarchical organization and how they work in the public realm. These arrangements yield conformity to law without a centralized hierarchy of command that is highly visible in its overt operations. How does such a system work?

5. Alexis de Tocqueville, *Democracy in America*, ed. Phillipes Broadly (New York: Alfred A. Knopf, 1966), p. 70.
6. Ibid.

Tocqueville views the germ of the American political system as grounded in the covenantal theology of the Puritans. This covenantal theology was not only a religious doctrine, but, as Tocqueville recognizes, it "corresponded in many points with the most democratic and republican theories."[7] Principles of congregational organization among religious communities were extended to the governance of civil communities, where the people were sovereign. Through processes of constitutional decision making, people define and establish the terms and conditions of government. These principles became "the law of the laws."[8] In this process, "the township was organized before the state and the state before the union."[9] The structure of the federal government was "in fact nothing more than a summary of those republican principles which were current in the whole community, before it existed and independently of its existence."[10] This law of the laws was constitutional principles reiterated in many different political experiments to create a system of multiple and autonomous units of government to govern diverse and overlapping communities of relationships, in which each government was bound by constitutional provisions as enforceable rules of law.

In articulating the basic principles of this political theory, Tocqueville indicated that each individual is first his own governor: "he is free and responsible to God alone, for all that concerns himself."[11] Each individual obeys the collective decisions reached by the communities of which he is a part, "because he acknowledges the utility of an association with his fellow men and he knows that no such association can exist without a regulating force."[12] The principles applicable to individual governance can be extended to different political communities in a federal system. The township is independent in all that concerns itself alone, and is subordinate to the state only in those matters that it shares in common with other townships. The same principles apply in the relationships of the state to the nation. Principles of self-government are reiterated in the government of townships, counties, states, and the nation as a whole. Each government exercises limited jurisdiction defined by charters and constitutions as civil covenants.

The system of administration contained within this structure of governance had many points of contrast to the system of centralized administration in France. In the New England town, many independently elected officials were responsible for administering the affairs of the township subject to the general authority of the town meeting and an elected board of selectmen who exercised interim authority. In Tocqueville's words, these included the following:

The assessors rated the township; the collectors receive the taxes. A constable is appointed to keep the peace, to watch the streets and to execute the laws; the town clerk records the town votes, orders and grants. The treasurer keeps the funds. The overseers of the poor perform the difficult task of carrying out the poor-laws. Committee-men are appointed to attend the

7. Ibid., p. 71.
8. Ibid., p. 31.
9. Ibid., p. 40.
10. Ibid., p. 59.
11. Ibid., p. 64.

12. Ibid.

schools and public instruction; and the surveyors of highways, who take care of the greater and lesser roads of the township, complete the list of principal functionaries. But there are other petty officials still; such as the parish committees, who audit the expenses of public worship; fire wardens, who direct the effort of citizens in case of fire; tithing-men, hog reeves, fence-viewers, timber measures and sealers of weight and measures.[13]

In such a system of administration there were "almost as many functionaries as there are functions and," as Tocqueville put it, "the executive is disseminated in a multitude of hands."[14] No single administrative center of authority existed to coordinate the efforts of this multitude of officials. Each official was independently accountable to his constituency for reelection. There was a danger that the rule of law would be eroded by the deference of each official to the expedient interests of his constituents.

Tocqueville found the resolution to this problem in the ordinary courts of law. Remedies were available to any person to use the courts to compel administrative officials to discharge their responsibilities under law and to resolve conflicts among officials when conflicts reached a point of threatening harm to others. These courts of law, as Tocqueville observed, could "compel the elected functionaries to obey, without violating the rights of the electors."[15] This relationship is generalized in the following way: "The extension of judicial power in the political world ought to be in the exact ratio of the extension of the elective powers; if these two institutions do not go hand in hand, the state falls into anarchy or into servitude."[16]

Each administrative official thus faced two different institutional constraints in addition to the general rules of law that applied to his conduct. The constraint of election required him to be sensitive to the needs of his constituents that controlled his election. The other constraint was exercised by the courts of law in response to actions initiated by any person adversely affected. Failure to fulfill the requirements of law exposed each official to personal liability for his actions, subject to appeal to higher courts. Within the bounds of these constraints, American administrative officials enjoyed substantial discretion in rendering service and exercising entrepreneurship on behalf of the community of which they were members.

Based on Tocqueville's analysis, the American system of government might be viewed as arrangements for the discharge of public trusts bearing upon the interests that diverse, overlapping communities of people share. The exercise of fiduciary relationships in such a system of public trust is based on a combination of votes and vetoes. Votes are used to commission trust relationships; vetoes are used to constrain, limit, and hold those relationships accountable to a public trust. Electoral controls, legislative controls, and judicial controls go hand in hand with substantial independent discretion on the part of administrative officials in the discharge of relationships. The whole system of relationships is bound together by a system of constitutional and ordinary law that is not formulated in a single code of law. Yet people are cognizant of the role of law in specifying and limiting trust rela-

13. Ibid., pp. 63-64.
14. Ibid., p. 81.
15. Ibid., p. 79.

16. Ibid.

tionships where each community is bound by a variable structure of legal relationships. Such circumstances give rise to the apparent paradox that, as we have already noted, struck Tocqueville: "In no country in the world does the law hold so absolute a language as in America; and in no country is the right of applying it vested in so many hands."[17]

By contrast, Tocqueville's analysis of French bureaucracy indicates contrary effects that are yielded by large-scale, highly integrated bureaucracies. A uniform code of law is applied to diverse environmental and cultural conditions. Instead of being a means of maintaining a rational legal order in society, the highly centralized system of French bureaucracy is found by Tocqueville to be characterized by rigid rules and lax enforcement.[18] A method for accommodating uniform rules to diverse circumstances is for officials in a bureaucracy to waive the rule of law. Citizens come to view law as a serious obstacle to enterprise and demand the right to have the law waived in their own circumstances. Officials are viewed as unreasonable and arbitrary when the law is waived in some cases and not in others. Law is no longer viewed as a means of maintaining stable and orderly relationships in mutually productive communities of relationships. Instead, the highly centralized system of French bureaucracy, applying a single uniform code of law, contributes to the erosion of the rule of law. Such circumstances become conducive to patterns of corruption when favorable decisions become available at the price of a bribe. Corruption in turn leads to efforts to impose more rigid rules to combat corruption. This gives rise to pathological cycles in which uniform rules are accommodated by lax enforcement, lax enforcement by corruption, corruption by more rigid rules, and more rigid rules by lax enforcement. The cycle goes on without end, interspersed with coups d'etat and revolutions in which each set of new rulers demands complete authority to root out corruption by imposing rigid controls.

PUBLIC CHOICE THEORY
AND NONHIERARCHICAL
COORDINATIONS IN A
MODERN PUBLIC ECONOMY

In the course of the last two decades an effort to apply economic reasoning to nonmarket decision making, and thus to the public sector, has arrived at general formulations consistent with Tocqueville's characterization of nonbureaucratic forms of administration, but based on quite different theoretical grounds. Tocqueville's focus was on a system of administration characteristic of New England towns. The application of economic reasoning to public-sector problems, instead, began with a theory of goods.[19]

Attributes of goods

Certain attributes of goods have long been identified as important in the formulation of classical economic market theory. Among these were exclusion, subtractibility of consumption, and unitization or measurability of goods.

17. Ibid., p. 71.
18. Alexis de Tocqueville, *The Old Regime and the French Revolution* (Garden City, NY: Doubleday, Anchor Books, 1955), pp. 61-72, 67.

19. Mancur Olson, *Logic of Collective Action* (Cambridge, MA: Harvard University Press, 1965), still represents a good initial treatment of the relationship of collective action to a theory of goods.

Exclusion was essential to market organization, in the sense that a potential user could be excluded from acquiring or using goods or services until that user had met the terms and conditions of a vendor who was prepared to supply them. Subtractibility of consumption was essential to price theory if individual choice was to prevail. A good was subtractible in consumption if use by one individual precluded its use by other individuals. Goods subject to joint use by several individuals required calculation of joint interests and were not compatible with the assumptions of price theory. Measurability was an important aspect bearing upon an exchange of units that could be substituted for one another and were subject to cardinal scales of measurement.

The shift of focus to public choice in the application of economic reasoning to nonmarket decision making implied that nonexclusion, jointness of use, and serious difficulties in applying cardinal scales of measurement had to be treated as basic attributes of goods and services associated with public economies. Early attention was variously applied to nonexclusion and jointness of use on an assumption that these would be treated on a single public-private continuum. When the different attributes or characteristics of goods are viewed as variables that apply independently to goods and services, it is possible to avoid the presumption of a single dichotomy and to move toward more extended typologies of goods and services. Where characteristics associated with exclusion and jointness of use are independently dichotomized and arranged in a two-by-two matrix, a typology of goods can be conceptualized as indicated in Figure 1.

Where exclusion is feasible some form of pricing is possible, even where jointness of use occurs. Thus pricing mechanisms can be applied to the use of many public facilities such as toll roads, bridges, public theaters, museums, and so on. Where exclusion fails, or is too costly to attain, market arrangements of the traditional type, that apply to individuals as potential buyers of goods and services, are no longer feasible, and some form of nonmarket or collective organization must be introduced. Individuals have no incentive to pay for that which is freely available. Taxes become a substitute for prices to assure that each person contributes a proportionate share to the cost of procuring a public good or service and foreclose the holdout problem.

Where jointness of use occurs, problems exist in regulating use among the community of users. Conduct appropriate for an audience at a rock-and-roll concert for example, may be quite inappropriate for the audience at a symphony concert. The capacity of a proprietor to exclude individuals who do not conform to acceptable standards of propriety may be sufficient to allow for the operation of private theaters; but problems in regulating patterns of use in other publicly used facilities, such as roads and highways, may require closer forms of surveillance in the exercise of public powers.

Common-pool resources are characterized by circumstances in which exclusion is infeasible but use of the resources is subtractible. These circumstances typically apply to water supplies, fisheries, oil pools, and so on. The capture of any one fish in a fishery precludes its capture by anyone else. The failure of exclusion implies that market arrangements are infeasible, and that the use of such resources is potentially subject to a holdout strategy that can eventuate in a

FIGURE 1
ATTRIBUTES OF GOODS

| | Jointness of Use or Consumption ||
	Separable Use	Joint Use
Exclusion — Feasible	Private Goods: bread, milk, automobiles, haircuts	Toll Goods: theaters, nightclubs, electric power, cable TV, telephone service, toll roads, toll bridges
Exclusion — Infeasible	Common-Pool Resources: oil extracted from an oil pool, fish taken from an ocean, water from a ground water basin	Public Goods: peace and security of a community, national defense, mosquito abatement, air pollution control, weather forecasts, common markets

SOURCE: Adapted from Vincent Ostrom and Elinor Ostrom, "Public Goods and Public Choice," in *Alternatives for Delivering Public Services: Toward Improved Performance*, ed. E. S. Savas (Boulder, CO: Westview Press, 1977), p. 12.

tragedy of the commons, unless appropriate institutional arrangements can be devised to gain joint management of the resource on behalf of the community of users.[20]

The public-goods case can be conceptualized as those circumstances in which both jointness of use and the failure of exclusion occur. Additional problems also arise as difficulties in attaining measurability of goods are considered. Direct measurement in like units of output is usually not feasible, although the development of qualitative measures is frequently possible.

If primary attention is given to the key defining characteristics of jointness of use and the failure of exclusion, it becomes apparent that these characteristics pertain primarily to organizing the consumption aspects of a public economy. Public powers of taxation are essential to foreclosing the holdout problem. Once payment of taxes is coerced by establishing penalties for nonpayment of taxes, alternative institutions such as elections become necessary for signaling demand; and institutions such as representation and rules for taking collective action become necessary to making decisions about the quantity and/or quality of a good or service to be supplied. Such decisions are equivalent to performing basic household functions in a public economy and apply to the collective organization of consumption functions in the public sector.[21]

20. Garret Hardin, "The Tragedy of the Commons," *Science*, 162:1243-48 (Dec. 1968), supplies a basic statement of the tragedy-of-the-commons argument regarding common-pool resources. Problems involved in developing common-pool resources are treated in Garret Hardin and John Baden, eds., *Managing the Commons* (San Francisco: W. H. Freeman, 1977).

21. It is interesting to observe that the German word *Haushalt* is used to refer both to a household

Once these collective consumption functions are competently organized, the choice of how to procure the supply of such goods or services can be made from a wide array of possibilities. A collectivity might, for example, organize its own production unit in which it would directly employ persons to assume responsibility for aggregating the factors of production and supply the services to the relevant community of people. Or, as an alternative, it might contract with a private vendor, a voluntary nonprofit association, or another public agency to supply to good or service. Or it might rely on a combination of those methods: use its own staff to supply some portion of a bundle of services, and contract with private vendors, nonprofit voluntary associations, or other government agencies for other portions of the service.

Contracting for services

The tradition of contracting for services by local units of government functioning as associations of consumers is a long-standing one. Contracting for public services occurred extensively in eighteenth-century England, as reported by Sidney and Beatrice Webb:

Up and down the country, in every conceivable service, the easiest way of getting done any continuous duty, seemed to be to "farm" it out, or put it out to contract to the man who offered the most advantageous terms. ... The stretch of highway could be repaired and kept in order by a contractor. The troublesome accumulation of garbage could be kept down by getting someone to contract for its removal, with no more demand on the time or labour of the unpaid official than the periodical payment of the "farmer's" account. The rows on rows of street lamps, which took the place of the swinging lanterns of the individual householder, could be made and fixed by contract, cleaned by contract and lit by contract. The collection of the public revenue could equally be "farmed"; and tolls and dues, from parish pounds and manorial cornmills up to municipal markets and turnpike roads, could be made the basis of contractural payments, leaving the contractor to incur all the labour and risk which would otherwise have fallen on the Local Authority or its gratuitously serving officers.[22]

The Webbs further report that the local associations and local government authorities contracting for service were stimulated by the following motive: "All they were concerned with ... was 'buying in the cheapest market', and getting the works done at the lowest possible monetary cost to the constituency that they taxed."[23]

Contracting for services under those circumstances has radical implications for using nonhierarchical principles of organization in a public economy. First, contracting for services implies that quasi-market conditions can exist in a public economy so long as the essential consumption functions are collectively organized. The market is not between vendors and individual users of public goods and services, but between vendors and collectivities functioning as associations of consumers. Under the quasi-market conditions of contracting for services, an association of consumers will confront the tasks of specify-

---

and to the public budget, implying conceptual similarities between consumption functions performed by households and collective expenditure decisions.

22. Sidney Webb and Beatrice Webb, *The Development of English Local Government, 1689-1835* (London: Oxford University Press, 1963), p. 114.

23. Ibid., p. 131.

ing the quantity or quality of service to be supplied, and monitoring the performance of the vendor in relation to its community of users. The collectivity will function like a consumer cooperative in which the executive staff operates more as a purchasing agent than as a producer of goods and services.

Second, contracting for services implies that a public economy will include a variety of associations and units of government that operate as collective consumption units, and a wide variety of private enterprises, voluntary nonprofit associations, and governmental agencies functioning as producers of public goods and services. The idea that a single unit of government will be responsible for supplying all different public services is no longer appropriate. Rather, a multiplicity of different types of organizations may concurrently serve any one community of users.

A proper understanding of the functional relationships involved will require analysts to think in terms of systems of interorganizational relationships, where the supply of any particular bundle of public goods and services will involve the joint activities of several collaborating agencies. As in the private sector, we can contemplate the organization of a public economy with a variety of public-service industries in which each industry may be composed of a large number of cooperative associations, units of government, private for-profit firms, private nonprofit associations, and government agencies.[24] We might further contemplate that the structure of particular public service industries might, in an extreme case, include a highly monopolized industry with only a single instrumentality responsible for organizing all consumption and production functions. Still other industries might include a large number of different types of agencies of varying sizes and functions. We would expect principles of bureaucratic organization to dominate only in the more highly monopolized public-service industries.

Third, contracting for services implies that coordination among the large number of diverse agencies and organizations in a public economy will occur through collateral coordination under mutually agreeable terms and conditions worked out by autonomous decision-making units, rather than through reliance on systematic patterns of dominance and subordination. Contractual arrangements are meaningful only where instrumentalities are independent or autonomous, capable of saying no, maintaining an arm's-length relationship when necessary, and undertaking cooperative arrangements when mutual advantage can be gained.

Where alternative options are available both among the potential vendors and among collective consumption units, patterns of cooperation occur within the constraint that other potential service arrangements are viable. The bargaining power of any one unit is constrained by the availability of other units to perform a like service. It is this condition that binds collaborative arrangements by the constraint of competitive options. If, as the Webbs report, it is possible for an equivalent service to be procured at a lower price, there are incentives to search out the vendor offering a lower price and realize a sav-

24. Vincent Ostrom and Elinor Ostrom, "A Behavioral Approach to the Study of Intergovernmental Relations," *The Annals* of the American Academy of Political and Social Science, 359:137-46 (May 1965).

ings for the constituency being taxed. Competitive rivalry creates the potential for driving the price for a service toward the true cost of rendering any particular service and for improving efficiency in organizing the supply of services among competing producers.

Fourth, contracting for public services implies that diverse size economies are more likely to be realized where different instrumentalities are available on both the consumption and production sides of economic relationships.[25] Economies of scale in producing different public goods and services are likely to vary among different types of services. Economies of scale in the production of elementary education, for example, are exhausted at a relatively small scale, while water supply under conditions of limited resources may involve much larger economies of scale. Similarly, the scale of the benefiting community of users may vary greatly among different types of services. Where diverse agencies exist, there is a greater likelihood of realizing a better match among diverse size economies and suffering fewer diseconomies.

Fifth, contracting for services implies that there are incentives to garner information about the costs and performance characteristics associated with different bundles of public goods and services under conditions in which costs and performance characteristics can be compared across different types of service agencies. In highly bureaucratic structures, by contrast, incentives exist to remove fixed costs from operating budgets and accounts. As a result, such factors as contributions to pension funds, expenditures for space and buildings, and payments in lieu of taxes are likely not to be taken into account in cost calculations. Where service is available among competing vendors, such factors begin to enter more consciously into cost calculations.

In turn, the performance achieved by the more efficient producers becomes the standard for measuring the performance of other agencies. Under those circumstances, the more efficient service instrumentalities begin to serve as yardsticks for measuring the performance of other service instrumentalities. This concept was first introduced in using the performance of publicly owned electrical utilities as a yardstick for assessing the performance of privately owned profitable utility companies. This pattern can also be reversed, using private vendors as a yardstick for assessing the performance of public agencies in any given public-service industry, such as the collection and disposal of solid waste.

Better cost accounting and performance evaluation, in turn, permit more explicit use of service charges and user taxes for the service being rendered. The introduction of user fees and user taxes creates incentives on the part of service users to take better account of the value of a service and to avoid the waste of scarce resources. All of those factors increase a sense of reality about cost calculations and performance characteristics in a public economy, and reduce the amount of fiscal illusion.

These characteristics of a public economy, organized on the basis of units of government viewed as associations of consumers capable of contracting for public services, imply structural

25. Vincent Ostrom and Elinor Ostrom, "Public Goods and Public Choices," in *Alternatives for Delivering Public Services: Toward Improved Performance,* ed. E. S. Savas (Boulder, CO: Westview Press, 1977), pp. 35-36.

characteristics and operating principles quite different from those that occur in a public economy organized by principles of bureaucratic organization. A critical problem arises in such a system of relationships when incentives for cooperation are insufficient to forestall serious problems of conflict. As a result, such a system of administration requires that serious attention be given to institutional arrangements that are capable of processing conflict and searching out resolutions under mutually agreeable terms and conditions. Principles of equity jurisprudence, where a master in equity is charged with the task of finding an equitable solution in accordance with the rules of equity, offer prospects for performing such functions of conflict resolution without having recourse to principles of bureaucratic organization. Such institutions are essential in a public economy organized on nonhierarchical principles, if externalities and the costs of potentially escalating conflicts are to be properly constrained.

Under those circumstances, public economies can be organized that rely extensively on nonhierarchical principles of organization. Each community can be constituted as a self-governing community in which principles of bureaucratic organization need apply only to those functions for which it relies exclusively on its own staff. Contracting and the development of mutual aid arrangements are the means of coordinating operations among equals rather than among superiors and subordinates. Intergovernmental arrangements in a federal system do not require the hierarchical management of subordinates through a system of bureaucratic domination. Law can still be made operable through ordinary courts of law. Conflicts of law can be resolved through processes of adjudication rather than by determination of the executive. The structure of countervailing vetoes in systems of checks and balances means that the exercise of authority is a fiduciary relationship in which the public trust is accountable to different judicial, legislative, executive, and political remedies. Law and principles of justice prevail because the right of applying them is broadly shared in society. The state is not external to society, ruling over society; but principles of self-government are reiterated to apply to many diverse and overlapping communities of interest. This is why Tocqueville advanced the thesis of the invisible hand as applying to organization of government in American society.

CONCLUSION

The dominant diagnosis of government failure in the twentieth century has attributed it to fragmentation of authority and to overlapping jurisdiction. Fragmentation of authority is assumed to confuse political responsibility in a democratic society. Political responsibility can be clearly identified, it is argued, only if there is one ultimate center of authority for all matters of government. Overlapping jurisdictions are assumed to be an evil because they imply duplication of services, and duplication of services implies waste and inefficiency in government.

So long as one accepts this mode of reasoning, the conclusions reached are intuitively obvious. But important advances in human knowledge often involve the conceptualization of counterintuitive relationships. It is intuitively obvious, for example, that the sun rises in the east, moves across the sky, and sets in the west. The Copernican revolution was based on a counterintuitive conceptualization of planetary movements in the solar system. So in the realm of politics, we must be prepared to consider counterintuitive explanations of political relationships.

The elimination of fragmentation of authority would imply the creation of a sovereign authority as the locus of an ultimate authority in society that can coerce others to obey its decisions but cannot itself be coerced by others in the society. The distinctive feature in the design of the American constitutional system was the establishment of a system of constitutional law that applied to the conduct of those who exercised governmental authority. This is why all assignments of authority in the American constitutional system were subject to limits. Specifying limits implies the potential exercise of veto capabilities, with authority both divided and shared among different decision structures. The elimination of fragmentation of authority implies the removal of limits on authority and the exercise of unlimited authority on the part of a single sovereign. The device of popular election may not be sufficient to hold governments accountable. Madison argued that auxiliary precautions were necessary. Those issues can be judged only with a fuller elaboration of theoretical arguments that appropriately specify the implications of different structures on the maintenance of political responsibility.

Overlapping jurisdictions are necessarily entailed in a federal system of government. The elimination of all overlapping jurisdictions would necessarily mean the elimination of federal arrangements. Systems of administration in a highly federalized system of government must necessarily rely on nonhierarchical modes of coordination among the diverse units of government. Federal structures imply that systems of administration must necessarily entail multiorganizational structures of relationships.

Woodrow Wilson argued that a basic pattern of bureaucratic administration, exemplified by French and Prussian administration, applies to all governments alike; but this is not a plausible thesis for highly federalized systems of government.[26] Tocqueville's recognition that the American system of administration was governed by principles different from those of the French system of bureaucratic administration provides a better point of departure for conceptualizing the principles of federal administration. The task of elaborating a federal theory of public administration will require much more extensive reliance on nonhierarchical forms of coordination in multiorganizational structures of relationships.

As Europe confronts the task of fashioning a European system of administration with reference to the European community, it will also be confronted with the task of exploring nonhierarchical modes of coordination and organization. Patterns of bureaucratic administration served a historical function in the fashioning of nation states; but new principles of administration are required as human societies have reference to the governance of diverse and autonomous communities of interest.

26. Woodrow Wilson, "The Study of Administration," *Political Science Quarterly*, 2:197-220, 202, 204-5 (June 1887).

Changing Public-Private Sector Relations: A Look at the United States

By BRUCE L.R. SMITH

ABSTRACT: One of the distinctive elements that accounts for the dynamism and innovative capacity of America's political institutions is the use of private organizations to accomplish public purposes. The nation has found it useful to contract out for services when bureaucratic obstacles thwart new policy objectives. Yet in recent years the country has seemed to lack exactly the qualities of dynamism, vitality, and innovative capacity in the public sector, in business, and in the voluntary sector that we have most cherished. The blame for this, in the view of some observers, rests with the blurring of the boundaries between public and private sectors that has characterized the postwar period. This article explores the paradoxical shift in attitudes on public-private sector relations against the background of contemporary ideological trends. The arguments for either a massive shifting of functions to private contractors or for the federal government to reabsorb major activities now carried out by contractors are equally unconvincing. The problem is to make the present system of shared responsibility among government, business, and the voluntary sector work more effectively, not to experiment with ideological solutions that would rearrange the nation's political and institutional landscapes.

Bruce L.R. Smith is a senior staff member, Advanced Study Program, the Brookings Institution. He received his Ph.D. in government from Harvard in 1964. After two years with the Rand Corporation, he taught for 13 years in the Department of Public Law and Government at Columbia. Before joining Brookings, he came to Washington, D.C., to serve as director, Policy Assessment Staff, Bureau of Oceans, International Environmental and Scientific Affairs, U.S. Department of State. He has consulted widely for state, local, and national government and international agencies, in the areas of public administration, science and technology policy, and business-government relations. His major publications include The Rand Corporation *(1966),* The Dilemma of Accountability in Modern Government *(ed. with D. C. Hague, 1971),* The Politics of School Decentralization *(with G. R. LaNoue, 1973),* The New Political Economy *(ed., 1975),* The State of Academic Science *(with J. Karlesky, 1977), and* Improving the Accountability and Performance of Government *(ed. with J. D. Carroll, 1982).*

A distinctive feature explaining the dynamism and innovative capacity of American political institutions is the use of private organizations to accomplish public purposes. The nation has found it useful to contract out for services when bureaucratic obstacles thwart the objectives of new programs. The rationales for resorting to novel public-private arrangements include the desire to set up programs rapidly, and hence to use an existing private institution rather than to create new government capacities; the ability to circumvent civil-service pay limitations or personnel ceilings; the avoidance of rigidities in working environment that interfere with the performance of a complex technological task; the relative ease of disbanding a nongovernment organization or terminating a temporary contractual relationship when the service is no longer needed; and other advantages.

America is constantly inventing itself, and the capacity to invent new ways of accomplishing the public's business has been a great strength. But in recent years something has seemed to go wrong. The country has seemed to lack exactly the qualities we most cherished—dynamism, vitality, innovative capacity—in government, in business, and in the voluntary sector. The links between government and the private sector, instead of fostering change and creative responses to problems, are now blamed for the malaise that afflicts the nation. This paradox is the theme of this article. The aim is to analyze the shift in attitudes on public-private sector relations and to do so against the background of contemporary ideological trends. To accomplish this task, we need to see the problem in its larger historical and political context.

THE PUBLIC-PRIVATE DISTINCTION AND AMERICAN CONSTITUTIONALISM

The distinction between the public and the private sectors is a central feature of American thought and practice in the art of self-government. The concept of the private sector is linked to the idea of limited government. Constitutional government exists because there is a sphere of human action not subject to public control, a domain of individual liberties and self-expression protected against infringement by the state. The energy in our society comes from the private sector, and government must not stifle the creative impulses of free citizens. The idea blends with other elements—checks and balances within the formal structure of government, an economy propelled by the dynamic forces of the marketplace, an active role for private philanthropy—to form a set of ideas that can be loosely identified as the American creed.[1]

Strains and contradictions, of course, have always existed in the nation's political thought. Disputes over bigness in government and/or in industry, over the boundaries of national and state power, over the institutional roles of the different branches of government, over the meaning of state action, and numerous other issues have been continuing features of the American constitutional scene. There is no static set of beliefs that never changes. The balances to be struck among conflicting values within the political tradition have shifted at different times in the nation's history. New concerns have sharply modified the

1. Samuel P. Huntington, "Paradigms of American Politics: Beyond the One, the Two, and the Many," *Political Science Quarterly*, 89(1):1-26 (Mar. 1974).

meaning of central myths. Special circumstances—the Western frontier, the abundance enjoyed by a people of plenty, the timely appearance of a foreign enemy—have played a part in blunting challenges to traditional ideas and practices. The dexterous qualities of political leadership have also served to harmonize clashing group interests and to help preserve the appearance and the substance of national unity in times of rapid change.

AN END TO CONSENSUS?

Yet for all the turbulence and seeming disorder in national affairs, a dominant ideology has seemed to shape American attitudes toward authority. During much of the nation's history, the influence of a central core of belief can be clearly traced in the institutions of government and in the policymaking process. The major result of the ideology, deriving from the political philosophy of Locke and Montesquieu, and from the tradition of British dissent, has been to create a truncated kind of politics without extremes. European-style socialism, the large public sector and the welfare-state traditions of Europe, the centralization of power and control of the national economy sought by many Third World nations—in short, extremes of any kind—are simply ruled out and, indeed, are beyond the ken of many Americans.[2] The complaint of critics was that too narrow an adherence to the established creed frustrates public debate, obstructs needed change and the solution of practical problems, and prevents Americans from understanding the rest of the world. Other nations simply do not adhere to the notions of limited government inherent in traditional liberalism. A nation suffering from an insufficient statehood and frozen in time, according to critics, has been the consequence of the dominance of the American creed of limited government.

But there are admirers as well. Those who defend the distinctive American tradition extol the virtues of the absence of extremism in public debate, the generally moderate character of American politics, the consensus on values, and the respect for the rights of the private individual. For many observers, it is absurd to think of an excess of stability in governmental institutions. How can there be too much stability, restraint, and moderation, given the nature of human beings in society and the destructive impulses of the human soul? If our relatively moderate politics continues to set the United States apart from other nations, so much the better for us and the worse for others. While critics deplored and admirers rhapsodized over the American tradition, they seemed to agree that a distinctive philosophy of limited government existed and that it had powerfully influenced the nation's political and constitutional framework. For much of the nation's history, this picture of reality seemed serviceable enough, providing a recognizable grasp of events even to ideological opponents and marking off the main lines of public debate.

All of this has now drastically changed. The American consensus has been stretched beyond recognition by the tugs and pulls of an emerging ideological style of politics. Sharpening

---

2. Louis Hartz, *The Liberal Tradition in America* (New York: Harcourt Brace Jovanovich, 1962); Bernard Bailyn, *The Ideological Origins of the American Revolution* (Cambridge, MA: Harvard University Press, 1967); James Young, *The Washington Community* (New York: Columbia University Press, 1966).

ideological conflicts have appeared within the political parties, in the attitudes of the wider attentive public, and in the general electorate.[3] American politics, if once thought to be frozen into too narrow a range of policy debate, now seems to have an agenda of vast scope. The framework of debate has been not simplified, but vastly complicated, by the value cleavages that cut in strange ways through the political landscape. Strong advocates of the return of functions to the private sector, for example, at times insist that intimate family matters, such as birth control, abortion, prayers in school, and other areas once considered to be private in character, should be subject to stringent public control.

The federal establishment, once small in size and marginal in its impact, has become a significant factor in the nation's economic life. By 1980, the regular federal budget reached $700 billion, credit authorizations grew to $175 billion, and guaranteed loans were $225 million—exceeding $1 trillion when considered together.[4] The federal budget alone, without considering off-budget items or state and local government expenditures, constituted 21 percent of the gross national product at the start of President Ronald Reagan's term of office.

America has become a "reluctant welfare state."[5] That is, expenditures for welfare and other social services grew sharply, but without a large-scale, centralized bureaucracy to administer the programs. Voluntary associations and state and local governments have played an important part in the evolving administrative system. Americans have sought a high-service society while preserving the appearance of a limited government role. Private institutions in the process have grown increasingly dependent on public funds, a trend affecting universities, cultural institutions, health and human service organizations, neighborhood associations, and a wide variety of other voluntary entities.

The blurring of lines between the public and the private sectors—by now a common theme in the public administration literature—has involved both the for-profit and the not-for-profit private sectors.[6] Government's involve-

---

3. Nelson W. Polsby, "Contemporary Transformations of American Politics: Thoughts on the Research Agendas of Political Scientists," *Political Science Quarterly*, 96(4):551-70 (Winter 1981-82); E. C. Ladd and C. D. Hadley, *Transformations of the American Party System: Political Coalitions from the New Deal to the 1970's* (New York: W. W. Norton, 1975); R. Rubin, *Party Dynamics: The Democratic Coalition and the Politics of Change* (New York: Oxford University Press, 1976); W. P. Shively, "The Development of Party Identification Among Adults: Exploration of a Functional Model," *American Political Science Review*, 73(4):1039-54 (Dec. 1979); P. E. Converse and G. B. Markus, "Plus ca Change: The New CPS Election Study Panel," *American Political Science Review*, 73(1):32-49 (Mar. 1979).

4. Elmer B. Staats, "Governmental Performance in Perspective: Achievements and Challenges," in *Improving the Accountability and Performance of Government*, eds. Bruce L.R. Smith and James D. Carroll (Washington, DC: Brookings Institution, 1982), pp. 19-34.

5. Harold L. Wilensky and Charles N. Lebeaux, *Industrial Society and Social Welfare* (New York: Free Press, 1965), p. xiv; Harold L. Wilensky, *The Welfare State and Equality: Structural and Ideological Roots of Public Expenditures* (Berkeley: University of California Press, 1975).

6. Don K. Price, *Government and Science, Their Dynamic Relation in American Democracy* (New York: New York University Press, 1954); J. Stefan Dupré and Sanford A. Lakoff, *Science and the Nation, Policy and Politics* (Englewood

ment at times reverses traditional roles of risk taking, entrepreneurship, and innovation in American society. The government agency, through the device of the administrative contact, assumes a major share of the risks of a complex undertaking, provides the venture capital, and even acts as the consumer of the goods or services produced. Many charitable organizations have taken on growing public responsibilities, in the process broadening their range of services but acquiring some of the bureaucratic disabilities that afflict the formal government.

The web of administrative relationships thus created in various policy areas has become deeply embroiled in political controversy. The productivity of American industry, many believe, has fallen because businesspeople have gotten used to government handouts and have lost the true spirit of entrepreneurship. The solution, in their view, is for government to get out of the economy, as planner, regulator, financier, or whatever—except, of course, in defense—and to let the energies of the marketplace lift the nation to a new level of prosperity. Similarly, officials of leading private universities several years ago began to wonder what had gone wrong in the partnership with government when funds for the support of research appeared to bring unwarranted intrusions into hiring policies, admission of students, and other jealously guarded internal management preroga-

tives. A Jewish or a Lutheran nursing home, long accustomed to serving a special clientele, could come into conflict with federal mandates against discrimination once Medicare funds became a source of support. From the government's side, doubts also arose about the wisdom and propriety of administrative procedures that parceled out authority to private parties without clear management controls and guarantees that public purposes would be fully served.

The confusion over public and private responsibilities lies at the heart of the ideological disarray and the feelings of breakdown in the contemporary political scene. What are the new rules of the game if there no longer are clear lines of demarcation between what is properly a public function and what is private? Are there any limits to the authority of government if it can reach into the inner workings of the economy, the policies of private organizations, and intimate family matters? By creating intricate new administrative arrangements, have we bogged the governing system down in ever deeper layers of bureaucracy? How did we reach the present state of affairs, and can any sense be made of recent developments as a guide to future action? There are times in the life of a nation when it must define itself anew in some fundamental sense. We seem to have reached such a point. Even hardheaded realists with little taste for theory and slight regard for the virtues of consistency in political action seem troubled by the absence of a "public philosophy" and yearn for some measure of coherence in events. Participants as well as observers apparently feel the need for a restatement of fundamental principles, a crisper vision of our larger social purposes and of the appropriate mechanisms of collective action.

Cliffs, NJ: Prentice-Hall, 1962); Bruce L.R. Smith and Douglas C. Hague, eds., *The Dilemma of Accountability in Modern Government: Independence vs. Control* (New York: St. Martin's Press, 1971); Lester M. Salamon, "Rethinking Public Administration: Third Party Government and the Changing Forms of Government Action," *Public Policy,* 29(3):255-75 (Summer 1981).

THE AMBIVALENT LEGACY OF THE NEW DEAL

The New Deal era is particularly relevant for helping us to understand the present state of affairs. The New Deal is notable, first of all, for the constitutional revolution that opened the way for an enormous expansion of national power. The power to tax and spend for the general welfare, the demise of substantive due process and the expansion of governmental authority under the commerce clause, and the elimination of the constitutional no man's land between federal and state power are among the dramatic developments that transformed the role of government in American society. No longer was there only a narrow and closed category of private interests that were subject to government regulation. The authority of government could now reach to nearly any part of the economy. The Supreme Court no longer saw itself as having the duty, under the Constitution, to protect the substantive liberties of private corporate persons.

These constitutional battles of yesteryear now seem to have gathered a layer of dust, like old photo albums in the attic. Nostalgia comes easier than hard analysis of the remarkable changes wrought in our constitutional system. But the New Deal era marked a milestone in the evolution toward a constitution of powers rather than a constitution of rights. The system of checks and balances within the federal government was altered so that the "popular" branches were largely free to combat the nation's economic ills without judicial curbs. One check in the system of checks and balances, in other words, was removed. In theory, this would permit more vigorous, speedy, and far-reaching remedial action by government in times of national economic emergency.

The Republicans in Congress, for their part, saw the Supreme Court's retreat from a major role in guiding the nation's economic destiny as a threat to constitutional balance, to fundamental liberties, and to their own political interests. Their answer was to launch the drive, which eventually culminated in the Administrative Procedures Act of 1946, to impose procedural restraints on the vast bureaucracy created by the New Deal. The intention was to curb the potential abuses of governmental power. The result was, in fact, an unsatisfactory judicialization of administrative action. Thus the procedural regularities that were a substitute for constitutional adjudication in limiting arbitrary governmental power played a part later in imposing bureaucratic rigidities on the private sector and in preventing the easy, informal, and nonadversarial relationship between government and business that has evolved in other Western nations.

The federal establishment took shape during the New Deal, acquiring virtually its present size in civilian employment by 1940, its major institutional features, and its operating character. The growth that has occurred since the New Deal has been not in the size of the federal establishment itself, but rather in the vast increase in federal outlays for transfer payments, grants to state and local government, to private-sector contractors, and in the remaining penumbra of the formal government. This development is not a departure from the New Deal tradition; it is a reflection of and a logical outcome of the New Deal's administrative style. FDR, suspicious of the existing old-line bureaucracy, was easily persuaded that new agencies, government corporations, off-budget approaches, and other arrangements to circumvent the regular bureaucracy wherever possible were the answer to the nation's pressing problems.

These arrangements were gradually brought into coherent working relations with the rest of the executive establishment—the Government Corporation Control Act of 1945 was a notable step in that process—but a pluralist, loose structure of government lacking a clear center of gravity was already institutionalized by the late 1930s. The growth of America's government, in short, did not take place along the lines of centralized, hierarchical bureaucracies as described in the classic writing of Max Weber. Innovation, experimentation, and responsiveness to change were present in abundant measure. The problems came later, in sorting out the tangled lines of authority, focusing energies too often dissipated in contradictory policy initiatives, and sustaining attention long enough to get something accomplished. The New Deal was able to implement governmental change in the short run; the era was a success story for the goals of responsiveness to change and marshaling energies quickly for important public purposes. But the government was, in a sense, too responsive. Every quiver in the body politic led to a new initiative. The major problems lay in relating myriad small changes to each other, sustaining initiatives so that they did not fizzle out in futility, and orchestrating the creative energies unleashed within the executive establishment by the transition from an eighteenth-century to a modern state.

The one source of central direction was the president. But FDR did not rate presidential management among his highest priorities. His administrative style encouraged conflicts among subordinates, overlapping responsibilities, and lack of clear jurisdictional lines. This approach served his short-run interests but also fostered freewheeling policy entrepreneurship and the growth of multiple centers of power within the bureaucracy. The growth of the institutionalized presidency, with strong staff support for the chief executive, came late and was not adequate to serve the needs of the office. The pattern of a president struggling, with inadequate supporting resources, to impose his will on the executive branch through guile, agility, and improvisation was established.

The president's problems in dealing with the executive agencies help to define, and of course are defined by, the pattern of executive-legislative relations. FDR did not present himself to the Congress as manager of the executive branch, partly because the Congress would not allow it, having already staked out large chunks of executive territory as its own and aspiring to a still larger role in the internal affairs of departments, but also partly because he did not wish to. He dealt with congressional leaders, much as he did with his own administration, through cajolery, temporary coalitions, and adroit compromise in response to the points of greatest pressure and on the issues he cared most about at the time. He did not set the legislative agenda, except for a brief period, and he did not see it as a routine responsibility of the office to act as leader of his party in the Congress or to present on a regular basis comprehensive programs for the Congress to review.

While the New Deal thus witnessed the emergence of modern government, it was a government at cross-purposes with itself, lacking a strong center of gravity and not capable of charting a clear policy course. There were many policy initiatives carried forward, but they lacked cohesion. The machinery of government was untidy, and the integrative forces in the whole system were weak. Partial interests, united into alliances of congressional committees, executive bureaus, and the private constituencies benefiting from the programs were stronger than general interests. The resulting fragmentation of authority, later to be deplored as "interest group liberalism," became incorporated into the American version of the welfare state.[7]

THE POSTWAR ERA AND ATTACKS ON THE MIXED PUBLIC-PRIVATE ECONOMY

The coming of World War II—the last of our wars to have had beneficial effects on the nation's economy—lifted the country out of the economic stagnation of the 1930s, which had deepened once again toward the end of the decade. The war swept the nation to an unprecedented prosperity, and the prosperity did much to foster the illusion that the New Deal, Keynesian economics, and governmental policies had "solved" the problem of prosperity.[8] In the postwar era, American leadership and enterprise dominated the reconstruction of the world economy. For a time things went our way. The dollar was stong, American products penetrated everywhere, and in the great expansion of trade that brought decades of prosperity to the world it seemed natural that the problems of the thirties were ancient history.

The reality was different. For a generation we were able to enjoy a free ride because of our dominant postwar position. U.S. industry's leading role in world markets contributed to domestic prosperity, but also delayed the necessity of facing hard choices. How could one argue with a winning combination? American industry produced the economic growth that permitted the expansion of government programs, growing support for the voluntary sector, and investment in the new technologies that would guarantee continued growth. The mixed system of public- and private-sector initiatives seemed to be working well and could hardly have major flaws.

The first signs of serious disaffection with the prevailing mood began to appear with the failures of macroeconomic policy in the late 1960s. Inflation set off by the Vietnam war shook the confidence of many Americans and threatened the economic security prevailing since the war. Small postwar downturns in the business cycle had caused problems, but nothing of the magnitude of the stagflation that bought widespread doubts about the nation's future. Meanwhile the rates of increase in the productivity of American manufacturing, for the first time, showed declines.[9] Competition from Japan and Europe, in both domestic and foreign

---

7. Theodore J. Lowi, *The End of Liberalism: Ideology, Policy, and the Crisis of Public Authority* (New York: W. W. Norton, 1969), p. 46.

8. The high point of our self-confidence was perhaps reached when fine tuning of the economy was a popular concept. See Walter Heller, *New Dimensions of Political Economy* (Cambridge, MA: Harvard University Press, 1966).

9. Edward F. Denison, *Accounting for Slower Economic Growth: The United States in the 1970's* (Washington, DC: Brookings Institution, 1979).

markets, was by now a reality. The oil shocks in 1973-74 and 1978-79 aggravated the adverse economic trends and contributed to the slump affecting the world economy.

The most powerful political force growing out of these developments was a strong, ideologically oriented conservative movement. The difference between the new movements and traditional conservatism lay in the strength and coherence of their ideological approach to issues. Particular anger was directed against the mixed public-private sector as a kind of Trojan horse for socialism, notably in the United States but also in Britain, Canada, and Australia. One of the early actions of the Thatcher government in Britain, for example, was to launch an investigation of quangos—quasi-nongovernmental organizations—which were considered to be more dangerous than outright socialist measures.[10] The quangos were disguised and hidden ways, the critics believed, to shackle the economy and to burden society with welfare arrangements, and were difficult to recognize for what they were until it was too late. In all three countries the critics attacked, with varying intensity, arrangements that blended public and private functions, and they sought to reestablish clear boundaries between the traditional sectors.

But it was not an ideological minority alone that mounted a challenge to the quangos and to the mixed public-private economy. No minority, however determined, can achieve power or impose its will on policy in the Western democracies without appealing to the broad base of moderate opinion. In America, the conservative critics who attacked the welfare state had company. Many moderates, as the economic hard times came in the 1970s, felt that the size of government was partly to blame—big government, handouts, large deficits, high taxes, inflation, and unemployment all seemed to be tied together. There was a feeling even among people who did not fully share the conservative viewpoint that things had somehow gone too far. The answer lay in the scaling down of commitments, the elimination of new ventures, and the retreat from recent social experimentation. Many people who would not support drastic cuts in public services, or repeal of the most important health and welfare programs, at least wanted marginal changes to reduce costs and prevent the growth of additional programs. New services, recent program innovations, and novel institutional arrangements were especially vulnerable in this climate.

A specific grievance of profit-making companies, which became more insistent as the economic slump deepened, was that governmental funds flowing to nonprofit institutions amounted to unfair competition. Business could provide better services and people would be willing to pay for them if it were not for the low cost or even free services provided by nonprofit institutions with public support. These institutions developed their own constituencies, which resisted changes in programs and proved to be harder to dismantle than traditional bureaucracies because they were not prohibited from direct political activity, as were civil servants.

As nonprofit organizations began to increase their own user fees in the face of

---

10. *Report on Non-Departmental Public Bodies,* CMND 7977 (London: Her Majesty's Stationery Office, Jan. 1980).

rising costs and declining support, the argument that the not-for-profit sector provides distinctive charitable service needing public support began to weaken in health, nursing homes, transportation, and other service areas. Competition became the rallying cry, and proprietary institutions made some notable inroads in some areas in which traditional public agencies and voluntary institutions were once the predominant providers.

The gains made by the profit-making sector were in some cases at the expense of nonprofit institutions. In other cases the competition was directed mainly against traditional government agencies. This competition is reflected both in private entry into previous monopoly markets—for example, Federal Express and electronic mail—and in private companies seeking to perform services on contract for a unit of government—for example, municipal garbage disposal. In this latter case the private firm seeks to reprivatize, but with the government still as the customer.

Public employees have increasingly joined the camp of the critics as well. The stringent circumstances that stimulated profit-making firms to call for competition in service delivery also encouraged career officials to be more wary about contracting. It is easy to welcome contract arrangements when budgets are growing; such programs provide needed staff assistance, enhance the importance of one's organization, create supportive clientele groups, and avoid delay. But with tight budgets and cutbacks the order of the day, the civil servant's first inclination is to preserve his or her own organization. Funds available for contracting out are liable to be cut first, if this can legally and politically be done. Hard times lead to playing it safe and avoiding risk. New program initiatives are eschewed. A county welfare department, for example, might argue that all of the services provided by funds passed through to voluntary organizations presuppose a core group of caseworkers in close touch with the clients and able to determine how well client needs are being met, and that without competent government employees the whole system of contracting out for services will fall apart.

Such an argument is not merely self-interest. Critics in growing numbers have begun to doubt the effectiveness of contracting arrangements. The cost, complexity, and opportunities for fiscal impropriety will often increase as private organizations become involved in the administration of a program. Additional layers of financial management need to be coordinated. A dense web of constituency relationships develops with which program managers must deal. A recurrent theme is that government has gotten itself tangled up by trying to do too much and by relying too much on devices to disguise its role.[11] There is a great need to improve traditional management within government, not to invent ever more subtle means to circumvent the stifling routines and other ills of bureaucracy. Government, also, may be forced to reenter program areas in which efforts to stimulate private-sector initiatives have failed—and at greater public cost than if the government had administered the program directly in the first place.

The net result of these developments is the more skeptical, even hostile, climate that exists today toward the new

11. See the excellent argument of Yair Aharoni, *The No-Risk Society* (Chatham, NJ: Chatham House, 1981).

political economy. Ideological opposition from conservatives, the business desire to penetrate new markets, cautious second thoughts within the ranks of the civil servants, and a perception of deep disarray in policy on the part of the attentive public all have played a part, against the background of economic recession, in shaping a new climate. The 1980 presidential election has sharpened, but has not resolved, the debate on the underlying issues. President Reagan has achieved some cuts in federal government expenditures, but the more sweeping cutbacks have remained only proposals as of the fall of 1982. The future shape of tax revenues, government expenditures, regulatory reform measures, and other integral parts of the administration's program still cannot be determined. The president certainly has given clear indication that he intends to "get government off the backs" of the American people, and that he wants a larger role for the private sector. But, like the New Deal, the Reagan administration contains conflicting policy directions that have not been fully sorted out. The administration's initiatives of course will also have to contend in the wider political arena. Compromises will be forced on the administration from the outside. The nation has therefore initiated, not concluded, its debate on the appropriate ends and means of government action.

WHAT NEXT?

Roughly speaking, there are four broad alternatives for the nation at this point: first, we could seek to restore a patched-up version of the American consensus. This might imply, among other things, a return approximately to the 1950s—not the 1920s—in terms of government's role in society: a strong defense; aid to education, such as the National Defense Education Act; support for rebuilding the country's infrastructure, such as the Interstate Highway Program; social security, plus the basic health programs of the 1960s; federal battles against states' rights in energy exploration; and modest but significant programs in a number of other areas. I confess to a special fondness for the America of the 1950s and applaud the revisionist scholarship that has recognized the outstanding leadership of President Dwight Eisenhower.[12] However, a return to the 1950s is as unlikely as a return to the limited government ideology of the founding fathers.

America has a permanent high-mobilization society—the first of its kind in the world—in which the energies of a free society are mobilized on a scale possible before only in wartime. The remarkable fact is that this has been done within a basic framework of respect for individual liberties. People want too much from life—and the complexities of domestic and international affairs are too great—for the national government to shrivel back to the insufficient statehood of the pre-New Deal era. The old American creed of limited government cannot be reconstructed. The effort to hang on to traditional ideas and practices, even while vastly broadening the range of responsibilities assigned to government, has marked the political history of our generation. The effort has produced the present discontent: the nation has tried, but has failed,

12. See Waldemar A. Nielsen, *The Endangered Sector* (New York: Columbia University Press, 1980).

to patch together successfully the old system of belief.

Second, the nation can embark on an ideological crusade, substituting clearly defined positions on a whole range of issues for the traditionally moderate style of American politics. Nothing is more understandable than, faced with a confusing reality and discordance between theory and practice, for an individual or group to embrace the comforting assurance of total commitment to an ideology. This removes the necessity for thought on a wide range of issues and seems to assure consistency of action. Consistency lets people know what to expect and enables them to plan for the future. Business particularly values continuity of policy. The difficulty is that the muddy normative issues of high policy do not lend themselves to ideological solutions. The problems facing modern government are too complex, too diverse, and too numerous to be resolved by slogans or pat formulas. To approach all problems from an ideological perspective is to invite frustration and irrationality. Moreover, those who suppose that the clash of political extremes produces a benign compromise should reflect more deeply on the experience of nations with ideological extremes. The extremes average out to chaos or to tyranny more often than to accommodation.

Third, the nation may choose to disengage from the arduous work of citizenship in the single-minded pursuit of private interests and self-realization. This course of action has some obvious appeal; it realistically focuses on life as it is actually lived, and reflects a healthy distrust of political hyperactivity. But ultimately this point of view is unsatisfactory as a general guide to action because of its abdication of citizenship.

There are too many ways in which the citizen collides with the state for withdrawal to be possible. The individual as well as the community will be impoverished by failures of citizenship. The nation needs more, not less, communication among its different estates. Business and government, voluntary institutions and government, and business and voluntary institutions need to be concerned with each other's problems and to understand how to help each other. Turning away from citizenship would only enhance the misunderstandings and mutual suspicions that have poisoned our public life.

The only remaining alternative is for the nation to enter into a process of dialogue and reflection leading to a new public philosophy. The general principles that might provide a starting point for debate would begin with the recognition of the organic division of society into three major estates: government, business, and the voluntary sector. These three clusters of institutions represent the core actors in our society. They are prominent forces around which myriad interests coalesce, and in their aggregation they determine the directions in which society will move.

THE THREE ESTATES
IN AMERICAN SOCIETY

The three great strata of American society overlap at the edges, competing against one another and displacing one another from time to time, but each having a central core that remains untouched by the collisions at the margins. Americans want this competition and overlap of function as the price to be paid for a dynamic society. But they do not want upheavals that threaten to rearrange the political landscape into totally unfamiliar patterns. Along with the competition, there is also a substantial measure of cooperation among the three estates, a forebearance and mutual support based on the recognition that joint effort is required to achieve nearly any important national goal.

The next step is to identify what is needed within each sector to improve its performance and, by strengthening itself, to make the system as a whole stronger. In the government sector, the strengthening of executive authority is a major need. The presidency, as it has evolved, still lacks the resources needed for effective management of the executive branch. The whole drift of events, particularly since the Watergate era, has been in the direction of dissipating presidential authority. We created the modern presidency in an imperfect form, with too many expectations and too few resources to do the job, and then proceeded to make it even harder for the president through curbs on his authority and detailed legislative intervention into the administrative process. The answer to the malaise of the federal government surely lies in strengthening the president's ability to manage the executive establishment. This implies more, not fewer, staff resources for the president, and it also implies stronger central management in most of the executive departments and agencies. With stronger central management within the executive branch would come more disciplined behavior vis-à-vis the Congress, removing the Congress from its misplaced role as micromanager of federal programs and freeing the energies of the members for policy dialogue with the president.

The arguments for either a massive shedding of functions to private contractors or for the federal government to reabsorb major activities now carried out by independent enterprises or contractors are unconvincing. Most of the calls for privatization—a term never precisely defined—come in the context of municipal government. But there are also those who wish to see the federal government, after limiting the areas in which it functions, remove itself as well from operations in the interest of performing more effectively a broad policy role. This view declares as prescription what has to a large extent already happened, and is blind to the many problems resulting from the already extensive use of outside institutions to carry out public functions. The problem is to make the system work, not to strain it further with new experimentation. Making the present system work means, among other things, better line management, improved civil-service morale, more—not less—attention to implementation, closer linkages between policy ends and means, and the right balance between too many administrative controls and too few. Vast new efforts to privatize functions could lead to disaster in either of two directions: giving away what should not be given away, or imposing unnecessary controls that stifle private initiative.

Government has shown that it can do many things well, and we should not disrupt the performance of essential tasks within the public service. But it would be equally misplaced to expect government to perform directly the vast range of functions now carried out by public enterprise or by administrative contract. No one can seriously propose that the public sector should suddenly double in size or that our problems would miraculously disappear if much of the complicated apparatus of service delivery involving private institutions were converted into direct government operations.

The voluntary sector is currently hard pressed and faces a paradoxical situation. On the one hand, it is urged to take on increasing responsibilities in the wake of cutbacks in federal, state, and municipal programs, but at the same time it is affected by those cutbacks. The sector must do more and do it with less. But when the dust settles after the current debate, the important mission of the voluntary sector should be clear to all Americans and its future more secure than ever, for many of the things that Americans cherish the most— education, the performing arts, religion, esoteric human services, social action, international relief—are unique strengths of the voluntary sector.[13] Competition with profit-making companies will force a redefinition of the nonprofit role in some areas, notably in health, nursing homes, and human services, but this will leave untouched the heart of the voluntary sector. One cannot imagine, for example, that business will take over a major share of family counseling services for troubled adolescents, or that a public bureaucracy can provide such services as effectively as a community-based voluntary organization. A recent New York State Commission found that voluntary-sector institutions provide superior services at lower costs than government agencies for a range of human services.[14] Voluntary-sector efforts will remain a critical factor in the nation's life because they have simply proved to be the best way to perform a range of important services.

The business sector, for its part, has to make changes to increase its competitiveness in world markets and at home against imports from Europe and Japan. Like the government and the voluntary sectors, it must learn to function in a leaner, more efficient fashion in a more complex and uncertain environment. There is some truth to the proposition that certain areas of the economy have been insulated from competition in recent years, partly as a result of government regulatory policy, and have in consequence been less innovative and dynamic than they might otherwise have been. The deregulatory movement, which has already brought dramatic changes to transportation, communications, and banking, seems bound to unleash creative new energies in the economy. Business has seemed to learn that the route to prosperity is not through government assistance but through its own capacity to generate products, markets, cost-saving innovations, and management improvements. Much of what business sought from government along the lines of incentives to encourage capital formation has, in any event, been achieved in the first two years of the Reagan presidency. Basically, the stage is set for an economic recovery. American business, while unlikely ever again to experience the unprecedentedly favorable circumstances of the last two decades following World War II, nevertheless enjoys a strong position vis-à-vis its chief competitors.

In this context, the United States needs not to abandon its mixed economy but rather to let it work. Deregulation should continue, but within an

13. Fred Greenstein, *The Hidden Hand Presidency* (New York: Basic Books, 1982).
14. Ronald Smothers, "State-Run Residences for Retarded Reported Inferior and More Costly," *New York Times*, 29 Aug. 1982, p. 1.

orderly framework to prevent needless disruptions. There are natural limits to the process; for example, safety considerations prevent a total deregulation of the airlines. Public concern for the environment prevents an excessive relaxation of health, environmental, occupational-safety, and other measures. Industry has not sought removal of environmental standards because it understands that a dramatic swing away from regulation could be followed by a swing back at another time. Some government subsidy programs to private industry, especially in the energy field, have been cut back, and others very likely will be trimmed. But a wholesale withdrawal of government from a role in the economy cannot and should not occur. Too many values important to American life are bound up with the government's role, not least the value of assisting the private economy in times of major distress.

Finally, a basic reason for maintaining the partnership between business and government is the fact that international economic considerations have become so critically important for the nation. Whether one considers the impact of imports domestically or the drive to expand exports as a major source of future markets, the government will need to be involved—not as an adversary but as a partner of business. The truly free international marketplace does not exist. Thus while the United States has sought and should continue to seek competitive markets both at home and abroad, there is a strong need for American government and business to work closely together in order to protect U.S. interests in the world economy. It should clearly not be a government responsibility to pick winners, nor should government have merely a passive spectator role.[15] Devising a solution within the American traditions of pluralism and a mixed economy will be a major challenge for the next decade.

FLEXIBILITY AND CHANGE IN THE AMERICAN GOVERNING SYSTEM: A RETROSPECT

Change has been present in abundant measure in the American governing system. The changes have been profound in the purposes sought by government and in the administrative means chosen to achieve the ends. The flexibility of means has facilitated the achievement of new substantive goals of policy. A new administration, blocked or thinking itself thwarted by a stubborn bureaucracy, has frequently been able to invent new ways to accomplish its purposes. Thus the complaints about unresponsiveness of American institutions to change from one perspective are unfounded. There may be too much change, which can happen too easily, for our own good—and those who deplore its lack usually want faster progress toward their preferred goals, or a more rapid return to earlier verities. That such hyperchange is made difficult by the fragmented structure of government should be seen as an important asset, desired by the Constitution's framers.

But this view is too simple. From another perspective, there is a problem of responsiveness, a problem caused in part by the inventiveness of policymakers and administrators in circumventing the existing system. As each new technique—the government enterprise of the 1930s, the not-for-profit institu-

15. Chalmers Johnson, *MITI and the Japanese Miracle: The Growth of Industrial Policy, 1925-1972* (Stanford, CA: Stanford University Press, 1982).

tions of the 1950s and 1960s, the off-budget spending tactics, the cooperative agreement to replace the grant, special revenue bonds for municipalities, and the like—has been added to the administrative repertoire, a new layer of complexity has been created. This complexity has finally resulted in such a layering of new devices upon the old as to threaten confusion and futility. It is in this sense of having taken too many shortcuts, of embracing too quickly new administrative practices without regard for their integration into the existing framework, that we have burdened the governing system. New initiatives are still possible, but effective implementation is difficult. The parts, that is, the small initiatives, war against the whole, that is, the capacity to redirect broad energies for major purposes. The absence of strong central management from the president and from department heads encourages new ideas but discourages sustained attention to problems and effective follow-through.

The nation will need even greater inventiveness in the future to make our loose-jointed and extraordinarily complex governing system work. A full review of the range of administrative devices employed in the modern contract state is not possible in this article. However, a few general lessons should be kept in mind to help avoid the improvisations that bring short-run benefits but long-run cumulative problems. Government should never contract out essential policymaking functions, critical aspects of strategic planning, or essential systems-management tasks—these must remain with accountable officials. Government agencies should not become so dependent on outside staff that they are unable to chart the main directions of policy for their departments. Close interaction with contractors is essential to assure a mutually understood definition of the task to be accomplished once the agency enters into a contract arrangement. But the kind of supervision exercised, as with subordinate units within the government department, should encourage creative performance rather than self-protection and risk avoidance. The contract state is here to stay. The need for highly professional skills in the policy process inevitably encourages the use of outside expertise as well as experimentation with novel management techniques within the government. In the end, the best safeguard against becoming trapped by the inherited complexity of our governing institutions is to keep inventing them anew.

Intergovernmental Redirection

By DONALD H. HAIDER

ABSTRACT: Intergovernmental reformers have long attempted to remedy the system's more apparent defects, especially the recent buildup in federal-state-local relations as Washington's involvement became broader and deeper. These remedies have included incremental and procedural changes, rationalization of federal aid and program delivery instruments, and total overhaul of the system through functional realignment. Efforts in the past have proved only marginally successful, essentially due to the fact that Congress had become the dominant architect and defender of the system. The world of intergovernmental relations changed dramatically from 1978 on, due to the poor performance of the economy, antitax and antispending sentiment, public-sector retrenchment, and fiscal deterioration at the federal level. Decentralization, competition, and fragmentation characterize the contemporary do-it-yourself federalism. President Reagan's proposed swap, turnback, and trust-fund package of New Federalism seeks to capture these changes in a system realignment. I examine these changes in light of whither intergovernmental relations go in the 1980s.

Donald H. Haider is professor of public management and director of the public and nonprofit management program at the Northwestern University Kellogg Graduate School of Management. He has served in the federal government as a White House fellow, and a congressional fellow, and as deputy assistant secretary of the U.S. Treasury for state and local finance. He also served as the chief financial officer of the City of Chicago. Haider has written extensively on intergovernmental relations and public finance.

THE federal system is overburdened with programs and regulations—inefficient, dysfunctional, and lacking any degree of accountability. This view of contemporary federalism is supported not just by intergovernmental scholars, but also by governors, mayors, state legislators, and county officials.[1]

Dire warnings concerning the fate of federalism have been characteristic of its study throughout the century. John Burgess, the recognized father of political science, found the prevailing doctrine of federalism to be unworkable in theory and in practice.[2]

One hundred years later, the Advisory Commission on Intergovernmental Relations (ACIR), in a comprehensive study of "The Federal Role in the Federal System," concluded that the "current network of intergovernmental relations has become dangerously overloaded to the point that America's most trumpeted traditional traits—flexibility and workability—are critically endangered."[3]

In a strict constitutional sense, federalism is a means by which the national government shares authority and power with the states or, as James Madison asserted in the *Federalist Papers,* the proposed constitution is "neither a national nor federal constitution, but a composition of both." The Constitution was silent as to how this partnership that would transcend structure or form of political organization was to unfold.

What is important to federalism's evolution is that the principle of partnership extended beyond the states to local governments, and later to a host of public, quasi-public, and private actors—institutions, groups, interests, and individuals. As this occurred, the chronic debates over legalism, principles, and national-state emphasis would be superseded by explanatory models, metaphors, and adjectives to illustrate federalism in action—creative, conflictual, combative, bamboo, screen door, picket fence, and chaotic. The concept of federalism became "muddied and made imprecise," replaced by the system's more behavioral aspects of persons occupying various positions in state-local government, interlocal relations, and questions of management, finance, and public policy.[4]

New-style federalism, then, is called intergovernmental relations. In its unfolding over the past 20 years, as the federal role became "bigger, broader, and deeper," a fundamental issue that unites scholars and practitioners alike is how to make this constantly changing partnership work. In theory and in practice, the agenda remains largely unchanged as to basic questions of its workings: (1) Who does what? (2) Who pays the bill? (3) Who is responsible?[5]

THE PROBLEM RESTATED

As significant as the evolutionary development in intergovernmental relations has been to shaping the federal sys-

---

1. The Advisory Commission on Intergovernmental Relations (ACIR), *The Federal Role in the Federal System: Hearings on the Federal Role* (Washington, DC: ACIR, 1980), p. 50.

2. John W. Burgess, "The American Commonwealth: Changes in Its Relations to the Nation," *Political Science Quarterly,* 1:9-33 (1881).

3. ACIR, *A Crisis of Confidence and Competence* (Washington, DC: ACIR, 1981), pp. 3-7.

4. See Deil S. Wright, *Understanding Intergovernmental Relations* (North Scituate, MA: Duxbury Press, 1978), p. 8.

5. Carl W. Stenberg, "Beyond the Days of Wine and Roses: Intergovernmental Management in a Cutback Environment," *Public Administration Review,* 41(1):10-19 (Jan. 1981).

tem prior to the 1960s, the effects of the federal government's involvement in all facets of American life since then have been profound and pervasive. The 16-year period of 1964-80 was marked by political instability and economic volatility, and sweeping changes in values and attitudes. Great hopes of solving social ills under President Johnson's Great Society programs were followed by much disillusionment, a divisive war, and social turbulence.

Federal aid to state and local governments increased from $7 billion in fiscal year 1960 to $90 billion in fiscal year 1980, for an annual growth rate of 15 percent. The number of federal programs grew from 130 to 500 in this period, operating through a bewildering maze of instruments for conducting the public's business: general revenue sharing, block grants, project grants, cooperative agreements, tax incentives, loans and loan guarantees, and contracts. Virtually all states and general-purpose local governments became participants in federal programs, as did special districts, planning agencies, nonprofit organizations, neighborhood bodies, and private institutions.

New instrumentalities for implementing public policy, more or less autonomous from general-purpose units of government, participated in government's growth and expansion, which, in turn, were based on a non-zero-sum game of a growth-oriented economy. Much competition and conflict followed, as well as rampant confusion and uncertainty as to participants' roles, responsibilities, and funding. Problems large and small became intergovernmentalized, from mass transit to bikeways, clean water to jellyfish control, education for the disadvantaged to displaced homemakers.

Regulatory proliferation followed program proliferation as the federal government used its largesse to leverage recipients into achieving social-policy goals, whether in the environment, affirmative action, citizen participation, and the like. By 1980, some 59 cross-cutting conditions and requirements uniformly applied to all grant programs regardless of purpose, burdening recipients with a stream of compliance and reporting requirements.

The sheer size, growth, and near incomprehensibility of government produced torrents of criticism from its alleged beneficiaries. Annual meetings by the governors, mayors, county officials, and state legislators came to be dominated by concerns over the unworkability of the intergovernmental grant morass. The ACIR, painfully and laboriously, documented the shortcomings of the federal grant system throughout this period. Congressional committees, the Office of Management and Budget, the General Accounting Office, the Commission on Federal Paperwork, and independent research institutions such as Brookings, the American Enterprise Institute, the Urban Institute, and others joined in the clamor for reform.[6]

INTERGOVERNMENTAL REFORMERS

To deal with these interrelated problems of narrow grant proliferation, federal intrusion into problems large and small, overregulation, and grant duplication and red tape, proponents of reform generally agreed upon a fivefold strategy for improving the system: simplification, consolidation, sensible con-

6. ACIR, *The Federal Role in the Federal System: An Agenda for Restoring Confidence and Competence* (Washington, DC: ACIR, 1981), ch. 4.

ditioning, effective evaluation, and reallocation of roles.

Intergovernmental reform had become a conspicuous public-policy issue by 1966-67. Some attribute this concern to the ACIR, congressional hearings on failings of the Great Society programs, and the growing influence of Washington-based public-interest groups such as the National Governors Association, the U.S. Conference of Mayors, the National League of Cities, the National Association of Counties, and the National Conference of State Legislatures. Others looked to the Democrats' midterm losses in the 1966 elections and the growing disenchantment with Great Society excesses as the cause.[7]

Whatever the exact date, reformers generally lined up into three broad camps that embraced academics and practitioners, pundits and politicians alike. The three included (1) incremental reformers, (2) structural consolidationists, and (3) functional realigners. Some reformers fell into all three categories, viewing reform as a continuum, from process changes to system overhaul. More pragmatic reformers pushed on all three fronts, seeking breakthroughs in whatever direction offered least resistance. In most cases fundamental assumptions concerning the cause of the intergovernmental problems were left unstated, as were expectations as to who would benefit from reform. Each camp brought its own agenda and values to the reform litany.

President Lyndon Johnson perhaps epitomized the incrementalist

7. See Donald Haider, *When Governments Come to Washington: Governors, Mayors, and Intergovernmental Lobbying* (New York: Free Press, 1974), ch. 2.

approach, a pattern that would be repeated by President Jimmy Carter from 1977 to 1980. Beginning in late 1966 with a presidential directive to federal officials requesting them to advise and consult with governors and mayors on the intergovernmental programs, President Johnson pursued strategies followed by all his successors. These included (1) simplifying federal grant practices, (2) improving communications between federal officials and state-local chief executives on federal grants, and (3) enhancing the discretion and authority of these nonfederal officials in managing intergovernmental programs. Budget Circular A-85 specified an advise and review process. Circular A-95 and Councils of Government provided for an areawide review and comment process on federal grants. The Intergovernmental Cooperation Act of 1968 called for intergovernmental policy coordination.

To incrementalists, remedies lay with a process aimed at increased interagency and intergovernmental coordination and communication. Many of President Nixon's intergovernmental reforms flowed from the Johnson effort: federal assistance review (FAR), chief executive review and comment (CERC), new coordinators through a departmental under secretaries' working group, and federal-regional office consolidation. President Carter, too, followed the procedural, incrementalist approach, relying on grant simplification, reorganization, audit and regulatory changes, and grant consolidation. His assistant for intergovernmental affairs became extensively involved in state-local officials' casework. The Carter administration invested considerable effort in regulatory reform, planning grant consolidation, compliance certification, and general reduction in the burden of paperwork.[8]

Such reforms invariably swam upstream. Devoid of a strong central management agency to pressure, monitor, or otherwise compel federal agency compliance with presidential directives, White House firefighting and handholding entangled the president and his staff in the intergovernmental thicket. Presidents soon found themselves embroiled in local political squabbles and treading dangerously on congressional turf. In the meantime, the march of new categorical grant programs continued unabated, and the state-local constituency redoubled their insatiable appetite for increased federal funding without strings.

The structural reformists moved beyond procedural reforms in the expectation that grant consolidation and block grants would overcome the more apparent defects of narrow categorical grants and greatly simplify administration. Two block grants were enacted during the Johnson presidency in health and law enforcement, and three under President Nixon in employment training, community development, and Title XX social services. Prior to the Reagan administration, President Nixon sought the most extensive overhaul of the federal grant system to date when his proposals for reorganizing the executive branch and nearly all domestic programs incurred fierce and successful opposition from Congress.

What President Nixon and his successor, Gerald Ford, discovered was that grant consolidation and block grants had a price. The whole was far greater than the sum of the parts. Grant beneficiaries demanded to be held harmless from loss of funds and authority, and a new higher funding threshold would be the cost for consolidating functionally related categorical programs and expanding recipient discretion. Mayors wanted federal aid to bypass state governments, governors demanded that all funds flow through the states, and counties wanted funds independent of states and municipalities.

Block grants differed from narrow categoricals insofar as they furthered some broad national purpose. Funds generally flowed to a general-purpose government unit in accordance with a statutory allocation formula for a recipient's discretionary use in a broad functional area. They aimed at achieving much of what reformers desired—decentralization, simplification, consolidation, generalist as opposed to specialist or bureaucratic involvement, and greater discretionary use.

However, block grants proved to be neither the panacea that supporters thought nor, for that matter, as terrible as their most ardent critics predicted. Between 1966 and 1980, only five were enacted. Congress moved to recategorize the block grants after a time—limiting their usefulness and alleged benefits.[9] President Ford's extensive block-grant proposals made little headway with Congress when he

---

8. See Richard P. Nathan, *The Plot that Failed: Nixon and the Administrative Presidency* (New York: John Wiley, 1975), ch. 2; and *The Budget of the U.S. Government, Fiscal Year 1982, Special Analyses,* H (Washington, DC: Office of Management and Budget, 1981), pp. 239-47.

9. For a research summary on block grants, see *Intergovernmental Perspective,* 7(2):8-17 (Spring 1981).

refused to raise aggregate funding for these programs to win opponents over. Given this unfavorable congressional reception, President Carter proposed no additional block grants and instead opted for modest grant consolidation in several related program areas.

The functional realigners, tempered by President Eisenhower's ill-fated efforts aimed at returning federal-state programs and revenues to support them to the states exclusively, recognized early on that the more radical the reform the greater the opposition. The ACIR's advocacy of federal assumption of welfare programs and costs in return for turning back to state-local responsibility the hundreds of narrow categorical programs, gained considerable support from big-city mayors and large urban-state governors. Realignment proposals invariably fell apart over issues of costs, specific turnbacks, and winners and losers. Much of Congress was simply uninterested in such sweeping changes.

Indeed, Richard Nixon went farther than any president prior to Ronald Reagan in seeking intergovernmental restructuring. His 1971 State of the Union Message pleaded the case for New Federalism, a sorting out and rearranging of responsibilities among various government levels. Nixon's Family Assistance Plan attempted to reform welfare by packaging income-transfer programs into a guaranteed-income approach, as opposed to the Great Society patchwork of income support, social services, and bureaucratic welfare programs. He also proposed to devolve power and to decentralize authority through an annual $5 billion general revenue-sharing program plus an $11 billion special revenue sharing that consolidated more than 100 existing federal-aid programs into six broad functional areas.

Try as he did through buy outs, impoundment, and executive fiat, Mr. Nixon's efforts stopped far short of system overhaul. The mix of federal aid had been broadened through the addition of general revenue sharing and block grants, but these had been built on top of a seemingly imperturbable grant base at an enormous cost in federal expenditures. President Carter further added to this base through various antirecession assistance programs that became the foundation for his new Public-Private Partnership and short-lived urban policies. His efforts to target and tailor federal aid fell victim to economic constraints and to distributional politics.

In this presidential tug-of-war over grant reform, Presidents Ford and Nixon advocated block grants to curb categorical growth and state government as the basic delivery mechanism. Presidents Johnson and Carter promoted direct federal-local ties and expanded participation by the private and nonprofit sectors. Each found reform difficult and set against the iron triangle of interest groups, congressional committees, and executive agencies that formed around domestic programs.

However, the aggregate effort of functional realigners produced few changes and incurred mostly defeats in the 1970s simply because Congress had become the dominant architect of the federal grant system during this period. Set against successive administrative efforts to simplify, expedite, and otherwise streamline the grant allocation system, Congress increased the number of categorical grants, rejected consolidation, recategorized existing block-grant programs, expanded the scope of cross-cutting conditions and regulations, and greatly expanded its control over domestic program administration.

THE INTERGOVERNMENTAL DEBATE CHANGES

The debate over reforming the intergovernmental system shifted substantially in the late 1970s due to four interrelated factors: the poor condition of the economy; public attitudes about government taxation and spending; pervasive public-sector retrenchment; and fiscal deterioration at the federal level. No longer would one consider whether federal aid to states and localities would be reduced, but rather by how much, in what areas, and with what consequences. No longer would one question whether reduced aid meant that state and local governments would be more on their own, but rather how much more on their own.

Much of the explosive involvement of the federal government in the state-local arena was built on future-growth oriented assumptions. The fine tuners and full-employment advocates of the 1960s envisioned an expanding economic pie of which the federal share would enable domestic programs to achieve their goals, provided that state-local partners also contributed to such efforts. But the high-growth/low-inflation economy of the 1960s was followed by low growth and high inflation in the 1970s. The 2 percent inflation levels of the early 1960s were followed by 6-10 percent levels in the 1970s. Unemployment levels moved from 3-5 percent levels in the 1960s to 6-10 percent levels in the 1970s and early 1980s. Four recessions racked the economy in the 1969-82 period.

For the federal government, the expenditure momentum of the 1960s carried into the 1970s with at least three fundamental differences. First, the budgetary growth proved incompatible with the revenue limits of lower real growth in the economy. Next, the uneven growth and unforeseen inflation of the 1970s propelled expenditure growth rates to a point where they consistently outpaced revenues in good as well as bad economic years. Third, more of the federal budget became uncontrollable due to entitlement payments such as social security, indexation of benefits, and multiyear purchase of goods and services. This expenditure momentum was maintained by deficit spending—more than $400 billion worth between 1960 and 1980. Once government was confronted by chronic inflation, deficits became a conspicuous target as a key contributor to economic problems.

Attitudes about government also shifted dramatically from the 1960s to the 1970s regarding taxes, waste, regulation, trust in government, and other key indicators of declining support for government spending. Much of this change stemmed from economic factors such as inflation, relative decline in real disposable income, job insecurity, and rising interest rates and borrowing costs. Watergate and an unpopular war also contributed. Between 1964 and 1978, the percentage of the citizenry believing that government wastes a lot of tax dollars rose from 48 percent to 79 percent. The ACIR's survey of public attitudes toward governments and taxes found that the federal income tax rated as the worst tax dating from 1979, when it replaced the property tax. The rating for support of local government moved past that for the national government.[10]

10. ACIR, *1981, Changing Public Attitudes on Government and Taxes* (Washington, DC: ACIR, 1981), pp. 3-5.

Whatever the complex factors underpinning changes in public opinion about government, these attitudes spilled over to widespread citizen action aimed at limiting government spending and taxing. The most publicized tax revolt occurred with the 1978 passage of Proposition 13, an amendment to the California constitution that sharply reduced state and local taxes. Proposition 13 was preceded and superseded by tax and spending limitations throughout the country.

However, the slowing of government growth came before Proposition 13 and other celebrated tax revolts such as Massachusetts 2½. As the ACIR has documented in the great slowdown in the state and local public sectors, the transition from fast growth to slow decline developed in a grass-roots fashion. The growth in real per capita spending stopped first at the local level in 1974, then at the state level in 1976, and topped off at the federal level in 1978.[11] Figure 1 illustrates this progression and retraction over the 36-year period 1954-80.

Thus, after growing at a rate almost three times as fast as the total economy, the state-local sector moved to a no-growth posture in the late 1970s, which means that its current growth is not keeping pace with either the sluggish economy or the high rates of inflation. State and local spending peaked as a proportion of gross national product in 1975, and has declined since then about 10 percent.

Finally, the entire intergovernmental debate changed as the economic growth slowed, public-sector retrenchment set in, and public attitudes turned distinctly against renewed spending and increased taxation. Congress seized the antispending initiative in 1979-80 when it rejected President Carter's proposed targeted fiscal assistance and countercyclical programs and, next, eliminated state governments from the three-year extension of general revenue sharing. It rejected the use of state-local governments as instruments of macroeconomic economic policy during economic recessions. The march of new categorical grant programs largely ceased; federal aid to state-local governments peaked in constant dollars in 1978, and would face successive years of decline in current dollars from 1981 on.

The golden fiscal era for the federal government ended, and with it ended many of the intergovernmental reforms so intensely pushed by various camps since the mid-1960s. Instead, the federal government entered its own period of fiscal stress, propelled by demand for defense-related purchases, social security, and transfer-type payments. Federal grants would be the inevitable casualty of scarcer federal resources and increased budget conflict for the foreseeable future.

Once on a decremental federal-aid path, reformers reverted to new or revised strategies, but this time aimed at the multiple causes of government growth—the hyperresponsiveness of the 1970s to pressure groups and general budget bloat. Bolstered by the tax limitation movement, one reform element moved to curb future expenditure growth. For each of the fiscal ills—high tax burdens, excessive spending, budget deficits—there was an attendant response: cut taxes, impose tax and spending controls, and mandate balanced budgets. Some sought ad hoc adjustments or statutory controls to

11. ACIR, *Significant Features of Fiscal Federalism, 1980-81 Edition* (Washington, DC: ACIR, 1981), pp. 7-9.

FIGURE 1
THE DECLINE IN "REAL" STATE-LOCAL SPENDING
(decline in local spending commencing 1975; state spending, 1977; federal aid flows, 1979)

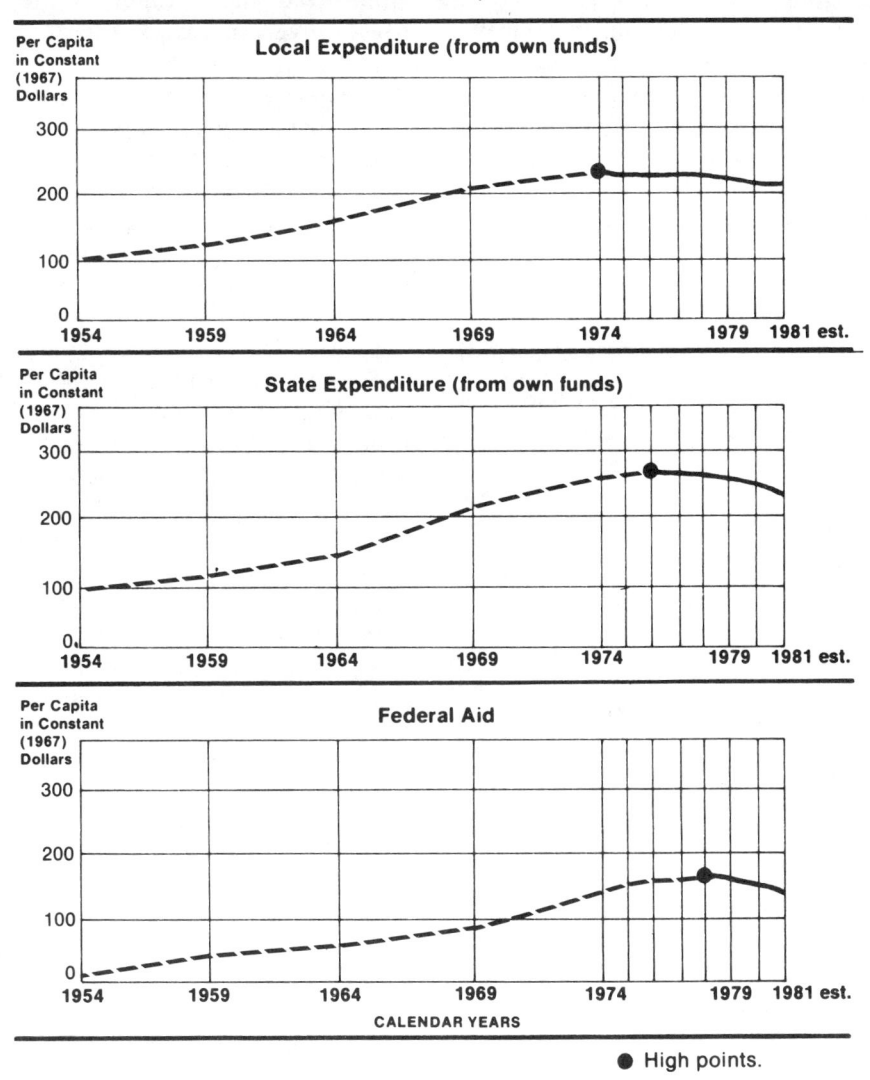

[Three line graphs showing Per Capita in Constant (1967) Dollars on the y-axis (0 to 300+) and Calendar Years on the x-axis (1954 to 1981 est.):
- Local Expenditure (from own funds): high point around 1974
- State Expenditure (from own funds): high point around 1975-76
- Federal Aid: high point around 1978]

● High points.

SOURCE: ACIR, *Significant Features of Fiscal Federalism, 1980-81 Edition* (Washington, DC: ACIR, 1981), p. 9.

attack the three public ills; others opted for direct constitutional controls subject to extraordinary majority rule.

Another school searched for institutional and political means toward achieving a "decongested, disciplined, administrable, and accountable system" short of constitutional and statutory reform. These changes included functional trade-offs between federal and state-local governments, substantial deregulation, strengthening of political parties and congressional leadership, and other formal and informal remedies associated with the president and Congress.[12]

The push for a constitutional amendment to require future balanced budgets carried the antispending sentiment to Congress, where, although defeated in 1982, it strengthened the existing budget process. It also provided credibility to President Reagan's proposals to sort out roles and responsibilities in the federal system.

REAGAN'S NEW FEDERALISM

The turn in intergovernmental relations occurred prior to the election of President Ronald Reagan in 1980, but his presidency accelerated trends and shifts already under way. From the very onset, Reagan indicated his desires to curb the size and influence of the federal establishment and to transform intergovernmental relations. His goals were indicated early on, when he stated, "Everything that can be run more efficiently by state and local governments we shall turn over to local governments, along with the funding sources to pay for it."[13]

Indeed, President Reagan's New Federalism proposals should not be separated from his economic recovery package, which contained four elements: reduced government spending, lower individual and business taxes, deregulation and regulatory reform, and stabilized monetary growth. The implementation of these programs reduced federal aid, altered state and local governments' tax and debt-management policies, and otherwise transferred many responsibilities to these governments. These changes would be intensified by the severe 1981-82 recession that brought national unemployment above 10 percent for the first time since 1940, and produced the most acute fiscal strain experienced by many governments since the 1930s. Tight monetary policy kept borrowing and interest rates at record-high levels and greatly reduced state-local borrowing in the credit markets.

President Reagan's New Federalism passed through three stages of development in 1981-82, with another and perhaps final stage awaiting the results of the 1982 midterm election both at the national and state-local levels.

The first stage in 1981 involved a combination of grant consolidation and deregulation accompanied by extensive budget cutting and a multiyear tax cut that would produce an estimated $500 billion federal revenue loss over the 1982-85 period. President Reagan proposed the consolidation of 90 categorical grants into seven block grants, and Congress, during the budget reconciliation process, consolidated 57 categoricals into nine new or modified block grants with a budget authority of over $7.5 billion.[14] Aggregate federal aid for state-local governments was reduced by $3.5 billion from fiscal year 1981 to fiscal year 1982, with further reductions proposed for fiscal year 1983. If enacted, as Table 1 indicates, federal aid for state and local governments, as opposed to aid for individuals, would be reduced by

---

12. ACIR, *An Agenda for Restoring Confidence and Competence,* ch. 4.

13. Acceptance Speech of Ronald Reagan at the Republican National Convention, Detroit, MI, 26 July 1980.

14. See The White House, *Federalism: The First 10 Months—A Report from the President* (Washington, DC: The White House, 1981).

TABLE 1
FEDERAL AID TO STATE AND LOCAL GOVERNMENTS (billions of dollars)

YEAR	TOTAL	TO INDIVIDUALS	FOR STATE-LOCAL GOVERNMENTS
1978	77.9	26.2	51.7
1979	82.9	29.1	53.8
1980	91.5	34.2	57.3
1981	94.8	39.9	54.8
1982 (estimated)	91.2	41.5	49.7
1983 (proposed)	81.4	37.6	43.9

SOURCE: *The Budget of the U.S. Government, Fiscal Year 1983, Special Analyses,* H (Washington, DC: Office of Management and Budget, 1982), p. 17.

more than $13 billion over a three-year period. This amounts to more than a 25 percent reduction in current dollars and a 40 percent reduction in constant dollars.

The impact of Reagan's first stage went far beyond mere budget cuts in federal aid to states and localities. Other federal program reductions increased demands on state and local governments —food stamps, trade adjustment assistance, and so on—as did recession-related pressures for welfare and unemployment assistance. The federal tax cut altered federal depreciation schedules, which, in turn, affected the vast majority of states in which tax codes were wedded to the federal tax structure. Changes in the tax code—capital gains, effective tax brackets, and the tax-exempt all-savers plan—not only altered the demand for tax-exempt debt, but also drove up the yield ratios for tax-exempt versus taxable debt from the 65-75 percent historical range to the 80-85 percent range. Market access for state-local borrowers narrowed, borrowing costs increased substantially, and maturities of debt shortened. Reduced federal assistance for capital infrastructure—roads, bridges, and so on—meant that states and localities would have to finance more of their construction, replacement, and maintenance costs from their own funds.[15]

The second stage of Reagan's New Federalism began in February 1982, when the president proposed a $50 billion transfer of federal programs to state and local governments over an eight-year phased transition. The costs would be offset by funds from a $28 billion per year trust fund financed from existing federal excise taxes on alcohol, tobacco, oil, and gasoline. Realignment of the federal system would be accomplished by a swap of program responsibilities— federalized medicaid for state-run Aid to Families with Dependent Children (AFDC) and food stamps—plus a turn-back of 40 federally financed programs, such as education and transportation, to be financed initially from the trust fund and later by states and localities on an optional basis. No state would be a loser or winner in the early stages of the swap-turnback based on the total federal-state-local expenditures for the returned programs minus net medicaid costs.

15. See Merrill, Lynch, Pierce, Fenner, and Smith, *The Effects of the Reagan Administration's Economic Recovery Plan on the Credit Standing of State and Local Governments* (New York: Merrill, Lynch, Dec. 1981); and *National Tax Journal: New Directions in Federal Tax and Expenditure Policies,* 35(3):231-306 (Sept. 1982).

President Reagan wrapped the aggregate agenda of intergovernmental reforms into a comprehensive package that will, as he stated, "in a single stroke" accomplish a realignment that would radically overhaul the way this nation provides public services and put an end to decades of concentration of power in Washington.[16] Beyond statements of principle or theory, Reagan's concrete plan produced swift reaction and criticism from fundamental interests that had shaped intergovernmental relations over the past 20 years: Democrats and Republicans, liberals and conservatives, northerners and southerners, governors and mayors.

Much debate turned on whether the states are able or willing to assume new responsibilities, and where additional resources could be generated. The more formidable stumbling block, however, involved issues of equity—who takes care of poor people, poor cities, and poor states. Short of federal responsibility and redistribution of resources for those least well off, such issues remained ambiguous, if not unanswered by the Reagan package.[17]

In August 1982, the president reworked a slimmed-down package of turnbacks, swaps, and trust funds to meet objections of governors, state legislators, and local officials. The nation's governors, in turn, softened their objections to specific turnbacks other than income-support programs. Local officials, especially big-city mayors, sensed from the onset that they would be shortchanged by any alteration of the direct federal-local-aid pipeline. However, much of this change was already under way.

Following months of negotiation between the White House and teams representing governors, state legislators, mayors, and county officials, the realignment package came unglued. Although the newer package retained federal asumption of the food stamps program, federal takeover of the $18 billion a year state portion of medicaid costs, opposed by the Office of Management and Budget, was split into two plans—one federally run, and one a full-service federal-state program. This retreat from full medicaid takeover, among other issues, caused the National Governors Association to decide on drafting its own New Federalism reform package for submission to Congress in 1983. Without the governors' support, President Reagan's proposals would have little or no chance of even gaining a congressional hearing.[18]

Far from dead, the New Federalism debate moved off center stage to await the outcome of the 1982 midterm elections that would greatly affect the president's working coalition in the Congress and his gubernatorial constituency. Reconciliation of the governors' demands for federalization of income-support programs and permanent trust fund or revenue source to support turnbacks would be difficult to achieve, fiscally or philosophically, for the Reagan administration. Moreover, even if a workable consensus were achievable, Congress, as the principal architect of intergovernmental relations, would have to be moved to adopt the plan. As long as Congress can take credit for individual programs and giving away

16. Rochelle Stanfield, "Reagan's New Federalism," *National Journal*, 9:357 (27 Feb. 1982).

17. A. J. Davis and S. K. Howard, "Perspectives on a 'New Day' for Federalism," *Intergovernmental Perspective*, 8(2):9-21 (Spring 1982).

18. See David Broder's coverage of the National Governors Association 1982 Annual Meeting, *Washington Post*, 10-12 Aug. 1982, p. 1.

funds in small portions, its inclination is to continue doing so, particularly when reinforced by interests that stand to gain more by concentrating pressure on Washington than by having to win over voters, bureaucrats, and elected officials in widely scattered state and local jurisdictions.

Events and trends since the mid-1970s have had far-reaching impacts upon the state-local component of intergovernmental relations. Following a decade of fiscal modernization in which states developed balanced and diversified revenue sources—the income and sales tax—they faced the new economic and political realities of the 1980s. Constrained by tax and spending limits and reductions in the 20-25 percent of their revenues previously derived from federal aid, their elastic revenue sources proved vulnerable to economic recessions and slow economic growth.

Caught between recession-induced shortfalls in revenues and federal unloading of responsibilities upon them, states faced record-low budget surpluses and record-high tax increases for 1981-82 to fill revenue-expenditure gaps. Nearly all states reduced their expenditures in this period to maintain balanced budgets, some as drastically as recession-racked Michigan, which cut real spending by more than 20 percent since 1980. States increased taxes by nearly $4 billion in 1981—a 10-year high—and are expected to raise them to another record-high increase of $7 billion in 1982.

Local governments have been even further constrained, caught between the hard place of federal-state cutbacks and the rock of voter resistance to property taxes—localities' dominant revenue source. Local governments had become increasingly dependent on higher government revenues to support capital and operating budgets. The reliance rate of nearly all medium and larger cities on federal aid, for example, grew dramatically through the 1970s, reaching dependency levels for such cities as St. Louis, Newark, Philadelphia, Cleveland, and Detroit, in which federal aid exceeded 50 percent of their own-source general revenues. Consequently, set against declining federal aid and static to slow-growing state aid, municipalities too cut budgets, deferred maintenance of their capital plants, increased fees and service charges, and faced chronic fiscal strain.

In short, what reformers thought would be a rational, planned, and methodical unfolding of intergovernmental relations—structure, finance, and management—turned out to be something quite different. Such factors as resource constraints, demographic shifts, economic volatility, and rapid transformation of our economy and labor force have accelerated change faster than public policy could respond.

Nearly 20 years have passed since an administration and the Congress undertook together a comprehensive effort to define and debate national purposes. President Reagan's New Federalism and the response by governors and state-local leaders to it suggest a beginning, but only that. In the meantime, the intergovernmental system reflects much turmoil, fragmentation, and enhanced competition among regions, states, and localities. We have moved, as it were, from a strong, quasi-centralized federalism to a weak, highly decentralized, do-it-yourself federalism.

CONCLUDING OBSERVATIONS

Future directions in intergovernmental relations smack of vast uncertainties.

"Knowledge experts," notes the ACIR, "were quite unable to foresee even the broad outlines of the changes in American federalism that occurred over the past 20 years."[19] We are viewing not only an exceedingly complex system, but also one in a constant state of flux. Unanticipated changes have been the rule; planned changes, as intergovernmental reformers have learned, are the exception.

The deterioration of the national government's fiscal position and gradual strengthening of the state-local sector, comparatively speaking, took several decades to emerge fully. How durable this role reversal proves to be will be largely a function of future economic growth and state government response to its current pivotal role as resource provider and its assumption of new responsibilities. Continued demographic, income, and economic shifts—Frostbelt to Sunbelt, urban to rural, manufacturing to service industry—will exacerbate interjurisdictional competition and regional tensions. Just as defense and social security—income programs—will place a rising demand on future federal resources, so will capital infrastructure and basic service provision command a high priority on state-local resources.

What we are experiencing is not a quiet revolution in intergovernmental change, but rather one punctuated by much noise and movement, as the public sorts out what it wants government to do and how much it is willing to pay. As all government levels are constrained by various fiscal shackles, much change will occur in how governments conduct their business—roles and responsibilities, accountability, and management. And after all, these are changes that intergovernmental reformers advocated in the first place, and they well may come about due to forces and pressures unforeseen by most in the past but likely to be with us well into the future. In sum, we have entered an entirely new era of government and intergovernmental relations.

19. ACIR, *The Future of Federalism in the 1980s* (Washington, DC: ACIR, July 1981), p. 8.

The Presidency and Political Change

By LESTER G. SELIGMAN

ABSTRACT: At a time when the president is attempting a drastic change in economic policy, it is appropriate to examine the development of his role in economic policy. As in so many other aspects of the modern presidency, the administration of Franklin D. Roosevelt is the watershed. He expanded the president's role as economic policymaker in an unchallenged executive response to the crisis of the Depression. The institutionalization of that role was a process involving several stages that unfolded in succeeding administrations. One stage was the role's definition and legitimation by Congress in the Employment Act of 1946, which defined a new governmental commitment to economic intervention to achieve maximum employment. The same act created the Council of Economic Advisers (CEA) and placed it in the Executive Office of the President. Since then, the CEA has played a vital part in economic policy. Its importance contributed to a train of economic policy staff agencies that grew as the president's economic policy role expanded with the emergence of such new problems as economic growth, poverty, inflation, stagflation, and foreign economic policy. Throughout this evolution, a constituency of economic policy crystallized, which contributed to the institutionalization of the president's role. President Reagan's efforts to reverse economic policy direction may be difficult, because some of the political institutional supports his predecessors could rely on have undergone considerable change and are now problematical.

Lester G. Seligman, professor of political science at the University of Illinois in Champaign-Urbana since 1973, received his B.A. and Ph.D. (1947) at the University of Chicago. He taught there from 1948 to 1954, when he joined the University of Oregon. His consistent research interest has been political leadership and political elites in the United States and compared with other nations. He is the author of Leadership in a New Nation *(1964), coauthor with E. Cornwell of* The New Deal Mosaic *(1965), and coauthor of* Patterns of Recruitment *(1974). He is past president of the Presidency Research Group (1980), an association of scholars concerned with the American presidency and other chief executives.*

HOW have presidents contributed to political change? This question is especially timely today, when the president is attempting a profound reorientation of government's relationship to the economy. Not since the New Deal has a president attempted such a drastic political change. Franklin D. Roosevelt's New Deal introduced a set of economic policies that make the federal government responsible for social welfare and also the regulator of some aspects of the economy. President Reagan has been pursuing an opposite objective based on a revived economic theory, variously called "supply-side economics" and "Reaganomics," designed to reduce the government's role in the economy. Both presidents were and are innovators who deviated from the paths of their predecessors.

Mr. Reagan's program is discontinuous with those of his predecessors in at least two respects. First, he is trying to reverse the gradual expansion of the government's role as regulator of the economy. Second, unlike those of many of his predecessors, his program is more explicit. Every one of our contemporary presidents—those since FDR—has been an activist, more or less declaring that his administration had a mandate to impart a particular direction to governmental policy. Truman's Fair Deal, Eisenhower's New Republicanism, Kennedy's New Frontier, and Johnson's Great Society suggested the spirit of the change each sought to achieve during his administration. Yet sometimes these objectives were only vaguely defined. This is not so in the case of Mr. Reagan's objectives. He has not only articulated an outlook, but has also stipulated specific policies that would radically alter the economic, social, and political direction of the last half century.

Yet in another respect, Mr. Reagan has also followed the path of his predecessors by making the presidency the source and driving force behind economic policy. Not too long ago presidents abjured such a role. If they had attempted it, they would have been sternly resisted by the Congress, and by many economic interest groups and public opinion as well. Today, the primacy of the president's role as the architect of overall economic policy is generally accepted, even though the Congress has not relinquished a role for itself in that area.

This presidential role has become institutionalized and legitimated. Public opinion attests to that. A Gallup Poll conducted in 1980 measuring public attitudes toward the presidency disclosed that two of the leading three public expectations were that a president should provide leadership (24 percent) and solve economic problems (17 percent).[1] Other studies of public opinion confirm that role for the president by showing that the state of the economy is the single most important factor in determining the president's popularity.[2]

Mr. Reagan is trying to undo the commitment of the government to active intervention in the economy on behalf of greater welfare, equalization of opportunity, and income redistribu-

1. Frank Kessler, *The Dilemmas of Presidential Leadership: Of Caretakers and Kings* (Englewood Cliffs, NJ: Prentice-Hall, 1982), p. 300.
2. Kristin Monroe and Dona Laughlin, "Economic Influences on Presidential Popularity among Key Political and Socio-Economic Groups: A Review of the Evidence and Some New Findings" (Paper delivered at the American Political Science Association Convention, Washington, DC, August 1980); Edward R. Tufte, *Political Control of the Economy* (Princeton, NJ: Princeton University Press, 1978).

tion. We had come to believe that in half a century this commitment had become rooted in the national consensus. President Reagan's efforts to dismantle this system therefore test the depth of acceptance of the policies of the last 50 years. Now is a good time to analyze the evolution of that change and the president's role in it. This article will focus on three facets of the change: (1) the substantive change in the president's role in economic policy; (2) the concomitant administrative changes in the office of the presidency, which have institutionalized the role; and (3) the political components of that change, specifically, the politics of presidential support and the extent of its compatibility with the change in the president's role. By focusing on these three facets, I hope to shed light on the president's part in political change. Is he an instigator of change, or does he merely react to and ratify it?

This question does not admit of a simple answer. In part it depends on what is meant by innovations. If we accept Herbert Simon's statement that the primary function of the chief executive is to take the lead in meeting the problems and opportunities that arise,[3] then Franklin D. Roosevelt's policies and his impact on the presidential office were certainly innovative. Yet on close examination, many of the supposedly innovative policies and programs of the New Deal did not originate with the president or his administration. To cite but a few examples, Roosevelt's agricultural policies may be traced back to proposals made during the administration of Calvin Coolidge; his initial program for economic recovery, the National Recovery Administration

3. Herbert Simon, Donald W. Smithburg, and Victor A. Thompson, *Public Administration* (New York: Knopf, 1950), p. 537.

(NRA), drew on governmental experience during World War I and the growth of trade associations the government fostered during the twenties; the Tennessee Valley Authority originated with Progressive Senator George Norris as an advocate of the long-standing movement for public power; and the Wagner Labor Act was fathered by Senator Robert Wagner. Roosevelt was therefore less a policy innovator than a catalyst accelerating their adoption. But innovation includes not just originality or its short-run effects, but also its durability and long-run consequences. In that light, innovation is not so much a matter of originality, but an evolutionary process: each president's contribution may be innovative or not, but the long-run cumulative result of the process is a significant innovation.

THE OVERALL PROCESS OF CHANGE: FROM INITIATION TO INSTITUTIONALIZATION

An analysis of change must differentiate between ephemeral changes that seem to leave few traces, and those that endure and become institutionalized. The development of the contemporary presidency has provided many examples of both, such as the transitory National Resources Planning Board under FDR, the Office of Drug Abuse under Nixon, and administrative practices such as the planning-programming-budgeting (PPB) system under Lyndon Johnson. But the presidential press conferences and the White House staff, to cite only two, took hold and evolved. The significant and persistent ones involved changes in presidential roles, because they changed presidential responsibilities, engendered new public expectations, and created new presidential constituencies. I believe that such durable changes are the products of a particular process; change is not dichotomous but continuous, as I will attempt to show. New presidential roles, from their initiation to their institutionalization, undergo several phases or thresholds during which they evolve and transform the presidency itself. This process of institutionalization also tells us a great deal about change in our political system.

The meaning of institutionalization

The term "the institutionalized presidency" has become a stock phrase that has acquired several meanings. One definition makes it synonymous with the growth of the White House staff and the Executive Office of the President. Another meaning refers to a methodical and formalized presidential managerial style. Thus Theodore Sorenson, describing Kennedy's mode of operation, wrote: "From the outset he abandoned the notion of a collective, institutionalized presidency. He abandoned the practice of the cabinet and the National Security Council making group decisions like corporate boards of directors. He abolished the practice of White House staff meetings and weekly cabinet meetings."[4] Still others use the term—and this is its most widely used meaning—to refer to pluralizing the presidency, so that the president's responsibilities are now discharged on his behalf by a number of staff officials in specialized offices. In this sense the institutionalized presidency reflects the actions of a corporate entity that ascribes its actions to the president.

The concept of institutionalization, which is widely used in the social sciences, has a somewhat different meaning in this context. Institutionalized behavior refers to the establishment of the prescribed ways in which roles are expected to be performed, in contrast to the idiosyncratic behavior of individuals.[5] Talcott Parsons defined the "institutional structure of a social system as the totality of morally sanctioned statuses and roles which regulate the relations of persons to one another through locating them in the structure and defining the legitimate expectations of their attitudes and behavior."[6] Philip Selznick added a new dimension by treating institutionalization as a stage in organizational development when an organization becomes valued in itself and is no longer expendable.[7]

The process of institutionalization

In the light of these definitions, I shall define institutionalization of the presidency as a process of several phases that involves the acquisition of new roles associated with an administrative staff designed to assist the president in fulfilling them. That staff becomes a key element in the president's decision making. In many ways, the administrative staff becomes a key part of each president's administration in order to be effective, and the president becomes dependent on his staff to enhance his effectiveness. In addition, the president and his staff

---

4. Theodore C. Sorenson, *Kennedy* (New York: Bantam, 1966), p. 281.

5. Charles Perrow, *Complex Organizations* (Glenview, IL: Scott Foresman, 1972), p. 75.

6. Talcott Parsons, *Essays in Sociological Theory Pure and Applied* (New York: Free Press, 1949), p. 276.

7. Philip Selznick, *Leadership in Administration* (Evanston, IL: Row, Peterson, 1957), p. 19.

are part of an evolving decision-making structure in particular policy areas.

Further, such role institutionalization cannot take place without the creation of a presidential constituency that expects and demands policies and provides political support. A durable coalition, including groups in Congress, interest groups, and bureaucratic agencies, must develop permanent stakes in the presidential role and provide support for its continuation. Without such a constituency, the presidential role will atrophy or will be acquired by others—congressional leaders, bureaucratic agencies, interest groups, or all three in alliance. Such a constituency makes the presidential role responsive and accountable and sustains its political importance. As the culmination of the process of institutionalization, this new role becomes an integral and indissoluble part of the presidency, universally expected of the president and blending with the president's other roles.

THE PHASES OF INSTITUTIONALIZED CHANGE

The process of presidential institutionalization unfolds in five phases: (1) initiation, (2) programmatic definition, (3) succession, (4) coordination, and (5) assimilation. These phases do not necessarily occur in this sequence. Each phase contributes a special component that contributes to the institutionalization of the president's role.

The first phase: crisis and role initiation

During the first phase, the president acquires his new role. Usually such initiation arises as an outcome of a crisis.[8]

8. Richard M. Pious, *The American Presidency* (New York: Basic Books, 1979), pp. 151, 152.

The typical pattern is as follows: a crisis arises that threatens national welfare or security. Everyone turns to the presidency for decision, for, as John Locke pointed out long ago, under crisis conditions power gravitates to the executive because he can make decisions quickly and mobilize the resources of the society. The president, after consulting with a group of his advisers and some congressional leaders, decides on a course of action and turns to Congress for its quick approval, or by Executive Order creates a new office or agency to deal with the crisis. Under the exigency of a crisis, the president's course of action is readily accepted.

It is not surprising that at such a time innovations occur. Prevailing policies are inadequate to deal with the crisis. New solutions are sought. Ideals that have been ignored or rejected in the past are seen in a new light as potential solutions. The usual resistances to innovation—custom, tradition, vested interests—give way as the resolution of the crisis acquires unchallenged priority and efficacy becomes the sole criterion.

The degree of support the president's new role has at its origin is crucial to its institutionalization. If it is well supported, then the president will enjoy greater latitude in defining his new role. If the initiation of the role occasions much conflict and has shaky support at its inception, then controversy will continue when the president tries to implement it.

The second or programmatic phase

When the crisis is over, a programmatic phase begins. From various quarters, Congress, interest groups, bureaucratic agencies, come suggestions that legislation is necessary to prevent the recurrence of such a crisis. Various legislative proposals suggest the new role of the president, propose a permanent agency, define the scope of its authority and the structure of its organization, and assign to the president responsibility to implement the program. They report to Congress on progress or policies that are necessary to anticipate situations that may prove dangerous.

The third phase:
  succession

The phase of succession refers to the change of administration and tests whether the president's role will continue. This phase is critical because the president who follows the initiating president may view the role differently and appoint his own people to administer the program. In the balance is the extent to which he will continue the policies and practices of his predecessor. Moreover, this phase is especially critical if the successor president belongs to the opposite party and espouses opposite policies. Then the new role and the staff apparatus created to carry it out face a test of survival.

The fourth phase:
  coordination

During this phase, the staff that has been created to assist the president in his new role must clarify its relationships with Congress, with its relevant committees, and with other executive agencies that play a part in the decision making in that policy. Relationships have to be worked out so that excessive conflict does not undermine the staff or the president's effectiveness.

The fifth phase:
  role assimilation

During this final phase, the president's role has become accepted not only as a vital function of the presidency, but as a national necessity. When this phase or threshold is reached, a coordinated structure for making policy has emerged that provides the presidency with information and policy recommendations. The president's role has expanded considerably from its definition when it was initiated.

This model of the phases of institutionalization fits several significant new presidential roles of the last 50 years. The crisis of the Depression and the reconversion problem at the end of World War II resulted in the enactment of the Employment Act of 1946, which assigned the president a permanent role in economic policy; the Sputnik crisis in 1957 was followed by the Space Program and the Science and Technology Program, assigning the president a new role of fostering scientific and technological development. Environmental-contamination crisis brought about legislation for clean air and water and the Environmental Protection Agency. Also approximating this pattern is the crisis of civil rights and the legislation and administrative agencies that were its outgrowth. The common denominator in all these changes is the crystallization of a new role for the presidency, a new administrative apparatus, and a new presidential constituency.

THE ADMINISTRATIVE
DEVELOPMENT OF THE
PRESIDENT'S ROLE
AS ECONOMIC POLICYMAKER

Each of these phases will be illustrated by the history and experience of the president's role in macroeconomic policy and the development of the Council of Economic Advisers (CEA). This presidential role was chosen to illustrate the process because it is perhaps the most important new role of the contemporary presidency, having grown steadily in importance and complexity since its inception.

The first phase: role initiation

The depression that began in 1929 devastated the country. Some 25 percent of the labor force was unemployed. State and local governments and private agencies could not cope with the massive dislocation that resulted. Franklin D. Roosevelt, who became president in 1933, had been governor of New York and as such had introduced several relief policies into that state. On assuming the presidency, he brought with him a group of economic advisers, later called "the brain trust," that had served him in Albany. They played an active part in formulating the New Deal measures that Roosevelt introduced to bring about recovery and relief. These and later measures did not follow a consistent economic theory. Policies were devised that dealt with specific problems in each sector of the economy, together making up a political coalition that FDR called a "concert of interests."

During World War II, federal management of the economy increased to mobilize the country's resources. New agencies were created, many housed in the Executive Office of the President, that were charged with allocating scarce resources under wartime conditions. Price controls and rationing were instituted, as well as policies designed to channel resources and manpower into defense industries.

The second or programmatic phase

The experience during these two severe crises, the Depression and the war, generated a new role for the president as the architect of economic policy and administrator of a sector in the economy subject directly or indirectly to public regulation. As the war drew to a close, concern arose that the termination of hostilities would bring a recurrence of depression as millions of men, demobilized from the armed forces, sought employment. During the war, the labor force had been fully employed and demonstrated that our productive capacity was remarkable. Congress therefore began to consider various proposals to deal with problems of wartime reconversion. Not until 1946 was an acceptable bill hammered out, the historic Employment Act. In that law, Congress declared a new governmental commitment to achieving and maintaining maximum employment. To that end, Congress required the president to submit regular reports on the status of the economy and to recommend policies that might close the gap between the prevailing level of employment and the level of full employment. To assist the president in preparing such reports, the act created the Council of Economic Advisers, consisting of three economists appointed by the president with senatorial confirmation and to be located in the Executive Office of the President. To consider these reports, the bill created a joint committee of both houses of Congress. This bill thus defined the president's role as that of preparing regularly an economic agenda, while also retaining for Congress a role in economic policy.[9]

9. L. G. Seligman, "Presidential Leadership: The Inner Circle and Institutionalization," *Jour-*

The initial administration of the act under President Truman was turbulent, as ambiguities in the president's role and that of the council became apparent. The president doubted the usefulness of the objective analyses of economic conditions that the council's chairman supplied him. For its part, the council was uncertain as to whether its role was to provide neutral diagnoses or to make recommendations that took into account their political feasibility from the president's standpoint. The resultant confusion over the council's role diminished the regard of Congress for the president and his new economic advisers.

The third phase: succession

When Eisenhower became president, he was committed to reducing the government's role in the economy. A new and critical phase began, because the continuity of the president's role was at stake under an economic outlook opposed to the welfare-state orientation of his predecessor. Eisenhower was primarily concerned with price stability rather than with economic growth and full employment.[10]

With the succession of presidents came a succession in the membership of the CEA. It seemed almost as if the president and his economic advisers were starting anew. For several reasons, the succession strengthened the president's role and the importance of his economic advisers. First, the president's role was not discretionary and was prescribed by law. Second, the role involved issues of inflation and unemployment that were critical to the president's political support. Third, in order to deal with these issues, the president needed technical advice, which made the CEA essential. As a result, the CEA and the president were established on a firmer basis than hitherto. The president worked closely with the chairman of his CEA, Dr. Arthur Burns, and Congress developed a new respect for the council and for the quality of its work.

The fourth phase: attempts at administrative coordination

Steps that contributed to institutionalization also derived from the relationships between the CEA and other agencies involved in economic policy. Over the years, the CEA actively participated in a network of economic policy with other executive agencies, including those in the Executive Office of the President, giving advice on a wide range of policies from pollution to communication. These lines of communication became sufficiently coherent that each successive CEA chairman did not have to start from scratch. The council chairman and members participated in negotiations on legislation originating in the executive, and in membership in various councils, committees, task forces, and other interagency groups. Through such relationships, the CEA defined its scope and boundaries and eventually came to terms with its potential bureaucratic competitors in the structure of economic policymaking and advice to the president. Once such boundaries were recognized, tacit bargains were

---

nal of Politics, 18:410-26 (1956); Edward J. Flash, *Economic Advice and Presidential Leadership: The Council of Economic Advisers* (New York: Columbia University Press, 1965).

10. A. F. Friedlander, "Macro-Policy Goals in the Post-War Period," *Quarterly Journal of Economics,* 87:25-43 (Feb. 1973).

struck to protect them. A standing bargain based on mutual exchange and mutual benefit emerged. As Walter Heller stated, "Only as the network of relations within the Executive Office of the President, with White House assistants, and with Cabinet and subcabinet members, was gradually built would the council feel that its position in the economic policy process was reasonably secure. . . . I can only hope that enough of tradition is developing so that the process of reconstructing this network in another administration one day will come rather more easily than it did to us."[11]

The relationship the CEA established with other agencies enhanced its usefulness. For example, the CEA and the Bureau of the Budget—later the Office of Management and Budget (OMB)—became natural allies. The council's forecasts guided the bureau's projections of federal expenditures, just as the latter's information about various programs could enlighten the council's economic diagnoses and projections. Second, the heads of the Bureau of the Budget and the CEA were often on the same side, opposing the point of view of Treasury economists.

The relationship between the CEA chairman and his colleagues with principal members of the White House staff was essential to keeping economic policy high on the president's agenda. As issues of economic policy came to the White House, whether or not the CEA would be consulted depended on principal White House staff members. Thus Joseph Califano, when he was LBJ's principal domestic-policy coordinator, often referred matters to Chairmen Heller and Okun. Similarly, under Nixon, George Shultz, the head of OMB, played a key role in involving Herbert Stein, the CEA chairman, in the active flow of economic advice to the president.

The emergence of the Troika illustrates how patterns of relationships evolved. During the Eisenhower administration, the heads of three agencies—the Treasury Department, the Bureau of the Budget (BOB), and the CEA—realizing their common concerns with economic forecasts and fiscal policy, and reluctant to confront a president who disliked disagreement, began to meet informally along with members of their staffs. Each agency was concerned with preparing estimates that were component parts of overall fiscal policy. The Treasury estimated government revenue, the BOB estimated government expenditures, and the CEA forecast gross national product, employment levels, and other economic indicators. A consistent fiscal policy required that estimates of government expenditures and revenue be considered together. The objective of the meetings was therefore to reach agreement on recommendations to be made to the president. These informal meetings became regularized during the Kennedy administration and continued during succeeding presidencies because the presidents wanted coordinated policies. Less often, the chairman of the Federal Reserve Board met with the Troika, which was then called the Quadriad, to coordinate monetary policy with fiscal policy.

During the Nixon years, policymaking on economic matters was centralized in the White House and involved the CEA in a new set of interagency relationships. The Troika achieved some

---

11. Walter Heller, *New Dimensions of Political Economy* (Cambridge, MA: Harvard University Press, 1966), p. 55.

coordination of monetary and fiscal policy but "beyond domestic, fiscal and monetary policy lay a vast realm of economic policy issues which were handled in a wide variety of ways."[12] Problems of international economic policy had become urgent, and so the Council on International Economic Policy (CIEP), made up of cabinet officials, was established in 1971. This proved ineffective, however. Shortly after the election of 1972, Nixon created the Council on Economic Policy in the White House, with responsibility to coordinate both domestic and foreign economic policy. The secretary of the Treasury, George Shultz, was appointed assistant to the president for economic policy and chairman of the new council as well as of the CIEP. The new council, which included the chairman of the CEA, met daily to coordinate various economic issues.

President Ford continued the council and added a Council of Wage and Price Stability to focus on the problem of holding the line against inflation. Jimmy Carter revised the set-up by establishing an Economic Policy Group (EPG) that was entrusted with three tasks: (1) coordination of interagency staff work on economic issues; (2) review of economic policy issues and formulation of option papers for presidential decision; and (3) oversight of the implementation of decisions made and policies adopted. The secretary of the Treasury and the chairman of the CEA were appointed cochairmen of the group. The latter withdrew after a time, and the secretary of the Treasury became the chairman. The CEA played an active role in this group, contributing a macroeconomic perspective, contrasting with the special bureaucratic interests of the other members.

12. Ibid., p. 25.

The Council of Economic Affairs, which meets twice weekly, was created in the Reagan administration. Weidenbaum was also a member of the Budget Review Board, with Reagan, Meese, Baker, and Stockman. Once a quarter, a White House Economic Policy Advisory Board meets, made up of prominent conservative economists like Alan Greenspan and Herbert Stein.[13]

The Troika and the developments in economic-policy machinery since then indicate that the continuation of the presidential advisory agency depends in part on its relationships with other agencies. If the agency succeeds in working out complementary relationships with other agencies in the same policy area, its status with the president will be enhanced. If other agencies regard the advisory agency as a threat, then it may become a liability to the president.

The fifth phase: role assimilation

In the decades after World War II, economic problems became increasingly significant. It was a period of great economic growth, but not economic stability. In the 30 years from 1948 to 1980, eight recessions of generally increasing gravity occurred. In the words of one economist, "Inflation started walking in the 1950s, trotting in the 1960s and galloping in the next decade. In 1978-1979 inflation rose to 13% while unemployment hovered between six and eight percent. From 1950 to 1980, consumer prices rose to 350%."[14]

As economic issues came to the forefront on the government agenda, so

13. Dom Bonafede, "CEA and Reaganomics," *National Journal*, 6 Feb. 1982, p. 247.
14. Melville Ulmer, "What Economists Know," *Commentary*, 74(1):3-57, 55 (July 1982).

public interest in economic policy grew. The programs of the Great Society drew public attention to such issues as poverty, the costs of medical care, the needs of public transportation, and the problems of cities. The new issues of environmental protection challenged the hitherto unquestioned goals of economic growth. The energy crises of the seventies dramatized our new economic interdependence with other nations. The mass media gave increasing attention to presidential actions and statements about economic policy. Thus when presidential economic policies faltered or failed, the statements of critics made front-page news and nightly television newscasts. Economists watched presidential economic policy closely and expressed their reactions promptly in the press and on Capitol Hill. As a result, the president's economic policy increased his political vulnerability.

On another level, a significant aspect of the growth in the presidential role was the president's acquisition of new clienteles. Organized interests that became beneficiaries of welfare policies or other governmental benefits turned to the White House to press their claims. But the president also invited group liaison in order to bolster his political support. As a result, from FDR on, presidents began to create special offices in the White House to maintain regular relations with various groups. This trend was formalized by the creation of the Office of Public Liaison under President Nixon, and the office his successors maintained with some organizational alterations. Thus successive presidents recognized the importance of support from groups and public opinion in building a coalition of support for economic policies, and as leverage with Congress, the bureaucracy, and the media.

Economic policy is politics. As Charles Schultze, the former chairman of CEA under President Carter, stated,

The economist turned policy advisor will quickly discover that in the councils where economic advice for the policy maker is formulated one-half to two-thirds of the discussion has little to do with economics, at least in the conventionally defined sense. A large part of the discussion centers around political feasibilities, legislative strategy, optimum timing, effects on public opinion.[15]

The importance of such coalitions of support was illustrated in two major instances of major economic policy. One was the celebrated Kennedy Tax Cut in 1964. The process of enactment took all of two years, while policy was debated within the administration, with leading figures in Congress, especially Wilbur Mills, chairman of the House Ways and Means Committee, and with various groups representing business and labor.[16] Similarly, when the CEA proposed to President Johnson that a tax surcharge be imposed in order to offset the mounting costs of the Vietnam war, Johnson initially rejected it because a supporting coalition in Congress could not be mobilized without exacting a quid pro quo that Johnson was not willing to pay. Later, Johnson negotiated a better deal for himself.

Just as the president's role required coalitions of support, so has his role become institutionalized as it has evoked greater challenge from Congress. Thus as an outgrowth of the presi-

15. Bonafede, "CEA and Reaganomics."
16. Laurence O'Brien, *No Final Victories* (Garden City, NY: Doubleday, 1974), p. 84; Herbert Stein, *The Fiscal Revolution in America* (Chicago: University of Chicago Press, 1969), ch. 17.

dent's increasingly important role in fiscal policy, Congress adopted in 1974 a new procedure for formulating its own budget. As a result, in principle, Congress placed itself in a better position to hold the president's budget and its own budget to better account. Thus the institutionalization of the president's economic role contributed in some ways to greater accountability.

POLITICAL CHANGE AND THE POLITICS OF THE PRESIDENCY

The analysis of presidential role institutionalization indicates that the political change associated with growth of federal responsibility over the economy involved several phases and complex interrelationships. Crises may accelerate political change, but the implementation of change is a less dramatic and more subtle process. If the metaphor of crisis is a flood, then the metaphor of institutionalized change is a stream.

This process is illustrated in the growth of presidential responsibility for economic policy. The concern with economic problems and the monitoring it required was a response to public and group expectations and demands that the government intervene not only to correct the imbalances of inflation or unemployment, but also to anticipate and prevent future dislocations. This change in public expectations and demands did not come about because the president zealously sought his new role, but because a new political coalition in the electorate and group leaders and leaders in Congress demanded it.

Today, President Reagan's attempt to revolutionize economic policy is somewhat paradoxical. A role institutionalized to increase governmental responsibility for welfare and to regulate the economy is being used to reverse that direction. Is the president's primacy in economic policy so linked to welfare policy that it can be used to induce movement in the opposite direction? Evidence to date indicates that some aspects of change were more easily reversed than others. Supply-siders, rather than Keynesians, were appointed to the Council of Economic Advisers. Other key figures in economic policy—the director of OMB and the secretary of the treasury—were appointed who were advocates, if not zealots, for the new economic direction. However, the stumbling blocks are (1) the effectiveness of the policy, and (2) constituency support. Can a steadfast coalition in support of the counterrevolution be developed? The evidence so far would lead to a negative answer, for reasons related to our analysis and recent developments in the politics of the presidency.

The president's effectiveness in his role as a policymaker and the institutionalization of his role have depended on sustained political support. But it is characteristic in U.S. politics to give the president a new role and then to make conditional the resources he needs to fulfill it. The politics of the presidency today makes broad policy changes more difficult because the presidency lacks the stable coalitional support that is necessary. Recent developments in the president's relationship to Congress and his political party are the principal reason.

The late Arthur Okun, an outstanding economist and former chairman of the CEA under Lyndon Johnson, called the Council of Economic Advisers "a pressure group for economic rationality."[17] But the politics of economic pol-

17. Remark made in interview with the author.

icy and the politics of the presidency make it especially difficult today for the president to win support for broad and consistent economic policy.

The political base for the president's economic role and the commitment of the government to intervention in the economy was the new majority coalition that crystallized in the Democratic party in 1936. That coalition, consisting principally of metropolitan voters, including ethnic minorities and organized labor, held together from the mid-thirties until it began to weaken by 1968. In Congress, with the exception of two brief periods, the Democrats dominated both houses. The representatives of this electoral coalition provided support for most New Deal legislation. For example, it was the coalition of labor and liberals that was instrumental in the enactment of the Employment Act of 1946.[18]

During the late fifties, this same coalition in Congress laid the groundwork for the legislation that was discussed during the New Frontier and enacted during the Great Society. When the new and unprecedented issues of stagflation arose in the seventies, they coincided with the erosion of this coalition. The difficulties presidents have encountered since then in dealing with economic policy result in large part from the weakening of that coalition.

In recent years, political parties have declined. In many ways, their role in the presidential selection process has diminished. The recent reforms, especially in the Democratic party, have led to an increase in direct primaries, which have given candidates, rather than state party organizations, the most active role in the winning of popular endorsements and delegates committed to them. As a result, candidates have built their own campaign organizations to build the coalitions of elite and popular support to win nominations and general elections. Another factor is the increased use of political consultants in campaign organizations, replacing the role of traditional party officials and campaign workers. As a result of these developments, a gradual disengagement between presidential candidates and their party organizations has taken place.

The effects of these developments is also apparent in presidential governing. Ever since FDR, presidents have been assigning greater staff resources toward building their own governing coalitions, often in conflict with their own party coalition in the electorate or in Congress. For example, the Office of Congressional Relations has been growing steadily in every presidential administration since its inception as an office in the White House under President Eisenhower. Of no less importance is the steady expansion of the number of White House officials charged with the special task of maintaining liaison with particular interest groups and ethnic minorities. With these developments has come greater White House use of polling agencies to gauge the shifts in public attitudes toward the president and his policies. This goes along with the attention presidents have given to the extensive use of the media for the purpose of mobilizing public opinion and generating grass-roots pressure that will impel hesitant or recalcitrant members of Congress to support his programs.

Trends in Congress have also aggravated the attenuation of party ties.

18. Stephen K. Bailey, *Congress Makes a Law* (New York: Columbia University Press, 1950).

Increasingly, members of Congress see themselves as agents performing services for their constituencies, channeling funds from the U.S. Treasury to projects in their districts, or intervening with the bureaucracy as caseworkers on behalf of their constituency clients. Voters respond by favoring the incumbent member of Congress, even though he or she may be of the party opposite to that of the voters in the district. The presidential coattail, once the sign of party attachment, no longer seems to carry much weight. Members of Congress, like presidents, are in business for themselves.

The growth in the number of interest groups has also contributed to fragmentation. As the scope of government has expanded, various groups have been formed to obtain favored positions or to protect their interests.

The result of these changes is that the president's coalition of support is less a party coalition than one that a presidential candidate has mobilized in the course of his nomination and election. Because this coalition rests on fragile party identifications, it is unstable. Moreover, the presidential coalition is made up of core support, often too narrow to sustain presidential policy. It contains too many incongruous elements, the divisiveness of party nomination battles and the fickle peripheral support gained during the general election. For these reasons, today more than ever before, presidents have difficulty sustaining consistent policy. In the absence of durable coalitions, the process of role institutionalization faces new difficulties. Ad hoc support is insufficient to support the continuity that institutionalized change requires.

CONCLUSION

Some aspects of presidential role institutionalization and political change have been analyzed. They indicate how the presidency has become a principal instrument of change, because it has become the focal institution during crises. But in the aftermath of crises, prophylactic policies require the expert advice and continual administrative implementation that only the presidency can provide. The result is the emergence of a new role for the presidency, the evolution of which involves several phases, during which a decision-making set of relationships unfolds. Concomitantly, a presidential constituency also emerges that turns to the White House for policy initiation and implementation. The president's need for coalitional support has become a vital necessity. Yet this has become more difficult to achieve as the presidency has become more disengaged from its party and more dependent on the coalitions it can mobilize. This is evident today, as President Reagan attempts to reverse governmental economic direction.

Integration and Fragmentation: Key Themes of Congressional Change

By WALTER J. OLESZEK

ABSTRACT: Congress is a fragmented, decentralized, and undisciplined institution. These essential qualities constitute both its strength and its weakness. On the one hand, Congress's fragmentation, as manifested by features such as bicameralism and collegial decision making, promote its representative and oversight roles. On the other hand, Congress has a difficult time getting its policymaking act together because it lacks sufficient integrative mechanisms, such as party and procedural devices, that would aggregate issues and interests. Throughout congressional history, the themes of integration and fragmentation have warred against each other with the forces of dispersal typically being victorious. This article's objective is to highlight certain complexities and anomalies in structural and procedural changes designed to constrain or impose order on Congress's diffused power. Two recent developments—committee modernization and renewed interest in oversight of administrative activities—provide the case material for the analysis.

Walter J. Oleszek is on the staff of the Congressional Research Service, Library of Congress. He is the author or coauthor of Congress against Itself, Congressional Procedures and the Policy Process, *and* Congress and Its Members.

NOTE: The views expressed here are the author's and not those of the Congressional Research Service.

CONGRESS is a fragmented, decentralized, and undisciplined institution. These essential qualities constitute both its strength and its weakness. On the one hand, Congress's fragmentation, as manifested by features such as bicameralism and collegial decision making, promote its representative and oversight roles. On the other hand, Congress has a hard time getting its policymaking act together because it lacks sufficient integrative mechanisms, such as party and procedural devices, that would aggregate issues and interests. Throughout congressional history, the themes of integration and fragmentation have warred against each other, with the forces of dispersal typically being victorious.

Unsurprisingly, Congress's untidiness opens it to sharp criticism from many quarters. Cartoonists, scholars, journalists, and even its own members fault Congress for its foibles and inadequacies. "Nobody in the House of Representatives is anybody else's boss," one representative has noted. "And what that means is that efficiency will always be much less than in a more hierarchically organized or in a financially organized place."[1]

Many other factors account for Congress's generally negative ratings. The public has its own conflicting set of images of Congress. Some, for example, want an efficient Congress, with disciplined parties to formulate clearly defined policies that the majority can enact into law. Others propose that Congress and the president be equal partners in policymaking. Still others advocate that either Congress or the president can be preeminent in national decision making. If Congress does not act in a way that comports with various notions of appropriate legislative behavior, it is open to such criticisms from these notions' advocates.

Similar results occur with congressional change. Like the proverbial half-full—or half-empty?—glass, members' views toward institutional developments are shaped in part by their vantage points. Innovations that strengthen party leaders, for instance, might be opposed by committee chairpersons who cherish their autonomy. Change, in short, is seldom neutral, particularly when it affects the distribution of power: who has it, who wants it, and who gets it.

To some members, change would bring authentic improvements. To others, it suggests cosmetic and ephemeral developments. This split vision is somewhat akin to what Humpty Dumpty told Alice in Lewis Carroll's *Through the Looking-Glass:* "When I use a word it means just what I choose it to mean—neither more nor less." Likewise in Congress, whether change is "reform" depends on who provides the definition.

In recent years, many proposals have surfaced to promote Congress's ability to develop policy or to review executive agencies in a systematic manner. Integration is an attractive concept that conveys unity, efficiency, coordination, and, in general, a comprehensive approach to policymaking. By comparison, fragmentation seems inherently unattractive. It connotes inefficiency, slowness, narrowness of perspective, and, in general, a piecemeal approach to policymaking. Little wonder that members and political observers commonly support organizational changes that emphasize integration over fragmentation.

Yet the framers of the Constitution stressed the values of fragmentation for Congress. They did not list efficiency,

---

1. "Flaws of Congress: Freshmen's Size-Up," *U.S. News and World Report,* 5 Oct. 1981, p. 47.

hierarchy, or speed as special legislative virtues. Instead, Alexander Hamilton noted that "promptitude of decision is oftener an evil than a benefit. The differences of opinion, and the jarrings of parties in [Congress], though they may sometimes obstruct salutary plans, yet often promote deliberation and circumspection; and serve to check excesses in the majority."[2] In short, Congress at its best is organized disorder.

It is an institution where members' different views on issues clash and compete over what is the public interest. The public interest means in practice what can attract a majority of the House and Senate. To be sure, this is a messy and complicated state of affairs, especially when there are vigorous exchanges among members and committees and between the House and Senate, the two parties, and Congress and the White House.

Some members are attracted to the purported virtues of the hierarchical executive branch: coordination, secrecy, information, coherency, and dispatch. Senator Daniel P. Moynihan, Democrat from New York, referred to this as the "Iron Law of Emulation." Whenever any branch of government acquires a "new technique which enhances its power in relation to the other branches, that technique will soon be adopted by those other branches as well," he said.[3] Congress, for instance, created its own staff bureaucracy to keep up with that of the executive. There are risks to Congress whenever changes are sought that revamp its basic nature.

Legislative changes are notable for producing mixed results and unexpected consequences. This article's objective is to highlight certain complexities and anomalies in structural and procedural changes designed to constrain or impose order on Congress's diffused power. Two recent developments—committee modernization and renewed interest in oversight of administrative activities—provide the case material for the analysis.

COMMITTEE REALIGNMENT

Committees are the centers of legislative policymaking, oversight, and education. They also serve as arenas for individual career advancement. Members believe, wrote a scholar, that favorable assignments can enhance their reelection prospects, increase their influence within the chamber, and assure their participation in preferred policymaking areas.[4] No wonder representatives and senators are interested in the organization, management, and performance of their committees and subcommittees. Members understand the importance of the committee system, the workshop of Congress, and want to ensure its ability to respond effectively to political and policy issues.

During the past decade, Congress tried three times—the House in 1973-74, the Senate in 1976-77, and the House in 1979-80—to restructure the committee system. The first House attempt at jurisdictional realignment had limited success; the Senate's committee revision was somewhat more successful; and the second House effort was a complete failure.[5] Despite the different outcomes, the

---

2. *Federalist,* no. 69, in *The Federalist,* ed. Henry B. Dawson (New York: Scribner, 1876), p. 491.

3. Daniel P. Moynihan, "Imperial Government," *Commentary,* 65:26 (June 1978).

4. Richard F. Fenno, Jr., *Congressmen in Committees* (Boston: Little, Brown, 1973), pp. 1-14.

5. See Roger H. Davidson and Walter J. Oleszek, *Congress against Itself* (Bloomington:

objectives of the three committee reviews were virtually identical. In a word, the objective was unification.

The three groups of committee reformers identified a selected number of fundamental issues facing the nation and surveyed how the committee system addressed them. They found major policy areas, such as energy, environment, health, and transportation, scattered among scores of committees and subcommittees. The 1979-80 House panel, for example, found that 83 house committees and subcommittees exercised some jurisdiction over energy. Its recommendation: establish a separate Committee on Energy to consolidate authority.[6]

In all three instances, adopting the unification approach placed committee reformers at odds with large numbers of their colleagues. To be sure, members understand that change brings in its wake both costs and benefits. A dilemma of the reformers is that costs seem direct and personal while benefits appear indirect and diffuse. Legislators, in short, have divergent perspectives on the multiple dimensions of organizational change: institutional, substantive, and political.

Divergent perspectives

Institutionally, members look at the committee system and see different things. Advocates of change perceive committees that are outmoded, imbalanced in workload, jurisdictionally fragmented, and unnecessarily duplicative. Representative Richard Bolling, Democrat from Missouri, architect of the 1973-74 committee revision plan, wrote an extensive bill of complaints:

> The present committee system . . . fails the House of Representatives in four ways: (1) the system cripples the Speaker by denying him operational leadership of the House; (2) the system neither receives, utilizes nor generates adequate information; (3) the committee system does not consider the economy from a macroeconomic point of view; and (4) it does not facilitate coordinated policies, nor does it coordinate emerging issues, because the jurisdictions of House committees are outdated.[7]

By this account, committee reorganization would not only promote cohesive policymaking but would also strengthen the floor leadership's ability to influence the direction of committee activities.

Opponents of significant committee realignment value Congress's overlapping jurisdictions and weak central party leadership. Representative John Dingell, Democrat from Michigan, a leading opponent of both the 1973-74 and 1979-80 House realignment attempts, put the issue this way:

> I am not altogether in favor of the idea that the Congress should abate its process and practice of having overlapping jurisdictions. I happen to think from the competition between these overlaps and overlapping committees and subcommittees, oftentimes we are able to approach questions from entirely different viewpoints leading to perhaps a better appreciation of problems, more vigorous oversight, better cooperation between the committees and ultimately bet-

---

Indiana University Press, 1977); Judith H. Parris, "The Senate Reorganizes Its Committees, 1977," *Political Science Quarterly*, 79:319-37 (Summer 1979); and Timothy Lee Peckinpaugh, "Reform of Congressional Energy Committee Jurisdiction: A Study of Parochial Politics," *Claremont Journal of Public Affairs*, 8:12-24 (Summer 1981).

6. U.S. House, Select Committee on Committees, *To Establish a Standing Committee on Energy*, House Report 96-741, 96th Cong., 2d sess., 1980.

7. Richard Bolling, "Committees in the House," *The Annals* of the American Academy of Political and Social Science, 411:3 (Jan. 1974).

ter statutes and better implementation of the statute by the executive.[8]

Instead of wholesale reorganization, these members suggest that problems with the committee system be handled in retail fashion, through coordinating devices such as multiple referrals—sending the same bill to several panels—joint hearings, or the creation of ad hoc panels, such as the 1977 House Ad Hoc Energy Committee that considered President Carter's energy initiatives.[9]

Substantively, members disagree on how broad as well as narrow subjects should be addressed in any revamped committee system. Even issues that appear narrow have many components. Is alcoholism, for example, a health or education or labor or advertising problem? Broader topics raise more fundamental concerns. Energy and environment represent cases in point.

The 1973-74 House reformers recommended creation of a new Energy and Environment Committee. Panel members were to be chosen carefully to ensure balance between the two policy interests. Committee members could then fight out issues within the panel's confines and report legislation to the House floor that could be debated systematically by the contending sides.

The Senate reformers took an entirely different approach. After considering a combined panel, the reform group recommended assigning responsibility for energy and environment to separate panels, noting in its report:

The Select Committee devoted substantial study to the relationship between energy and environmental jurisdictions. It carefully weighed the option of creating a single Energy and Environment Committee, but decided against it on the grounds the workload of such a committee would be staggering, and totally consolidated jurisdiction over both energy and environment might lead to policies dominated by one point of view. While the Select Committee seeks balanced consolidation of jurisdictions, it recognizes the dangers and impracticalities of overconsolidation.[10]

In sum, what seemed an appropriate policy mix to House reformers was found in the Senate to be overconsolidation.

Politically, perspectives on committee reorganization are colored by many concerns, two of which are especially critical. First, jurisdictional changes affect directly the responsibilities of committees and the careers of their members and staff aides. Unsurprisingly, those who lose jurisdiction are among the strongest opponents of realignment. As then Majority Leader—later Speaker—Thomas P. O'Neill observed after the 1974 House adopted a watered-down revision plan: "The name of the game is power and the boys don't want to give it up."[11]

Second, jurisdictional realignment is opposed by affected interest groups. Outside interests mobilize against committee reorganizations that threaten their relationships with existing panels. "Carefully nurtured contacts with key congressmen and their aides, as well as

---

8. U.S. House, *Workshop on Congressional Oversight and Investigations,* House Document 96-217, 96th Cong., 1st sess., 1979, p. 176.

9. Bruce I. Oppenheimer, "Policy Effects of U.S. House Reform: Decentralization and the Capacity to Resolve Energy Issues," *Legislative Studies Quarterly,* 5:5-30 (Feb. 1980).

10. U.S. Senate, Temporary Select Committee to Study the Senate Committee System, *First Report,* Senate Report 94-1395, 94th Cong., 2d sess., 1976, p. 85. Another consideration involved the preservation of chairmanships for two senior Democrats: Henry Jackson, WA (Energy), and Jennings Randolph, WV (Environment).

11. "The Democrats, Given the Chance to Reform, Don't," *New York Times,* 12 May 1974, part IV, p. 3.

years of selective campaign contributions," explained a journalist, "will all come loose when a new, unfamiliar committee takes jurisdiction."[12]

Indeed, large-scale committee realignments provoke sharp disagreements about what constitutes an effective committee system. There is little consensus among members concerning the criteria for an ideal committee system. To be sure, many members support the abstract notion of fundamental committee change. But a specific plan presents a complex and contradictory mixture of policy, political, substantive, personal, and symbolic considerations that cross-pressure even advocates of change.

Future prospects

Congress is an adaptive and flexible institution. Change is part of its very essence. Every two years, for example, the November elections trigger organizational and operational changes in almost every House and Senate committee. The future of deliberate and comprehensive committee modernization is unclear, however. There are at least three possibilities.

First, Congress may continue to conduct business as usual with its current committee arrangements. "The House has lived on glue and bailing wire throughout the 1970s," wrote Representative Bill Frenzel, Republican from Minnesota, "and so it may be expected to survive on the same in the 1980s."[13]

Second, either chamber, independently or concurrently, may again attempt a major overhaul of committee structure. Complaints from members disadvantaged by the existing system, the stresses and strains of coping with a growing and complex workload, challenges from the White House, or severe public disenchantment with Congress are among the factors that might combine to instigate the endeavor. No doubt there will be uncertainty again among members as they vote, perhaps many for the first time, on competing views of the committee system.

Finally, Congress may innovate and emphasize coordinative devices and procedures—the aforementioned multiple referrals, ad hoc panels, and the like—to accommodate issues that crosscut jurisdictional lines. Party leaders and groups, perhaps even Congress's relatively centralized budget process, may have untapped coordinating potential. In this regard, the significance of the congressional budget process merits further discussion. As one scholar recently declared: "A potent centralizing and coordinating force had been established to counter the long-dominant centrifugal trends within the congressional power structure."[14]

In 1974, Congress integrated its fragmented budgetary process in part because its power of the purse was threatened by the impoundment actions of President Nixon. Two objectives of the change were to reclaim lost authority and to bring coherence and fiscal discipline to the way congressional committees handle the president's budget. The centralization occurred, however, not by merging any of the authorizing, appropriating, or taxing committees. To take authority away from any panel that had it would have been too contro-

12. Quoted in Davidson and Oleszek, *Congress against Itself,* p. 196.
13. Bill Frenzel, "House Reforms and Why They Haven't Worked," *Commonsense,* 3:47 (Winter 1980).

14. James L. Sundquist, *The Decline and Resurgence of Congress* (Washington, DC: Brookings Institution, 1981), p. 231.

versial and difficult. Instead, new House and Senate budget committees were created to take overall charge of Congress's uncoordinated financial procedures. These budgetary innovations are "one of the most important government reforms in decades," observed Stuart Eizenstat, President Carter's chief domestic aide. Congress has "set up a competing power system which makes it more difficult for the President to have his way."[15]

Things did not work out that way, however. In 1981, President Reagan turned the Congressional Budget and Impoundment Control Act against Congress itself. He helped persuade his congressional GOP allies to employ the act's reconciliation procedure—requiring House and Senate committees to reduce spending according to fiscal instructions contained in a budget resolution—and thus force Congress in one huge bill to make dramatic financial cuts in numerous governmental social programs. "Without reconciliation," said Senate Budget Committee Chairman Pete Domenici, Republican from New Mexico, "it would be absolutely impossible to cut the budget by this dimension"—nearly $140 billion over three years.[16]

Reconciliation short-circuited the House and Senate's piecemeal process of hearings, markups, and deliberations by its committees. The Senate, led by the GOP for the first time in 26 years, deferred to its Budget Committee, which followed the White House. The Democrat-led House committees were steamrollered by President Reagan's skillful mobilization of Republican and conservative Democratic votes and public backing for his economic plan. Parliamentary government reigned for a time in Congress as presidential budgets won quick approval and circumvented the normal routine of lengthy review and modification of executive recommendations.

After the dust had settled, many members wondered whether Congress was really reconciled to reconciliation. "Nobody is particularly happy about this procedure," said Representative Barber Conable, Republican from New York.[17] At least two lessons can be derived from the experience. First, political forces count as much as or more than legal controls in determining which branch exercises predominant influence. Second, members can never be certain how congressional changes will evolve, perform, or work out in practice. As one analyst wrote:

Congress wouldn't be Congress if it always knew what it was doing. Many of the things that were recently undone in obscurity, misunderstanding and deceit were probably enacted in similar circumstances. As for the timing and scope of the reconciliation package, they reflected the changed political climate. Nothing in the 1974 Congressional Budget Act said these things couldn't happen.[18]

DEVELOPMENTS IN OVERSIGHT

The president has an explicit constitutional obligation to ensure that laws are faithfully executed. Implicitly, Congress has a similar obligation to monitor and scrutinize program implementation by federal administrators. It performs this function through control of the

---

15. Quoted in Roger H. Davidson and Walter J. Oleszek, *Congress and Its Members* (Washington, DC: Congressional Quarterly Press, 1981), p. 312.
16. Ibid., p. 333.
17. Ibid, p. 334.
18. Ibid.

purse strings, committee hearings and investigations, enactment of legislative vetoes—statutory provisions that permit either or both the House and Senate, or their committees in some instances, to approve or disapprove proposed executive action—and scores of other activities. Given the size, diversity, and reach of the executive establishment, Congress needs a variety of review techniques to hold federal officials accountable for their actions and decisions.

Recent changes

In 1964, a scholar defined oversight as "review after the fact. It includes inquiries about policies that are or have been in effect, investigations of past administrative actions, and the calling of executive officers to account for their financial transactions."[19] A dozen years later the definition was substantially broadened to mean "behavior by legislators and their staffs, individually or collectively, which results in an impact, intended or not, on bureaucratic behavior."[20] The sweep of the latter definition mirrors much that happened to the country and to legislative-executive relations in the interval.

A narrow vision of oversight no longer seemed appropriate to many in the aftermath of the Vietnam war, the Watergate affair, and the breakdown of trust between the branches. "For us, it is conventional wisdom that the President of the United States lies," stated a House member. "That was unthinkable before the 60's."[21] Additionally, public concern about escalating federal expenditures, government waste and fraud, fiscal scarcity, and the proliferation of regulations, as well as the election of many members skeptical about the national government's ability to resolve problems, provided renewed interest in legislative oversight.

Congressional party leaders urged committees and colleagues to stress oversight. "I think more attention to oversight ought to be a major thrust of the 96th Congress," said the House majority whip.[22] There was an upsurge of committee oversight activity in both chambers.[23] In November 1979, for example, Speaker O'Neill compared the growth in the number and percentage of oversight meetings during the first 11 months of the Ninety-fourth (1975-79), Ninety-fifth (1977-79), and Ninety-sixth Congresses (1979-81). Table 1 describes this development.

Heightened sensitivity to oversight encouraged both chambers during the 1970s to adopt numerous rule changes designed to promote vigorous reviews of executive performance. The House, for instance, directed its committees to create oversight subcommittees and prepare biennial oversight plans. For its part, the Senate instructed committees to evaluate the regulatory impact of carrying out the measures they report and to conduct comprehensive policy oversight of broad subject areas. Explained

19. Joseph P. Harris, *Congressional Control of Administration* (Washington DC: Brookings Institution, 1964), p. 9.

20. Morris S. Ogul, *Congress Oversees the Bureaucracy: Studies in Legislative Supervision* (Pittsburgh: University of Pittsburgh Press, 1976), p. 11.

21. Steven V. Roberts, "Congress, a Critical Coterie on Foreign Policy," *New York Times*, 5 Apr. 1982, p. A20.

22. Mary Russell, "New Congress to Emphasize Oversight," *Washington Post*, 26 Dec. 1978, p. A7.

23. See, for example, Joel D. Aberbach, "Changes in Congressional Oversight." *American Behavioral Scientist*, 22:493-515 (May-June 1979).

TABLE 1
NUMBER OF HOUSE COMMITTEE OVERSIGHT MEETINGS

TYPE OF MEETING	94th CONGRESS	95th CONGRESS	96th CONGRESS
Oversight	868	1117	1339
All other	1845	2196	2075
Percentage of oversight to total meetings	32.0	33.7	39.2

SOURCE: Data provided to the Speaker by the 1979-80 House Select Committee on Committees. Meetings include hearings.

Senator Adlai Stevenson, Democrat from Illinois:

Standing committees are directed and permitted to undertake investigations and make recommendations in broad policy areas—for example, nutrition, aging, environmental protection, or consumer affairs—even though they lack legislative jurisdiction over some aspects of the subject. Such oversight authority involves subjects that generally cut across the jurisdictions of several committees. Presently, no single committee has a comprehensive overview of these policy areas. [This rule change] corrects that. It assigns certain committees the right to undertake comprehensive review of broad policy issues.[24]

Congress also fortified its analytical capability for oversight. There has been a veritable staff explosion on Capitol Hill. With more eyes and ears, Congress theoretically is better equipped to monitor and supervise administrative performance. In 1947, for example, the House had 167 and the Senate 232 committee staffers. By 1980, the figures were 1918 and 1108, respectively. So many committee and personal aides have been recruited in recent years that the House and Senate have had to construct new office buildings and convert former hotels, apartments, and federal buildings into offices. Even if Congress manages to retrench its staff, a trend begun in 1981, it is not likely to return to the old days because it needs independent expertise and talent to handle a burgeoning array of issues.

Finally, the resurgence in oversight is reflected in Congress's assertiveness toward recent presidents. There are scores of new legal constraints on executive authority. For example, during the past decade numerous statutes were passed restricting war powers, impoundments, Central Intelligence Agency activities, and arms trade abroad. Further, inspectors general were created to investigate and audit agencies and to report their uncensored findings directly to Congress.

Divergent perspectives

There is little question that Congress has augmented its statutory authority, staff resources, budget, and institutional role in oversight. Further, the available statistical evidence highlights increases in committee review activity. Yet numerous members still believe that oversight is Congress's neglected function.[25] "Members like to create and leg-

24. 123 *Congressional Record,* 1 Feb. 1977, 2897.

25. See U.S. House, Select Committee on Committees, *Final Report,* House Report 96-866, 96th Cong., 2d sess., 1980, pp. 286-87.

islate," Speaker O'Neill said, "but we have shied from both the word and deed of oversight."[26] Several factors help to explain why doing more in oversight is often perceived as doing less.

First, there is no clear consensus about how to measure oversight, quantitatively or qualitatively. As a result, congressional anxiety about its ability to review the massive executive establishment remains high. Quantitatively, no one really knows how much oversight Congress is doing. It is clear, however, that undercounting characterizes statistical analyses of oversight no matter what definition of that activity is employed. Part of the problem is that legislative review is a ubiquitous activity carried out by many entities: committees, member offices, legislative support agencies such as the General Accounting Office, and committee and personal staff aides. Almost any committee hearing, for instance, even ones ostensibly devoted to new legislation, might devote considerable attention to reviewing past policy implementation. Noted Senator Moynihan about the Senate's advice and consent responsibilities:

The confirmation process is important not only because it gives the Senate a chance to make an independent evaluation of the qualifications of the nominee, but also because it offers a major opportunity for the exercise of the congressional oversight function. It enables us to take stock of where we have been and where we are headed.[27]

Qualitatively, there is little agreement among members on the criteria that separate effective from ineffective oversight. To illustrate, one House member lauded a particular subcommittee's thorough and continuous review of the Food and Drug Administration. There is "no better model . . . on how to be a watchdog and detective," he said.[28] Declared another representative: that subcommittee spent "8 years nickel-diming around whether you take those pills off the shelf."[29] In sum, one member's effective oversight is another member's waste of time.

Second, some legislators hold oversight objectives that appear impossible to meet. These members want Congress to conduct comprehensive reviews of the entire federal establishment. Oversight "doesn't exist in any serious sustained, systematic basis by Congress," remarked a representative.[30] Critics find Congress's selective and unsystematic oversight approach generally unsatisfactory even if there is more of it.

Third, many members and committees believe they have minimal impact on bureaucracy. "Fighting the redtape and the overregulation of bureaucratic rule-making and guideline writing," said House Majority Leader Jim Wright, Democrat from Texas, is "almost like trying to fight a pillow. You can hit it—knock it over in the corner—and it just lies there and regroups. You feel sometimes as though you were trying to wrestle an octopus. No sooner do you get a hammerlock on one of the tentacles than the other seven are strangling you."[31]

---

26. See U.S. House, *Workshop on Congressional Oversight and Investigations*, p. 3.

27. 128 *Congressional Record*, daily ed., 9 June 1982, S6493.

28. 121 *Congressional Record*, 9 Apr. 1975, E1625.

29. U.S. House, Select Committee on Committees, *Committee Organization in the House*, 3 vols., House Document 94-187, 94th Cong., 1st sess. 1973, 2:267.

30. Ibid., p. 261.

31. See U.S. House, *Workshop on Congressional Oversight and Investigations*, p. 5.

When legislators denounce bureaucracy, they often mean that certain agencies or officials are not responding to biases or values that they hold. Charges of runaway bureaucracy are shaped in part by negative committee and member judgments about the benefits of specific federal activities. To be sure, the reverse phenomenon is prevalent on Capitol Hill.

Those who are program advocates in the beginning become program protectors along the way. They may criticize here and there, cut back or defer fund authorizations as circumstances dictate, call for evaluations and reports when trouble spots appear, but they do not propose to jettison the programs they have authorized, and continue to authorize over the years.[32]

Finally, oversight may produce more questions than answers. Congress finds it easier "to highlight what's going wrong and to blame it on someone," declared Senator Lawton Chiles, Democrat from Florida, "than to try to determine what to do about it."[33] In short, more oversight can still mean that agency problems remain uncorrected.

Future prospects

Congressional concern about big bureaucracy, the adequacy of traditional review techniques, and programs or agencies slipping through the cracks because of infrequent monitoring has prompted members to sponsor more systematic approaches to oversight. Called by various titles—"sunset," "legislative veto," and "sunrise," for example—these approaches share the essential objective of permitting Congress and its committees to schedule comprehensive reviews of most federal programs and agencies on a regular basis. None of these omnibus approaches has yet been enacted into law. A review of one of the ideas—sunset—spotlights some of the strengths and weaknesses generic to the broad review proposals.

Sunset legislation has been the subject of extensive hearings and debate on Capitol Hill at least since the mid-1970s. Introduced in the wake of public and member dissatisfaction with the bureaucracy, the measure's primary feature is the establishment of a systematic procedure for the mandatory review of similar federal programs over a designated time period. A current version recommends a 10-year cycle for program reviews. The object of sunset, said Representative Lee Hamilton, Democrat from Indiana, is to have "Congress determine which programs are needed and which are not, and to eliminate those programs that have outlived their usefulness or have duplicated the functions of other programs."[34] A sunset bill passed the Senate in late 1978 by an 87-to-1 vote, a symbolic action because there was no time left for the House to act on the legislation.

Enthusiasm for major sunset legislation dropped among many members by the 1980s. "Sunset is an idea whose time has come and gone," declared Senator Thomas Eagleton, Democrat from Missouri. He even called himself a "misbegotten fool" for having voted for sunset in 1978.[35] Several factors account for the

---

32. Herbert Roback, "Program Evaluation by and for the Congress," *Bureaucrat,* 5:27 (Apr. 1976).

33. See U.S. House, *Workshop on Congressional Oversight and Investigations,* p. 144.

34. 125 *Congressional Record,* 4 Apr. 1979, E1518.

35. David Ignatius, "Sunset Bill Sets Up Test of Wills in Senate between Young Members and

turnabout. Among them are member concerns about enormous workload increases and the likelihood of larger staffs to perform sunset reviews; interest group pressures to exempt their favorite programs from the mandatory review process; and the broad scope of the legislation.

Less ambitious sunset proposals might pass Congress in the future. House and Senate committees, for example, might be required by law or rule to establish sunset review agendas that contain their oversight priorities for every Congress. Or sunset review provisions could appear in more statutes. The legislation that created the Department of Energy in 1978 (P.L. 95-91) obligated it to conduct a sunset review of itself.

Another prospective development involves third-party government. "The central reality of most federal programs today is that the lion's share of discretionary authority is vested not in federal officials, but in one or another of a wide array of non-federal implementers," wrote an analyst.[36] The nonfederal implementers include businesses, hospitals, universities, and state or local governments. The renewed thrust contained in President Reagan's New Federalism might accelerate the shift of authority and revenue to localities. Congress's task is to determine how and to what extent essentially independent entities not directly answerable to it are to be held accountable for managing federal responsibilities.

Finally, the conventional wisdom is that members lack electoral and political incentives for oversight. That function appears to be on the back burner behind members' lawmaking and representative responsibilities. However, in an era marked by resource scarcity, more press and media coverage of bureaucratic activities, and public disenchantment with governmental performance, committees and members may find greater rewards in devoting time to supervisory work. In 1975, Representative Benjamin Rosenthal, Democrat from New York, for example, relinquished his subcommittee chairmanship on the Foreign Affairs Committee to concentrate instead on oversight as a subcommittee chairman—Commerce, Consumer, and Monetary Affairs—on the Government Operations Committee—almost exclusively a review panel. He chose, apparently, to do oversight that has back-home impact rather than the more distant review of foreign affairs.

Furthermore, there is sentiment in Congress and the nation that there are too many laws. "We over-legislated. There is no question about that," observed Speaker O'Neill.[37] As a result, the 1980s might be a period when Congress produces fewer laws than before but more reviews of executive agencies and programs. Committees and members understand that there is written and unwritten national policy. The first involves the usually arduous task of getting proposed laws through the procedural maze of Congress. The second means using oversight to change informally the way administrators are implementing existing laws. The latter approach might be employed more fre-

---

Old-Timers," *Wall Street Journal,* 16 June 1980, p. 8.

36. Lester M. Salamon, "Rise of Third-Party Government," *Washington Post,* 29 June 1980; reprinted in 126 *Congressional Record,* 1 July 1980, E3320.

37. Julia Malone, "O'Neill Sees a New Mood in Washington Country," *Christian Science Monitor,* 11 May 1982, p. 15.

quently to redirect executive decision making.

CONCLUSION

Purposeful innovation in Congress often depends on whether members perceive a problem, agree on its causes and its solutions, mobilize to do something about it, and strive to overcome significant barriers to change. This combination of circumstances helped produce numerous changes that characterize the contemporary Congress: greater dispersal of authority, more openness, larger staffs, individualism, increased assertiveness toward the executive branch, and much more.

Evidences of significant change on Capitol Hill are legion. Less clear, however, are the collective and cumulative consequences of these developments. To assess what has been gained by change against what has been lost is not easy. Thus the observation in the mid-1960s of Gerald Ford, then House Republican leader, still rings true: "'Reform' is a tricky word; change *per se* is not necessarily the same as progress."[38]

Part of the dilemma of change is knowing when there is too much or too little of something, such as integration or fragmentation. The signs usually occur when the House and Senate or the two parties decide to redress or repair perceived inadequacies. Both chambers and parties, for example, took steps during the past decade to diffuse influence among scores of committees, groups, staff aides, and members. Predictably, numerous members and scholars today argue for some recentralization of the dispersed authority. Actions in one era provoke reactions that help shape the agenda of change for future Congresses.

Finally, Congress is fundamentally a fragmented institution and part of a larger political system filled with fragmentation: separation of powers, checks and balances, and federalism, to name a few. To be sure, calls to streamline Congress, eliminate committee duplication, or revitalize oversight have large appeal to legislator and citizen alike. The caveat is to ensure that such changes continue to permit Congress to exercise its own special brand of rationality. As a scholar wrote more than two decades ago, contrasting the tension between the White House and Congress, we should

abandon the fiction . . . that we have on the one hand an Executive devoted to high principle, and a Legislature whose majority simply refuse to live up to it, and confront the possibility that what we have is in fact two *conceptions* of high principle about which reasonable men may legitimately differ.[39]

---

38. Gerald R. Ford, "Introduction," in *We Propose: A Modern Congress,* ed. Mary McInnis (New York: McGraw-Hill, 1966), p. xii.

39. Willmoore Kendall, "The Two Majorities," *Midwest Journal of Political Science,* 4:317-45 (Nov. 1960); reprinted in *Congress and the President,* ed. Ronald C. Moe (Pacific Palisades, CA: Goodyear, 1971), p. 289.

Book Department

	PAGE
INTERNATIONAL RELATIONS AND POLITICS	207
AFRICA, ASIA, AND LATIN AMERICA	211
EUROPE	220
UNITED STATES	224
SOCIOLOGY	233
ECONOMICS	242

INTERNATIONAL RELATIONS AND POLITICS

RICHARD B. BILDER. *Managing the Risks of International Agreement.* Pp. xi, 302. Madison: University of Wisconsin Press, 1981. $22.50.

International agreements are viewed by the public, and indeed by most lawyers and diplomats, as a means of ending conflict and dispute, as evidence of international cooperation that will benefit the contracting states. Such agreements, however, are not without serious pitfalls. Often such agreements mask unresolved differences and create significant risks for the parties involved. The question of how to manage and limit these risks and still obtain the desired benefits of agreement is the subject of a well-thought-out new book by Professor Richard Bilder of the University of Wisconsin.

Professor Bilder's thesis is a simple one: that the risks of agreement can be reduced by a clear recognition of what those risks are. Depending on the respective interests of the parties involved and the subject matter to be covered by the agreement, it may be possible to use a variety of techniques both to increase the prospects for performance by other parties and to eliminate the hazards that apply to a particular international situation.

One of the most important risks in a negotiation between states is that the expected value of an agreement will subsequently change. Often in these circumstances one party or the other will feel justified in ignoring the agreement if it feels that the other party is receiving a disproportionate amount of the benefits involved. Bilder even notes instances in which states will terminate or violate agreements that remain beneficial to them if they perceive that another party to the agreement has benefited on a much broader scale. Elemental fairness is thus an almost essential ingredient.

Methods of maintaining or reevaluating the relative benefits are numerous: by use of guarantees, by joint or simultaneous performance, by setting floors or ceilings on performance, by setting levels of performance by reference to an objective standard, by reference to third-party evaluation, by providing prompt methods of revision or amendment. Bilder lists and categorizes these and a number of other approaches to risk management and often does so with reference to a particular agreement or negotiation between two or more countries.

Bilder's discussion of risk-management principles, although aimed at negotiations between sovereign states, has considerable application in the commercial context as well. The same sorts of concerns that trouble diplomats with regard to international agreements often exist for corporate negotiators as well, for example, the binding nature of the agreement, default procedures, dispute settlement, use of ambiguity, and waiver and withdrawal provisions. There is an obvious parallel in the early warning or verification sorts of devices that Bilder discusses with regard to arms limitation and cease-fire agreements, and the kinds of financial barometers, such as quarterly financial reports and plant inspections, that give advance warnings of possible default in the corporate and financial context.

Bilder's discussion of risk factors is straightforward, sound, and extremely well organized. It does, however, lack some of the real-life flavor that would have made the book's impact even stronger. While Bilder does refer to specific recent agreements and negotiations in passing, often with reference to the Kissinger years at the State Department, he could have strengthened the book considerably by breathing some life into the negotiating situations he describes. Perhaps the most instructive way of doing this would have been to analyze in depth all of the risk-management considerations that arise in one or two particularly complex recent negotiations.

Bilder closes his book with several caveats concerning the risks of risk management. As he notes, it is sometimes better, in the heat of negotiations, to ignore the carefully planned pace of negotiations and push for the elemental agreement that is the real basis for the negotiations in the first place. In these cases the most important element of international agreement comes quickly into place—the need for mutual trust, not as a substitute for the risk-management concepts that Bilder discusses, but as a necessary complement to successful and constructive agreement between nations.

JAMES R. SILKENAT
Member of the
   District of Columbia Bar
Washington, D.C.

GREGORY FLYNN et al. *The Internal Fabric of Western Security.* Pp. xiii, 250. London: Croom Helm, 1982. $32.50.

How times have changed! Following World War II and until the 1970s, the United States exercised an unquestioned hegemony over the security policies of its Atlantic allies. However, U.S. involvement in Vietnam and the accompanying social revolution of the 1960s forced Western European citizenry to evaluate their external security considerations—could the United States be depended upon to come to the defense of its European allies? If the answer was negative, then how much of a country's resources should be devoted to military security? Overnight, domestic considerations, which had theretofore been relegated to a position of lesser importance in the foreign-policymaking process, now came to the fore.

To address this change, Gregory Flynn and his four coauthors have written a comprehensive analysis of the problems facing the Alliance. *The Internal Fabric of Western Security* has one paramount thesis—the economic and security relations among the partners of the Atlantic alliance, Great Britain, France, West Germany, and Italy, are becoming more constrained by domestic necessities. No longer can the governments of these nations ignore internal factors when they debate and formulate an external policy that has as its focus the restraint of the Soviet Union. Flynn lists three factors responsible for these uncertainties: rise of the Soviets from a continental to a global superpower; the ever-present energy problem; and the rising economic problems of unemployment, inflation, and debt payment. I would add three others: increasing world terrorism (Italy), the emergence of new governing groups (France), and the rising influence of Eurocommunism. At the nexus of these uncertainties is yet another uncertainty—the role of the United States in the security of its European allies. One common preconception is that part of the burden lies with the United States to help reverse the "domestication of the Alliance's foreign policy priorities and re-create confidence in U.S. forces." U.S. insistence on placing nuclear weapons in the heartland of Europe countered by Soviet resolve to do anything possible to destroy or at least minimize the cohesiveness of the Alliance and reduce Western European links to U.S. power further complicates the issue.

Mr. Flynn and his coauthors address this morass of uncertainties in a very commendable way. They establish the background of the problem, analyze in four chapters the predicaments each country confronts in formulating its external security policy, and draw a poignant conclusion—"The growing importance of these constraints [internal policies] and the European loss of confidence in the United States are the two critical new conditions that must be changed if the Allies are again to move toward reconciliation of their often differing perspectives."

While each of the four countries has a common external security problem, the Soviets, the internal policies of these countries are parametered by different uncertainties: West Germany—will *Ostpolitik* continue to be an overriding domestic consideration; France—where will *force de frappe* and withdrawal from NATO (1966) lead; Italy—do the Italians have an external enemy (Soviets) or an internal enemy (terrorism, communism); and Great Britain—how much of a continental miliary entaglement can it accept? For one interested in examining the probable relationship between the internal and external security agendas of the Atlantic alliance as it enters the 1980s, *The Internal Fabric of Western Security* is an excellent research source. I recommend it highly.

RICHARD E. JOHE

St. John's University
New York

RAGAEI EL MALLAKH, ed. *OPEC: Twenty Years and Beyond.* Pp. xxiii, 270. Boulder, CO: Westview Press, 1982. $26.25.

This work consists of a compendium of 17 essays that relate to economic, political, and social aspects of OPEC. Each essay is independent and does not rely on material presented in other parts of the book. When models or analyses require data, the data are presented in a self-contained form, even when similar data are used by other authors. As independent essays, each has its own conclusion; Mallakh does not have a general summary of findings or conclusions. The essays range in length from about 8 to 30 pages. Although Mallakh does not indicate how and why the essays were chosen for inclusion in the book, the compendium was put together to mark the twentieth anniversary (1960 to 1980) of the founding of OPEC.

Based on the individual biographies given for each of the contributors, the authors appear to be distinguished and well qualified to address the multifarious issues concerning OPEC. Although the political, academic, and business backgrounds of the authors are diverse, most have doctorates in law, political science, or economics from Western European, British, or American universities. Some of the authors have held academic or government positions in OPEC member countries; others have been affiliated with international bodies that oversee energy policy formulation; and still others have been associated with major American oil companies or American research institutes.

About two-thirds of the book is devoted to economic issues; the remaining one-third to sociopolitical and international questions. Most of the economic analyses relate to pricing issues. If one theme could be chosen to represent the findings of these analyses, it would be that in real terms—that is, ignoring inflation—the price of petroleum products supplied by OPEC members has not increased since the initial embargo in 1973. A second theme is that OPEC is not a cartel, nor does it possess monopoly powers over the price of oil.

The economic knowledge required by the reader to understand the chapters on the economic aspects of OPEC varies considerably. For example, F. Al-Chalabi and A. Al-Janabi address the issue of optimum production and pricing policies. They assume knowledge and do not explain the technical concepts they use. In contrast, W. J. Mead's analysis of crude-oil price behavior in the 1970s is readily understood because Mead carefully explains the notions of capital theory and property rights used for his theoretical foundations. Most of the topics that relate to pricing use simple econometric techniques, such as regression analysis.

One extremely interesting essay, by R. D. Zentner, covers the question of perceptions about OPEC. His data come from opinion polls and national surveys undertaken in the United States after 1973. His main finding is that few Americans understood the energy problem and that the American public was eager to find a scapegoat for high petroleum prices. I was disappointed that Zentner did not suggest that at least part of the confusion of the American public resulted from the leading nature of questions frequently asked by pollsters. His sample questions include polls using such phrases as "blame for the energy problem," or "price increases have been a 'rip-off' that take billions of dollars out of the pockets of consumers."

I recommend this book to a limited audience: social scientists and expecially economists who have a keen interest in the international oil market of the 1970s.

MARY A. HOLMAN
George Washington University
Washington, D.C.

BASHEER MEIBAR. *Political Culture, Foreign Policy, and Conflict: The Palestine Area Conflict System.* Pp. xiv, 312. Westport, CT: Greenwood Press, 1982. $29.95.

Basheer Meibar has, regrettably, failed in an effort to construct an all-encompassing analytical framework for understanding the conflict between Arabs and Jewish Israelis over Palestine/Eretz Israel. The primary fault is twofold. First, the analytical framework he introduces is far too complex to be wholly intelligible. He divides Arab belief systems into 108 possible varieties of potential relevance to the conflict in the area. Israeli political culture is said to be composed of 48 belief dimensions. Together these result in "8978 dyads of possible actors." Although Meibar mercifully does not try to explain all of these, he presents more than enough to confound the reader thoroughly and to diminish interest in his study. Consequently, rather than enlightening, he ends up obfuscating the existence of a few widely shared aspects of political culture that are important to the conflictual system he seeks to explain.

The second fault is that Meibar has little evident expertise in matters of Israeli political culture, despite its centrality to the conflict he hopes to explain. Remarkably, only 23 pages are devoted explicitly to this subject; and these are disastrous. The work of leading Israeli social scientists is ignored in favor of largely outdated efforts by others, several of whom wrote in the 1960s. Meibar's lack of understanding of Israel leads to several bizarre notions, to wit: there is extant in Israel an important Canaanite movement that seeks to divide the land of Canaan among its true descendants, Arab and Jewish, but not European; Israelis believe that the concept of the chosen people absolves them of moral obligations toward non-Jews; and Ben Gurion's call for Israel to be a "light unto the nations" is synonymous with an expansionist foreign policy, which can be likened to the so-called white man's burden. In sum, Meibar's rationalization for relying on secondary sources on Israel notwithstanding, he would have been much better off to learn about his subject firsthand, or, alternatively, simply to have produced a book on Arab political culture.

In closing, Greenwood Press deserves special mention for the outrageously high price for what is an unattractively designed book, lacking right-column justification, and including various imperfections.

DAVID H. ROSENBLOOM
The Maxwell School
Syracuse University
New York

ADAM WESTOBY. *Communism Since World War II*. Pp. xiii, 514. New York: St. Martin's Press, 1981. $32.50.

An unusually timely and well-written work on national and international communism, this book is, in Westoby's words, "a Global Political history of Communism from the Second World War to the Soviet invasion of Afghanistan and the birth of the free unions in Poland."

According to Westoby, communism since World War II has two connected objectives: Part I sketches the main developments in the political history of official communism, approximately since the dissolution of the Communist International in 1943. The narrative runs up to 1980. Part II takes up some of the problems of explanation raised by Part I. Though broadly distinct, the two parts complement each other.

However, the most obvious problem, according to Westoby, is that of sources. For very recent events he relies principally upon contemporary newspapers, especially the Soviet press. To begin with the USSR: *Izvestia* is the government organ; everything published therein may be regarded as official. *Pravda*, the semiofficial Party mouthpiece, is in reality the power behind the throne. It sets the tone in ideological matters, and its journalists are probably the best in the Soviet Union. To put it in commonplace English, whereas *Izvestia* represents the state, *Pravda* represents the communist "church."

Moreover, it is Westoby's view that the survival of the Soviet Union in World War II marked a turning point in world communism. In other words, the war was a blessing in disguise for communism. In spite of the German invasion of Russian territory, the Soviet Union emerged from the war stronger and better organized as a nation.

But with Marxism in power, states Westoby, a new despotism resulted—Stalinism. "The working class, destroyed and dispersed, lost all power to control events. . . . The dictatorship of the proletariat became that of the Party."

The Socialist Workers' Party leadership maintained that the crucial problems lay in the massive expropriations of property. They also claimed that mass mobilizations were everywhere an essential factor, forcing communist governments to overturn capitalism in Vietnam, China, Yugoslavia, and Soviet-occupied Eastern Europe. According to this view, workers' states were not established in Eastern Europe until 1948 or so, and in China not until 1951-52—that is, until the main economic overturns had occurred.

The origins of Communist dictatorship, its social anatomy, the struggle against it: these three problems—on which there is so little agreement—seem to me among the main ones upon which any renascence of socialism turns. Much work has already been done, some of which I discuss. . . . My wish is to make a small "input" to this process [p. xii].

I recommend this book highly, especially to scholars and advanced graduate students.

IVAR SPECTOR

University of Washington
Seattle

AFRICA, ASIA, AND LATIN AMERICA

TRILOKI N. KAUL. *Reminiscences: Discreet and Indiscreet*. Pp. 312. New Delhi: Lancers Publishers, 1982. Rs. 115/-.

"Tikki" Kaul is one of India's best-known and most experienced diplomats. He has already written a general book entitled *Diplomacy in Peace and War*, and two more specialized books on subjects with which he was personally involved—*India, China and Indochina* and *The Kissinger Years (Indo-US Relations)*. Now that he is a liberated diplomat he has written an even more comprehensive and more personal memoir, appropriately entitled *Reminiscences: Discreet and Indiscreet*. This covers his entire career as a public servant, extending over a period of 40 years—1936-76—with many comments and reflections on the last years of the British Raj and the independence struggle and on India's relations with the rest of the world since its independence—the era of *Swaraj*.

Born in Kashmir, Kaul was educated in Kashmir, Allahabad, and London, where he earned an LL.M. degree and passed the ICS examination. His return to India was an overland odyssey in a secondhand Ford, with three English companions. He served as an ICS officer in Uttar Pradesh for 10 years. In 1947 he transferred to the Indian Foreign Service and began a varied and active 30-year career in diplomacy. He served successively in the Soviet Union (1947-49), the United States (1949-50), and China (1950-54). In 1957-58 he was president of the International Commission for Supervision and Control in Vietnam. After serving as ambassador to Iran, deputy high commissioner to the United Kingdom—with the rank of ambassador—and ambassador to the Soviet Union, he was India's foreign secretary for several years. As ambassador to the United States in the era of Indira Gandhi and Nixon-Ford-Kissinger (1973-76), he had the difficult and thankless task of defending the Emergency in India (1975-77) to generally unsympathetic American leaders and audiences. Incidentally, he makes almost no mention of the Emergency in his *Reminiscences*. In his long and distinguished diplomatic career he had a major role in the negotiation of important agreements with China, Bangladesh, the Soviet Union, and the United States. Unfortunately, he provides few details about this important dimension of his diplomatic work.

His *Reminiscences* contain a good overview of many aspects of India's foreign policy, with particular emphasis on India's policy of nonalignment, in which he is a "true believer," and on India's relations with its subcontinental neighbors and with the superpowers. Most American readers will regard his approach as strongly pro-Soviet and rather anti-American, an interpretation to which he would take exception. But he obviously regards the Soviet Union as a better and more reliable friend of India than the United States. He devotes two chapters to the Indo-Soviet Treaty of August 1971, which, he insists, not only strengthened India during the crisis in South Asia in 1971, but also had "significance and importance for the period 1971-81," and beyond. "We must not weaken this strong friendship," he argues, "for the doubtful gains of a dangling offer from those who have let us down in the past." The reference to the United States is all too obvious. "There is a fundamental clash," he writes, "between Nixon's America as a global super power and Indira Gandhi's India, as a middle regional power." In his view, "Kissinger was a dangerous man to deal with," and Brzezinski "proved as bad as Kissinger if not worse." With Reagan in the White House he believes that "the prospects for Indo-US relations are grim." But he contends that "in the long run, . . . the prospects of Indo-US relations are not gloomy, if India becomes economically strong, politically stable and is able to defend her integrity and sovereignty."

"Tikki" Kaul, an interesting combination of staunch nationalist and dedicated internationalist, will undoubtedly continue to take an active interest in world affairs and to preach the necessity for India to put its own house in order, whether he is carrying out international assignments, such as participation in international conferences or his work with UNESCO, or serving as adviser or special troubleshooter for Indira Gandhi, whom he strongly supports, or living in isolated retirement in his small cottage, Hermitage, in the Himalayas.

NORMAN D. PALMER
University of Pennsylvania
Philadelphia

XU LIANGYING and FAN DAINIAN. *Science and Socialist Construction in China*. Translated by John. C.S. Wu. Edited by Pierre M. Perolle. Pp. xxvii, 225. Armonk, NY: M. E. Sharpe, 1982. $35.00.

Published in April 1957 in Chinese was a small volume on science, policy, and socialist construction in China. It had been written in 1956, following the formulation of a 12-year plan for the development of science and industrial technology, after the Maoist dictum, "Let a hundred schools of thought contend and a hundred flowers bloom." In June 1957, two months after publication, there began the turbulent movement opposing the whole program of modernizing scientific development. The authors were banished to rural agricultural village labor and the book disappeared in the turmoil. The present volume is a translation of that volume, which now constitutes both a historical documentation and a valid statement on science policy in the future.

The translation by John C.S. Wu follows the 1957 text literally. A few statements are dated: the Soviet Union no longer is a partner in development, some projects were completed despite opposition, and a few programs for the early 1960s no longer are elements of future policy. A foreword by the senior author, and the translation of his 1981 essay on the role of science and democracy, as an appendix, bring the policy statement up to date. A preface and a short introduction by the editor, Pierre M. Perolle, complete the volume. There are five chapters in the basic text of the translated volume.

Chapters 1, 3, and 5, and the appendix essay all are concerned with the roles of science, particularly in a socialist society. There is recognition of the need for practical versus basic science research, the impact of developing science on social ideologies, and the need for freedom in research efforts. Chapter 3 has some euphoric writing as a reaction to the new freedoms of 1956. The authors work skillfully within the Maoist-Marxist framework.

Chapter 4, the longest, contains the heart of the 1956 12-year program. It begins with plans for surveys of natural resources, and ranges widely. Industrial programs, the improvement of agricultural technologies and production, and transportation-communications systems development are laid out. Then follow pharmaceutical sciences-public health, the use of atomic energy, electronic technologies, computer technology and automation, rocket technology, and a few final bits. Within the commentary is the best outline of what Chinese science policy in the mid-1950s aimed at. After the 1978 National Science Conference, the statement is likely to be what current policy returns to. The translated essay in the appendix is a forthright statement that, were the winds of power to shift again, would serve as adequate cause for a second banishment of the author.

J. E. SPENCER

University of California
Los Angeles

PETER McDONOUGH. *Power and Ideology in Brazil.* Pp. xxxiv, 326. Princeton, NJ: Princeton University Press, 1981. $25.00. Paperbound, $7.95.

"Drawing on personal interviews with over 250 Brazilian leaders in industry, banking, politics, labor, the civil service, and the church, . . . challenges the conventional notion of elites in authoritarian regimes as unideological pragmatists . . . demonstrates that the Brazilian power structure is instead torn by complex, multi-dimensional cleavages as the elites attempt to reconcile the tradeoffs between economic accumulation and social equity, political order and liberty, and secular and sacred norms of community . . . also links these ideological tensions to the decay of authoritarianism in Brazil during the late 1970's" (book jacket copy).

McDonough goes beyond the obvious causes of erosion of authoritarianism in Brazil, that is, the unexpected international deterioration caused by the 1973 oil crisis and the work stoppages and strikes that followed the inability of the regime to distribute material benefits more widely during the rapid growth of 1968 to 1973. He instead focuses on the interelite rivalries and the tensions within the establishment itself that have helped undermine the dictatorial coalition.

The first third of the book deals with what elites think about one another and about political issues. This enables McDonough to reject the polar cases of unideological and unidimensional ideology of elites—the so-called structuralist and culturist schools of thought. His hypothesis is that Brazilian elites are multidimensional, that is, they think in terms of at least three axes of political choice that reflect conflict cleavages. For example, class ideology divides economic conservatives from social progressives, best personified by cleavages between urban labor and other elites. A second cleavage separates supporters of authoritarian order from supporters of decentralized decision making. McDonough stresses the lack of a simple convergence between accumulation-distribution and the order-autonomy axes, which, if true, would result in an extremely polarized, simple phenomenon. Instead, we find divergences, many of which are not left-right issues; Marxists and Catholics diverge on the left-right issues, but both condemn population planning. Finally, there are cleavages of a moral order on such collisions as between church and the military about torture, imprisonment, and social justice. Despite the disintegration of authoritarian rule, however, a transition to a pluralistic democratic state is not guaranteed. But the worst of the authoritarian state may be past in Brazil—troops in the streets and dissidents tortured and in prison. As McDonough says, "A cycle of democratic experimentation is under way." As of 1982 there is no censorship and political parties are able to form, even if under somewhat difficult and limiting constraints. This is encouraging to democrats and pluralists.

I recommend this book to students of Brazil and of politics and authoritarianism generally. Much cannot be summarized in this short space. Methodologically the approach is sound, given the limitations of social science. I would have liked to see environment included as an issue and I wish that McDonough had found terms other than "economist" and "politician" to define somewhat heterogeneous groups that are not necessarily descriptive of these professions. Finally, I wish that he had delved more deeply into the rift within the military itself. But such are the wishes of special interest groups, who, perhaps mistakenly, associate their own biases with the public interest.

DONALD L. HUDDLE
Rice University
Houston
Texas

BARBARA D. MILLER. *The Endangered Sex: Neglect of Female Children in Rural North India.* Pp. 201. Ithaca, NY: Cornell University Press, 1981. $17.50.

Barbara D. Miller is an anthropologist who is a senior research associate at the Local Revenue Administration of the Maxwell School of Public Affairs, Syracuse University. Her study was launched with a Woodrow Wilson Doctoral Fellowship in women's studies, a language fellowship from the American Institute of Indian Studies provided her the opportunity to use Indian libraries and talk to several scholars in India, and a grant from the Rockefeller-Ford Research Program on Population and Development Policy made the completion and writing of this book possible.

Miller notes the phenomenon of high juvenile sex ratios found in the rural population of North India, particularly among the higher castes. She wonders what accounts for this imbalance in the sex ratio of this particular region of the country, and she looks for the factors responsible for the noticeably higher mortality rate among girls.

The thrust of Miller's argument is that historical materials from the British period show that female infanticide was practiced widely in pre-twentieth-century India, particularly in the Northwest, and that this cultural practice continues in a muted form.

Examining evidence regarding regional variation in "nutrition, medical care, and love" of children, Miller declares that boys are very definitely favored in rural North

India, and that this is what leads to the relatively higher mortality of female children. Miller then relates the variation in sex ratios in North and South India to regional differences in women's work and worth, marriage costs and property inheritance, and son preference.

Miller concludes her study with the notion that if medical technology makes sex control possible at conception, this could pose tremendous danger to the females in North India. She reasons that "sex control at conception shares with female infanticide a great degree of 'efficiency' in increasing the maleness of the population—efficient in the sense that male offspring are obtained and female offspring tidily avoided.... Unless a concerted effort is made soon to counteract the forces promoting son preference, unless the victimization of North Indian daughters is slowed, then cultural sway will prevail, demanding the demise of fertility, of childbearing, of the female."

It appears that such an utterly alarmist notion is not a passing fancy of Miller's; she really believes in it. Note the main title of the book, *The Endangered Sex*. Miller feels fully supported in her reasoning by what she found in the historical materials concerning rural North India. She cites the following report, which appears in another author's study of female infanticide in India:

James Thomason accidentally discovered the practice [of female infanticide] in 1835, while he was engaged in revising the settlements of the Deogaon and Nizamabad paraganas in Azamgarh. . . . In conversation with some of the zamindars . . . he happened to refer to one of them as the son-in-law of another. This mistake raised a sarcastic laugh among them and a bystander briefly explained that he could not be a son-in-law since there were no daughters in the village. Thomason was told that the birth of a daughter was considered a most serious calamity and she was seldom allowed to live [p. 51].

Again, Miller writes:

From all reports available, it is clear that female infanticide in nineteenth-century India was practiced primarily in the higher social groups of the North, though this point is debatable. . . . No doubt, in the North, the problem is one of degree: it could be that in the most infanticide-endemic areas all castes practiced it to some extent, but it was clearly the higher social groups who were the most extreme, preserving no daughters at all [p. 55].

I do not mean to give the impression that Miller's scholarship is not good. It is simply the case that she is too credulous about the reliability of certain historical materials. The study does make a strong case for believing that the rather high juvenile sex ratios among certain caste groups in rural North India are a result of neglect of female children and a preference for male offspring.

This is a well-written and a good book that presents a picture of the powerful relationship between culture and differential mortality by sex. Its findings are of considerable significance for anthropologists, demographers, students of South Asia, policymakers, and those who are concerned about discrimination against women.

A word of caution to readers who are not demographers or are not otherwise knowledgeable about sex ratios. It is simply not the case that, as Miller states, "indeed, at age one, the proportion of the sexes is equal in the West." For this to be true, the male infant mortality rate would have to be about five times as high as the female infant mortality rate in the West, whereas it is only some 30 to 60 percent higher.

SURINDER K. MEHTA
University of Massachusetts
Amherst

MILTON SILVERMAN, PHILIP R. LEE, and MIA LYDECKER. *Prescriptions for Death: The Drugging of the Third World.* Pp. xviii, 186. Berkeley and Los Angeles: University of California Press. $16.95.

This book is a balanced treatment of a highly charged issue, written by researchers affiliated with the University of California Medical School at San Francisco. It has a typical design of evoking stress, concern, and anger by presenting a problem, followed by proposed remedial prescriptions. The title in a perhaps ironic way involves a bit of excessive advertising rhetoric of its own, for it suggests a more hard-hitting negative analysis than is actually found within the book. Silverman, Lee, and Lydecker recognize that drug sales in countries of squalor and poverty constitute an extraordinarily complex mix of benefits, costs, ignorance, and greed, with all participants, including publicly and privately owned multinational and domestic drug companies, Third World physicians and government officials, and even patients themselves, touched with shades of gray. There are few unrelieved villains or unsullied heroes in the tale they tell.

Their presentation can be understood on one level as a fast-paced, straightforward exercise in reporting detailing differences in the promotion of drugs over the world. The apparent pattern is that with many drugs, with many companies, in many countries there are insufficient warnings about adverse side effects, often with disastrous results. Their detailed cross-national, cross-company study with selected drugs takes up about half of the book, with the remainder directed to a discussion of bribery and Third World health professionals, a popular styled survey of world drug companies, and finally an appraisal of alternative strategies for reducing the worst features of drug marketing in developing nations.

This engrossing story can be viewed as a useful case study illustrating basic social science processes and conclusions. It vividly demonstrates, for example, that when informational asymmetries exist in massive fashion coupled with considerable deceitful self-interest reflected in the behavior of many participants, then competitive market practices lead in a perverse dynamic to unfortunate results rather than to the optimalities as proposed in elementary theory. Untrammeled free enterprise in these circumstances does not result in unalloyed social benefit. This analysis also shows that grinding poverty abstractly portrayed in seemingly dry data translates into graphic facts of malnutrition, drug shortages, deplorable water and sanitation deficiencies, and too few health professionals and hospitals. Squalor leads to terrible health circumstances by any number of routes, only one of which is that of faulty drugs misapplied to ignorant patients by relatively uninformed doctors, whose principal sources of information are the promotional materials of drug company sales representatives.

This book closes with notes of optimism for the prospect of evolving amelioration of many of the evils depicted in it. A fascinating ad hoc amalgam of forces and groups are at work to change drug marketing in poor countries. World Health Organization instrumentalities, the International Federation of Pharmaceutical Manufacturing Associations, health researchers such as the authors of this book, consumer interest groups over the world, and government and health care officials of developing nations are playing important roles. The unavoidable reality of a goldfish bowl of publicity, concern, and negotiation evokes stronger government regulation in developing countries, a likely World Health Organization code of marketing conduct, and increasingly effective self-regulation by the world's drug manufacturers.

Some may view an adaptation of company policy to myriad pressures as an unfortunate halfway move to socialism, but to me it appears to be a reasonable response to market and political demands by increasingly sophisticated managers. Developments toward more responsible marketing come from a combination of fear of further government action, the glare of unfavorable publicity, threats of costly court suits associated with drug malpractice, and the fact that there are persons of principled integrity in all groups involved in this fascinating political-economic evolution.

HAROLD L. JOHNSON
Emory University
Atlanta
Georgia

BRIAN H. SMITH. *The Church and Politics in Chile: Challenges to Modern Catholicism.* Pp. xiii, 383. Princeton, NJ: Princeton University Press, 1982. $30.00. Paperbound, $9.75.

Professor Smith's dissertation combines three elements: a historical account of Church-state relations in Chile since the two institutions separated in 1925; an empiricosociological view of Chilean Catholic attitudes; and the author's own value judgments via-à-vis the Church, recent Chilean governments, and economic models.

Smith's strong point is as a historian. He gives a fair and thorough presentation of the Church's role in successive periods: efforts to disassociate itself from the Conservative Party; opposition to the Christian Democrats in the 1930s, followed first by tolerance and then by virtual identification; the Church's struggle for self-survival and national unity during the Allende years; and its role since 1973 under an authoritarian, military regime. Although Smith does not make the point, the clearest conclusion is that the Cardinal and the episcopacy have successfully and diplomatically steered a middle course between political extremes while under constant fire from the left and the right, both within and without the Church.

The empirical material is composed of opinion polls carried out by Smith and others as well as interviews with participants identified with the Church. Other than the presentation of the opinions of the bishops—all 30 were interviewed—conclusions based on Smith's questionnaires, submitted to 72 priests, 33 nuns, and 51 laymen, are of dubious methodological value and serve only to distract from the book's thesis. The Church itself has carried out a poll of 160,000 practicing Chilean Catholics, the results of which, when published, should be meaningful, although, as with Smith's poll, multiple-choice questioning leaves much to be desired compared to in-depth analysis.

The weakest element of the book is the sprinkling throughout of often contradictory, frequently fallacious value judgments based on unexamined premises, without revealing any coherent personal philosophy, though Smith does top off his diffuse subjectivism with a totally unscholarly call for ecclesiastical action the next time the Church has an opportunity to assimilate or be assimilated by socialism.

Although Professor Smith, in his eagerness to reveal to us the Church Militant, utterly ignores the Church Spiritual, the book remains a valuable contribution to contemporary history. Further, it is bound to stir the reader, in one direction or another. And that is what books are all about.

DAVID M. BILLIKOPF

Santiago
Chile

CONRAD TOTMAN. *Japan Before Perry: A Short History.* Pp. xvi, 246. Berkeley: University of California Press, 1982. Paperbound, $6.95.

The English reading world has been well served by several generations of interpreters of Japan. Starting with Sir George Sansom, wide-ranging and excellent interpretive studies of Japanese history have appeared regularly, the newer ones enhancing and developing the older ones, rather than erasing their validity. Conrad Totman now joins this eminent group of historians with his fine *Japan Before Perry: A Short History.*

Professor Totman dispatches the prehistoric and Yamato periods quickly to move into a consideration of what he sees as the three great pre-Perry eras. Here he addresses the old problem of periodization that all historians of Japan have had to face. He divides the Japanese development into the traditional Classical, Medieval, and Pre-Modern Periods, but characterizes them as eras of "aristocratic bureaucracy," "political fluidity," and "integral bureaucracy," respectively. It is with the last of these, which covers the Tokugawa years, that he is most concerned; and it is here that his interpretation is most original. He argues that the

Tokugawa integrated the attention and interests of all segments of society into the concept of the state and its service. The merchant class, in particular, was thrust into an increasingly important role in the Japanese polity, which contrasted sharply with its traditionally depressed social position. The contrast between service and status, with merchants and others as well, created one of the dynamics that helped to propel Japan forward and also to wreck the stability the Tokugawas had achieved.

A subtheme that emerges late in the book but that assumes real importance is the development of ecological regulation in Japan. Totman traces restraints on the use of limited natural resources and careful husbanding of those resources as early as the seventeenth century and sees this control as responsible for the solid foundation from which Japan was able to leap into modernity.

Japanese history is fascinating material indeed. In the hands of one with Professor Totman's felicitous control over the language and infectious excitement in the subject, it could not fail. Let us have more Totman.

R. KENT LANCASTER
Goucher College
Towson
Maryland

PETER WILES, ed. *The New Communist Third World.* Pp. 392. New York: St. Martin's Press, 1981. $32.50.

International politics, Marxist ideology, and the search by underdeveloped countries for an economic path form the backbone of this composite study, called an essay in political economy. It resulted from a two-year project, backed by the Social Science Research Council, on commercial policies of the communist Third World. As edited, with general introduction and conclusions, 12 countries are grouped and discussed in categories such as the new communist Third World, the marginals, the independent Stalinists, such as Albania and North Korea, and the Third World within Comecon, such as Mongolia and Vietnam. Cuba is omitted since it has been extensively treated. Trade, aid, and balance of payments tables are interspersed, current through 1978-79.

Typical of a new Marxist-Leninist state is Ethiopia, with its single party, ideology, and means for retaining power. Wiles believes that there is no going back; you do not unbecome a communist state. Somalia is called "the one that got away," because it had not been on the communist road long enough to ride out the pressures of the conflict with Soviet-supported Ethiopia.

In terms of material aid most of the states reviewed have obtained significant free-world economic aid, welcoming it in the pragmatic—Leninist—realization that the USSR can only offer acceptable and abundant arms, which keeps their military strong and their elites in power. Two economic aid exceptions are the dogmatic—Stalinist—regimes, Albania and North Korea.

A curiosity is Yemen—Aden—which pragmatically avoids, in deference to rival Islamic sensitivities, official use of "Marxism" and "Leninism," while serving as a Soviet pillar in the Middle East. Yet the country managed with a large trade deficit and aid from the USSR, even Communist China, and Arab oil states.

By attempting to examine the variety of Third World states claiming varying allegiances to forms of communism, the authors have undertaken a formidable task. The economic information is well organized and compact. However, it is difficult to analyze the indigenous factors that give viability to political-ideological forms and military cadres in directing those regimes. Certainly the one-party system in areas with small democratic traditions is an attractive device, and Marxism can provide a justifying gloss. So long as its influence grows worldwide, the USSR or its Cuban surrogate can provide military support to power-holding elites. In a division between economic and political analysis the latter could have received fuller treatment. This is a worthwhile collection, but the price could be a real handicap.

ROY M. MELBOURNE
Chapel Hill
North Carolina

A. JEYARATNAM WILSON. *The Gaullist System in Asia: The Constitution of Sri Lanka.* Pp. xvii, 218. London: Macmillan Press, 1981. Distributed in the United States by Humanities Press, Atlantic Highlands, NJ. $50.00.

The structure and arrangement of political institutions do not by themselves ensure the stability and success of a political system. But along with the political culture, the level of economic development, and the values and traditions of a people, they do play a role. Parliamentary systems, for example, have been notoriously unstable in countries riven by ethnic, linguistic, religious, regional, and other primordial rivalries. The failure and collapse of parliamentary systems in so many developing Third World countries in Asia, Africa, and Latin America attest to this.

Sri Lanka's attempt to make its political institutions more compatible with the realities of its internal socioeconomic and political conditions is the subject of A. Jeyaratnam Wilson's valuable analysis of the country's 1978 constitution, which replaced the constitution of the First Republic, which lasted from 1972 to 1977. Professor Wilson was invited by the first elected president of the Second Republic, J. R. Jayewardene, to comment upon and criticize the draft of the new constitution in July 1978.

Wilson analyzes the origins of what he calls the Gaullist system, the socioeconomic setting of Sri Lanka, the process of constitution making, the attempt to modify yet protect fundamental liberties, the new system of proportional representation, and the institutions set up by the constitution: the executive presidency, the office of prime minister, parliament, the judiciary, and the public services.

Judiciously, Wilson analyzes the strengths and potential dangers of the new constitution. The centralization of power in the executive presidency, and its relative independence from the pressures of parliament, can make for stability, continuity, dynamism, and direction. But in the wrong hands it could degenerate into authoritarianism. As Wilson puts it:

Sri Lanka's hybrid constitutional child is perhaps ... the last obstacle to praetorianism and dictatorship.... The presidential system stands midway between classical democracy and contemporary authoritarianism. It could be the style for pluralistic developing societies. But there is the ever present prospect that it could degenerate into the Asian counterpart of Castroism or Bonapartism. The greatest problem is to maintain a just equilibrium.

So far this equilibrium has been maintained. In a postscript to the book, written in December 1979, Wilson lists the achievements of the new system under the wise and steady guidance of President J. R. Jayewardene: the disciplining of a chaotic labor situation, the curbing of political violence and various kinds of political extremism, the attempt to increase interethnic harmony through the recommendation to decentralize the administration and devolve subordinate lawmaking powers to elected administrative development councils so as to encourage local autonomy and economic development at the grass-roots level, the pruning of wasteful government expenditure, and the radical alteration of the socioeconomic environment.

As of now the momentum continues. The aim of the constitution, "to attract foreign investment and to convince international aid-givers that Sri Lanka is a safe bet," seems to have been achieved. But will this progress continue if Jayewardene and his United National Party are voted out of power at the next election and replaced by Mrs. Sirimavo Bandaranaike and the Sri Lanka Freedom Party? That is a vital question.

MINOO ADENWALLA
Lawrence University
Appleton
Wisconsin

EUROPE

FERNAND BRAUDEL. *The Structures of Everyday Life: The Limits of the Possible.* Translated by Sian Reynolds. Pp. 623. New York: Harper & Row, 1981. $30.00.

The Structure of Everyday Life—a revised edition of Braudel's *Capitalism and Material Life* (1967)—is the first volume of his three-volume *Civilization and Capitalism, 15th-18th Century.* As set forth in his *Afterthought on Material Civilization and Capitalism* (1977), the essential argument of structures is as follows:

To my mind, the fundamental characteristic of the preindustrial economy is the coexistence of the inflexibility, inertia, and slow motion characteristic of an economy that was still primitive, alongside trends—limited and in the minority, yet active and powerful—that were characteristic of modern growth. On the one hand, peasants lived in their villages in an almost autonomous way, virtually in an autarchy; on the other hand, a market-oriented economy and expanding capitalism began to spread out, gradually creating the very world in which we live, and, at that early date, prefigured our world. Thus we have two universes, two ways of life foreign to each other, yet whose respective wholes explain one another.

Braudel defines the fundamental historiographical principles of his *Structures* in his two-volume classic *The Mediterranean and the Mediterranean World in the Age of Philip II* (1949). Out of the tradition of the influential French historiographical school, the *Annales*, formed in the 1920s by Lucien Febvre and Marc Bloch, Braudel sets his sights on global history. For Braudel the writing of global history means first grasping the demographic, geographical, sociological, and economic structures of history, and only then articulating the world of change, events, and politics.

Paradoxically, Braudel's *Structures*, which aspires toward global history, under the inspiration of both positivism and Marxism, has its strength not as a work of global history but as a work of historical imagination. It brilliantly invites us to conjure the significance, interconnections, and possibilities of a world we cannot entirely know.

Through an array of maps, charts, and graphs as well as a marvelous succession of beautifully drawn vignettes composed of telling anecdotes, detail, and data, Braudel excites us to imagine the entirety of the world that was. His greatest contribution in this volume, as his title suggests, is that of the presentation of the realities of everyday life. In a chapter appropriately titled "Weight of Numbers," he estimates the world's population for three centuries, while also describing the scale of human institutions and the size of human numbers when measured against nature, space, and the continuing reoccurrence of famine, epidemic, and plague. In successive chapters, Braudel tells us how people ate and drank—Chapter 2, "Daily Bread," Chapter 3, "Superfluity and Sufficiency: Food and Drink"—and how they were housed and clothed—Chapter 4, "Superfluity and Sufficiency: Houses, Clothes and Fashion."

With the material order described, Braudel then sketches the emergence of the worlds of market and commercial capitalism that gave birth to our world of industrial capitalism. The last four chapters of the volume treat growing human technological power, the use and the spread of money, and the growth of towns and cities, especially the big cities of the eighteenth century.

Because Braudel invites us to imagine a whole world, and because we know that the origin of our world is in that world, we value *The Structures of Everyday Life* as well as await the translation of the two remaining volumes, *Les jeux de l'echange* and *Les temps du monde*, of his *Civilization and Capitalism, 15th-18th Century.*

JOSEPH A. AMATO
Southwest State University
Marshall
Minnesota

L. M. CULLEN. *The Emergence of Modern Ireland, 1600-1900.* Pp. 292. New York: Holmes & Meier, 1981. $37.50.

D. GEORGE BOYCE. *Nationalism in Ireland.* Pp. 441. Baltimore: Johns Hopkins University Press, 1982. $32.50.

"We are a parcel of mongrels. Spanish, Scottish, Welsh, English, and even a Jew or two," said George Bernard Shaw of the Irish. Despite the mythology surrounding the Irish race, Ireland endured several centuries of settlement and conquest by diverse groups. Irish pluralism is a central concern of both volumes under review. In *The Emergence of Modern Ireland*, L. M. Cullen examines the impact of modernization on the Irish economy and social fabric. With a canvas that extends from the close of the sixteenth century to the dawning of the twentieth, Cullen focuses on the regional, cultural, and sectarian tensions produced by "a haunting profusion of overlapping layers of indigenous and external settlement." Although D. George Boyce's chronology, ranging from the pre-Norman period to the present, is even broader than Cullen's, the former employs a more circumscribed conceptual framework. *Nationalism in Ireland*, despite some attention to social, cultural, and economic change, confines itself largely to an examination of nationalist ideology.

A central thesis permeates every chapter of the Boyce volume: the Irish have failed to fashion a nationalist ideology that acknowledges their heterogeneous origins. Irish nationalist ideology depicts a golden age of Gaelic culture and law before foreigners invaded Ireland. Even socialists have employed a variant of the orthodox version of Irish history for their purposes, characterizing property arrangements in the utopia of pre-Norman Ireland as primitive communism. But the Gaelic idyll is a creation of hagiography, not history. According to Boyce and the mainstream of modern scholarship, decentralized political power, localism, and fragmentation characterized Gaelic Ireland. Moreover, the Gaels were not indigenous to Ireland; they, like the Normans and later invaders, dispossessed earlier inhabitants. Subjugated groups often fashion myths into usable history, and Irish nationalists are thus not unique. The parochialism of Irish nationalist ideology and its noncomprehensive nature, however, contends Boyce, intensify sectarian and social strife.

Ironically, notes Boyce, Protestants rendered seminal and significant contributions to Irish nationalist ideology despite their ultimate exclusion from it. The first assertions of Ireland's constitutional rights emanated from the Anglo-Irish. Morever, Charles Stewart Parnell was merely the last, albeit the greatest, of the Protestant politicians who led the struggle for Irish freedom. And Anglo-Irish literary men played key roles in the nineteenth-century Gaelic revival. But, explains Boyce, tirades against England, the progenitor of Ireland's distress, came to include attacks against the power of Ireland's Protestant minority. In its mature form, Irish nationalism portrayed the Anglo-Irish as beneficiaries of policies pursued by English Protestants and, consequently, opponents of Irish nationalism, which by then subsumed statehood. Pluralistic concepts of Irish nationalism, argues Boyce, could not compete with the passion that unified Catholics around the belief that they constituted the true Ireland, legitimate heirs to an ancient and glorious Gaelic state.

Although Cullen also gives much attention to the multiple layers of Irish peoples, his focus is social and economic rather than political. In contrast to Boyce's narrative style, Cullen is innovative in regard to both content and interpretation. Few other monographs provide detailed analysis of the complex relationship between diet and lifestyle. Beyond illuminating the correlations among class, religion, and living standards, Cullen adroitly clarifies regional nuances.

Historians, implies Cullen, have too often distorted history by employing English persecution, the Great Famine, and Catholicism to explain nearly every aspect of Irish life. Cullen views Ireland's distinctive pattern of modernization as the primary circumstance in its evolution. Modernization in Ireland, he argues, began relatively late, occurred within a compressed time frame, and created sharp contrasts between new forms and old. Despite a veneer of traditionalism, modernization vitiated most continuities with the past.

Had Cullen contrasted Ireland's swift modernization with that of former colonies in the Third World, he might have modified his assertions of Irish exceptionalism. Nevertheless, *The Emergence of Modern Ireland* nicely complements *Nationalism in Ireland*. Cullen is original, provocative, and nontraditional, while Boyce demonstrates skill at synthesizing existing knowledge. In contrast to Cullen's boldness, assurance, and didacticism, Boyce acknowledges ellipses amid caveats that definitive interpretation must wait for more specialized studies. But Cullen, the social historian, and Boyce, the political historian, are not antagonists; they are allies. Clio demands the treasure of both generalists and specialists.

WILLIAM M. SIMONS
State University of New York
Oneonta

SIMA LIEBERMAN. *The Contemporary Spanish Economy: A Historical Perspective*. Pp. xiii, 378. Winchester, MA, and London: George Allen & Unwin, 1982. $33.50.

This book is a useful introduction to the economic history of contemporary Spain that attempts to demonstrate that social and political as well as purely economic factors have hindered the development of a modern industrial economy. Beginning his narrative with the medieval Reconquest, Professor Lieberman traces the persistence of traditional values and institutions in Spain, arguing that these have produced rigidities that have stood in the way of economic progress. The outlines of his account—based on the most recent secondary literature—are fundamentally correct, although sometimes marred by dubious assertions, such as, "There was no Spanish Renaissance in the sixteenth century." Occasionally, too, he relies excessively on controversial interpretations of recent Spanish history, such as those of Tamames and Preston, without acknowledging the debate surrounding those interpretations.

The focus of the book is of course on economic development. Perhaps the strongest section is the first, which describes the historical forces that created lingering imbalances in Spanish agriculture. Lieberman convincingly argues that the political influence of traditional landed elites has prevented the agricultural sector from responding positively to changes in consumer demand. The resulting scarcities have created inflationary pressures that have spilled over into other sectors.

The second section of the book examines Spanish industrial development. The Spanish bourgeoisie early became dependent on protectionism, culminating in the "autarky" of the 1940s and 1950s. Highly critical of *dirigisme* in any form, Lieberman points out that even after the economic liberalization of 1959, the government continued to protect small, uncompetitive industries. Economic prosperity was thus dependent on foreign investment, cheap labor, and the worldwide economic boom of the 1960s. A concluding section analyzes the collapse of the economic "miracle" since 1973 and pessimistically assesses the potential for renewed growth.

The major virtue of this book is that it brings together a mass of recent economic data from widely scattered published sources, many of them Spanish. Lieberman is only partially successful, however, in illuminating the connections between political and social structures on the one hand, and economic development on the other. The historical narrative occasionally takes on the tone of a conspiracy of elites against the people, an oversimplification that obscures the significance of a large traditionalist middle class, both urban and rural. In the concluding section, where the analysis is almost exclusively economic, some of Lieberman's prescriptions for growth do not take the post-Franco political situation sufficiently into account. Finally, although much of the raw data are comparative, Lieberman does not comment when the Spanish figures differ little from those of the rest of Europe, leaving the reader wondering just why the Spanish case is unique.

CAROLYN P. BOYD
University of Texas
Austin

DAVID VITAL. *Zionism: The Formative Years.* Pp. xviii, 514. New York: Oxford University Press, 1982. $30.00.

Scores of books have been written and published relative to the Zionist movement and the subsequent establishment of the State of Israel (Erez-Israel). Professor David Vital, a political scientist at the University of Tel-Aviv, has now come forth with a sequel to his earlier study, *The Origins of Zionism* (1975). Vital centers his attention primarily on Theodor Herzl, the Vienna journalist, and other Jewish leaders in Central and Eastern Europe, Ahad Ha-Am, Max Mandelstamm, Max Nordau, and Israel Zangwill, along with many others. He tells the story of Herzl's negotiations and conversations with Sultan Abd al-Hamid, William II, and Joseph Chamberlain, and the Zionist attempts to set up a Jewish state in the Ottoman Empire (Palestine), the Sinai region (El Arish), and East Africa. Herzl's experience in Central and Eastern Europe—and the Middle East—made him a natural advocate and led to his unrivaled leadership and domination, a position he retained until his death in 1904.

Professor Vital considers the period immediately following the first Basel Congress, 29-31 August 1897, to have been decisive in the history of political Zionism. The organization established by this congress was no more than rudimentary and the primary ideological legacy underwent little change. But the congress proclaimed that "Zionism aims at the creation of a home for the Jewish people in Palestine to be secured by public law." This was the one basic element on which the members of the congress were agreed. As Herzl stated later, "the Zionist's duty is the propagation of Zionism. So long as there is a Jew who is not a Zionist, we have our work to do—to turn him into one."

Herzl failed in his attempt to win support for a Zionist state but he left a legacy of organization and ideology that endured over the years. For six years, 1897-1903, Herzl dominated the Zionist movement, essentially without challenge. There was rather more of secular politics than orthodox Judaism among the Zionists of the late nineteenth and early twentieth centuries.

Although he provides little new material on the subject, Professor Vital writes with masterly command of historical data. Anyone who now writes of Zionism seeking knowledge of the background of European nationalism will welcome Professor Vital's responsibly written book. Its contribution as a background to the study of the Palestine problem is at once evident. One need not agree with some aspects of Vital's story in order to appreciate the superb character of this volume. A useful appendix contains notes and statistical data on the Sixth Congress, 23-28 August 1903, and a select bibliography on the Herzlian Supremacy, Russian Jewry, Russia, and the Russian Zionists.

HARRY N. HOWARD
Bethesda
Maryland

ALEXANDER YANOV. *The Origins of Autocracy: Ivan the Terrible in Russian History.* Translated by Stephen Dunn. Pp. xvi, 339. Berkeley: University of California Press, 1981. $19.95.

This is a book written on several levels. First of all, it is a study of the origins of the autocratic state in early Russia. Central to this process were the activities of Tsar Ivan IV, the Terrible, most significantly by way of the violent and terrorist revolution from above of the mid-1560s—the Oprichnina system to destroy the tsar's enemies.

Second, there is a detailed presentation of what the author calls "Ivaniana": the impact of Ivan the Terrible's policies on many generations of historians, mainly Russian, and their all too frequent justification of Ivan's tyrannies. These include classical tsarist writers, prerevolutionary Marxists, and more recent Soviet historians. All the well-known names from Shcherbatov and Karamzin show up. Much of this discussion, while stimulating, goes over lots of old ground as to why a strong, even all-powerful, state came into existence in Russia.

Finally, the connection is drawn between the Russia of Ivan the Terrible and Stalin's Russia. Stalin becomes the twentieth-century version of the Terrible Tsar.

What happened happened. If the behavior of Ivan the Terrible's Oprichniki can still be interpreted in various ways, the behavior of Stalin's Oprichniki does not permit two opinions. In order to evaluate it, we do not need either "documented facts" or "the light of Marxist methodology". We were there. We know that we have before us not only beasts and hangmen, but also people to whom the tradition gives a basis for being proud of their corruption.

Stalin is quoted as follows: "Ivan IV was a great and wise ruler, who guarded the country from the penetration of foreign influence and strove to unify Russia."

Yanov is a Soviet intellectual and freelance political writer who fled to the United States, we are told, "because of both censorship and the KGB." His book is both shrewd and passionate. But even as one sympathizes with his hatred for Russian tyrannies, past and present, it is clear that he is himself so deeply immersed in an emotional nationalism and attachment to fatherland that his cause is marred—for a cause is fundamentally what this learned tirade of a book is about. Incidentally, the perennial question of the tsar's possible madness is not discussed.

In general, the translation by Stephen Dunn reads smoothly. The Selected Bibliography is spotty and uneven. Many titles given in Russian are also available in English, and many standard works on Ivan the Terrible are omitted.

DAVID HECHT

Pace University
New York

UNITED STATES

VIRGINIUS DABNEY. *The Jefferson Scandals: A Rebuttal.* Pp. x, 154. New York: Dodd, Mead & Company, 1981. $8.95.

This book is a landmark. It caps an intellectual process that has bewildered students for some time, to no scholarly end. Sir Max Beloff, reviewing in *Encounter* the literary occasion for Dabney's book, Fawn N. Brodie's *Thomas Jefferson: An Intimate History* (1974), complained that Americans were oversensitive to their presidents' reputations. If Beloff had employed Brodie's method in tracing a conjectural relationship between Queen Victoria and one of her gardeners, he would have lost his credibility in English journals. And yet there is as much psychohistorical basis for conjecture about Victoria in the vast library touching on her life, and in the hiatuses of her days and hours, as in Jefferson's. Victoria's routines and nonevidence, widowhood, natural impulses, and interpretation of words in letters and speech rank about with those of Jefferson.

Beloff patently errs in respect to American sensibility about presidents; one need only recall attitudes toward Lyndon Johnson, Richard Nixon, the Gerald Ford of alleged gaffes and physical blunderings, and even John F. Kennedy. Brodie's book is a Book of the Month Club selection; Barbara Chase-Riboud's *Sally Hemings* (1979), a lengthy, intense novel purportedly describing a secret 38-year liaison between Jefferson and a Monticello slave and her five natural children, is a Literary Guild selection. Both authors were widely interviewed and approved. A television series has been bruited, based on the avowed fiction.

The fact that the Jefferson scandals have required so elaborate an inquiry as Dabney's is indicative of a far more basic condition: the status of history in our national debates. It is one thing to recall the slanders of James T. Callender, a former stipendiary of Jefferson's, who turned against him and set down vengeful fancies. It is even no more than one thing that Callender's malice should have been utilized by Jefferson's Federalist foes, and later, sadly, by abolitionists building a case against slavery.

It is another thing, however, that the wide coverage given Brodie's readings in Jefferson, and the frank concoctions of Chase-Riboud based on Brodie, should have required of Dabney a patient tracing of rumors and inaccuracies about a figure who had exacted the study of generations of scholars. The goal was not merely to demean Jefferson as a calculated hypocrite and trickster, but to demean the nation for such faults. It is generally conceded that the probe into Jefferson's sex life dwindles to insignificance as his achievements are recounted. The entire concern has been to direct attention away from those achievements, as from those of the nation he helped found. It cannot be too often repeated, in present circumstances, that those achievements include the abolition of slavery at a fearful human cost, made heavier by awareness that there are today, by estimates of the Antislavery Society of England, some 50 to more than 100 million slaves in the world, to say nothing of poverty and traditions that amount to little more than enslavement.

The phenomenon of the Jefferson scandals is not quite history. It would be all but scandalous to review the responses of litterateurs and even scholars to Brodie's 66 pages of notes or Chase-Riboud's vivid and drawn-out constructions. The *New Republic* critic, for example, honored the "careful supposition" of the latter, and the *National Review* commentator found "tragedy for all" in her pages, the "all" referring to the Jefferson of the writer's fancy. Professor Woodward of Yale University, for the *New York Times*, thought Dabney's "a brief for the defense rather than ... a work of pure scholarship," not indicating what Dabney might have done that he failed to do. If the burden of proof continues to be on scholars rather than on partisans, then a Princeton enterprise to collect Jefferson's writings in 65 volumes—reported by the *Times* as in jeopardy, thanks to Reagan cuts—might yet fail of consummation.

LOUIS FILLER

Ovid
Michigan

JAMES R. ECCLES. *The Hatch Act and the American Bureaucracy*. Pp. xiii, 318. New York: Vantage Press, 1981. $14.95.

Despite an old adage to the contrary, it is sometimes possible to judge a book by its cover, or at least by its dust jacket. On the jacket of this book there is an eagle—not a majestic American eagle soaring above, but an eagle grounded by a ball and chain. James R. Eccles, the author of this study, is a career civil servant who has spent more than a quarter of a century experiencing what he writes about. As he sees it, he and the other eight million civil service employees of government are victims of a discriminatory law that divests each of them of precious rights, thus rendering them a group of second-class citizens. Symbolically speaking, then, there are millions of American eagles who are grounded. "In 1790, there were 4,000,000 citizens of the United States of America," writes Eccles passionately. "Less than half of the citizens who today are politically proscribed under the Hatch Act created this great nation of political liberty."

"An Act to Prevent Pernicious Political Activities" has been the law of the land—the very controversial law of the land—since 1939. Section 9 of this act, which is the real subject of Eccles's study, prevents civil servants from participating in partisan politics. While the act itself was intended as a reform measure, it is Eccles's contention that the remedy has been far worse than the supposed illness it sought to cure. Indeed, in the author's view, section 9 is clearly unconstitutional, since it denies basic First Amendment rights.

Historiographically, Eccles might be termed a kind of latter-day progressive. Like Charles A. Beard, Carl Becker, Vernon

Parrington, and other progressive writers earlier in this century, Eccles sees history in distinctly practical terms: he writes about the past in order to inform the present and reform the future. By focusing on the original debate that accompanied the passage of the Hatch Act and on the unsuccessful attempts to repeal it since, Eccles provides a useful primer for those still interested in repeal. The numbers of those so interested will doubtless increase due to the publication of this book, as well they should, for Eccles's case is well made. Clearly, it is time that the eagle was unchained.

ROBERT P. HAY
Marquette University
Milwaukee
Wisconsin

JOHN GAVENTA. *Power and Powerlessness: Quiescence and Rebellion in an Appalachian Valley.* Pp. xi, 267. Urbana: University of Illinois Press, 1982. $7.95.

Why do people acquiesce to conditions of injustice and inequity? That is the pivotal question raised by John Gaventa in his study of power relations in a mining community in Central Appalachia. Gaventa argues that power and powerlessness can be understood only through historical analysis, that case studies of decision making by their very method tend to emphasize either consensus or coercion when power arrangements are developmental and cumulative. For him, acquiescence emerges only after an elite first establishes dominance over a nonelite, then blocks access to political participation, and finally forges an ideological hegemony through the controlling of information and placing of limits on what the community actually debates and discusses. The powerless gradually become quiescent through continued defeat and a learning process that convinces them that conditions could not be otherwise.

Gaventa backs his theory with a 100-year history of politics in the Clear Fork Valley of eastern Kentucky and Tennessee. He documents the literal colonialization of the region by a British company, American Association, Ltd., in the 1880s, the role played by the local middle class in promoting loyalty to the area's patron, fleeting labor militancy in the early 1930s, the undemocratic practices of the United Mine Workers union, how fear has influenced elections, and the slight changes in political awareness and confidence effected by community organizing drives in the 1960s and early 1970s. Gaventa shows that the inhabitants of the Clear Fork Valley have never experienced genuine democracy and that they have believed and acted accordingly.

Gaventa's book is replete with insight, interesting detail, and disturbing findings; it is deserving of the many awards that have been bestowed on it, and it undoubtedly will serve as a critical reference point for future studies. *Power and Powerlessness*, however, is not without its faults. The subtleties of Gaventa's arguments are often difficult to follow; his historical overview is uneven and adds little to the existing secondary literature on Appalachia, and generalizations hardly seem warranted from his very particular case history. More important, the people of the community under study and their work and personal lives are surprisingly absent from this sympathetic, but at times overly analytic work. Gaventa does not present an ethnography or sociology of the region. Since he eschews a cultural approach, the reader never learns whether the culture autonomously fashioned by the men and women of the area acts as a buffer to the powers that be and whether that culture is and has been a source of both their strength and powerlessness. That kind of dialectical sense is missing in this book.

WALTER LICHT
University of Pennsylvania
Philadelphia

GERALD L. HOUSEMAN. *City of the Right: Urban Applications of American Conservative Thought.* Pp. viii, 207. Westport, CT: Greenwood Press, 1982. $25.00.

Intellectuals promoting a particular orthodoxy can be a potent force for political change. Their philosophical murmur and pointed debate can give reason and direction to changing popular moods. Since the 1930s liberal thinkers gained such ascendancy as popular demands for greater economic security and social welfare benefits grew; the result was a governmental revolution, new national power, and a proliferation of innovative public policies. Today that liberal experience has been opened to severe questioning and its legacy in the form of established policies and governmental arrangements has come under attack. This time a shift toward political conservatism has emerged and conservative writers with a wide following have entered the political limelight to give reason, substance, and ideals to the new national mood. Just what these people say about one of America's most controversial problems—its cities— is the subject of this volume by Gerald L. Houseman. What is the philosophical vision of the new conservatism? What policies to address the plight of the nation's cities do they offer? How will they reshape our urban destiny? These are the focal questions of *City of the Right.*

Houseman describes and evaluates the writings of five conservative authors whose work has won a considerable following among those on the right, particularly within the Reagan administration. The works of William F. Buckley, Irving Kristol, Edward C. Banfield, Milton Friedman, and novelist Ayn Rand are surveyed in separate chapters; Houseman considers each author's basic political philosophy as well as his or her urban vision and specific policy recommendations for particular urban problems, such as unemployment, law and order, housing, racial justice, crime, and poverty. Throughout these chapters and in the book's concluding segment, Houseman attempts to point out themes that define the conservatism of this group and its urban outlook. He also evaluates the philosophical ideas of these authors and the relevance of many of their specific proposals for cities.

From nearly every perspective Houseman finds the conservatism of his subjects and their specific ideas for cities wanting. With their varied backgrounds—journalist, academician, literary gadfly, or novelist—the writers reveal certain distinctive ideas about the meaning of conservatism and its relevance to the city. But in general Houseman finds them unsympathetic and often even hostile to cities and their people, motivated by inegalitarian considerations and downright mean-spirited. Captivated by the shopworn myth of laissez-faire economics, which acts as philosophical glue and dominates these authors' outlook on society, conservatism's political orthodoxy is shown to be shallow, contradictory, and selfish. While conservatives claim to defend individualism in theory, Houseman argues that their antiliberal sentiments actually assault individual liberties and rights in practice. In fact, latent racism frequently creeps into their thinking once urban problems can no longer be conceived in terms of their favored economic categories of analysis. Except for Friedman and Banfield, the new conservatives have failed to develop many detailed proposals for dealing with specific urban problems. Given this group's biases and hostility toward so much of the urban way of life, the reader might well conclude that this is fortunate.

A book that so thoroughly damns contemporary conservative thought will no doubt offend many. However, even the most ardent liberal will find that this volume leaves much to be desired. Although Houseman often successfully describes the essence of these writers as he meanders through their work, his analysis and evaluation seems shallow and unconvincing. Particularly lacking is a rigorous, in-depth probing of the conservative philosophy that leads these writers to the conclusions that Houseman finds so repulsive. Common themes, such as inequality, concern for religion, capitalism, free markets, and so on, are pointed out as common terms of reference making up conservatism, but the larger logic and framework that underpins and activates this mode of thought is left unexplored. Beyond pointing to some common values in conservatism, Houseman's analysis too often comes down to taking quick potshots at conservative ideas, calling attention to their simplicity, their lack of empirical foundation, their inconsistency with their other ideas, or their logically horrifying social consequences. In the end no real thesis emerges. The reader is left with little firm sense of conservatism as an intellectual force and is unprepared for Houseman's highly caustic conclusions.

PAUL KANTOR

Fordham University
Bronx
New York

HERBERT A. JOHNSON. *Essays on New York Colonial Legal History.* Pp. viii, 269. Westport, CT: Greenwood Press, 1981. $29.95.

In this volume the accomplished legal historian Herbert A. Johnson has combined eight of his published essays with a new bibliography. The essays are diverse. Photographically copied, they differ in format and apparatus. Some address a general, and others a specialized, audience. Nonspecialists, including this reviewer, will find the volume useful for understanding its field.

Johnson begins with a general introduction to scholarship in American colonial legal history. He observes that early studies emphasized institutional continuity or Turnerian adaptation, but usually avoided reductionism. His seven essays on early New York law maintain balance. Their very heterogeneity gives the collection a comprehensive flavor. They afford glimpses into the life of the legal profession, the variety of legal and court systems, and issues ranging from constitutional to procedural. The reader becomes aware of, although not erudite about, the varied milieu of the eighteenth-century jurist.

The collection also introduces readers to the history of law before the courts kept regular records of written decisions. Oral tradition supplemented English reports, and law developed peculiarly. English common law gradually displaced local Dutch and Puritan codes. For most, but not all, purposes, English law as of 1691 became the basis of New York law, but courts received later British statutes selectively and unsystematically. Pioneering researchers must explore "topics for which the documentation is slender and conclusions can only be tentative in nature." Johnson considers "unimaginative and poorly-motivated" historians the greatest obstacle to this research.

In several essays Johnson suggests that legal development contributed to the imperial crisis of the 1760s. A professional elite emerged that was prepared to debate constitutional questions in a cosmopolitan context. A customs case illustrated statutory obsolescence that prompted stricter British measures. A procedural question generated a constitutional controversy between royal and provincial officials. An attempt to adopt many British statutes wholesale, which the Privy Council disallowed, paralleled the similarly contested claim to the undiminished rights of Englishmen in the colonies. "In many ways," Johnson concludes, "the American Revolution was a lawyers' rebellion."

The 45-page topically organized bibliography of historical works about law in all the American colonies will in itself make this volume an important resource for scholars and general readers. The bibliography, like the collection of essays, will serve as an introduction to scholarship to date and a springboard for future investigation.

JACK P. MADDEX, Jr.

University of Oregon
Eugene

ANDREW LEVINE. *Liberal Democracy: A Critique of Its Theory.* Pp. 216. New York: Columbia University Press, 1981. $25.00.

Liberals hold, as Mill put it, that there is a circle around each individual that no government should overstep. Democrats hold that political matters should be decided collectively. Levine refers to the theory that these two can be combined as "liberal democracy." He concludes that the theory of liberal democracy has not adequately established the combination. And he doubts that it can be done.

Here are his criticisms. Essentially, the dominant theory "is overwhelmingly liberal and only very tenuously democratic." The majority are not allowed to tamper much with the liberal principle that government be minimal. However, freedom can be limited not only by the acts of individuals but also by the ways in which social institutions are arranged. Levine believes that the usual theory ignores the effect of institutional restrictions, while paying great attention to coercion by individuals. He then argues that representative democracy is clearly not adequate democracy: representatives become professionals and represent their own reelection more than anything else. In addition to the usual objections, a theory of representation must face the difficulties raised by the Arrow problem: there is no single best way to count the votes.

Given the liberal concern with freedom, Levine holds that there should be rapt attention to the matter of measuring degrees of individual freedom. The dominant theory ignores the question, he finds. The other basic gap in the theory, for him, is the complete lack of interest in measuring and dealing with degrees of exploitation of individuals. Levine holds that a seriously democratic theory would not avoid the subject of human exploitation; it would not leave that territory to the Marxists.

Since his subject is not the practice of liberal democracies, but their theory, one might expect more analysis of the sources of the theory. The classical authors—Hobbes, Mill, Bentham—are mentioned without much reference. Levine calls Kant and Rousseau the "idealist" opponents of his subject. Of contemporaries, David Gautier, Amartya Sen, Isaiah Berlin, and C. B. McPherson get most attention. The essay is essentially his own analysis of what he calls "the core theory" of liberal democracy, with little specification of the literature and none of the practice.

The subject seems to call for a serious consideration of U.S. constitutional law, particularly in the chapter on rights. Not here. We have little sense of reality unless we connect with legislative and judicial activity. There cannot be politics without law. I suspect that the next generation of writers on political theory will have jurisprudence as their second language. Not only does Levine ignore legal theory, but his self-imposed restriction to theory without practice leaves him with the same abstractness that he charges against the developers of liberal democracy.

One could wish for more attention to other matters that are not in fashion, but are significant for Levine's subject—for example, Mill's book on political economy and Kant's philosophy of history. The typical reader of this book has probably memorized Mill's essay, "On Liberty," but does not know the material in his longer work. Kant's focus on individual ambivalence is a theoretical matter that destroys most comments about his political viewpoint. Kant does not take individuals to be morally perfectable. Actually, he holds that individual selfishness, greed, and envy are the necessary elements in humankind's progress. In view of Levine's earlier work on Kant and Rousseau, it is odd that he lumps them together. Their ideas on human nature have little in common.

The strong parts of the book are the criticisms of representation rather than direct decision making and the stress on the theoretical importance of exploitation and degrees of freedom. While not original, these topics are sharply handled. The book stands as an interesting reminder of the unfinished business of liberal democratic theory.

SIDNEY AXINN
Temple University
Philadelphia

ARTHUR S. LINK et al., eds., *The Papers of Woodrow Wilson,* vol. 38. Pp. xxvi, 716. Princeton, NJ: Princeton University Press, 1982. $30.00.

This volume highlights Wilson's campaign for reelection and his vindication at the polls following the dark moment when it appeared he had lost the presidency to Charles Evans Hughes. Readers must, of course, seek elsewhere to discern why the electorate seemed to turn to Hughes in the crisis, even though they held Congress for the Democrats. Indeed, readers will be hard put to see a crisis at all. There are loose ends to be tied up with Mexico, which take up a substantial number of these pages, almost as many as those given the war in Europe. A cordial letter from Kaiser Wilhelm II all but seems to strike a balance in the peace explorations for which Wilson takes credit in the campaign. The clear tilt of his government toward Great Britain—what is called "benevolent neutrality" in one place—evident in earlier volumes is all but absent here. Famous is Wilson's public scorn of Irish-Americans who sought to bully him into anti-British pronouncements.

Meanwhile, he has recommended, picking up from the Democratic Party Platform, an "extension of suffrage by the states upon the same terms as to men," backtracking on his old antisuffragist views. In talking to the National American Woman Suffrage Association, he cites its inevitable victory and urges it to consider that it "can afford a little while to wait." He impresses its leader, Anna Howard Shaw, who notices he has not asked for enfranchised women's votes and has seemed statesmanlike. He has already resolved the great threat of a railroad strike—Henry Ford and others had warned that such a strike would close down their factories—by forcing from the industrialists the concession of an eight-hour day, and he has already added to his Council of National Defense Advisory Commission none other than Samuel Gompers. This would seem— it seemed so to Gompers—to put labor into government; but the AFL chieftain's crucial role in the coming war intervention ultimately contributed to his decline in labor annals.

Meanwhile, the war grinds on in Europe. It is little reflected in the White House or personal correspondence. A Republican plan to buy and publicize Wilson's letters to Mary Allen Hulbert, discussed in volume 35, is frustrated by the lady, but does evoke an odd draft of a letter to her by Wilson, pretending to be someone else, which she says in her own memoir she did not "choose" to answer. There is no question that the publication of those letters would have ended Wilson's term of office.

Wilson had a plan for leaving office immediately if he was defeated at the polls, and one can read tension in his and his aides' assessments of possibilities. But once this crisis is past, Wilson and his alter ego House are more loose-jointed, with potentialities that even from hindsight are alarming and tragic. Great Britain has continued peremptory over American shipping, and has offended public opinion at home. Wilson cannot help noticing—and his own sensitivities inform him—that the British are dragging their feet in the pursuit of peace. They have blacklisted American firms— outraging the business community—and censored American mail. Anglophile Ambassador Page pleads England's cause, and Wilson himself fears a too "argumentative" tone in dealing with England. Peace proposals hinge on how the war is going. House is against proposals while England seems to be "winning." Later he fears that England might reject peace offers and Germany accept, giving the Germans a case for unrestricted submarine warfare. House notes in his diary that Wilson "went so far as to say if the Allies wanted war with us we would not shrink from it."

House sets down fantastic perspectives, reminding the reader that he is the anonymous author of *Philip Dru, Administrator* (1912), in which he boldly imagined long-term war. He now sees the possibility of Great Britain destroying the American fleet and landing troops from Japan "in sufficient number to hold certain parts of the United States." Wilson agrees, but adds that "they . . . would have to stop somewhere." It is a mind-boggling prospect, as this volume draws to a close.

LOUIS FILLER

Ovid
Michigan

WILLIAM McGAUGHEY, Jr. *A Shorter Workweek in the 1980's.* Pp. xiii, 308. White Bear Lake, MN: Thistlerose Publications, 1981. $6.95.

The major theme developed by McGaughey is that American society is now ready for a shorter workweek. The book reviews the history of labor, when work meant from sunup to sundown, or a minimum of a 12-hour day.

Labor's long and historic struggle for a shorter workweek was crystallized when Henry Ford inaugurated in 1926 the 5-day, 40-hour workweek without any reduction in wages. Since then, this policy has become a fixed pattern in the world of work. McGaughey argues that it is now time for change, and he projects a further reduction of the workweek to a 35-hour, 5-day week, not the 32-hour, 4-day schedule. To bring this about, Representative John Conyers of Michigan introduced in 1978 HR-1784, the Conyers Bill, which would update the Fair Labor Standards Act of 1938 and introduce a process of gradual change. The bill was pigeonholed and the 40-hour week is still with us today. So far so good.

If McGaughey's major thesis were only a reduced work schedule, it might have been duly applauded. However, what he really is opposed to is the entire program of the welfare state that has been developed since the beginning of the Roosevelt New Deal era. Specifically, he condemns the pattern of chronic joblessness as stemming from unemployment compensation. But this is only the beginning. He blames the housing shortage, government pensions, medicare and medicaid, food stamps, social security, and various social problems on the 40-hour workweek! Furthermore, he has few kind words for college professors, especially economists. He further suggests that a shorter workweek is the panacea for alcoholism, cigarette and drug use, juvenile delinquency, high crime rates, and myriad other social problems plaguing contemporary American society.

Space does not permit any refutation of this illogical and irrelevant presentation. The criticism will be limited to the structure and organization of the book. First, McGaughey bases his material largely on current newspaper and journal articles. Popular magazines such as *Time, Newsweek,* and *U.S. News and World Report,* and local newspapers in Minnesota as well as the *New York Times* and the *Wall Street Journal* are quoted very frequently. For example, in Chapter 1, there are 20 citations of the *Wall Street Journal.* Obviously, no thought has been given either to the business biases or to the partisanship of the quoted articles.

Second, there are no theories, major or subordinate, utilized as a framework for the book.

Third, secondary data, most commonly from the *Monthly Labor Review,* are utilized by McGaughey without any awareness of the purpose and limitations of the original data.

Finally, there is a good deal of editorializing, if not outright preaching, about the merits of the reduced workweek. At best, this text is a good example of the conservative, antiliberal, and rightist views of a self-appointed spokesman for the world of work.

MARTIN E. DANZIG

City University of New York
Kingsborough

DOUGLAS MUZZIO. *Watergate Games: Strategies, Choices, Outcomes.* Pp. x, 205. New York: New York University Press, 1982. $17.95.

Noting that what is absent in the literature about Watergate are attempts at "explanation as Abraham Kaplan defines the term," Douglas Muzzio attempts to provide an explanation of Watergate that "shows that on the basis of what we know, the something to be explained could not be otherwise." Whether he succeeds in this grand scheme is difficult to judge. However, he certainly does provide one of the most coherent, succinct, and revealing accounts of Watergate I have read. As Muzzio points out, there has, until now, been no theoretical framework within which to fit the complex events known as the Watergate affair, and his intention is to begin bridging the explanation gap by "applying game theory to Watergate events."

It appears to me that the main questions one might have about this book are not substantive, then, but methodological. Does the game-theoretic model—with its emphasis on rational actors, acting consciously, in the light of more or less full information, attempting to maximize net expectable utilities for themselves or their team, unconstrained by moral or ethical norms—provide the most plausible one for understanding the way the Watergate affair unfolded? Even Leon Jaworski was moved to comment about Muzzio's book that it "is a striking condensation of the Watergate escapade in a unique setting and posing challenging inquiries of strategy." Jaworski, one of the special prosecutors in the Watergate events, could not bring himself to admit that Muzzio had accomplished his objective—perhaps because to admit that he had is in some sense to forgo forever the claim that the principal actors in Watergate acted out of anything but sheer self-interest: all the principal actors were psychological and/or ethical egoists. Thus Archibald Cox is seen as a "masterful strategist"; John Sirica, as a man who "redefined the consequences of continued silence"; Elliot Richardson, as a man whose canonization was "unjustified"; and, somewhat surprisingly, Richard Nixon is the only person who is redeemed modestly by this model of analysis. As the dust jacket on the book says, "He fell not because he was 'mad' or 'needed to fail.' He acted rationally in response to events and actions by other Watergate players."

Perhaps it is because so many of the players in the Watergate games behaved as rational egoists that Muzzio's account appears to be so accurate. On the other hand, as one reads this account, one cannot help asking the question, Is this account so convincing because it is postdictive and after the fact, or is it so convincing because it is the one true account that explains Watergate? I think that the truth lies somewhere in between. Muzzio's analysis has the appearance of logical explanation simply because he uses a method that imposes an abstract form on the evolving events. Just as logicians can use truth tables to ascertain the truth value of complex truth-functional propositions, and statisticians can use tree diagrams to array the probable outcomes of everything from drawing aces from a deck of cards to throwing a deuce on a die, so game theoreticians can use tree diagrams to array all of the options open to players in various games, including the Watergate games. Just because we can array the probabilities in a sequence of events does not mean, however, that we can predict which order that sequence will follow—simply because we cannot know all the variables influencing individual players and events. So while Muzzio's account eliminates many of the logical surprises in Watergate, there are still a great number of empirical surprises—surprises one could not have reduced to any explanatory account simply because they were too numerous. In short, Muzzio's account may have fallen short of showing how "the something to be explained could not be otherwise." I hasten to add that those interested in understanding Watergate cannot afford to ignore *Watergate Games*: it comes so close to accomplishing the objectives of its author that wrestling with the judgment of whether or not it succeeds is a worthwhile activity in itself.

STEPHEN W. WHITE
East Tennessee State University
Johnson City

HENRY SHUE. *Basic Rights: Subsistence, Affluence, and U.S. Foreign Policy.* Pp. xiii, 231. Princeton, NJ: Princeton University Press, 1980. $17.50. Paperbound, $4.95.

Henry Shue, senior research associate at the Center for Philosophy and Public Policy, University of Maryland, estimates that nearly one billion people worldwide live below the level of minimal subsistence. These people exist without adequate food and clothing, and without minimal preventative health care. The realization of this suffering in the world elicits anger from Shue. Nevertheless, he writes, his intention is to develop an applied philosophical argument that rationally defends the basic rights of people to a decent standard of living and to physical security. Explicit in his defense of basic rights is his contention that the United States must undertake profound changes in its foreign policy, beginning with the ratification of the International Covenant of Economic, Social and Cultural Rights. Furthermore, Shue feels that the United States, in order to defend the basic rights of deprived people, should cease all economic and military assistance to governments engaged in the systematic deprivation of subsistence rights.

In his call for a radical transformation in American foreign policy, Shue argues that policymakers should not, as they have in the past, make sharp distinctions between violations of civil and political rights and violations of economic and social rights. In turn, Shue rejects the traditional dichotomy between positive rights and negative rights as "intellectually bankrupt." All moral rights, he states, have negative and positive aspects. The right to physical security, for instance, implies not only that a person's physical security must not be violated, but that it must be protected as well. In the past, the role of protecting these rights fell to each individual nation. Now, Shue posits, the close dependency created by an international economy means that affluent nations must assume the primary duty of aiding and protecting the basic rights of people in all nations. Only in this way will the basic rights of all people be protected.

Shue's book is terse, well written, and carefully illustrated with specific examples. It is also provocative. Radicals will complain that Shue has not addressed the central issue of whether the economic and social systems of affluent nations and Third World nations must be changed if basic rights are actually to be protected. In turn, realists in foreign policy will question whether Shue's goal of a perfect world would, in the end, only create more havoc. Such critics will recall the words of John Adams, who wrote during the French Revolution: "Too many ... pant for equality of persons and property. The impracticability of this, God Almighty has decreed, and the advocates for liberty, who attempt it, will surely suffer for it."

DONALD T. CRITCHLOW
MICHAEL A. PAYNE
University of Dayton
Ohio

SOCIOLOGY

ERNEST L. ABEL. *Marihuana: The First Twelve Thousand Years.* Pp. xi, 289. New York: Plenum Press, 1980. $17.95.

This book seems especially timely in light of the recent recommendation by a National Academy of Sciences committee that marijuana be decriminalized. Their report comes 10 years after that of another scientific panel that also urged the lifting of criminal penalties for personal possession or use of marijuana. Both reports met with the same fate: they were rejected by the federal administration in power at the time—both, by the way, conservative ideologically.

Abel's book sheds light on why decriminalization is such a bone of contention, specifically, on why marijuana use and possession should remain a crime despite scientific evidence that it is no more intoxicating or harmful than alcohol.

This book, however, is not a treatise on decriminalization. Rather, it is far more comprehensive, with a probable appeal for many different audiences, including social scientists. The book cannot be labeled simply a history of marijuana, either, although the title suggests that indeed. It defies categorization, exploring a range of topics—from hemp in international commerce to hashish in literature to the association of marijuana with socially suppressed groups.

Readers will appreciate a scholarly approach to a subject that has often been treated with more prejudice than reason. Abel researched the area thoroughly, going far and wide through literary works, history books, medical and legal journals, and newspapers. Yet without underestimating the effort, one gathers that it was not terribly difficult to locate relevant material, given that marijuana has played a feature role in human civilization.

In finding out about marijuana historically and cross-culturally, one often acquires a knowledge of entire societies, for the cannabis plant, with its great array of uses, is a feature of the total pattern of existence. So essential was it in early China, for example, that certain religious ceremonies evolved to ensure its abundance.

We learn that the culture of the Far East was more compatible with socially sanctioned marijuana use than that of the West. Conversely, when the dominant values of a particular society were closest so what has become known as the Protestant Ethic, marijuana has been perceived as a threat and accordingly outlawed. Marijuana became a popular alternative to alcohol among American college students in the 1960s—a time when fundamental values were being questioned and there was an increase in experimentation with different lifestyles. Although the generation of the 1960s subsequently joined the cultural mainstream, marijuana use has not abated and has spread to younger groups. Perhaps this goes along with a greater tolerance of escapism in all its various forms—from pot smoking to video games.

A serendipitous outcome of the research effort to find out the extent to which marijuana was a harmful substance was the discovery of therapeutic qualities. To some degree this was a case of rediscovering the wheel, since the therapeutic value of cannabis was recognized in other societies at other times. A new element, however, was that, with modern technology, the specific active ingredient—1-delta-9-trans-tetrahydrocannabinol (Δ^9-THC)—could be isolated.

Abel suggests in the title that, having been with human beings for 12,000 years, marijuana is likely to remain for the next 12,000, provided that human civilization can survive that long. Then again, if a prudent social policy toward marijuana use can evolve—indicative of more rational social policies in general—perhaps human beings will collectively have that kind of longevity.

MAUREEN SEARLE
University of Kentucky
Lexington

JEFFREY C. ALEXANDER. *Theoretical Logic in Sociology, Vol. 1: Positivism, Presuppositions, and Current Controversies.* Pp. xx, 234. Berkeley and Los Angeles: University of California Press, 1982. $25.00.

This is an ambitious work that could have a significant effect on the direction of sociology in the 1980s. Alexander argues that recent positivistic trends have weakened theoretical analysis, produced confused self-understanding among theorists, and had a generally trivializing effect on the discipline. To revive the subject we must revive its theoretical heritage, establishing the proper role of general theory in scientific practice and making a thorough study of the most general presuppositions underlying all intellectual work in sociology.

This book is the first in a projected sequence of four, all under the general title *Theoretical Logic in Sociology*. Alexander begins by drawing on postpositivist writers such as Thomas Kuhn, Michael Polanyi, and Gerald Holton to outline a conception of science that resists reducing theoretical statement to induction from observation—the positivist position—or to ideological commitment—Marxism and much critical theory. Whether the components of science, such as models, concepts, definitions, laws, and so on, can really be ordered on a single continuum of generality-specificity between the "metaphysical and empirical environments," as Alexander suggests, is highly debatable. His locating ideological orientations between presuppositions and models, for example, is too restricting and potentially misleading since many questions here are more radical than he indicates. Nonetheless Alexander's account of science and the role of general theory is uncommonly cogent and includes many sharp observations on the current state of sociology.

The power of Alexander's work lies in his integrated conceptualization of theoretical logic as dealing with general presuppositions that must be both general and decisive. Alexander argues that the presuppositions are essential for sociology, namely, those of action and order. In the present volume his discussion is quite abstract, yet loaded with acumen. The next three volumes will deal with Marx and Durkheim, Weber, and Parsons, respectively, in which Alexander will analyze, as it were, these presuppositions at work. His intent is to explicate the most general yet discriminating presuppositions behind all theoretical sociology so that we can rationally transcend present parochialisms. We might anticipate that the way Alexander sets up his discussion serves to avoid many issues crucial to contemporary theorists, such as the current linguistic turn, for example, or the conceptualization of global systems. We can only fairly evaluate his strategy, however, after publication of all four volumes. What we can assert at this point is that anyone interested in the current state of sociology should study *Positivism, Presuppositions, and Current Controversies*. It includes some of the best theoretical discourse of recent years. The publisher is also to be congratulated on a handsome production.

ADRIAN C. HAYES
State University of New York
Albany

DEBORAH BELLE, ed. *Lives in Stress: Women and Depression.* Pp. 247. Beverly Hills, CA: Sage Publications, 1982. $22.50. Paperbound, $9.95.

Lives in Stress is a report on depression and its causes among low-income women, the result of a preliminary study conducted by the Stress and Families Project in 1978 and funded by the National Institute of Mental Health. While it is widely recognized that more women than men suffer from depression, this phenomenon has usually been studied among middle-class women and without regard to the environmental context of women's lives. The Stress and Families Project took note of the fact that among women, low-income mothers were, as a group, disproportionately victims of depression; its directors emphasized the factors in low-income environments that contributed to stress and depression. "As long as women are disproportionately represented in low-income groups, they will also be disproportionately represented among the depressed." This focus is of particular interest in light of recent census figures that indicate that the number of low-income households headed by women is increasing.

A total of 43 Boston low-income mothers were interviewed at length and their family situations observed by project investigators. These women represented a cross section of the population in terms of race and marital status. The data obtained are analyzed in 14 chapters, each the report of a different author on such topics as the importance of support networks for women's mental well-being, strategies of coping, and child-rearing philosophies. A primary conclusion of the project is that among low-income mothers, "those with particularly low or unreliable incomes, those who have been unable to secure the kind of paid employment they have sought, those without confidantes and child-care help, and those with a history of change and loss in childhood appear to be at high risk" for depression. Assistance in alleviating these problems should be the most effective way to minimize the risk of depression. This conclusion is perhaps obvious, but discouraging in the light of recent and proposed budget cuts in programs for the disadvantaged, such as CETA job training.

The study itself breaks no new ground. Each chapter is primarily a summary of current thinking on the particular topic, and indicates only perfunctorily the findings of the Stress and Families Project investigators, which confirm the current theories. For instance, Zur-Szpiro and Longfellow report that support from fathers is indeed related to reduced stress among mothers.

It is to be expected that no new conclusions would likely emerge from a study of such limited scope, but the authors have failed to exploit what could have been a virtue of such a limited but intensive study. The rapport the authors claim emerged between the investigators and the investigated is nowhere in evidence; a detailed picture of the personalities and problems faced by the women involved would have humanized the subject matter and removed the conclusions from the realm of statistics. Nevertheless, *Lives in Stress* could serve as a useful introduction to women's studies for its succinct restatements of current scholarship, its excellent bibliographies, and its stress on the need to look at women's problems in terms of the environment women inhabit.

CHARLOTTE L. BEAHAN
Murray State University
Kentucky

THEODORE M. BENDITT. *Rights*. Pp. ix, 148. Totowa, NJ: Rowman & Littlefield, Barnes & Noble Books, 1982. $22.50.

Words often assume an existence of their own, separate from the ideas in conjunction with which they first appeared. One particular term may come to stand for a variety of concepts: it may shed a meaning with which it has long been closely associated; it may attract an idea formerly carried by a different term; or it may come to convey an entirely new intellectual construction. Some of these metamorphoses are barely perceptible while occurring, others by contrast are willful manipulations.

Such a widely trusted abstract word is "rights." Admirable and fruitful as it may be in the context of philosophy, often through juristic concepts, the language of legal symbolization, it has been permitted to move away from the meaning it originally held. "Rights" are generally defined as "powers of free action," while in a juristic context a "right" is a capacity residing in one person controlling with the assent and assistance of the state the actions of others. Thus, a "right" is what a person is entitled to have, to do, or to receive from others within the limits prescribed by law.

And yet Professor Benditt, chairman of the Department of Philosophy at the University of Alabama in Birmingham, in this remarkable reference book, provides a handy source of adrenalin to those who believe that rights are so much more than these juristic concepts.

Here is an entirely new kind of reference book, for it presents a comprehensive probing and provocative discussion of an abstract subject with a clarity of examples, making the subject understandable reading while drawing no discernible conclusion.

Clearly the proliferation of civil rights and the rights of privacy color Benditt's masterful discussion of the "Importance of Rights" in his introduction. His analyses include the kinds and characteristics of right, absolute or prima facie, theories such as the will theory and rights as claims and entitlements, and concludes with the benefit theory.

There follows a series of chapters containing detailed treatments of philosophical concepts regarding the relationship of rights to morals, law, society, economics, and politics. Chapter 2 discusses the utilitarian theory of rights through the entrenchment of rules and rights, often relying on learned treatises of eminent philosophers.

Particularly enlightening is Chapter 3, which is a study of the conflicting of rights, such as the right to know and another's right to privacy. This incisive chapter discusses how rights may or may not be outweighed by or overridden by moral and practical considerations, mainly the distinction between general and special rights. Featured is a hierarchy of "rights" and "obligations."

Benditt then moves gracefully, in Chapters 4 and 5, to a discussion of the economic aspects and rights and duties of compensation and beneficence. Included is a stimulating argument on alternatives to institutions and contract.

Chapters 7 and 8 are most relevant to our times, as Benditt delves into the modern social structure, arguing effectively for the individual's rights against society and the rights of protection and enforcement. Intertwined are the arguments for and against the collective as the foundation for success or failure depending on the general economic life of the society.

In his none-too-optimistic concluding chapter, Benditt shares views on "Rights in Law." Most provocative is his section on "Legal Rights in Government and Largess," which stresses the growth of government to a point that great numbers of people derive from it a portion of their well-being. Often these benefits, including technological change, are caused by forces far beyond the control of the individual. This largess often leads to a diminution or trade-off of rights for dependency. His final observations deal with the court's recognition of the benefits state.

Written in an incisive style, Professor Benditt's book will join other treatises on humankind's determination to govern the individual's mind, being, and conduct in interpersonal and intergovernmental affairs as a work of enduring value.

   HON. GERALD L. SBARBORO
Circuit Court of Cook County
Illinois

DAVID R. HEISE, ed. *Microcomputers in Social Research*. Pp. 139. Special issue of *Sociological Methods & Research*, Vol. 9, No. 4. Beverly Hills, CA: Sage Publications, 1981. No price.

JAMES B. TAYLOR. *Using Microcomputers in Social Agencies*. Pp. 119. Beverly Hills, CA: Sage Publications, 1981. $7.50.

Microcomputers did not exist in their present forms before about 1977. The growth and use of microcomputers since that date has been nothing if not spectacular. While the PET was the first unit with resident full floating-point BASIC that enjoyed good sales, at the present time the leading sellers seem to be Radio Shack and Apple. The three units together have created many new research and teaching possibilities since access to the small machines has freed users from artificial restrictions imposed by computer bureaucracies.

Heise has edited a collection of seven essays addressed to social science professionals who are familiar with what mainframe computers can do with large data packages such as SPSS or SAS. Each article explains how microcomputers can handle the same jobs for much less money and effort than can a large IBM-type computer. The best article is by Tracy Collins, who explains not only the cost of the system, but includes sample output from statistical packages for the Apple. As a sociologist who also sold computers, Collins gives practical advice to sociologists who may wish to purchase their own systems to enjoy unlimited access to data analysis. Other articles describe data base management, keeping your bibliography on the computer, and how to use the computer while in the field collecting raw data. In short, this journal special issue is essential for professors who need to know what microcomputers can do for them.

Taylor has written a different type of book. Taylor assumes that the reader needs to know how a computer, large or small, may be useful to an administrator. He defines terms such as RAM, ROM, CRT, CPU, and the like. The advice is exact, even including a chapter on how a computer consultant would advise a client on how to set up a microcomputer system and which printer to use.

If there is any fault with either of these works, it is the authors' collective tendency to ignore what can go wrong when using a microcomputer. Collins, for example, neglects to mention that she went broke selling computers due to some very strange and difficult practices in the way new computer companies operate. In general, the art is not advanced enough yet for users to remain completely ignorant of the way computers work, as is possible while using SPSS. Most microcomputer users still have to learn some BASIC, even if they are working with a professional programmer. After having developed four packages for microcomputers, I still end up redoing a good bit of what professional programmers do for me. Even casual users will find themselves drawn more heavily into concerns about the way computers operate than they may wish. On the other hand, the freedom microcomputers can give sociologists and other social scientists for data analysis and teaching makes them well worth any extra effort required. Beginners will probably wish to purchase both these works.

GEORGE H. CONKLIN
North Carolina Central University
Durham

GAIL WARSHOFSKY LAPIDUS, ed. *Women, Work, and Family in the Soviet Union.* Pp. xlvi, 311. Armonk, NY: M. E. Sharpe, 1982. $22.50.

This collection of 17 essays by Soviet writers discusses various aspects of the subject indicated by the title. The essays are grouped in three sections: (1) "Levels and Patterns of Female Employment"; (2) "The Impact of Female Employment on the Family"; and (3) "A Policy Agenda for the 1980s." An introduction by the editor, Harvard trained and a professor at the University of California, Berkeley, a Selected Bibliography—mostly Soviet Russian, with some English titles—and appendix matter—Soviet laws, reports, decrees—round off the book. Among acknowledgments by the editor is one "to the Rockefeller Foundation for the opportunity to complete the project in the lovely setting of the Villa Serbelloni."

Professor Lapidus notes that "this volume is designed to offer an overview of current Soviet concerns by presenting a selection of the best recent Soviet writings on these subjects in English translation." Actually some of these pieces are not quite so recent, a few even going back to 1975.

Lapidus is shrewd to observe that

the reassessment of earlier assumptions and policies [that is, that the "woman question" had been solved in the USSR] which began in the mid-1960s was prompted by the emergence of two serious and interrelated problems. First and foremost was the declining birthrate. Its ominous implications for future political and military power, for the supply of labor resources, for the balance between the productive and the dependent age cohorts in the total population, and above all for the ethnic structure of the USSR brought demographic problems to the foreground of political concern.

Further fuel for this concern comes from the fact that "sharply declining birthrates have already made the single-child family the norm in the urban regions of the European USSR." And further: "The only remaining major untapped reserves of female labor are found in the Central Asian and Transcaucasian republics."

The ongoing problem for working women of combining work and household duties is explored in a 1975 essay by E. V. Porokhniuk and M. S. Shepeleva. Clearly this task has not as yet been solved, nor will it likely ever be so long as Soviet husbands and fathers do as little as they do to help out with family duties.

Many of these essays offer interesting, even valuable information. However, it is really tiresome by now to have liberal sprinklings of quotations from Lenin serve as the ichor flowing though the body of this collection.

The volume has its share of errors, including curious disparities in dates and of names. No index is included.

DAVID HECHT

Pace University
New York

GORDON D. MORGAN. *America Without Ethnicity*. Pp. 137. Port Washington, NY: Kennikat Press, 1981. $17.50.

America Without Ethnicity could be subtitled "The Defeat of a Straw Man." Morgan equates ethnic pluralism with separatism. He states that pluralism is based on fear and insecurity, that pluralism asserts chosenness or specialness, and that ethnic areas are pathologies never formed by choice. He claims that cultural pluralism is a bogus theory and a conservative racist apology for the status quo, that it would sap the country's strength by division, and would lead a society toward fascism to control the competing demands.

Morgan recognizes that positive perspectives of pluralism exist. He quotes Edgar Epps's statement that some writers "stress values of respect for diversity in cultural pluralism" and George Ritzer's that "pluralism . . . implies recognition of cultural equality among ethnic groups, not the superiority of one." Nevertheless, these statements seem to have no modifying effect on Morgan's opinion. He says that "pluralists vigorously deny that out of this hodgepodge of great cultural differences emerged one people" and that Michael Novaks and Andrew Greeley admonish ethnics to abandon the belief that they will ever be accepted in America. I suggest Greeley's "Who's a Chauvinist?" (*Contemporary Sociology*) for another interpretation.

There are disturbing claims, for example: that anti-immigration legislation did not necessarily reflect objections to the different lifestyles and values of immigrants—what about the *Congressional Record*?; that social membership obviously does not affect one's ability to buy a house if one has the money because it is illegal for sellers to discriminate—what about reality?; that, economically, ethnic status means lower class or poverty and that all successful ethnics give up ethnicity as soon as they can—what about Jews, Japanese, Chinese, Cubans? Morgan divinely impugns the motives of others, Pettigrew, Coleman, and this reviewer. This book is not an accurate portrayal of ethnic pluralism. Ethnic pluralism can be negative if carried to an absurd extreme, but so can almost anything.

ABRAHAM D. LAVENDER

University of Miami
Coral Gables
Florida

ERDMAN PALMORE. *Social Patterns in Normal Aging: Findings from the Duke Longitudinal Study*. Pp. 135. Durham, NC: Duke University Press, 1981. $19.75.

This is the first of a series of monographs that will review the findings of the Duke Longitudinal Studies. The principal purpose of the Duke Longitudinal Studies was to measure changes in persons as they age. The study began in 1955 with a panel of 270 noninstitutionalized men and women aged 60 to 94 from the Durham, North Carolina, area. Eleven examinations were conducted on these persons over a 21-year period. Beginning in 1968, a second study was begun as a supplement to the first study. The second study utilized a stratified random sample of 502 persons aged 45-69, drawn principally from the membership list of the major health insurance association in the Durham area. This panel was examined four times over an eight-year period.

This first monograph from the Duke studies reviews existing theories and findings on social patterns in normal aging, and presents the findings of the Duke studies that are relevant to current theory. The major issues addressed are disengagement, activity, and continuity theories—the Duke data support portions of each of these theories; age, period, and cohort effects as related to age stratification; minority group theory; life events and stress; and homogeneity versus heterogeneity—that is, whether persons become more alike or more different as they age. Methodologically, the most interesting aspect is Palmore's use of a cross-sequential design in order to distinguish the effects of age, period, and cohort—something that cannot be accomplished with the commonly used cross-sectional design.

Social Patterns in Normal Aging is an important contribution to gerontological research, both in terms of methodology and in terms of the data that it reports. Data reported include the following areas: socioeconomic status, retirement, social activity, social networks, sexual behavior, and life satisfaction of study participants.

While the generalizability of the data may be subject to some mild questions, this is an important and careful report of able research. Generally the findings are more hopeful than earlier studies might have suggested they would be. Thus, although about two-thirds of the participants in the Duke studies retired for involuntary reasons—poor health or compulsory retirement policies—retirement for most had little effect upon life satisfaction. About half of married males maintained sexual activity until their mid-seventies, while social activity was maintained for many participants until they reached their eighties.

This is an important resource for both research and classroom use, and its findings will be hailed by anyone concerned with the study of aging.

GEORGE R. SHARWELL
University of South Carolina
Columbia

DAVID A.J. RICHARDS. *Sex, Drugs, Death, and the Law: An Essay on Human Rights and Overcriminalization.* Pp. xii, 316. Totowa, NJ: Rowman & Littlefield, 1982. $26.95.

Arguments about whether the criminal law should be employed in attempts to control or eliminate so-called victimless offenses have generally been made from different philosophical perspectives by the contending sides. Proponents of using the criminal law generally argue that the immorality of such activities alone justifies state intervention. Opponents typically concede that the activities are immoral but, reasoning as utilitarians, claim that governmental attempts to eliminate such activities through criminalization are ineffective, waste scarce resources, and lead to undesirable secondary consequences. In *Sex, Drugs, Death, and the Law*, Richards confronts the moralists on their own ground with an antiutilitarian theory. He shows that utilitarian arguments have failed both philosophically, in not responding to the moralists' claims that immoral behavior should be prohibited despite the high practical costs, and politically, in failing to persuade legislatures to decriminalize victimless offenses. Decriminalization, where it has occurred, has been the product of changing morality, not of the persuasiveness of utilitarian criticism.

Richards grounds his theoretical structure on the work of John Rawls, claiming that a group of people in the hypothetical original position—having equal liberty and empirical knowledge about the world but lacking any knowledge of their own specific situations, values, or identity—would rationally develop a set of principles of justice that would maximize the situation of the person in the minimum condition. This contractarian theory gives great weight to humans as rational creatures who formulate and pursue individual life plans. Persons are treated as equals under such a scheme, having equal freedom to hold values and arrange their life plans limited only by principles of obligation and duty to which they would agree, such as not inflicting harm on others, mutual aid, consideration, and paternalism.

Richards finds this theory superior to utilitarianism as a basis for lawmaking because under it the higher-order interests of people are fairly protected. Utilitarianism, in its method of aggregating the pleasures and pains of all members of the society to determine the best set of laws, fails to recognize that pleasures have meaning only in the context of individual life plans. Richards's intent is to maximize human autonomy rather than aggregate pleasure. He believes that autonomy ought to be limited only when other competing rights are threatened.

From this contractarian foundation Richards examines the legal prohibitions against homosexuality, prostitution, drug use, and suicide. In each case he finds that the constitutional right to privacy affirmatively prohibits the intervention of the state that currently exists in the form of criminalization. For each of these behaviors the philosophical roots of the prohibitions are shown to be located in peculiar interpretations of Christian doctrine by Augustine, Thomas Aquinas, Thomas More, or the Calvinists—interpretations that Richards finds to be inconsistent with preexisting Jewish or Christian morality. Further, each of the prohibitions is based on a set of assumptions about the illogical, morally degrading, and physically destructive nature of the activity concerned—assumptions that have generally been shown to be false when subjected to empirical validation.

This book is an important contribution to the debate about the proper role of the state regarding victimless offenses. The author's background as both a lawyer and philosopher is evident in the impressive range of sources employed and in the sophistication of the criticism of both philosophical tracts and legal decisions bearing on the right to privacy. To challenge Richards seriously involves attacking his method, which means attacking John Rawls. Though the original-position method of Rawls has been rigorously criticized, Richards's argument based on the right to privacy cannot be easily dismissed. His historical and empirical assessment of the legal prohibitions of victimless offenses remains as a serious challenge to existing law because this assessment so thoroughly and convincingly supports his position that these prohibitions are based on weak moral foundations.

JOSEPH E. JACOBY
Bowling Green State University
Ohio

W. TIMOTHY WEAVER. *The Contest for Educational Resources.* Pp. xv, 188. Lexington, MA: Lexington Books, 1982. $22.95.

Lyndon Johnson's Great Society initiative of the 1960s was designed to close the gap between the haves and the have-nots. For those of us who were encouraged by this effort, *The Contest for Educational Resources* is convincingly discouraging. Dr. Weaver sums up one of his major points:

It is as though the major social classes are riding up an occupational escalator, all advancing, with those in the middle taking a few steps up and a few down as the escalator moves, but on the whole the groups at the extremes remain intact, immobile and highly distinguishable as groups [p. 43].

Weaver's description of the struggle for economic resources and educational attainment as a contest appears to be particularly appropriate. He indicates, for example, that "the system in equilibrium serves a private interest: maintaining the relative advantage of upper-status families." Governmental decisions—as occurred in the 1960s—to increase the funds available for lower-SES individuals eventually led to even more funds being channeled into middle- and upper-SES families. The latter occurred in the 1970s.

An excellent description of the equality-efficiency paradigm is provided throughout the book. This paradigm is, of course, an important and long-standing debate. The contest that is waged always exists between these two approaches to the allocation of educational resources.

Weaver's final two chapters include numerous value-laden statements centering around the meritocratic ideal. These chapters are very well written and could easily stand alone for their treatment of the issues inherent in this complex subject. Weaver points out the futility of the additive policy—that is, the simple allocation of educational funds to the lower-SES individual. As he emphasizes, the system simply responds by pouring more money into the programs for higher-SES individuals. He indicates that displacement makes more sense in the long run: "Some places reserved now for the sons and daughters of the wealthy would be taken by the more capable poor."

The only criticism of Weaver's work lies in the fact that he has crammed so much into one volume. A series of two or three monographs would have been more readable. This is not a major problem, but it should act as an indicator for the reader that this book is heavy reading. It is certainly recommended for those interested in our schooling system.

WILLIAM A. HARRINGTON
West End
North Carolina

ECONOMICS

W. PATRICK BEATON, JON H. WEYLAND, and NANCY NEUMAN. *Energy Forecasting for Planners: Transportation Models.* Pp. 281. Piscataway, NJ: Rutgers University Center for Urban Policy Research, 1982. $17.95.

First, the good news: *Energy Forecasting for Planners* sets out a step-by-step procedure to forecast gasoline consumption that could be implemented by many governmental authorities. Now the bad news: in their own implementation, for the counties of New Jersey, they do it wrong.

There are, according to the authors, essentially two ways to develop a forecasting model. The first, analogous to numerous consumer-demand studies, is to study gasoline consumption directly, relating it to its economic and social determinants. The second, the way selected by the present study, is to get at the matter indirectly. Suppose we knew the population (P) of the state or area in question, and could estimate regional average fuel economy, that is, average vehicle miles per gallon (F). Then the only behavioral necessity would be to forecast per capita miles driven (M). Given this, an estimate of gasoline consumption is just $(P \times M)/F$. In effect, the book explains how to get estimates of F and M.

The book opens with an informative review, first of the statistics of fuel consumption and its detail at the national level, and then of the previous literature. The Houthakker-Taylor stock adjustment direct demand model is explained, and more recent developments in techniques are surveyed, with particular reference to gasoline consumption. This is followed by a survey of state-sponsored models. It should be noted in this connection that later chapters also contain useful compendia of data sources at the state level. This material—about 40 percent of the book—is a valuable research tool.

That said, it must be noted that there may be some substantial problems with the econometrics in the original work of the authors. First, it appears that the researchers were in the grip of a malign computer program that would not allow them to estimate 20 coefficients. Second, there is the role of dummy variables. The authors surmised quite reasonably that intercepts in their equations might differ over New Jersey counties. Thus they created a set of county dummy variables to allow for this. But nowhere are the coefficients of these reported; indeed, their results in Exhibit 6.1 show a single intercept for the preferred equation. Though it is hard to be certain, it appears that their forecasting also ignored this information. No explanation is given.

Third, the authors seem to have little appreciation for that part of econometrics known as specification analysis. This forces them to go through some extraordinarily convoluted procedures to choose a preferred equation, estimating 25 equations including randomly generated subsets of all the dummy variables, then picking that equation whose coefficients of the 11 reported independent variables were closest to the means of the 11 coefficients over the 25 equations. What this is supposed to attain is not clear. The problem of model selection is far from trivial, but procedures do exist for making informed choices among, for example, nested submodels, and even, more recently, among nonnested models.

Overall, the econometrics gives one the impression of a group of researchers who want to use the techniques, but are fundamentally uncertain of the theoretical underpinnings. Two examples: an extension of the basic single-equation model to a recursive structure is discussed, but the authors, in the midst of their sloppy notation—look at the indices—neglect to mention the single feature that makes all this work, namely, mutual independence of the three disturbance vectors. Second, in their appendix on techniques in stating that the least-squares estimator is best linear unbiased, the requirement of a scalar covariance matrix is omitted. The role of normality is not made clear in the subsequent discussion of efficiency either.

What then can be salvaged from this effort? Despite these comments, the book still retains a good deal of value. This inheres primarily in the compendia of data sources, the review of the literature, and, to the extent that one ignores the econometrics, the step-by-step forecasting and scenario-development procedures. Much can be learned from this. But in the final analysis, everything depends on the researcher's understanding his or her tools. And here the book is sadly deficient.

PHILIP A. VITON
University of Pennsylvania
Philadelphia

ROBERT W. BURCHELL and DAVID LISTOKIN, eds. *Energy and Land Use.* Pp. 601. Piscataway, NJ: Rutgers University Center for Urban Policy Research, 1982. $25.00.

Energy and Land Use is written for land-use planners, as it deals primarily with how metropolitan land use can be or is being affected by solar/conservation technologies and high energy prices. This is not a book for the energy specialist seeking insight into the land-use impacts of mining, processing, and utilizing conventional energy resources. More specifically the volume primarily consists of 27 invited essays grouped around the following subjects: energy and the city; land-use measures to limit energy consumption; land-use measures to assure adequate energy supply; and implementation of conservation/solar technologies at the local, state, and federal levels.

The overall impression the reader gets is that existing metropolitan land-use patterns have proved surprisingly resistant to change in the face of high energy prices; and that while energy considerations can no longer be ignored in land-use decisions, they rarely can be considered dominant considerations either. The public desires that led to urban sprawl in the first place still exist, as do some of the disincentives for change facing key interest groups, such as home builders. The number of communities that have adopted far-reaching or comprehensive land-use plans on the basis of energy considerations, as revealed in this book, remains strikingly small.

Nonetheless, one gets the sense that energy consciousness is inexorably making definite, even if undramatic, inroads in public perceptions that are leading to change. Data collected by North Carolina researchers show that many builders are incorporating various energy efficiency features in the construction of new homes, on the basis of consumer demand. The glacial pace of these changes does not satisfy those writers in this volume who desire radical land-use changes either to conserve energy or to implement other social agenda. Gradual improvements in building and automobile energy efficiencies are, however, developing a momentum that will be difficult to reverse.

Perhaps the most valuable contribution in this book—at least for the novice in this field—is the excellent literature review of existing metropolitan land use and energy research provided by the editors in their extensive introduction. Unfortunately, few of the subsequent essays offer fresh empirical evidence to extend or modify the findings noted in the literature review. The excessive length of the book and the obvious lack of careful editing also detract from the value of the book. In short, this book offers considerable insight into the subject of land use and energy, but the reader must wade through a lot of verbiage to find it.

JACK N. BARKENBUS
Oak Ridge Associated Universities
Tennessee

KENNETH W. DAM. *The Rules of the Game: Reform and Evolution in the International Monetary System.* Pp. xviii, 382. Chicago: University of Chicago Press, 1982. $27.00.

Kenneth Dam provides us with both a careful history of the development of the international monetary system from the gold standard era to 1980 and an analysis of the legal foundations of the institutions that made the system function. This marriage works. By concentrating on the legal aspects of the monetary system and especially on the changing legal basis for the International Monetary Fund (IMF), Dam has found a convincing structure for historical events.

The plan of the book is impressive and tight. It begins with two brief background chapters: the first reviews the myths and the reality of the pre-World War I gold standard and the second reviews the monetary events of the interwar period. This is followed by an analysis of the legal, economic, and diplomatic compromises that resulted in the formation of the IMF. Special attention is given to the IMF Articles of Agreement and to the legal implications of the compromise wording of important sections. The next section traces the evolution of the IMF up to the dollar float of 1973. This evolution occurred within the legal structure of the original Articles of Agreement and Dam shows how the IMF staff and executive board were able to use the ambiguities generated by the compromise language to enhance the IMF's world role.

Since 1973 the IMF has had to adjust to a world in which many of the major currencies have floating exchange rates and in which the reserve support function of the IMF has been, in theory at least, less useful. Other major events have included the decline of gold, the rise of the SDR, and the increased concern of the IMF with the less developed nations. The final chapters of the book address these issues in light of the diplomatic and legal maneuverings that resulted in the Second Amendment to the Articles of Agreement, the results of the Committee of 20 and the Jamaica Agreement.

The book is carefully organized and clearly written, and provides many insights into the development of today's IMF. The sections in the more recent history are especially useful since much of this material had not been previously integrated. The use of the development of the legal rules as the main theme provides considerable cohesiveness. This is a valuable piece of work.

GEORGE T. McCANDLESS, Jr.
Dartmouth College
Hanover
New Hampshire

CARL P. SIMON and ANN D. WITTE. *Beating the System: The Underground Economy.* Pp. xvi, 304. Boston: Auburn House Publishing, 1982. $21.95. Paperbound, $12.95.

Simon and Witte's goal, in this work, which grew out of a paper prepared for the Joint Economic Committee's Special Study on Economic Change, is to use national income accounting concepts to estimate the size of the underground economy. Income tax evasion, avoidance of excise taxes on cigarettes, illegal immigration, theft and fencing of stolen goods, and drug trade—heroin, cocaine, and marijuana—fraud arson, illegal gambling, loan sharking, and prostitution are the evasive or illegal activities resulting in underpayment of taxes and underreporting of national income that are discussed.

Those readers who hope for a definitive estimate of the size of the much-discussed underground economy will be disappointed. Neither the sector-by-sector approach taken by Simon and Witte nor their careful use of the existing literature allows them to improve substantially upon the various rough and ready macroeconomic estimates that have been widely reported in the popular press. Thus they conclude that the national income generated in the underground economy was between 9 and 16 percent of the reported national income for 1974 and it has grown at a rate of approximately 10 percent per annum in the years since then. This is within the range guessed at by others and, because there is so much guesswork involved, the cautious reader is likely to wind up concluding that the underground economy is big, but will be uncertain about how big.

While readers hoping for precise numbers that may be used with confidence will be disappointed, those who want a survey of what we do know about the underground economy will find the book rewarding. For each of the activities listed at the beginning of this review, Simon and Witte have combed the literature of the popular press and of professional social science to find out what there is to know. If one wants to learn more about the economic organization of any of the activities covered, this is the place to begin.

For the social scientist there is also an unintended but interesting methodological conclusion to be drawn. In spite of Simon and Witte's careful attempt to use a microeconomic framework for their analysis, the real substance of the study is derived from what they call "ethnographic accounts." The economic analysis that they provide often seems a fifth wheel. This is not true of some of their use of national income accounting concepts. It is, for example, probably worth pointing out that the "theft industry" can be seen as a sector that provides a distributive service. Estimates of the incomes of the thieves and fences, but not the total value of stolen goods, is therefore the national income generated in this sector. However, when Simon and Witte attempt to describe aspects of the underground economy as monopolistic or competitive or to use cost-benefit analysis, the analysis seems unnecessary and the conclusions lame. However, the important point is that the worthwhile substance of the book derives from studies that have been based on ethnographic techniques and, because the traditional turf of anthropologists and sociologists is more likely to include prostitutes and gamblers, we know more about that exotic part of the underground. We know, apparently, very little about the small retailer who underreports sales and evades taxes and very little about corporate tax evasion. Not until we have ethnographies that tell us more about the financially improper behavior of proper people will we be able to judge accurately the size of the underground economy.

In the meantime, Simon and Witte have done a good job of describing what we do know.

ANNE MAYHEW
University of Tennessee
Knoxville

OTHER BOOKS

ALMOND, GABRIEL A., MARVIN CHODOROW, and ROY HARVEY PEARCE, eds. *Progress and Its Discontents.* Pp. xiv, 565. Berkeley: University of California Press, 1982. $27.50.

BALINSKI, MICHEL L. and H. PEYTON YOUNG. *Fair Representation: Meeting the Ideal of One Man, One Vote.* Pp. xi, 191. New Haven, CT: Yale University Press, 1982. $27.50.

BERTON, PETER, PAUL F. LANGER, and GEORGE O. TOTTEN, eds. *The Russian Impact on Japan: Literature and Social Thought—Two Essays by Nobori Shomu and Akamatsu Katsumaro.* Pp. 143. Los Angeles: University of Southern California Press, 1981. $9.50. Paperbound, $6.50.

BIENKOWSKI, W. *Theory and Reality: The Development of Social Systems.* Trans. Jane Cave. Pp. 303. London: Allison & Busby, 1982. Distributed by Schocken Books, New York. $17.95. Paperbound, $9.95.

BOTTOMORE, TOM, STEFAN NOWAK, and MAGDALENA SOKOLOWSKA, eds. *Sociology: The State of the Art.* Pp. 378. Beverly Hills, CA: Sage Publications, 1982. $27.50. Paperbound, $12.95.

BREZHNEV, LEONID ILYICH. *Memoirs.* Trans. Penny Dole. Pp. 41. New York: Pergamon Press, 1982. $9.50.

BROCK, WILLIAM R. *Scotus Americanus: A Survey of the Sources for Links Between Scotland and America in the 18th Century.* Pp. viii, 293. Edinburgh: Edinburgh University Press, 1982. Distributed by Columbia University Press, New York. $20.00.

BROWN, HARRY JAMES and FREDERICK D. WILLIAMS, eds. *The Diary of James A. Garfield, Vol. IV: 1878-1881.* Pp. 689. East Lansing: Michigan State University Press, 1982. $40.00.

BUKHARIN, I. I. *Selected Writings on the State and the Transition to Socialism.* Trans. and ed. Richard B. Day. Pp. lviii, 351. Armonk, NY: M. E. Sharpe, 1982. $30.00.

BURKHAUSER, RICHARD and ROBERT H. HAVEMAN. *Disability and Work: The Economics of American Policy.* Pp. vii, 131. Baltimore: Johns Hopkins University Press, 1982. No price.

BURT, RICHARD, ed. *Arms Control and Defense Postures in the Eighties.* Pp. x, 230. Boulder, CO: Westview Press, 1982. $25.00.

BUTLER, EDGAR W. and JAMES B. PICK. *Geothermal Energy Development: Problems and Prospects in the Imperial Valley of California.* Pp. xix, 361. New York: Plenum Press, 1982. $39.50.

CHERNENKO, KONSTANTINE. *Selected Speeches and Writings.* Trans. Y. S. Shirkov. Pp. x, 296. Elmsford, NY: Pergamon Press, 1982. $30.00.

CLAPHAM, CHRISTOPHER, ed. *Private Patronage and Public Power: Political Clientelism in the Modern State.* Pp. 222. New York: St. Martin's Press, 1982. $25.00.

COHEN, IRA H. *Ideology and Unconsciousness: Reich, Freud, and Marx.* Pp. ix, 235. New York: New York University Press, 1982. Distributed by Columbia University Press, New York. $32.50.

COHEN, RAYMOND. *International Politics: The Rules of the Game.* Pp. vi, 186. New York: Longman, 1981. $7.50.

CORNWALL, JOHN. *Modern Capitalism: Its Growth and Transformation.* Pp. xii, 226. Armonk, NY: M. E. Sharpe, 1982. Paperbound, $13.95.

deLUCIA, RUSSEL et al. *Energy Planning for Developing Countries: A Study of Bangladesh.* Pp. xx, 298. Baltimore: Johns Hopkins University Press, 1982. $24.00.

DIPPIE, BRIAN W. *The Vanishing American: White Attitudes and U.S. Indian Policy.* Pp. xvii, 423. Middletown, CT: Wesleyan University Press, 1982. Distributed by Columbia University Press, New York. $24.95.

DUNBAUGH, EDWIN L. *The Era of the Joy Line: A Saga of Steamboating on Long Island Sound.* Pp. xxv, 363. Westport, CT: Greenwood Press, 1982. $27.50.

FALK, RICHARD, SAMUEL S. KIM, and SAUL H. MENDLOVITZ, eds. *Toward a Just World Order (Studies on a Just World Order, Vol. 1).* Pp. x, 652. Boulder, CO: Westview Press, 1982. $35.00. Paperbound, $16.50.

FERRAROTTI, FRANCO. *Max Weber and the Destiny of Reason.* Trans. John Fraser. pp. xviii, 133. Armonk, NY: M. E. Sharpe, 1982. Paperbound, $10.95.

FIRESTONE, BERNARD J. *The Quest for Nuclear Stability: John F. Kennedy and the Soviet Union.* Pp. x, 176. Westport, CT: Greenwood Press, 1982. $27.50.

FRASER, JOHN. *Italy: Society in Crisis/Society in Transformation.* Pp. vii, 307. Boston: Routledge & Kegan Paul, 1981. $27.50.

GOEBEL, JULIUS. *The Struggle for the Falkland Islands: A Study in Legal and Diplomatic History.* Pp. xxx, 482. New Haven, CT: Yale University Press, 1982. $35.00. Paperbound, $10.95.

GOPALAKRISHNAN, CHENNAT. *Natural Resources and Energy: Theory and Policy.* Pp. xiii, 138. Ann Arbor, MI: Ann Arbor Science Publishers, 1980. No price.

GORDON, GEORGE J. *Public Administration in America: Second Edition.* Pp. xv, 623. New York: St. Martin's Press, 1982. $17.95.

GORMAN, ROBERT A. *Neo-Marxism: The Meanings of Modern Radicalism.* Pp. x, 309. Westport, CT: Greenwood Press, 1982. $35.00.

GOVE, WALTER R., ed. *Deviance and Mental Illness.* Pp. 303. Beverly Hills, CA: Sage Publications, 1982. $25.00. Paperbound, $12.50.

HARRISON, DAVID. *The White Tribe of Africa: South Africa in Perspective.* Pp. vii, 307. Berkeley: University of California Press, 1982. $16.95.

HEAL, M. J. *The Presidential Quest: Candidates and Images in American Political Culture, 1787-1852.* Pp. xi, 268. New York: Longman, 1982. Paperbound, $11.95.

HUFBAUER, KARL. *The Formation of the German Chemical Community (1720-1795).* Pp. viii, 312. Berkeley: University of California Press, 1982. $40.00. Paperbound, $14.95.

JORDAN, TERESA. *Cowgirls: Women of the American West.* Pp. xxxi, 301. Garden City, NY: Anchor Press, Doubleday, 1982. $19.95.

KIGER, JOSEPH C., ed. *Research Institutions and Learned Societies* (The Greenwood Encyclopedia of American Institutions, No. 5). Pp. xxv, 551. Westport, CT: Greenwood Press, 1982. $45.00.

KIRK, RUSSELL. *The Portable Conservative Reader.* Pp. xl, 723. New York: Viking Press and Penguin Books, 1982. Paperbound, $6.95.

KNIGHT, THOMAS. *Technology's Future.* Pp. xiii, 249. Malabar, FL: Robert E. Krieger Publishing, 1982. $11.50.

KRAUSE, ELLIOTT A. *Division of Labor: A Political Perspective.* Pp. xiii, 203. Westport, CT: Greenwood Press, 1982. $27.50.

KRENTZ, PETER. *The Thirty at Athens.* Pp. 164. Ithaca, NY: Cornell University Press, 1982. $17.50.

KRUSKAL, WILLIAM H., ed. *The Social Sciences: Their Nature and Uses.* Pp. xv, 166. Chicago: University of Chicago Press, 1982. $12.00.

LASH, NICHOLAS. *A Matter of Hope: A Theologian's Reflections on the Thought of Karl Marx.* Pp. 312. Notre Dame, IN: University of Notre Dame Press, 1982. $19.95.

LEWY, GUENTER. *False Consciousness: An Essay on Mystification.* Pp. ix, 134. New Brunswick, NJ: Transaction Books, 1982. $17.95.

MacFARLANE, L. J. *Issues in British Politics Since 1945, Second Edition.* Pp. x, 181. New York: Longman, 1981. Paperbound, $6.95.

MENAKER, ESTHER. *Otto Rank: A Rediscovered Legacy.* Pp. xvii, 166. New York: Columbia University Press, 1982. $22.50.

MOULIN, HERVE. *Game Theory for the Social Sciences.* Pp. 304. New York: New York University Press, 1982. $30.00. Paperbound, $12.50.

NAIRN, TOM. *The Break-Up of Britain: Crisis and Neo-Nationalism. Second, Expanded Edition.* Pp. 409. London: NLB. 1982. Distributed by Schocken Books, New York. $24.00. Paperbound, $9.50.

NASH, MICHAEL. *Conflict and Accommodation: Coal Miners, Steel Workers, and Socialism, 1890-1920* (Contributions in Labor History, No. 11). Pp. xix, 197. Westport, CT: Greenwood Press, 1982. $27.50.

NELSON, DANIEL and STEPHEN WHITE, eds. *Communist Legislatures in Comparative Perspective.* Pp. ix, 201. Albany: State University of New York Press, 1982. $33.50. Paperbound, $10.95.

NEWMAN, BARRIE and MALCOLM DANDO, eds. *Nuclear Deterrence: Implications and Policy Options for the 1980's.* Pp. xii, 249. Tunbridge Wells, Kent: Castle House Publications, 1982. Distributed by Humanities Press, Atlantic Highlands, NJ. $31.50.

OLSON, DAVID H. and ROXANNE MARKOFF, eds. *Inventory of Marriage and Family Literature, Vol. III.* Pp. 510. Beverly Hills, CA: Sage Publications, 1982. $75.00. Paperbound, $35.00.

PARDESI, GHANSHYAM, ed. *Contemporary Peace Research.* Pp. xi, 374. Atlantic Highlands, NJ: Humanities Press, 1982. $32.25.

PEILLON, MICHEL. *Contemporary Irish Society: An Introduction.* Pp. 231. Dublin: Gill & Macmillan, 1982. Distributed by Humanities Press, Atlantic Highlands, NJ. $10.00.

ROSSI, PETER H. and STEVEN L. NOCK, eds. *Measuring Social Judgments: The Factorial Survey Approach.* Pp. 255. Beverly Hills, CA: Sage Publications, 1982. $22.50.

SANDOZ, ELLIS, ed. *Eric Voegelin's Thought: A Critical Appraisal.* Pp. xv, 208. Durham, NC: Duke University Press, 1982. $24.75.

SCHNEIDER, WILLIAM H. *An Empire for the Masses: The French Popular Image of Africa, 1870-1900.* Pp. xxi, 222. Westport, CT: Greenwood Press, 1982. $29.95.

SCOTT, ANDREW M. *The Revolution in Statecraft: Intervention in an Age of Interdependence.* Pp. xvii, 214. Durham, NC: Duke Press Policy Studies Paperbacks, 1982. $9.75.

SELDEN, MARK and VICTOR LIPPIT, eds. *The Transition to Socialism in China.* Pp. ix, 326. Armonk, NY: M. E. Sharpe, 1982. $25.00. Paperbound, $12.95.

SHARKANSKY, IRA. *Public Administration: Agencies, Policies, and Politics.* Pp. xv, 393. San Francisco: W. H. Freeman, 1982. $19.95.

SHUBIK, MARTIN. *Game Theory in the Social Sciences: Concepts and Solutions.* Pp. 514. Cambridge: MIT Press, 1982. No price.

SMITH, ROBERT C. *Equal Employment Opportunity: A Comparative Microanalysis of Boston and Houston.* Pp. xiii, 94. Totowa, NJ: Allanheld Osmun, 1982. $18.50.

SNIDERMAN, PAUL M. *A Question of Loyalty.* Pp. x, 186. Berkeley: University of California Press, 1982. $18.95. Paperbound, $6.95.

SOMMERVILLE, C. JOHN. *The Rise and Fall of Childhood.* Pp. 255. Beverly Hills, CA: Sage Publications, 1982. $22.00. Paperbound, $10.95.

STEINBERG, STEPHEN. *The Ethnic Myth: Race, Ethnicity, and Class in America.* Pp. x, 277. Boston: Beacon Press, 1982. $8.95.

STEWART, V. LORNE, ed. *Justice and Troubled Children Around the World, Vol. IV.* Pp. xix, 146. New York: New York University Press, 1982. $22.50.

STONEMAN, COLIN, ed. *Zimbabwe's Inheritance.* Pp. xiii, 234. New York: St. Martin's Press, 1982. $25.00.

STREMLAU, JOHN J., ed. *The Foreign Policy Priorities of Third World States.* Pp. xii, 174. Boulder, CO: Westview Press, 1982. $15.00. Paperbound, $8.00.

SULLIVAN, WILLIAM M. *Reconstructing Public Philosophy.* Pp. xiv, 238. Berkeley: University of California Press, 1982. $19.95.

THOMPSON, JAMES J., Jr. *Tried as by Fire: Southern Baptists and the Religious Controversies of the 1920s.* Pp. xv, 224. Macon, GA: Mercer University Press, 1982. $13.95.

TIFFIN, SUSAN. *In Whose Best Interest? Child Welfare Reform in the Progressive Era* (Contributions to the Study of Childhood and Youth). Pp. 310. Westport, CT: Greenwood Press, 1982. $29.95.

TIKHONOV, N. A. *Selected Speeches and Writings.* Pp. xxii, 421. Elmsford, NY: Pergamon Press, 1982. $50.00.

TIMASHKOVA, O. K. *Scandinavian Social-Democracy Today.* Trans. B. Meerovich. Pp. 271. Moscow: Progress Publishers, 1981. Distributed by Imported Publications, Chicago. $7.00.

WOLIN, RICHARD. *Walter Benjamin: An Aesthetic of Redemption.* Pp. xvi, 316. New York: Columbia University Press, 1982. $19.95.

ZEITZ, DOROTHY. *Women Who Embezzle or Defraud: A Study of Convicted Felons.* Pp. xii, 157. New York: Praeger Publishers, 1981. No price.

ERRATA

In the September 1982 *Annals,* vol. 463, there are several errors in the question-and-answer session following Robert W. Taylor and Harry E. Vanden's "Defining Terrorism in El Salvador: 'La Matanza.'" On p. 117, lines 29-34 of column 1 should read, "The point is, as a matter of fact, that the villagers are not killed by bullets from the FMLN—and it would be the FMLN, which is the military arm of the FDR, and not the FDR itself." On p. 118, column 2, the comment attributed to Taylor should be attributed to Vanden, and in the fourth line from the bottom of that paragraph, "capitol" should read "capital."

INDEX

Aberbach, Joel D., 33, 47
Acheson, Dean, 27, 31
Administrative Procedures Act (1946), 154
Agriculture, U.S. Department of, 25, 30, 82, 86, 131
Anderson, Patrick, 26
Anthony, Robert, 92
Antideficiency Act, 87

Ball, George W., 31, 38
Beard, Charles, 70
Bennis, Warren, 123
Blumenthal, Michael, 29
Bolling, Richard, 90, 196
Boorstin, Daniel J., 68
Britain, public administration in, 17, 18, 24-25, 43-59, 157
Brock, Bill, 106
Brown, Harold, 28
Budget, Bureau of the, 26, 79, 88, 89, 187
    see also Office of Management and Budget
Burgess, John, 166
Burns, Arthur, 186

Caiden, Naomi, 100
Califano, Joseph, 28, 37, 86, 187
Campbell, Alan K., 33
Caputo, David, 33
Carlucci, Frank, 87
Carter, Jimmy, 25, 26, 27, 28, 33, 35, 65, 81, 82, 86, 168, 170, 172, 188, 197, 199
CHANGING PUBLIC-PRIVATE SECTOR RELATIONS: A LOOK AT THE UNITED STATES, Bruce L.R. Smith, 149-64.
Chelimsky, Eleanor, 19
CHELIMSKY, ELEANOR, Program Evaluation and Appropriate Governmental Change, 103-18
Chiles, Lawton, 203
Civil service, career executives in the, 18, 23-41, 43-59, 61-76, 88-89, 92-93
Civil Service Commission, U.S., 73, 89
    see also Office of Personnel Management
Civil Service Reform Act (CCRA) (1978), 35, 36, 73, 93
Cole, Richard, 33
Commerce, U.S. Department of, 25, 29, 32, 81, 82, 85
Comprehensive Employment and Training Act (CETA), 116
Conable, Barber, 199
Congressional Budget Act (1974), 105

Congressional Budget and Impoundment Control Act, 199
Contracting for services, government, 20, 98, 143-46, 149-64
Coolidge, Calvin, 181
Council of Economic Advisers (CEA), 185-91

Dam, Kenneth W., 37, 38
Dean, Alan L., 18
DEAN, ALAN L., The Management of Executive Departments, 77-90
Defense, U.S. Department of (DOD), 29, 30, 84, 85
Department of Transportation Act (1966), 79, 83
Departments, executive branch, 18, 25, 28, 30, 77-90
d'Estaing, Valerie Giscard, 51
Dillon, Douglas, 28
Dingell, John, 196
Domenici, Pete, 199
Drucker, Peter F., 94, 95

Eagleton, Thomas, 203
Education, U.S. Department of, 80, 81, 131
Eisenhower, Dwight D., 27, 159, 170, 180, 186, 187, 191
Eizenstat, Stuart, 199
Employment Act (1976), 184, 185, 191
Energy, U.S. Department of, 80, 204

Federalism, 20, 135-47, 165-78
Fesler, James W., 18
FESLER, JAMES W., Politics, Policy, and Bureaucracy at the Top, 23-41
Ford, Gerald, 26, 169, 170, 188, 205
France, public administration in, 17, 18, 24-25, 43-59, 137, 138, 140, 147
Freedom of Information Act, 68
Frenzel, Bill, 198

Gaus, John, 101
Gawthrop, Louis C., 13, 19
GAWTHROP, LOUIS C., Organizing for Change, 119-34
General Accounting Office (GAO), 83, 98, 105, 109, 114, 116, 167, 202
    Institute for Program Evaluation (IPE), 109, 114, 116, 117
GILBERT, CHARLES E., Preface, 9-21
Government Corporation Control Act (1945), 155
Great Society (Johnson administration), 20, 167, 168, 170, 180, 189, 191

Greenspan, Alan, 188
Grémion, Catherine, 50, 52

Haider, Donald H., 20
HAIDER, DONALD H., Intergovernmental Redirection, 165-78
Haig, Alexander, 28
Hall, Gene, 110
Hall, Peter A., 18
HALL, PETER A., Policy Innovation and the Structure of the State: The Politics-Administration Nexus in France and Britain, 43-59
Hamilton, Lee, 203
Harriman, Averell, 28
Hatry, Harry, 97
Health, Education and Welfare (HEW), U.S. Department of, 28, 29, 79, 81, 85, 86, 87, 131
 see also Health and Human Services, U.S. Department of
Health and Human Services (HHS), U.S. Department of, 81
Heclo, Hugh, 31, 32, 35
Heller, Walter, 187
Helmer, John, 39
Herzberg, Frederick, 94
Hoffmann, Stanley, 53
Hoover Commission, first, 79, 88, 90
Hoover, Herbert, 70
Housing and Urban Development (HUD), U.S. Department of, 30, 79, 85, 95, 131

Ickes, Harold, 81
INTEGRATION AND FRAGMENTATION: KEY THEMES OF CONGRESSIONAL CHANGE, Walter J. Oleszek, 193-205
Intergovernmental Cooperation Act (1968), 168
Intergovernmental Personnel Act, 94
INTERGOVERNMENTAL REDIRECTION, Donald H. Haider, 165-78
Interior, U.S. Department of, 80, 81, 84

Johnson, Lyndon B., 26, 28, 30, 167, 168, 169, 170, 180, 181, 187, 189, 190
Justice, U.S. Department of, 29, 85, 93, 96

Kennedy, John F., 38, 45, 88, 180, 182, 187
Kramer, Fred A., 18
KRAMER, FRED A., Public Management in the 1980s and Beyond, 91-102

Labor, U.S. Department of, 29, 81
Levine, Charles, 101
Light, Paul C., 39
Lovett, Robert, 28

Madison, James, 68, 125, 147, 166
Malek, Frederick, 40
MANAGEMENT OF EXECUTIVE DEPARTMENTS, THE, Alan L. Dean, 77-90
Marshall, George, 27
McGregor, Douglas, 94
McGregor, Eugene B., Jr., 18
McGREGOR, EUGENE B., Jr., The Public-Service Problem, 61-76
Mills, Wilbur, 189
Mitterand, Francois, 44, 54
Monnet, Jean, 52
Mosher, Frederick, 93
Moynihan, Daniel P., 106, 195, 202

National Defense Education Act, 159
New Deal, 17, 154-56, 159, 180, 181, 185, 191
New Federalism, 170, 174-77, 204
Nixon, Richard, 26, 27, 30, 33, 40, 79, 81, 89, 107, 136, 168, 169, 170, 181, 187, 188, 189, 198
NONHIERARCHICAL APPROACHES TO THE ORGANIZATION OF PUBLIC ACTIVITY, Vincent Ostrom, 135-47
Norris, George, 181

Ordiorne, George, 96
Office of Management and Budget (OMB), 25, 26-27, 70, 80, 89, 95, 137, 167, 176, 187, 190
 see also Budget, Bureau of the
Office of Personnel Management (OPM), 73, 89
 see also Civil Service Commission, U.S.
Okun, Arthur, 187, 190
Oleszek, Walter J., 16
OLESZEK, WALTER, J., Integration and Fragmentation: Key Themes of Congressional Change, 193-205
O'Neill, Thomas, P., 197, 200, 202, 204
ORGANIZING FOR CHANGE, Louis C. Gawthrop, 119-34
Ostrom, Vincent, 13, 20
OSTROM, VINCENT, Nonhierarchical Approaches to the Organization of Public Activity, 135-47

Parsons, Talcott, 182
Pendleton Act (1883), 73
POLICY INNOVATION AND THE STRUCTURE OF THE STATE: THE POLITICS-ADMINISTRATION NEXUS IN FRANCE AND BRITAIN, Peter A. Hall, 43-59
POLITICS, POLICY, AND BUREAUCRACY AT THE TOP, James W. Fesler, 23-41
PRESIDENCY AND POLITICAL CHANGE, THE, Lester G. Seligman, 179-92

Presidency, U.S., 16, 39, 155, 161, 179-92
Program evaluation, 19, 89-90, 96-97, 98, 103-18, 145
PROGRAM EVALUATION AND APPROPRIATE GOVERNMENTAL CHANGE, Elanor Chelimsky, 103-18
PUBLIC MANAGEMENT IN THE 1980s AND BEYOND, Fred A. Kramer, 91-102
PUBLIC-SERVICE PROBLEM, THE, Eugene B. McGregor, Jr., 61-76

Reagan, Ronald, 25, 26, 27, 34, 38, 44, 81, 152, 159, 170, 174-77, 180, 181, 188, 190, 192, 199, 204
Richard Elliot, 28, 38, 85
Rockman, Bert, 33
Roosevelt, Franklin D., 26, 82, 88, 154, 155, 180, 181, 185, 189, 191
Rosenthal, Benjamin, 204
Roth-Bolling bills, 90
Roth, William V., 90, 106, 114

Savas, E. S., 98
Sayre, Wallace, 93
Schlesinger, James, 28
Schultze, Charles, 189
Seligman, Lester G., 16
SELIGMAN, LESTER G., The Presidency and Political Change, 179-92
Selznick, Philip, 182
Senior Executive Service (SES), 18, 24, 34, 35-36, 73-75, 93
Schultz, George, 28, 37, 38, 187, 188
Simon, Herbert, 46, 126, 129, 181
Smith, Bruce L.R., 20

SMITH, BRUCE L.R., Changing Public-Private Sector Relations: A Look at the United States, 149-64
Sorenson, Theodore, 182
Staats, Elmer, 33
Stans, Maurice, 32
State, U.S. Department of, 30, 78, 80, 93
Stein, Herbert, 187, 188
Stevenson, Adlai, 201
Stillman, Richard, 93
Stockman, David, 100, 188
Suleiman, Ezra, 52
Sundquist, James L., 40, 41, 136, 137

Thatcher, Margaret, 44, 157
Tocqueville, Alexis de, 137-40, 146, 147
Transportation, U.S. Department of (DOT), 79, 82-84, 86, 87, 131
Treasury, U.S. Department of, 29, 78, 80, 85, 86, 187, 188, 192
Truman, Harry, 65, 180, 186

Vance, Rufus, 28
Volpe, John, 87

Wagner Labor Act, 181
Wagner, Robert, 181
Webb, Beatrice, 143
Webb, James, 69
Webb, Sidney, 143
Weber, Max, 124, 125, 155
Weidenbaum, Murray L., 106, 188
Weinberger, Caspar, 28, 85, 87
Wildavsky, Aaron, 100, 126
Wilson, Woodrow, 62, 65, 68, 71, 72, 76, 147
Wright, Jim, 202

Who Gets What from Government
by Benjamin I. Page

"Page's admirably clear and careful survey is a potent antidote to the supply-side nonsense on which the calamities of Reaganomics are shakily founded. Anyone to the left of Milton Friedman will be impressed by the extent of unnecessary favoritism which we display to the already inordinately rich and the parallel neglect of the interests of low income Americans."—**Robert Lekachman** "Readers from every part of the political spectrum will learn more about the issue of economic inequality even when they disagree with Page's position."—**Joseph J. Minarik** "An uncommonly incisive analysis....This is an important book, one that might well set the agenda for the future of social policy."—**Herbert Gintis** $15.95

When Government Speaks
Law, Politics, and Government Expression in America
by Mark G. Yudof

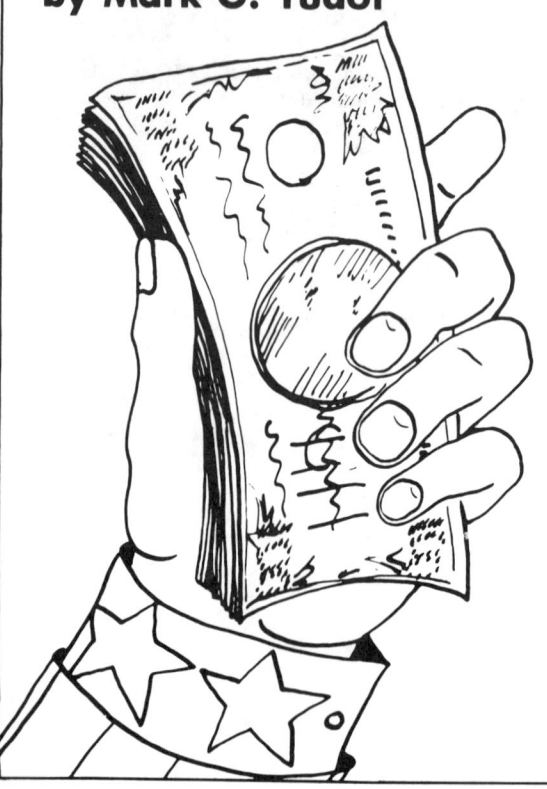

"Focusing on government regulation of private expression, First Amendment scholars long have neglected the issues created by government-supported expression itself, issues that range from disputes over public school courses and libraries to public broadcasting and campaign subsidies. Yudof's informed analysis of these diverse issues makes a most valuable contribution toward an increasingly crucial concern of democratic theory."—**Hans A. Linde,** Associate Justice, Oregon Supreme Court $25.50

The United States and the Berlin Blockade, 1948–1949
A Study in Crisis Decision-Making
by Avi Shlaim
Combining the approaches of political science and history to analyze the decision-making behavior of the United States during the critical superpower confrontation precipitated by the Soviet blockade of Berlin in 1948, Shlaim focuses on the impact of crisis-induced stress upon the performance of the makers of foreign policy. $38.00

Communism in Kerala
by T.J. Nossiter
In a framework of political history from the Freedom Struggle to the present, Nossiter examines communists' aims and record in Kerala's government; their attitudes toward parliamentary processes; national-state relations; and communism's electoral base and future prospects. He stresses the regional character of Kerala's communism and its synthesis of tradition, theory, and expediency. $35.00

Education, Race, and Social Change in South Africa
Edited by John A. Marcum
This book provides a concise overview of South African higher education and its politics and concludes with suggestions for actions the United States government, corporations, foundations, and universities might take to further higher education of South African blacks. The overview and suggestions are partly based on interviews with South African educators and others conducted by a team of American educators sponsored by the U.S./South Africa Leadership Exchange program. $25.00 hardcover, $6.50 paperback

Emotion and High Politics
Personal Relations at the Summit in Late Nineteenth-Century Britain and Germany
by Judith M. Hughes
A psychoanalytic explanation of why British and German leaders from the 1880s on failed to understand one another. Stressing the pre-oedipal mothering relationship, it argues that tempers rooted in childhood produced two contrasting patterns of behavior which set up an almost insuperable barrier to mutual comprehension. $28.50

The Management of Marine Regions
The North Pacific
by Edward Miles, Stephen Gibbs, David Fluharty, Christine Dawson, David Teeter, et al.

Atlas of Marine Use in the North Pacific Region
by Edward Miles, John Sherman, David Fluharty, Stephen Gibbs, Shoichi Tanaka, Masao Oda, et al.
The *Atlas* and its companion volume *The Management of Marine Regions* should prove an indispensable source for decisionmakers and for all those with an interest in the region's resources. *Management:* $38.50 until 6/30/83, $50.00 thereafter. *Atlas:* Large format, full-color, screw-post hinged, $125.00 until 6/30/83, $150.00 thereafter

Available at bookstores or from

University of California Press
Berkeley 94720

Ninety years of scholarly excellence

MAKING BUREAUCRACIES WORK

edited by **Carol H. Weiss,** *Harvard University*
and **Allen H. Barton,** *Columbia University*

Making Bureaucracies Work examines reforms that have been instituted or advocated to improve government agency performance in the United States. The contributors identify strategies that hold promise for making public bureaucracies more effective, and mechanisms that generate more negative consequences than gains. Together they offer directions to efforts to make government agencies more effective, efficient, and response to the needs of the citizenry.

"Articles by established authorities, from the perspective of their specialties endeavor to diagnose the nature of our bureaucratic maladies. Seven chapters measure the effectiveness of governmental performance. Six deal with the issues of responsibility and political accountability with stress on such well-worn nostrums as legislative oversight, judicial review, political controls, decentralization, greater public participation, and even a proposal for a constitutional limitation on governmental spending. Obviously, these are well-traveled paths of research, and yet the individual essays provide a rich diversity of insight. Can means be found to improve the functioning of our bureaucracies? The book responds affirmatively..."

—*Choice*

"This is a comprehensive anthology of 17 highly current selections relating to the general theme of reform in public administration. Addressing the two critical issues of administrative inefficiency and lack of accountability, the editors have successfully covered many important facets of their theme and have assembled an outstanding supplementary text."

—*Journal of Politics*

Sage Focus Editions, Volume 22
1980 / 312 pages / $25.00 (h) / $12.50 (p)

SAGE PUBLICATIONS, INC.
275 South Beverly Drive
Beverly Hills, California 90212

SAGE PUBLICATIONS LTD
28 Banner Street
London EC1Y 8QE, England